)

11

1

2

*International Relations
then and now*

International Relations then and now

Origins and trends in interpretation

WILLIAM C. OLSON

Professor and Former Dean
School of International Service
The American University
Washington

A. J. R. GROOM

Professor of International Relations
University of Kent at Canterbury
and Centre for Conflict Analysis

 HarperCollins*Academic*
An imprint of HarperCollins*Publishers*

Published by
HarperCollins *Academic*
77–85 Fulham Palace Road
Hammersmith
London W6 8JB
UK

First published in 1991

British Library Cataloguing in Publication Data

Olson, William C. (William Clinton, *1920–*)
  International relations then and now: origins and trends
  in interpretation.
1. Foreign relations, history
I. Title II. Groom, A. J. R. (Arthur John Richard), *1938–*
  327.09

  ISBN 0-04-445101-6

Typeset in 10 on 12 point Bembo by CentraCet, Cambridge
and printed in Great Britain by Billing and Sons, London and Worcester

For
Betsy and Antoinette

Contents

Preface   xi

Acknowledgements   xiii

1   The antecedents   1

PART ONE   *'Then': the formative years*   17

2   The "international" idea and the reordering of Europe,
    1776–1848   19

3   Transforming the world: Marx, the peace movement
    and war   37

4   The period of the first consensus: a quest for peace   56

5   The impact of the collapse of the League system   79

6   The second consensus: the quest for power   104

Appendix A   Books on general international relations,
             1916–31   130

Appendix B   General international relations works of the
             1932–44 period   131

Appendix C   "Mainstream" texts during the second consensus
             1945–62   133

PART TWO   *'Now': contending paradigms*   135

7   A pause for reflection   137

8   Breaking the mould   142

9   World society approaches   183

10   Structural approaches to international relations   222

11   Realism resurgent?   262

12   Paradigms in perspective: conflict, international political
     economy and the return to theory   285

PART THREE   *Epilogue*   313

13   Future imperfectly   315

References   329

Index   348

Preface

At the turn of our century the philosopher Santayana noted that 'those who cannot remember the past are condemned to repeat it'.[1] This is true for academe as well as statecraft, for disciplines as well as books. As we see it, the function of this little book is to open up a panorama of past and present ideas about international relations, both as politics and as conception, to those who are fascinated by the unfolding of world events and have already taken the trouble to inform themselves about what is going on and why.

This 'advanced beginner' may be a university student, a young foreign service officer, a new don, perhaps a researcher or a serious journalist. Young or old, he or she may be a member of what Gabriel Almond terms[2] 'the attentive public', the intelligent layman who wants to be better informed not only about the present, but the past, especially the ideas that have shaped the way philosophers and practitioners look at international affairs. Our book is a sort of intellectual map to guide one from ancient insights to contemporary debates.

Emphasis in the book is on two dimensions: one of space, the other of time. Most recent work in International Relations (hereinafter referred to as IR) has been in English, including translation of much of consequence from Ibn Khaldun to Raymond Aron, just as the distinguished Danish scholar, Niels Amstrup, chose to present his superb recent monograph, 'The study of international relations: old or new?' (Institute of Political Science, University of Aarhus, March 1989, 58 pp.) in that language. Yet, as there are signs that this particular manifestation of ethnocentrism is beginning to give way to a truly international basis of theory, we are already planning a second edition reflective of this transformation.

As for time, we have struggled in the first half of the book to produce an abbreviated pre-history up to the end of the Age of Enlightenment, and have then taken five chapters to cover most of the last two centuries. The second half of the book interprets the state of the study of IR today (by which we mean from about 1960). This segment has been divided topically rather than sequentially, simply because it is too early to tell which of the several current approaches will prevail. Throughout we have proceeded on the assumption that facts do not speak for themselves. Lord Keynes was right when he pointed out that facts tell us what our theories suggest they should reveal. It behooves us therefore to know our theories and the version of reality that is implied by them. As reality changes, theory tends to change with it.

One other point, on style. We have tried to take to heart the advice given to writers fifty years ago by William Strunk and E. B. White: to use language to clarify and to promote understanding, not to obscure. We have tried to avoid the pitfalls of 'jargon'. But where a new scholarly term reflects something more clearly than ten old ones do, we use it.

So onward into the past, the better to understand the present and – just possibly – to prepare for future worlds.

Acknowledgements

Although the writing of any book entails a modicum of pain as any author, successful or otherwise, will attest, we have both enjoyed writing this book for the opportunity it has given us to read where we had not read before and re-read what we had often first read long ago; for the collegiality and friendship of working together; for the professional support, criticism, comment and encouragement of our friends; and, above all, to learn a little more of what our subject has to offer. Our hope in this 'little book', as we have affectionately come to call it, is to convey to you our sense of intellectual adventure and to share the stimulus and insight that we derived from writing it.

We could not have had the opportunity to prepare this volume without the benefit of study leave from our home institutions. For this we are very grateful to The American University in Washington and the University of Kent at Canterbury. In particular this enabled us to meet on a number of occasions both in Britain and the United States. We wish to thank the faculty of the School of International Service for granting a sabbatical leave following Professor Olson's seven-year term as Dean to enable him to become a writer again. For providing a place for a year as a Visiting Research Fellow in the Royal Institute of International Affairs, we are grateful to the Director, Admiral Sir James Eberle. To acknowledge properly the help received from Chatham House (often in the Canteen) would take a page of names, but the head Librarian, Nicole Gallimore, and her chief assistant, John Montgomery, were especially keen in seeking out the myriad titles and references required for a book like this. The head of computer services, Maria Lathia, graciously made room in her day to print out drafts. The Institute's Director of Studies, William Wallace, and Professor Edward Kolodziej of the University of Illinois, a fellow visitor and former colleague at the Library of Congress, constructively assessed early chapters. Doug McDaniel, a doctoral candidate at the School of International Service, painstakingly checked footnotes while a research assistant at Chatham House in 1988–9.

On his return to The School of International Service, Professor Olson shared his part of the book with his doctoral seminars on the development of the study of International Relations. While all the members certainly contributed, two were particularly helpful: Ginger Smith proofread the entire manuscript and John Petrou was exceedingly generous with his time, drawing upon expert bibliographical assistance from Linda Stevens of the University of Maryland. Colleagues at The American University shared their knowledge and wisdom in reviewing the text as it went along. Special thanks are due to other friends whose comments proved especially useful: Theodore Couloumbis of the University of Thessaloniki in Greece; Burkart Holzner, Director of the University Center for International Studies of the University of Pittsburgh; James Wolfe of the University of Southern Mississippi; Barry Hughes of the Graduate School of International Studies at the University of Denver; Harold Jacobson of the University of Michigan; and the Foxes. As a creator as well as a user of knowledge about IR, the comments of William T. R. Fox were as incisive as they were lengthy, confirmed and supplemented by Annette Baker Fox (sadly for all of us in the profession, Bill has since passed away; it may be that his observations for this modest volume constitute his last intellectual contribution). Lee Schwartz (geography), Tom Farer (international law), and Louis Goodman (sociology) lent their specialized expertise, and other colleagues at The American University, Albert Mott (intellectual history), William Cromwell (world politics), Hamid Mowlana (global communication) and Stephen Gallup (European history) worked their way through the whole manuscript, all finding potholes and bumps in need of repair on the road to completion. N. G. Onuf went beyond the call of collegial duty by commenting upon the entire manuscript at no less than three stages, including this final one. Fellow members with William Olson of the Cambridge University/British International Studies Association 'Studies in International Relations' Editorial Board, especially Roger Tooze of North Staffordshire Polytechnic and the chair, Steve Smith of East Anglia, provided expert counsel.

The new president of the Council on Foreign Relations, Peter

Tarnoff, was particularly helpful toward the end in scrutinizing the sections of the early contributions of the CFR to the development of the study of international relations, William Wallace performing a similar essential role with reference to the early days of Chatham House.

Professor Groom's study leave began with a visit to the United States en route for New Zealand and a term as William Evans Visiting Fellow in the Department of Political Studies at the University of Otago. In that happy atmosphere the reading for several chapters was undertaken. Warm thanks are due to Professor Jim Flynn for extending the invitation and to his colleagues Professor Richard Mulgan, Dr Anthony Wood and Dr Ramesh Thakur for their hospitality, both intellectual and practical. The drafting of those chapters was done while a Visiting Fellow for a term at the Department of International Relations of the Australian National University in Canberra. Professor J. L. Richardson provided quiet but sustained support and Dr Richard Higgott brimmed with ideas and, like many of his colleagues, lent books. Dr Richard Little, on study leave from the University of Lancaster, fielded many queries with his customary skill, aplomb and great forbearance. At home, Professor Groom had the benefit of the comments and criticisms of his friends in the IR team at the University of Kent and the Centre for Conflict Analysis. They are too numerous to name individually, but particular thanks are due to Michael Banks, Chris Brown, Stephen Chan, A. V. S. de Rueck, Mark Hoffman, Vivienne Jabri, Margot Light, Keith Webb and Andrew Williams.

We have been 'takers', from the literature, from our colleagues and from our friends; it is now time to 'give' back our best. In so doing we are greatly in debt to many people for their ideas, advice and concern; but we alone are responsible for any errors of fact or judgement for which we take whatever blame accrues thereby.

Finally, family and staff members saved the day because of their skill at the word processor: Olson son-in-law Christopher E. L. Laxton, daughter–author Annie, and SIS assistants Kelly King and Patrick Llerna. Research Fellow Raphael Flores provided needed bibliographic help. By her own commitment to getting a job done and done well, Betsy Olson was nothing less than an inspiration to keep at a task that from time to time seemed to lose its urgency. In

Canberra Barbara Owen-Jones and in Canterbury Elizabeth Dowling went far beyond the line of duty in making available their secretarial skills. We are much indebted to them. Antoinette, Anna and Helen Groom were, as ever, ideal travelling companions, through life as well as to the Antipodes.

Through it all the co-authors have, somewhat to their surprise, remained warm friends, vastly expanding their understanding of the discipline to which they have given their professional lives by travelling together on this voyage of discovery.

Canterbury and Washington, DC
May 1990

*International Relations
then and now*

1 *The antecedents*

> . . . I shall be content if the future student of these events, or of other similar events which are likely in human nature to occur in after ages, finds my narrative to them useful. (Thucydides, *The History of the Peloponnesian War*, c. 413 BC)[3]

The systematic study of the relations of states had begun to take shape by the middle of the seventeenth century. Even in antiquity, there had been a great deal of thought about world society, which was to have its effect upon what the discipline is today. These were its antecedents. Masterpieces of the past cannot be ignored by the serious student seeking insights into understanding contemporary international relations; even in Pharaonic literature, we can find references to the Kadish treaty during the era of Ramses II that reflect modern concerns.

Ancient diplomacy and philosophy

Thucydides' noted work could well have been entitled the "diplomacy" of the Peloponnesian war, which was so long in coming, so long in ending, between certain Greek states and their systems of alliances. Inasmuch as Thucydides developed no systematic theory of interstate relations, its principal value for our purposes lies in his description of the negotiations, the policy alternatives, the strategic concepts, the diplomatic skills (or lack of them) exhibited by plenipotentiaries as Athens tried first to avoid the war and then to win it. While important and lasting elements of IR are to be found in Thucydides' writing, notably lessons which derive from the confrontation of land power and sea power, it was Herodotus who has been described as the first historian "to set an example of universality" in his treatment of the Greek states in their relations with one another.

The view that "man is the measure of all things," is attributed to the sophist Protagoras, an antecedent of contemporary behavioralist thought, especially in relation to perception and images. When Socrates proclaimed himself "a citizen of the world," he shared the cosmopolitanism of the Stoics. Though he showed little interest in inter-state relations except by implication, Aristotle demonstrated the connection between ethics and politics which preoccupies such writers as Joseph Nye and Kenneth Thompson today, who like the great logician are careful not to equate justice and equality as many present-day political moralists tend to do. Plato anticipated Machiavelli, Hobbes, and Hans Morgenthau in his realism, "firmly representative of the collective Greek mind in apparently recognizing that war remained a central, if tragic, feature of international life."[4] Despite their philosophical differences, both Plato and Aristotle recognized that a consequence of unequal size among city-states was that "the strong would normally strive to become stronger and the weak seek to avoid becoming weaker."[5] Their contradictory views of justice between states led to schools of philosophy that prevailed for centuries. As Fred Parkinson has put it in his *Philosophy of International Relations*, this "cleavage between the normative and the empirical runs right through the history of thought in international relations."[6]

Ancient Asia remains an instructive source of ideas and experience concerning interstate relations. As early as 771 BC the important principle that treaties should be regarded as being between equals was recognized in China. During the "Age of Philosophers," Confucius (551–479 BC) and later his principal follower, Mencius, tried to promote government by moral virtue, just as Woodrow Wilson and Jawaharlal Nehru were to do on a world plane twenty-five centuries later. Late in the fourth century BC appeared the first more or less systematic treatise on interstate politics ever written, *The Book of the Lord of Shang*, or Kung-sun Yang, the exact date of which is uncertain because many Chinese scholars and statesmen over a period of time apparently contributed to its final form. In paving the way for the Ch'in dynasty, which ended in 221 BC, this great work, while promoting the rule of law to govern the relations of princes, precluded any role for an informed public in government. In the discipline of military science, the views of another Chinese thinker, Sun Tzu, are cited even today, both in terms of strategy and tactics, though hardly in terms of morality.

Meanwhile, far to the south and west in India, Prime Minister

Kautilya (321–296 BC), known as "The Crooked" because of his explicit rejection of any place for morality in politics, produced an influential treatise entitled *Arthasastra*. Kautilya anticipated Machiavelli fifteen centuries later by describing how heads of state actually conduct their relations with one another rather than how they should. In contrast to this somewhat cynical guide came the dramatic renunciation of armed conquest by the Emperor Asoka (265–238 BC) after leading his forces to one of the bloodiest victories in early Indian history. Converted to Buddhism, Asoka then advocated conquest by persuasion and reason. Though regarded as one of the wisest emperors of all time, his exemplary reign unfortunately was followed by "confused centuries of invasions, conflicts, and conquests."[7] In the longer run, that compilation of Hindu wisdom over the centuries, the *Bhagavadgita*, justifies the reconciliation of actual participation in war with spiritual peace, a position resembling "conscientious participation" in the Second World War.

In reviewing ancient thought, Kal Holsti of the University of British Columbia has pointed out that China and Greece represent two of the three periods of inter-state relations, out of dozens, that may be seen as particularly instructive because of their resemblance to the anarchical current world system of today. For this reason, the third was not the relatively unified Roman Empire, but what followed several centuries after its historic decline: Renaissance Italy. Marcus Aurelius, Epictetus, and others among Rome's political thinkers, although providing insights into the nature of power, had little to offer in comprehending or ordering inter-state contacts. The *jus gentium* of Imperial Rome represented a law of peoples, not of states. It was not international law, but "Roman law over *citizens* of other lands." The contributions of men like Frontinus or Vegitius were to the discipline of military science. Tacitus criticized the Empire principally for its internal nature, not relations beyond its borders, and Livy's *History of Rome* constituted a lengthy glorification of the Roman republic.

Antecedents in religious thought

In the Biblical tradition, the Old Testament represents a literature rich in political insight, all the way from the reference in *Genesis* to "their lands each with its own language, by the families, in their nations," to the words of the oracle in *Malachi* summoning "all the nations against Jerusalem in battle. . . ." The international relations of the children of Israel rested upon deep philosophical and religious foundations. Christ's critique of Rome as set forth in the majestic yet simple form of the Sermon on the Mount provided a guide to political behavior, however seldom it may have been followed by those in power throughout history. The devotion to peace of the early Christians, who believed in cooperation, underwent transformation by the third century after Christ when St Augustine considered the possibility of "just war." This is yet another ancient concept experiencing a revival today.

Much later, after the seventh century AD, the *Koran* provided many political guidelines for followers of Mohammed, such as for making peace, the observation of treaties, and militancy in the spread of Islam. In tenth-century Persia, the Muslim philosopher Al-Farabi saw politics essentially as a struggle of each against all. Another Islamic philosopher and thinker, a North African born in Arabia and raised in Spain, Ibn Khaldun (1332–1406), argued that while "human civilization requires political leadership for its organization,"[8] it seems also true that "savage nations are better able to achieve superiority than others."[9] Conceivably, similar ideas were abroad at about this same time in such places as Benin in Africa and in the Incan, Aztec, and Mayan empires in the Americas, where the Spaniards would have destroyed any such records. Further north, the Pilgrims found in the Iroquois not only the concept of nationhood but even formalized treaties between Indian "nations."

From the point of view of what might be termed the "linear" development of ideas about international relations, however, it is Europe that really matters in terms of how *world* politics as we conceptualize it today emerged. The legacy of the European nation-state system, despite many variations, has essentially been adopted as the world system in our time. Appropriate to the several essentially lawless centuries of the Dark Ages which followed Rome in the West is the term *Völkerwanderung* to describe menacing barbarian tribes constantly breaking what was left of the Roman legacy. The Greek legacy has come down to us perhaps more through the line of Arab scholars than European. The "Christian" period of world politics was not particularly peaceful; Europeans lived in a Holy Roman Empire, which belied all three terms that made up its title. Yet in the thirteenth century, St Thomas Aquinas saw the world as reflecting God's plan, which mortals must endeavour to comprehend and to which their temporal affairs should conform. It was in that same century that Europe saw what was perhaps the first of its many peace plans, that of Pierre Dubois (1250–1320) for pacifying Europe by enhancing the power of France at the expense of other states in order to recover the Holy Land.

Dante Alighieri soon produced his remarkable *De Monarchia (c. 1313)*, designed to secure unity through a world state under an emperor. Shortly thereafter, Marsilius of Padua followed with the first treatment of the problem of sovereignty, though he only went far enough to indicate that, as an interstate problem, it certainly deserved "rational inquiry."[10] Like Dubois, his overriding objective was revitalization of the Crusades, but his means to that end would require the princes of Christendom to strive toward a common goal. It would be some time before the ideal of a peace system as an end in itself would occur to the philosophers of Europe, although the farsighted Dutch philosopher, Desiderius Erasmus, did issue a *Plea of reason, religion and humanity against war* in 1518. Detached, objective foreign policy theory, which might challenge authority, seemed inappropriate to the Age of Absolutism.

The origins of international law

With the emergence of the state system in Europe, the fifteenth and sixteenth centuries witnessed early manifestations of international law as a discipline. This could not have occurred in Rome, whose empire had neither the need nor the use for it, or in medieval times, when law was rudimentary and local. Though hardly the father of the subject as some of his contemporaries claimed, Francisco de Vitoria (1480–1546) did do much to delineate

the *jus gentium* (now somewhat broadened from its original meaning), followed by another Spaniard, Francisco Suarez, early in the
next century. In Italy, the study of international law on a religious
foundation was advanced by the Italian diplomatist Ottaviano
Maggi in 1566. Shortly thereafter, his Protestant countryman,
Alberico Gentili, developed an entirely new concept, which saw
war more as a political than a religious matter, arguing in his study
of war in 1588 that "if men in another state live in a manner
different from that which we follow in our own state, they surely
do us no wrong."[11] At about the same time, the French philosopher
Jean Bodin defined sovereignty, a central concept in this field, as
unlimited power over citizens and subjects, unrestrained by law.
While Bodin's contribution was a milestone, principal credit for
advancing the discipline of international law as a practical concern
for the policy-makers of his day must go to Hugo Grotius
(1583–1645), whose career included a stint as an ambassador. Like
Plato, Aristotle, St Augustine and St Thomas Aquinas before him,
Grotius was progenitor of a whole school of thought, which has
adherents down to the present day. Writing during the Thirty
Years War, his work on the law of war (in which he counselled
moderation and, to a lesser degree, peace) derived its principles of
reason from the actual nature of world society in his day. The
definitive work for law between states for many years, *De Jure
Belli ac Pacis*, must take its place in the early development of the
discipline simply because international law was the context within
which IR subject matter was considered by scholars of that era. To
Grotius, clear rules must govern even wars: "violence is characteristic of wild beasts, and effort should be put forth . . . be tempered
with humanity, lest in imitating wild beasts too much we forget to
be human."[12]

    Even though international law may be considered the "root
discipline" of international relations, none of these savants of the
law gave much time to concocting peace plans. That was left to
others. Among the most significant of them (in terms of seminal
ideas, if not in terms of actually producing any striking alteration
in the power structure) was Emeric Crucé. Even though a book he
wrote in 1623 was regarded by Quincy Wright as the first truly
systematic study of international organization, it received far less
attention than the "Grand Design" of Henry IV, drawn upon and
revised by numerous authors over a considerable period of time.

Each author made changes according to his own political predisposition and objectives. The best known of these was the Duc de Sully, who in 1638 was trying to lay the groundwork for a Christian republic. The design, regarded by Sir Harry Hinsley as a "source of endless confusion," had been seen by some earlier writers as the forerunner of contemporary proposals for maintaining lasting peace among states. In point of fact, this and most other peace plans of the period were more hegemonic than universal in purpose.

Renaissance Italy: the anarchical precedent

Although it is no accident that one contemporary writer, Georg Schwarzenberger, called Niccolò Machiavelli "the father of realism in the study of international affairs,"[13] he was not as "Machiavellian" as is often thought. Having boldly advised "the Prince" in 1513 how to manage his affairs with other princes, based upon his own considerable diplomatic experience, he put forth seven years later more cautious views in discourses praising the Roman republic, which belied the sinister reputation earned for him by his earlier, more cynical book of advice. The political environment within which he wrote – a kaleidoscope of warring Italian city-states – parallels the current world system, at least in certain particulars. What were its characteristics? In the first place, neighbors who were outside the system were not necessarily considered barbarians. They were people with whom a prince might have to deal, hopefully at arms length, but perhaps at peril of losing some degree of independence (as the Milanese found out when, to enhance their security, they went outside the limited peninsular configuration to invite in French troops in the fifteenth century). Like the earlier systems, it was one of independent city states, but with each participant more insecure and unstable than those making up the ancient configurations. The Peace of Lodi in 1454 nevertheless reflected a sort of collective security system reminiscent of the time of the Delian League or the Ch'in dynasty. Within the Italian peninsula, the political system was characterized by diplomatic intrigue, conspiracy, betrayal, and amorality, all conveniently lumped together under the name of "Machiavellism."[14] If there was an ethic at all, it was to serve the state, or rather the interest of the Prince whose province it was; in a sense, *The Prince* was its book of rules.

The significance of Westphalia

The quest for alternative systems, however fanciful, must have been irresistible. In a sense, the inchoate Italian system extended itself to the rest of Europe, culminating in the bloody, militarily inconclusive Thirty Years' War in Central Europe (1618–48). More conclusive was the Peace of Westphalia which ended it, recognizing as it did a new state system based not upon the city but increasingly upon a wider territorial base, though not yet in every case the nation. To many students of the subject, "international relations" began at Westphalia essentially in the form which continues today, more than three centuries later.

Complex as their negotiations turned out to be, what the princes at Westphalia did was very simple, not unlike what had occurred in different circumstances and for very different reasons four hundred years earlier at Runnymede. To oversimplify, they defied the highest authority. Consisting of several bilateral understandings, the Westphalian agreements brought an end to the religious wars of the Reformation. They *legitimized* the new order, which now rested upon sovereign, independent states. At least in theory. No longer did princes have to seek the Pope or the Emperor's permission to deal with one another as equals. Theirs were competing interests with common norms. This demonstrated, if nothing else, that European diplomacy had matured after a century which was "one of the most formative periods of thought in international relations."[15]

Yet it is easy to read too much into what emerged from Westphalia. People from earliest times have tended to believe that history repeats itself, but as Frederick Schuman observed in one of the first widely used IR textbooks, "of course, it does not."[16] Similar circumstances do produce similar reactions, however, as Arnold Toynbee tried to demonstrate in his ambitious "challenge and response" theory. What Westphalia created was less a model than a profoundly significant and novel development in the relations of sovereign states and the analysis of those relations.

Within a few years, Baruch Spinoza was able to give unreserved acknowledgement to the existence of a system of sovereign states and to concentrate on the relationships between them. He regarded wars as legitimate, writing in 1677 that the sovereign "may live entirely as he pleases and is not bound by the will of another."[17] Though the study of international relations may be said to have had its origins at Westphalia because of the diplomatic and political phenomena that took place there, it should not be thought of in terms of a sudden revelation to those who thought they were establishing a revolutionary order. Nevertheless, the views of leading commentators on the state in its relations with others now take on more importance in the development of thought about the nature of what can at last technically be termed "international relations" than before Westphalia. Reasons of state now were seen to be more compelling in determining the actual behavior of Princes than the reason of nature of Grotius or the reason of humanity and religion of Erasmus. After all, it was in 1648 that the great Swedish statesman, Count Oxenstiern, wrote in a famous letter: "Dost thou not know, my son, with how little wisdom the world is governed?"

The central authority of the Papacy and the Holy Roman Emperor having been weakened, the more informal mechanisms of the balance of power now were strengthened. The state became the lodestone of political loyalty. At the same time men of vision, who could rise above the system and thus be less constrained than politicians, continued to think and to write opinions not bound entirely by the dictates of national interest. Three of these deserve particular notice. One was Baron Samuel von Pufendorf who, in contrast to Grotius, differentiated between ethics and law in an influential book published in 1672. Several decades later, a professor of the "law of nature and nations," Christian von Wolff, would appear, in his *Jus Gentium Methodo Scientifica Petractatum* (1749), to have been one of the first to adopt a kind of "scientific method" to which such modern thinkers as David Singer give so much weight. More important than either Pufendorf or Wolff was Emmerich de Vattel (1714–67). In *Le Droit de Gens* in 1758 ("the first direct onslaught on the traditional international law")[18] Europe was urged to "form a political system in which the nations inhabiting this part of the world are bound together by their relations and varied interests into a single body," as it was no longer "a confused heap of detached parts. . . ."[19] He did not mention the still detached

other parts of the world, which would gradually become enmeshed
in the European colonial system and, in time, adopt many of its
characteristics upon becoming independent. In rejecting accepted
ideas about the law of nations, Vattel turned instead to "the well-
known principle of the balance of power, by which is meant an
arrangement of affairs so that no state shall be in a position to have
absolute mastery and dominate over the others,"[20] a shift in
emphasis that was to prove prophetic in the development of
classical theory in IR.

The state in international relations

But what of the state itself? What was its nature? What *should* it
be? Some intellectual giants grappled with the external dimensions
of the state as well as with its internal nature. Thomas Hobbes,
John Locke, and Jean-Jacques Rousseau concentrated upon governance, but they all also concerned themselves explicitly with the
state in relation to other states. Already a noted translator of
Thucydides (whom he called "the most Politik Historiographer
that ever writ"),[21] Hobbes published his famous *Leviathan* three
years after Westphalia. To him, states lived in a state of nature, a
hostile world lacking both cooperation and balance between states:
"neither if they cease from fighting, it is therefore to be called
Peace, but rather a breathing time, in which one enemy observing
the motion and the countenance of the other, values his security
not according to the Pacts, but the forces and counsels of his
adversary."[22] His term "the body politic" lends itself well to
international relations, avoiding both the utopian overtones of
"world society" and the cynical undercurrents of nationalism.
Some decades later Locke gained attention with his two treatises
on government (1690), which concentrated upon the philosophy
and organization of government and in which he made a distinction
between the state of war and that of nature. He did not, however,
develop the implications of this distinction for world politics.[23]
Although, of the three, only Locke had diplomatic experience,
Rousseau had more to say about international affairs. Early in the
eighteenth century, he endeavored to apply his renowned Social
Contract theory to states as they related to one another, which led
him to be confusing and contradictory. In one place he urged that

"all the European powers form among themselves a sort of system which unites them by the same religion, the same international law, by customs, literature, commerce, and by a kind of balance of power," but in another that "the pretended brotherhood of the nations . . . seems nothing but a term of derision" and "if the present system is founded on a rock, it is all the more on that account exposed to storms," which keep them in a "constant state of unrest."[24] Needless to say, it would not be all that difficult to argue that he was right on both counts, given the capriciousness of world politics that has already been noted.

Diplomacy and the balance of power

Known at the time for his conservative philosophy, David Hume's contribution to international thought is seen principally in his perceptive historical essay, "Of the balance of power" (1742), in which, as Stanley Hoffmann has pointed out, he demonstrated "an actue awareness of the advantages of such a system, of the delicacy of its operation, and of Britain's special position."[25] Like Voltaire (nom de plume of François-Marie Arouet), who wrote of a "Christian Europe" in 1751, Hume saw in the multiplicity of states of differing natures an element of common sense, which had in fact been practiced in the balancing process, a process whose principal instrument was diplomacy.

Hitherto hardly more than a form of "aristocratic cosmopolitanism," diplomacy itself matured. Cardinal Richelieu was the first to establish the art as a permanent activity and "not merely a hurried endeavor."[26] Later descriptions tended to concentrate upon procedure, style, and technique, or the symbols of diplomacy, but among these thinkers concerned in an innovative manner with the philosophy of interstate contact, three are noteworthy. Not surprisingly, their commentaries on the art followed the publication of the landmark philosophical treatises on the nature of government itself, of which foreign relations had become more and more a formalized feature. Nearly a hundred and fifty years after Gentili had described the nature and function of the legation, Abraham de Wicquefort reviewed the lessons of a lifetime in describing *The Ambassador and his Functions* in 1681. Though full of practical insights, he unfortunately exhibited neither the charm nor the

depth of understanding of Françoise de Callières. This grand
master of diplomatic method observed in *On the Manner of Negotiating with Princes* (1716) that "it is a fundamental error, and one
widely held, that a clever negotiator must be a master of deceit
. . . apart from the fact that a lie is unworthy of a great Ambassador, it actually does more harm than good. . . ."[27]

Drawing to some degree upon his experience as Secretary of
War, James (later Lord) Bolingbroke extended the concept of
diplomacy to encompass policy in several fascinating letters on the
study of history, written between 1735 and 1742. His *Idea of a
Patriot King* (1746) is significant for the contemporary student of
IR in that he endeavored to bring state and nation together in a
single context; the force of nationalism would become the chief
determinant of the politics of the latter part of the eighteenth
century. It culminated in wars where the *levée en masse* produced
massive contingents of troops so fiercely loyal to the French nation
and its Emperor Napoleon that a mighty coalition of other
European states would have to be drawn together to defeat
them.

The vision of peace

The writings of these pragmatic men of affairs (though only
Bolingbroke might be regarded as a specialist in foreign policy)
must not obscure the value of the admittedly more visionary work
of William Penn, John Bellers, and the oft-cited Abbé St Pierre,
however little their prescriptions actually affected the relations
between states in their time. A Quaker often in trouble with the
law in England for applying deep religious convictions, Penn left
his homeland to found a colony based upon pacifist principles in
America and there to consolidate his ideas about improving the old
world. In his *Essay towards the Present and Future Peace of Europe*
(1693), he was realistic enough to write that men "will hardly be
brought to think of peace unless their appetites be some way
gratified."[28] In a similar vein Bellers advanced reasons for a
"Christian Commonwealth" in 1710, laying down certain broad
principles for a peaceful international order. By very different (and,
to some, dubious) means Charles François Irénée Castel, the Abbé
St Pierre, drew upon the labors of many others (including Sully),

even changing his own ideas in successive drafts of a renowned project for achieving perpetual peace in Europe.

What is really at issue here is neither literary purity nor philosophical originality but rather the persistence of what Hinsley has termed "the pursuit of peace" as an approach to the study of international relations. The more men practiced, and through the discipline of military science perfected, the art of war, the more they longed for the possibility of peace. The trouble then was, as it is today, that peace is rarely if ever the ultimate value in the determination of the foreign policies of states. That value usually is self-preservation, and sometimes self-extension, based upon the notion of "national interest" (an elusive concept because it is subjective rather than objective). Most of the plans for general peace were designed as a means for serving the interest of a particular prince or state; not only great painters and composers had to have patrons to support their performance in that era. What is different about Penn is that he sought peace for its own sake, and not the self-interest of any particular State.

Difficult as it may be to say just when the Age of Enlightenment came to an end, it was certainly still in flower when Thomas Paine published *Common Sense* in 1776.[29] The openness that had encouraged scientific inquiry by such men of that age as René Descartes, Frances Bacon, and Isaac Newton also set the stage for innovation in many fields of thought. The "pre-history" of the discipline of international relations was about to be replaced by the internationalization of the political process, first in the form of a military coalition brought into being to restore the balance of power, to be followed by what came to be called the Concert of Europe.

Notes: Preface and Chapter 1

1 George Santayana, from *The Life of Reason* (1905–1906), Vol. I, *Reason and Common Sense*, cited in John McCormack, *George Santayana: a Biography* (New York: Alfred A. Knopf, 1987), p. 173.
2 Gabriel Almond, *The American People and Foreign Policy* (New York: Harcourt, Brace, 1950), *passim*.
3 Trans. by R. Crawley (London: Everyman's Library, 1910), p. 3.
4 Robert Purnell, "Theoretical approaches to international relations: the contribution of the Graeco-Roman world", in Trevor Taylor (ed.),

Approaches and Theory in International Relations (London: Longman, 1978), p. 27.

5 ibid., p. 25.

6 F. Parkinson, *The Philosophy of International Relations* (Beverly Hills and London: Sage, 1977), p. 11.

7 Frederick L. Schuman, *International Politics* (New York: McGraw-Hill, 1933), p. 32.

8 *The Mughaddimah* (An Introduction to History), trans. Franz Rosenthal (London: Routledge and Kegan Paul, 1967), p. 256.

9 ibid., p. 107.

10 Cited by Sir Harry Hinsley, *Power and the Pursuit of Peace: Theory and Practice in the History of Relations between States* (Cambridge: Cambridge University Press, 1967, first published in 1963), p. 15.

11 Cited by P. Savigear, "European political philosophy and international relations", in Taylor, *Approaches and Theory in International Relations*, p. 38.

12 ibid., p. 40.

13 Martin Wight, *Power Politics: An Introduction to the Study of International Relations and Post-War Planning* (London: Jonathan Cape, 1941), p. 97.

14 Friedrich Meinecke, *Machiavellism* (1957), cited in Hinsley, *Power and the Pursuit of Peace*, p. 368.

15 Parkinson, *Philosophy of International Relations*, p. 33.

16 ibid., p. 15.

17 ibid., p. 38.

18 Hinsley, *Power and the Pursuit of Peace*, p. 166.

19 E. De Vattel, [1758] *The Law of Nations* (New York: AMS Press, 1987).

20 ibid.

21 One of the leading contemporary writers on international systems has a similar view; Hinsley writes, "Thucydides is still the author of the best book on that subject," that subject being "international aggression, continuous, calculated, pathologically inspired." Hinsley, *Power and the Pursuit of Peace*, p. 275.

22 Parkinson, *Philosophy of IR*, p. 30.

23 Savigear, *European Political Philosophy*, p. 39.

24 Cited by Hinsley, *Power and the Pursuit of Peace*, p. 61.

25 "The balance of power," in *International Encyclopaedia of the Social Sciences*, ed. by David I. Sills (New York: Macmillan and the Free Press, 1968), p. 508.

26 Cited by Sir Harold Nicolson. *The Evolution of Diplomatic Method* (London: Constable, 1953), p. 50-1.

27 Cited by Nicolson, ibid., p. 63.

28 Cited by Hinsley, *Power and the Pursuit of Peace*, p. 41.

29 *Common Sense and the Crisis* (Garden City, New York: Anchor Books edition, 1973).

Further reading

Aristotle. *Politics* (trans. Benjamin Jowett), in *The Works of Aristotle*, ed. by W. D. Ross. Oxford: The Clarendon Press, 1921.

Callières, François de. [1716]. *On the Manner of Negotiating with Princes* (trans. A. F. Whyte). Boston: Houghton, Mifflin, 1919.

Erasmus, Desiderius. [1511]. *The Praise of Folly*. London: Reeves and Turner, 1876.

Grotius, Hugo. [1625]. *De Jure Belli ac Pacis* (trans. Kelsey). Oxford: Carnegie Endowment for International Peace, 1925.

Herodotus. *The History of Herodotus* (trans. George Rawlinson). London: Murray, 1880.

Hume, David. "Of the balance of power," in *Essays and Treatises on Several Subjects*. Edinburgh: Bell and Bradfute, and W. Blackwood, 1825.

Machiavelli, Niccolò. [1513]. *The Prince* (trans. and ed. by Thomas G. Bergin). New York: Appleton-Century-Crofts, 1947.

Nulle, Stebelton H.(ed.). *Classics of the Western World*: Vol. I. *The Ancient World*. New York: Harcourt, Brace and World, 1964.

Plato. *The Republic* (trans. Benjamin Jowett), in *The Dialogues of Plato*. Oxford: The Clarendon Press, 1953.

Rowen, Herbert H.(ed). *From Absolutism to Revolution 1648–1848*. New York: Macmillan, 1968.

St Augustine. [413–27]. *The City of God* from *Basic Writings of Saint Augustine* ed. by Whitney J. Oates. New York: Random House, 1948.

Sully, Duc de. *The Grand Design of Henry IV*. Boston: Ginn and Co., 1909.

Thompson, Karl F. *Classics of the Western World*: Vol. II, *Middle Ages, Renaissance, and Reformation*. New York: Harcourt, Brace and World, 1964.

PART ONE

'Then': the formative years

2 The "international" idea and the reordering of Europe, 1776–1848

> To whatever other criticisms they might be subject, the states-
> men who made the Treaty of Vienna could at any rate claim that
> they did what they set out to do. They did not go to the Austrian
> capital to create a new heaven and earth, but to produce order
> out of chaos. (Sir Charles Petrie, *Diplomatic History 1713–1933*)[1]

Had Albert Grosser of France been right in dubbing IR an
American speciality, it would be appropriate to begin our study at
about the time of the birth of "the first new nation."[2] But that is
really only coincidence. To be sure, the war of independence began
in 1776, but that was also the year of the publication of Adam
Smith's *Wealth of Nations* and shortly after that came the first use
of the term "international" by Jeremy Bentham.[3] As William T. R.
Fox has put it, "the word is symbolically important because it
registers the norm-expectation that the interstate system is becoming and ought to be an inter-nation-state system."[4]

To Bentham, the force of public opinion would make states keep
their pledges, so that "international integration was not so much
attainable and undesirable as utterly unnecessary."[5] To Smith, the
state could not be trusted anyway, so he advocated a system of
political economy based upon *laissez-faire*. Both understood the
interaction of economics and politics, an attribute too often lacking
in unidisciplinary approaches to IR today. Though dimly understood at the time, a third discipline, demography, which would have
profound implications for international relations, began to emerge
at this time with the publication in 1798 of Thomas Malthus's essay
on the principle of population. In the realm of public international
policy, Edmund Burke championed the traditional rights of "the
natives of Hindustan and those of Virginia"[6] against the Crown.

On the other side of the Atlantic, the concepts of the Declaration of Independence reflected the work of Edmund Burke, Jean-Jacques Rousseau, and other European thinkers, supplemented by those in *The Federalist Papers*, notably the ideas of Hamilton on national commerce and its implications for international relations. Curiously, in laying the foundations for the Constitutional phase of the American revolution, the basic principle of the separation of powers led to placing the term "Law of Nations" under the powers of Congress and the treaty powers of the Senate under the powers of the President. As we shall see in Chapter 3, application of the two-thirds rule to the Treaty of Versailles was to have an effect upon how the study of IR grew up. By the end of the eighteenth century, both through the philosophical insights of James Madison and Thomas Jefferson and the effective diplomacy of John Jay and Benjamin Franklin, an American contribution had begun in world affairs. These men shared a belief with many in England that lasting international peace was a possibility, though this was tempered by the view of those like George Washington who felt that America should steer clear of entanglements with Europe. A commonly held view was that, since no real conflict existed between the basic national interests of the respective actors, there need be no delay in creating a workable international order. Optimism, based upon the ideas of Bentham, Penn and others, continued to dominate thought in the two countries well into the nineteenth century. Britain was preoccupied with its emerging position of world leadership. America was preoccupied with its internal development. While relying upon the processes of traditional diplomacy, both were to experience the growth of a peace movement whose ideas would threaten that tradition. Both possessed the elemental security of the seas as a gift of nature that enabled them to share a broader vision.

On the Continent of Europe, the intellectual climate was very different indeed. Neither Rousseau, who thought that international conflict rendered impossible any real progress, nor Immanuel Kant, who took the opposite view that progress might well be achieved as a result of conflict, had shared this optimism. The Age of Enlightenment had come to a close with an eruption of violence which began with the French revolution and ended with the double defeat of Napoleon. There were emerging in Prussia thinkers whose preoccupation was war and the theory of war, just as the "century of peace" was getting under way. Yet even Napoleon had sought a confederation of Europe, which he hoped, vainly as it turned out, might be achieved by peaceful means. As we have seen, he was not the first to experience that frustration, but unlike Sully and the Abbé St Pierre, he possessed the means to realize his goals. He did not succeed, though it took a dramatic shifting of coalitions to beat him, the last of which lasted long enough to establish a working system to preserve the peace. One reason this endured (at least for a time) was that the defeated Power was to be made part of the system, which constituted an application of an important theory of international relations. Unhappily, that principle was neither perceived nor applied at the peace negotiations following the next general war a century later, though as the author of *A World Restored* (Henry Kissinger)[7] so well demonstrated, the lesson was not to be lost forever.

Another kind of theory, largely ignored by the policy-makers if not the intellectuals of the time, took the form of a renowned essay put forth in 1795 by Kant. One philosopher has characterized this as "the last link in an intellectual chain spanning the best part of the 18th century."[8] Never travelling more than forty miles from his home in Konigsberg, Kant nevertheless endeavored to create a practical plan for the abolition of war the world over. He argued that what was needed was less a treaty *of* peace to end the French revolutionary wars than a treaty *for* peace. As he himself put it in the final paragraph of *Perpetual Peace*, "it may well be said that this Treaty for universal and eternal peace constitutes not only a part, but the final objective in its entirety of law within the confines of common sense."[9] This represented a fairly widespread image of international relations in which good states (i.e., for Kant, republics) make peace by making good policies. But unlike Woodrow Wilson a century later, Kant had no power to influence events.

Instead, Napoleon's troops were to continue to march across the face of Europe seeking a quite different final objective. Once *l'Empéreur* was twice defeated and banished, peace was to be organized upon a traditional basis at the historic Congress of Vienna in 1815. Like the Peace of Westphalia a century and a half earlier, the Congress of Vienna followed a series of continental wars, but there was one great difference. The Thirty Years' War had left the continent exhausted, with vast tracts laid waste and economies ruined in a Europe which had already been disintegrating for a long time. Napoleon's wars did not. His own country had just gone through a liberal revolution as had the United States, their respective constitutions having been adopted within a few months of one another. Regimes which had fought long battles remained in power. In the emergent configuration, what could now be called the nation-state system would now dominate world politics.

There was another distinction. The influential thinkers of the Westphalia era – Spinoza, Vattel, Pufendorf – had written as individuals with no professional accountability, as outsiders commenting upon the system and advocating its reform. The new preeminent minds – Castlereagh, Metternich, Talleyrand – were themselves statesmen occupying positions of high responsibility in the states that made up the system, promoting its restoration once the disturber had been put down.

The new century would provide a rich legacy of thought, some profound, some in retrospect frivolous or cynical, on how international affairs should be, or actually were, conducted. The period between Westphalia and the defeat of Napoleon was characterized neither by peace nor by any systematic theory of international relations. That which followed was noteworthy for its lengthy period of general peace and at least the beginnings of an integrated field of study, growing principally out of the peace movement. This relative stability encouraged both intellectuals and ministers to think about the longer-range aspects of foreign policy and to concentrate upon harmony, law, and the active promotion of peace.

The statesmen-thinkers

Such fundamentally contrasting types of statesmen as the idealistic Alexander I of Russia and the practical Pitt the Younger of England argued – separately – for some sort of a league of governments, which would undertake to help one another prevent war and encourage international stability. As early as 1804, Pitt actually recommended in a state paper that the powers "should bind themselves mutually to protect and support each other against any attempt to infringe upon" their respective positions.[10] Whether because of these sometimes contradictory ideas or in spite of them, the statesmen of Vienna were to succeed in creating a relatively stable postwar order. But it was the balance of power rather than the peace plans of the centuries upon which practitioners were now to seize as the keystone of European security. That decisive international conference was to set in motion what had been regarded as a century of peace, a century which began with public opinion being ignored as something which could or should affect diplomacy but ended with its role being, if anything, exaggerated.

No overview of nineteenth-century thought concerning international relations can ignore the essentials of the power configuration emerging from the Congress of Vienna. Ideas for planning the peace as promulgated by Kant provided no more than a kind of backdrop for the events now taking place on the stage of conference diplomacy. It was the doers, the statesmen of the victorious Powers, who were to make the peace. The actors were the treaty makers, not the peace planners. As the eighteenth century gave way to the nineteenth, the dominant state system comprised five major Powers in Europe, a multiplicity of minor Powers, and a new state, as yet untried as a power, geographically outside Europe. That system had been challenged by a brilliant disturber, but France now renounced its claims to what Napoleon had conquered. A German confederation of some 38 states was established, with Prussia strengthened and Austria enabled to maintain its basic status with some gains here, some losses there. Britain enhanced its power, especially overseas but also by virtue of being able to manipulate the balance of power on the continent, apparently as it chose, a condition which produced the epithet "perfidious Albion." Russia gained both territory and prestige, its ruler regarded as the savior of Europe until his indecisive behavior cast doubt upon his right to any such role. In each instance it was to be the quality of thought as well as the political astuteness of the top negotiators which, given the power of their respective states that granted them the right to be there in the first place, determined the outcome of their deliberations.

Perhaps the most influential of these statesmen was Lord Castlereagh, the British Foreign Secretary. It was his conception of the European balance of power that was to prevail. A leading historian of the Congress of Vienna, C. K. Webster, observes that "for courage and common sense he has rarely been signalled among

British diplomatists . . . by working with intense energy, and utilizing to the full his unique opportunities, he acquired a great knowledge of Continental affairs, and became one of the least insular of British foreign ministers."[11] His intellectual stamp, which was on most of the Treaties, rested upon a few simple but well-conceived principles: first, lasting peace depended upon a real balance of power being established in Europe; second, France being confined to limits going back to ancient times; third, the continuation of the alliance after the peace settlement; fourth, a clear recognition that British interests should take into account the emerging plans for reconstructing the Continent of Europe. In order to achieve all this (and he did achieve most of it) he knew he would have to act as mediator between the other allied powers.

Both before and after Castlereagh's systematic thinking came to dominate the conference, it was Prince Clemens Metternich's more pragmatic approach to international relations which, day-by-day, set the actual pace. As a noted interpreter of international conferences, Sir Harold Nicolson, has put it, "in his attitude to internal and to external affairs the whole of Metternich's political theory can be summarized in the one word 'equilibrium'."[12] This was eloquently expressed in the following passages:

> Politics is the science of the vital interests of states, in its widest meaning . . . The great axioms of political science proceed from the knowledge of the true interests of *all* states; it is upon these general interests that rests the guarantee of their existence. The establishment of international relations on the basis of reciprocity . . . constitutes in our time the essence of politics, of which diplomacy is merely the daily application. Between the two there is in my opinion the same difference as between science and art.[13]

Or, as we might put it today, between theory and practice. Neither has much meaning without the other, whether one is thinking of "theory" in the sense of how things work or "theory" in the sense of how they ought to be made to work. After the Congress system had broken down and even its successor, the Quadruple Alliance (Prussia, Austria, Russia, England), had been abandoned by an England under George Canning increasingly antagonistic toward the so-called Holy Alliance, Metternich was forced to resign in the face of the revolutionary power of 1848. Now after nearly forty years as Austrian Foreign Minister, the venerable statesman bitterly observed, "I ruled Europe sometimes but I never governed Austria."[14] In the end it was his thought and his system rather than Castlereagh's that left its mark upon the conduct of international affairs.

The third principal actor's influence was brought to bear only later in the conference, because it was his lot to try to bring his country back into the center of European politics. As a tactician, Prince Charles de Talleyrand brilliantly succeeded but, as these words reveal, his views on the balance of power were more pragmatic than theoretical, more adaptive than consistent:

> If Europe were composed of states being so related to one another that the minimum of resisting power of the smallest were equal to maximum of aggressive power of the greatest, then there would be real equilibrium. But the situation in Europe is not, and will never be such.[15]

The French Minister's talents, writes Nicolson, "transcended opportunism, they amounted to genius."[16] Yet unless cynical realism constitutes an intellectual contribution, Talleyrand did little to advance the development of international relations as a coherent subject. Nor did the fourth actor, Tsar Alexander of Russia, whose mysticism, inconsistency, sense of guilt, and diplomatic limitations outweighed his genuine attempts at conciliation, his military achievements and even his early advocacy of a collective security system (to which he soberly but hardly prophetically referred as a "league"!).

Even though the period separating two great conferences – Vienna and Versailles – has often been referred to as the *Pax Britannica*, was this really a century of peace? If by "peace" is meant the absence of any fundamental, intended threat to the balance of power, the answer is "yes." If it means the absence of wars, even those involving the Great Powers in adjusting the balance by border changes, then the answer must be "no." The first answer is both more persuasive and more useful to the student of international relations, though it would never satisfy the peace seekers who became more activist as the century wore on. What needs to be understood is what was meant by the catch-phrase, *Pax*

Britannica. England, which had acquired strategic pieces of the French and Dutch colonial territories as a result of the Congress, had persuaded the ambassadors of Austria, Prussia and Russia to agree not even to discuss the question of British maritime rights during the negotiations. Whitehall would now be free to remain aloof or to intervene in continental affairs, whenever and wherever it wished, without necessarily committing itself to any other power in advance.

In light of the importance that was to be attached to public opinion after the next great peace conference, it is instructive to note its relative unimportance at the Congress of Vienna. Nevertheless, in a *Handbook*[17] released just after the First World War by the Foreign Office as being of probable use to those in the reading public concerned with international affairs, Webster noted the efforts by diplomatists to influence public opinion and, through public opinion, the negotiators at Vienna. There had been a real journalistic struggle in Prussia. Talleyrand was himself believed to have on more than one occasion stirred up dissension for his own purposes. The Tsar's ambassador in London was instructed that effort was to be made to influence public opinion in a direction favorable to Russian interests. Webster concluded that the total impact of these episodes was insignificant. Only the ideas of the plenipotentiaries mattered. An effective role in international affairs for potential challengers outside governments was to be postponed. Those in power neither wanted nor needed it; they merely ignored the public.

This did not mean that the governments always continued to support one another, as Castlereagh had hoped. Within less than a decade, the tidy Congress system had broken down, as had been predicted by one of the leading theorists of international relations of the time, Friedrich Gentz. Earlier he had attacked Kant's ideas, writing that "it is impossible to establish an eternal system of public law by means of a general treaty," and that the "question of the probable duration of this European League, which has temporarily overcome the gulf of competing political pretensions but cannot overcome it for ever, or even for very long, is thus the most important question facing statesmen."[18] What preserved peace was the interest of the Powers in preserving it, not a formal international organization which thereby was not even needed. What took the place of the Congress system was the "Concert of

Europe," an informal inter-state association which worked fairly well until the Crimean War (1853–1856). Once a coincidence of perceived interests gave way to contention, an order based upon consensus of value inevitably broke down. "History teaches us, and invariably we disregard her lesson," one authority has observed in what is almost a theorem: "that coalitions begin to disintegrate the moment that the common danger is removed."[19]

The philosophers

If the diplomatic interplay of the century may be said to have been ushered in by statesmen-thinkers, it also had its share of political philosophers who never held power, but, in the long run, were probably more influential for not doing so. Several widely-divergent authorities, David Ricardo and Friedrich List to name but two, were convinced that economics and politics cannot and should not be separated. Their views contributed to the history of ideas in the political economy of international relations that, with security studies, was to constitute one of the growing points of the discipline in the late twentieth century. While few would venture to claim that it could be a "science," the art of diplomacy was itself made more exact by the writings of Prince Czartowski, G. F. de Martens and Montague Bernard. And challenging the entire system by word and deed were numerous groups making up the peace movement, which in the second half of the nineteenth century had to be taken more seriously by foreign offices than it had been by the diplomats at Vienna, when as a "movement" it hardly existed. All of this was nourished in all its contradictions by a European society which allowed them all to exist and indeed, to a greater or lesser degree, to thrive. Totalitarianism was only to smother the human mind several generations later.

Most of these seminal writers about the state and politics writ large, while never holding responsible positions in government, accepted prevailing societal assumptions and values. Georg Hegel's philosophy of history, particularly his dialectical method of thinking (thesis, antithesis, synthesis), was different. He succeeded in doing what neither Kant nor Rousseau had attempted, which was to produce a comprehensive theory based on impersonal forces propelling humanity in a sort of preordained route of progress.

Hegel reversed the order in what Parkinson regards as the first theory of international relations to be conceived entirely in terms of social dynamics.[20] Contending that what *is* must be rational, Hegel saw the basis of history as what he regarded as divine and absolute reason, yet argued that as a result of the Enlightenment freedom had become general in the world, forging a kind of link in the course of world history.[21] War between states was simply a fact, neither to be praised nor condemned, so there was no point in moralizing about what should govern relationships between governments. This amoral approach to international relations reflected a break with the immediate past. Like Burke, Hegel was skeptical about formal agreements, such as treaties. Though he did write of something called "world spirit," he rejected the whole idea of international integration. Universal diplomatic custom was a better basis for bringing about order among states. For this reason Hegel concentrated upon the state and subordinated international relations, as would Marx, but for different reasons.

Conventional approaches to law and peace

Meanwhile several other conventional, that is state-centric, theories or approaches to international relations were being advanced. In the field of international law, for example, James Mill wrote an influential series of *Essays* for the *Encyclopaedia Britannica*, which placed considerable emphasis upon public opinion, or as he put it, "the approbation or disapprobation of mankind."[22] He even went so far as to advocate that steps be taken to educate public opinion, postulating that

> the book of the law of nations, and selections from the book of trials before the international tribunal, should form a subject of study in every school and a knowledge of them a necessary part of every man's education . . . a moral sentiment would grow up, which would, in time, act as a powerful restraining force upon the injustice of nations. . . .[23]

Yet, while he favored an international court with real power to treat offenses against the law of nations, Mill rejected any intention of backing up such a court by armed force. Another believer in the rule of law in the tradition of statesmen-scholars, though never a decision-maker like Castlereagh or John Quincy Adams, was an American international lawyer, Henry Wheaton (1785–1848), an experienced career diplomat widely known for the precision of his writing. In 1836, the year he became Minister in Berlin, he published the first of many editions of a widely read standard work, which was translated into several languages. One basic principle was put this way: "the peculiar subjects of international law are Nations, and those political societies of Men called States . . . a State is also distinguishable from a Nation, since the former may be composed of different races of Men, all subject to the same supreme authority."[24] Confirming Wheaton's efforts at promotion of an enlightened public opinion as a necessary step in achieving a rule of law in interstate relations was "Historicus" (Sir Vernon Harcourt) in addressing certain issues in international law. Highly influential over a period of many years, Sir James Lorimer, in his *Institutes of the Law of Nations* (1883), revealed himself a master of the middle ground in the field of international law between national independence and cosmopolitan values. He advocated both the loosest possible bonds in an international organization and a court whose awards should if necessary be enforced by an international army. The work of Lorimer, who as Professor of International Law at Edinburgh was not afraid to change his mind, represented what one authority calls the first serious attempt to define the juridical form of a European federation.

As at the Congress of Vienna, there were now statesmen who were serious thinkers preparing for another widely heralded conference in 1898. As a result, a good deal of cerebration was brought to bear among members of the inner circle in the Foreign Office upon the related questions of international law (in which most of them believed) and international government (in which most of them did not). However inaccurately, the Congress of Berlin in 1878 was characterized by *The Times* as the "first instance of a real Parliament of the Great Powers,"[25] but only a few years later, the desirability of such a parliament was apparently shared by the British Prime Minister. William Gladstone endeavored to revive the Concert of Europe in 1893 though a "Council of the Great Powers" (all of which at that time were still, but not for long, wholly or partly European). General belief in the feasibility of international cooperation through formal organization of powers with common values, however, was to wane after Bismarck was forced to resign. As for formal international organization, that potentially rich harvest was to remain in seed for a later generations. But that seed had been planted, at least in theory, during a century in which for the first time the idea of international institutions was seen as a feasible form of the relations among states.

Political economists and strategists

From an entirely different perspective, the political economists continued to stand out, some for their writing (such as List), some for their parliamentary skill (such as John Bright) and some for both (such as Richard Cobden).[26] They believed in as little government intervention as possible, either in domestic or foreign affairs. A Member of Parliament who founded a major opposition newspaper, Cobden argued in his *Free Trade as the Best Human Means for Securing Universal and Permanent Peace* (1842) that unfettered commerce would create such a powerful incentive for peace that men would prevent their governments from using war as the chosen instrument for serving their interests. Another Progressive Radical of the so-called Manchester School was Bright, a brilliant orator who wrote little but was much written about, particularly by Cobden. An early manifestation of functionalism (though it was not then called that), Bright's philosophy was based on three essential elements: first, existence of a "harmony of interests" among states, second, an intimate connection between peace and free trade, and third, abolition of the monopoly of trade, which Bright saw as being fundamental to what was termed "the colonial system." His parliamentary colleague Cobden even went so far as to contend that free trade constituted "the international law of the Almighty." The theory of peace, while still perhaps rudimentary, was advancing on several fronts, though there was as yet still no theory of international relations as such. Or at least it was not called that, though two kinds of theory had begun to emerge. One grew out of a need to *explain* the nature of power relations; the other reflected a deep desire to *change* it.

As for the theory of war, the nineteenth century also produced significant advances. One important thinker achieved notoriety for his maxim (which every student of international relations learns almost as a basic hypothesis, to be accepted or not as one chooses): "war is a mere continuation of politics by other means."[27] When Karl von Clausewitz wrote this in *Vom Kriege* (On War) in 1823, he spelled out a theory of war as an instrument of national policy. To this great German disciplinarian, peace seemed hardly more than a temporary respite from the normal, yet he warned against "the most soulless analysis, and as if in a horrid dream" trying to "connect this base of abstractions with facts belonging to the real world. Heaven preserve every theorist from such an undertaking."[28] Some years later, a Swiss who served in the French and Russian armies, Baron Antoine Henri Jomini, further systematized military science, concentrating not upon politics and diplomacy, but war itself. In his *Précis de l'Art de La Guerre* (1838), Jomini made a theoretical attempt to demonstrate that there is a fundamental principle in all operations of war, a principle which should preside over all measures adopted so that they may be successful. Jomini was at one time a paramount figure in his field in Europe, although unlike Clausewitz he may later have been neglected because he was referring to a type of war that was no longer relevant. Although neither a war theorist nor a military specialist, another nineteenth-century thinker deserves attention, if only because he came close to anticipating "conflict resolution," one of the principal "islands of theory" of the late twentieth century. An influential French authority, C. de Mougins de Rocquefort implied in 1889 that governments must reconcile themselves to the possibility of legitimate sanctions and compromises on national sovereignty if wars were ever to be prevented or contained.[29]

Closely related to thinking about war and strategy were questions of resources, land mass, and location. Alexis de Tocqueville had produced in 1832 a disturbingly prophetic study entitled *Democracy in America*. In some ways, he can be regarded as one of the first modern exponents of what came to be known as geopolitics, predicting that because of their respective size, position and resources, as well as their political institutions and capabilities, Russia and America would in time become the major power centers of the world (he also expressed grave reservations about the ability of democracies either logically to define a foreign policy or to adhere to it persistently once defined). In the context of defining goals for the peace movement in 1866, Michael Chevalier was to be perhaps the first to promote European unification expressly for the purpose of providing an essential counter-weight to what he called the "political colossus"[30] on the far side of the ocean.

Sociologists and historians

Long-range prediction in international relations also fascinated two much more influential writers of the time, Auguste Comte and Herbert Spencer. The founder of Western sociology, Comte was the first modern thinker to recommend the empirical investigation of the facts of society and politics along scientific lines. His critique of the widely known and by some highly regarded *Project* of the Abbé St Pierre revealed both a theory of international relations and of foreign policy:

> The idea of the worthy Abbé was in itself good, but it erred by the false combination by means of which he wished to carry it out, for he proposed a coalition of kings . . . He might as well have proposed that wolves should guard sheep . . . soon, by the power of public opinion, enlightened by the press . . . the people will actually govern.[31]

What Comte wanted was a League of Peoples, not of states. Like Comte, Spencer (who coined the term "survival of the fittest" in 1864) believed that the conflict between individuals and the world in which they live could only be resolved by applying ethical principles to contemporary society. But this had to be based upon knowledge acquired by free individuals, not the initiative of organized society. As about the same time, another sociologist, Lester Ward, was drawing distinctions between territorial groups called races, nations, or states. He was convinced that war would disappear as international understanding was developed through education (a concept later institutionalized in Archibald Macleish's preamble to the constitution of UNESCO, which begins with the words "as wars begin in the minds of men, it is in the minds of men that the defenses of peace must be constructed").

Historical interpretations provided useful insights for international relations, among them a study of British policy by Sir

John Seeley, in which he responded to the shock of the Franco-Prussian war by advocating that Europe federate,[32] and a series of essays on the study of history by Lord Acton, who is perhaps best known for the well-known expression "power corrupts, and absolute power corrupts absolutely."[33] In an insight which presaged the interdisciplinary nature of the future field of international relations, Acton noted the advantage of the complementarity and toleration provided by the heterogeneous nature of large states in terms of geography, culture, language, economics, and law.

The conventional consensus

Certain paradigms can be said to have been accepted by most, though certainly not all, of the nineteenth-century thinkers about the nature and the improvement of international relations. Despite sharp differences of opinion and even of action, consensus seemed to prevail on the presumably obvious, though increasingly challenged, legitimacy of the state. What were the elements of this consensus? In the first place, the state and its continued existence in any one of its existing forms was taken for granted, as it had been certainly since Westphalia. Second, even though strategists like Clausewitz and statesmen like Metternich expected war to occur from time to time among such states, there was a general acceptance of an essential interest among them in maintaining the existing order. The Progressive Radicals and classical economists went further in this view than others, particularly policy-makers who had to deal on a day-to-day basis with international disputes. Third, undergirded by a shared belief in international law, peace was regarded as the normal state of relationships. Even Bismarck's "blood and iron" use of force was designed more for internal German unification than expansion. Fourth, although the prime value remained the national interest, acceptance of the idea of the existence of some kind of an international interest had also been prevalent. Even the expression "harmony of interest" was often used to describe one of the underlying realities – or even principles – of the world political economy of the period, despite the all-too-evident competition between the powers for advantage. Finally, the sometimes almost mystical belief in the balance of power as the way of accommodating these contradictory values was widespread.

All this represented the conventional nineteenth-century world-view, and many of these consensual precepts were to continue to affect international thought right up to the totally unexpected outbreak of a general war early in the twentieth century. But all was not, in fact, well. The liberal revolts that broke out all over the Continent of Europe in 1848 gave evidence of an underlying discontent and reluctance to accept the prevailing value systems of elites in the respective countries which together made up European society. There were alternative paradigms or conceptual frameworks. One was a gradually changing peace movement. Another was Marxism, which seemed to burst suddenly upon the consciousness of society. And a third was nationalism. As Jeff Holzgrefe suggests in his challenging contribution on the origins of modern international relations theory, these are "pieces of the puzzle" of trying to ascertain who or what founded our discipline.[34]

Notes: Chapter 2

1 (London: Hollis and Carter, 1948), p. 125.
2 Cited by William T. R. Fox and Annette Baker Fox, "The teaching of international relations in the United States," *World Politics*, XIII, 3, April 1961, p. 339 n.
3 Wright, Quincy. *The Study of International Relations* (New York: Appleton-Century Crofts, Inc., 1955) p.3
4 Correspondence with Olson, July 1988.
5 Hinsley, *Power and the Pursuit of Peace*, p. 81.
6 R. J. Vincent, "Edmund Burke and the theory of international relations", *Review of International Studies*, 10, 3, July 1984, p. 216.
7 Henry Kissinger, *A World Restored* (New York: Grosset and Dunlap, 1964), p. 167.
8 Parkinson, *Philosophy of International Relations*, p. 70.
9 Cited by Parkinson, ibid., p. 68.
10 Sir Harold Nicolson, *The Congress of Vienna: A Study in Allied Unity: 1812–1822* (New York: Harcourt, Brace, 1946), pp. 241–2. Perhaps his earliest claim to fame as a writer came from his *Peacemaking 1919* (London: Constable, 1933), in which he describes the Versailles conference "as I experienced it myself," p. 6.
11 C. K. Webster, *The Congress of Vienna* (New York: Barnes and Noble, 1963), p. 30.
12 Nicolson, *Congress of Vienna*, p. 39.
13 ibid.
14 ibid., p. 274.
15 ibid., p. 155.

16 ibid., p. 154.
17 Webster, Sir Charles Kingsley, *The Congress of Vienna 1814–15*, Great Britain, Foreign Office, Historical Section. Peace Handbooks, Vol. 24, No. 153 (London: HMSO, 1920), pp. 93–7.
18 Hinsley, *Power and the Pursuit of Peace*, p. 198.
19 Nicolson, *Congress of Vienna*, p. 260.
20 Cited by Parkinson, *Philosophy of International Relations*, p. 75.
21 ibid., p. 76. See also Lewis P. Hinchman, *Hegel's Critique of the Enlightenment* (Gainesville, Fla: University Presses of Florida, 1984), esp. p. 125.
22 Hinsley, *Power and the Pursuit of Peace*, p. 88.
23 ibid., pp. 90–1.
24 Henry Wheaton, *Elements of International Law*, 8th edn. (Boston: Little, Brown, 1966), p. 29.
25 Hinsley, *Power and the Pursuit of Peace*, p. 137.
26 The views of both Bright and Cobden are perceptively reviewed in Part I of Hinsley, *Power and the Pursuit of Peace*, in "A history of internationalist theories," esp. pp. 96–124.
27 Karl von Clausewitz, *On War*, taken from the Penguin edition. Harmondsworth: Penguin, 1968, p. 119.
28 ibid., p. 250.
29 *De la Solution des Conflicts Internationaux*. Cited by Hinsley, *Power and the Pursuit of Peace*, p. 138.
30 Cited by Hinsley, ibid., p. 122.
31 Cited by Hinsley, ibid., p. 106.
32 *The Growth of British Policy* (Cambridge: Cambridge University Press, 1895). See Hinsley, *Power and the Pursuit of Peace*, p. 121.
33 In a letter to Bishop Creighton. Cited in *Oxford Dictionary of Quotations* (Oxford: Oxford University Press, 1979), p. 1.
34 Jeff Holzgrefe, "The origins of modern international relations theory," *Review of International Studies*, 15, 1, January 1989, p. 11.

Further reading

Bentham, Jeremy. *An Introduction to the Principles of Morals and Legislation*, ed. by J. H. Burns and H. L. A. Hart. London: Athlone Press, 1970.
Clausewitz, Karl von. [1823]. *On War*. London: Kegan Paul, 1911.
de Tocqueville, Alexis. [1832]. *Democracy in America* (trans. Henry Reeve). London and New York: Colonial, 1900.
Gentz, Friedrich. *Fragments on the Balance of Power*. London: Peltier, 1806.
Hobbes, Thomas. [1651]. *Leviathan*, in *The English Works of Thomas Hobbes*. London: John Bohn, 1839.
Kant, Immanuel. [1795] *Perpetual Peace*. (trans. Lewis L. Beck). Boston: World Peace Foundation, 1950. New York: Bobb Merrill, 1957.
List, Friedrich. [1841]. *The National System of Political Economy* (trans. Lloyd). London: Longman, 1904.

Lorimer, Sir James. *The Institutes of the Law of Nations*, 2 vols. Edinburgh: Blackwood, 1883.

May, Arthur. *The Age of Metternich 1814–1848*. New York: Henry Holt, 1933.

Mill, John Stuart. [1848]. *Principles of Political Economy*, 7th edn. Green and Co., 1871. London: Longman, 1909.

Petrie, Sir Charles. *Diplomatic History 1713–1933*. London: Hollis and Carter, 1948.

Ricardo, David. *The Principles of Political Economy and Taxation*. New York: Macmillan, 1895.

Smith, Adam. [1776]. *Selections from the Wealth of Nations*, ed. by George J. Stigler. New York: Appleton-Century-Crofts. 1957.

3 Transforming the world: Marx, the peace movement and war

> The philosophers have only interpreted the world, in various ways; the point, however, is to change it. (Karl Marx, "Theses on Feuerbach")

The idealist paradigm that would dominate the thinking about international affairs in the early part of the twentieth century had its origins, within the context of British liberalism, in the peace movement of the nineteenth century. More revolutionary was another alternative to convention, represented by Karl Marx, who opposed the entire system. Both declined to accept the state's judgement about the legitimacy of the military option and particularly the people's role in war. Different in kind from what had been seen before, these efforts were so organized that at least some of their manifestations promised to threaten the state itself in its pursuit of what its spokesmen regarded as "the national interest." Those spokesmen, then as now, regarded this principle as being beyond question (actually it was often merely beyond definition), and some went so far in their fervency as to constitute a third alternative to conventional values – a more virulent form of nationalism.

The Marxist alternative

Karl Marx, one of those who rejected the right of the bourgeois state to speak and to act for the people, expanded his ideas in England, but did not live to see them effectuated where he least expected it: in Russia. He and his principal collaborator, Friedrich Engels, have been characterized as the last of a number of thinkers on international affairs in the nineteenth century who placed great emphasis upon the meaning of historical progress.[2] When they wrote the first sentence of *The Communist Manifesto* in 1848 – "A spectre is haunting Europe: the spectre of communism" – many countries were either in revolt against the existing order or were about to be. The revolts turned out to be more liberal than communist, and for the most part they failed. The old order was given a new lease on life. In a sense, so was Marx, the most influential political thinker of the nineteenth century, and his ideas are still the source of debate, sometimes violent. In his commentary on political economy in 1859 (which incidentally was his only theoretical work relating the non-European world to his general philosophy of history,[3] Marx observed that "mankind always takes up only problems it can solve."[4] Engels agreed and acted upon that premise.

Two of their political ideas are of particular concern to students of the development of international thought. One was the conception of the state itself. The other was their interpretation of the relations between states. To Engels, who was a social Darwinist, the state was "the executive committee of the ruling class" which exploited the working class for its own advantage. Were there no classes, there would be no need for the state; it would "wither away." Before that could happen, however, there would have to be the overthrow of class society. Applied on a world plane, the class struggle would produce a stateless world without class antagonisms. Hence war was the only road to peace.

The state, far from providing the basis for international law, organization, and peace, was itself necessarily and by its very nature the enemy of peace. The system could not be improved nor could the balance of power be tinkered with; they had to be replaced. Yet Marx was, according to Hinsley "firmly attached to a belief in perpetual peace. If he said little about it it was because he believed that it would follow automatically upon the withering away of the state."[5] On a world level, Marxists regarded national economies merely as sub-systems of the wider capitalist system and thus the world as a class "battlefield between world bourgeoisie and world proletariat." What they regarded as "inevitable historical processes" would lead from primitive communism towards the feudal, bourgeois and proletarian state, leading ultimately to a world society that would be both classless and stateless. A rebel outside the system in the nineteenth century, Marx's ideas were to have a tremendous impact on the twentieth.

A related work of considerable significance was *Gemeinschaft und Gesellschaft* (community and society), published in 1887 by Ferdinand Tonnies when he was only thirty-two. Little noticed at first, it was to become a major work in both the theory and application of sociology to the state and the emerging capitalist economy. In discussing its tendency "to be cosmopolitan and unlimited in size," Tonnies postulated that the capitalist society "through a long process spreads itself over the totality of this people, indeed over the whole of mankind."[6] Though greatly influenced by Marx, Tonnies disagreed with him on what brings about social change.

Imperialism and nationalism were never principal preoccupations of Marx (who, incorrectly, saw nationalism in decline), but Marxist writers were later to deal extensively with both these phenomena, notably Nikolay Bukharin on imperialism and the world economy, Vladimir Ilyich Lenin in his famous work on imperialism as the highest stage of capitalism, and Karl Kautsky, who established the twin criteria of territory and language. But the Marxists were not the only philosophical activists of this period.

The peace movement as alternative

Certain segments of the peace movement, which flourished in England, France, the United States, the Netherlands, and other Western countries after the Crimean War, and particularly after the Franco-Prussian war, also opposed the existing state system. They felt that inherently it sanctioned war. The aggressive unifier of Italy, Giuseppe Garibaldi, was a leading figure in the International League of Peace and Liberty, set up in 1867 by Charles Lemonnier, an outspoken federalist advocate of a United States of Europe. In discussing this movement, Hinsley refers to "the strong undercurrent of distrust of government which marked even English and American liberal views," including such writers as Henry Thoreau and William Lloyd Garrison. In England, Bright, who was no Marxist, had argued in the 1850s that "wars were financed by the working class, which stood to lose most by them," while Cobden was convinced that "the intercourse between communities is nothing more than the intercourse of individuals in the aggregate"[7] to which the intervention of governments was but an obstacle. The Benthamites agreed, yet another group outside the conventional consensus went even further: the anarchists and near-anarchists. William Godwin (1756–1836) had seen the state as an institution whereby such privileged groups as the military and the diplomats – "all the train of artifices that has been invented to hold other nations at bay, to penetrate their secrets, to traverse their machinations, to form alliances and counter-alliances"[8] – sought to impose their will on the people. An international organization of governments would be only one more obvious manifestation of the state's effort to preserve its status.

Not all peace activists rejected international organization as an unnecessary evil. Some saw it as the only way to guarantee peace. In the United States, one of the most articulate, William Ladd, published a *Dissertation on a Congress of Nations* in 1832 and followed up with another essay on such a congress some eight years later. In 1843 the first Universal Peace Conference (a non-governmental enterprise despite its official-sounding title) took place in London, based upon a manifesto of the American Peace Society. Complementing Cobden, whose book relating to free trade and peace has already been noted, were William Ellery Channing, the founder of the Massachusetts Peace Society (later to become national) and Charles Sumner, who regarded the Constitution of the United States as proof that war as an institution in society could actually be outlawed. Both were writing, speaking and organizing with enthusiastic vigor.

The first of many journals produced by the peace movement appeared in 1819 under the auspices of a group calling itself the British Society for the Promotion of Permanent and Universal Peace, the name itself, *The Herald of Peace*, implying a certain expectation of a world bound to come. On the continent, the French Peace Society (La Société des Amis de la Morale Chrétienne), founded in 1821, had many branch societies by the 1890s, stimulated no doubt by Henri de Saint Simon in his *De La Réorganisation de la Société Européenne* a few years earlier.

From opposition to participation

By mid-century the ideas of the peace movement apparently began to have an effect upon governmental behavior, with the *Manchester Examiner* in 1853 stating that:

> The principles of the Peace Society, fanatical as they are, have unquestionably gained ground among us; statesmen shrink from war now, not only on account of its risks, its costs, its possible unpopularity, but from a new-born sense of the tremendous moral responsibility. . . .[9]

This sense was not confined to England. Western society had become more integrated and more representative, all of which "reconciled the mass of public opinion to the state . . . A new kind of publicist, not at loggerheads with the government, found an interest in the field of international relations."[10] This was the reverse side of the coin of the peace movement. Its main adherents were coming to believe that the road to peace ran through influencing public opinion in order to change public policy, not through challenging the state itself.

No such shift was taking place in the thinking of the Marxists, but only the more radical members of the peace movement were drawn to the Marxists' fundamental transformation approach. The movement as a whole came to occupy the middle ground between the opposition of Rousseau, Kant, Bentham, and their followers to any kind of formalized international organization at all and the equally radical advocacy by such writers as Penn, Bellers, and Saint-Simon of some form of federal union. The peace movement gradually had became part of the conventional nineteenth century, not an alternative to it in any basic manner. Some statesmen were now quite prepared to enter a confederation of some form or other. What had influenced the mainstream peace movement was the international political environment itself. Its adherents, looking at the world around them, concluded that the *grounds* for war had almost disappeared in the international relations of civilized states. That war existed at all was due simply to the "stupidity and criminality" of governments, and hence international organizations made up of those governments were undesirable because politicians could not be trusted. To these activists, the opinion of the public would exercise its benevolent influence which, with international law, would ensure peace. Given these happy premises, inter-state organization seemed hardly necessary.[11]

This conviction had produced a change of tactics in the peace movement: parliamentary participation. Cobden and Bright had already led the way in this, followed by such men as Senator Marcoartu of Spain and Professor Mancini, a member of the Chamber of Deputies in Rome, one of several thinkers instrumental in fostering the peace movement in Italy as a result of the shock of the Franco-Prussian war. That experience led to formation of societies in the Netherlands and Belgium as well. In the years before the Hague conferences at the turn of the century their efforts concentrated upon the promotion of arbitration at various assemblies, notably a congress of all the peace organizations in Paris in 1878 and the formation of the Inter-parliamentary Union in 1892. Speaking before the 1893 Congress, W. Evans Darby, the secretary of the British Peace Society, warned that what was necessary was to provide the state, not with policies, but with principles upon the basis of which goverments should then have the responsibility of making policy. Otherwise, the peace movement would be charged with "arrogant meddle-someness."[12] The effort to influence those in power took the form from 1900 onwards of inviting ministers to attend. Some did so, and received reports annually on the peace resolutions passed by successive congresses.

A recurring debate: idealism versus realism

These developments may now be seen as harbingers of what was to become the study of international relations, characterized by two drives. One was the desire to understand and to promote peace. The other was to accomplish this by influencing government policy, by making public opinion a factor in international relations. A striking example of two approaches to this and the related subject of morality in foreign policy is seen in dramatic speeches in the House of Commons following Ottoman suppression of Balkan peoples in 1875. Prime Minister Gladstone stated what might be called the idealist view:

My hope, therefore, is twofold. First, that, through the energetic attitude of the people of England, their Government may be led to declare distinctly, that it is for purposes of humanity alone that we have a fleet in Turkish waters. Secondly, that fleet will be so distributed as to enable its force to be most promptly and efficiently applied, in case of need, on Turkish soil, in concert with the other Powers, for the defence of innocent lives, and to prevent the repetition of those recent scenes, at which hell itself might almost blush.[13]

By contrast, Benjamin Disraeli put the national interest first in a classical "realist" statement:

We must remember that our connection with the East is not merely an affair of sentiment and tradition, but that we have urgent and substantial and enormous interests which we must guard and keep . . . We have, therefore, entered into an alliance – a defensive alliance – with Turkey, to guard her against any further attack from Russia. We believe that the result of this Convention will be order and tranquillity.[14]

One reason for citing this particular colloquy is that the real-ist–idealist debate would continue well into the next century as the discipline of IR came to maturity. The more difficult epistemological question is how one assesses the statesman who is idealist in rhetoric and realist in action. This is particularly difficult when "the national interest" is elevated to a high ethical plane.

Throughout the second half of the nineteenth century a number of intellectuals in several countries advanced theories of international relations, though few, if any, called them that. Among the most advanced was Gustave de Molinari who, in comparing the peace plans of St Pierre and Kant in a notable study published in Paris in 1857, linked the idea of a universal organization to a tribunal and an international police force which would have no domestic jurisdiction at all. In Britain, John Noble soon proposed a Supreme Court of Nations, Leone Levi (professor of international law at London) published a *Draft Project of a High Court of Arbitration*, and Lorimer challenged the assumption that any given status quo could ever be regarded as permanent, ridiculing the old Grand Design of Henry IV as being "as meaningless in the mouths of princes as of other people."[15] In Germany, J. K. Bluntschli anticipated in 1878 what was later to emerge as one of the basic principles of both the League of Nations and the United Nations. He argued that the independence of member states be protected, that voting be weighted in favor of Great Powers, that disputes be decided by majority vote and that, if such decisions had to be carried out by force, this should be the responsibility of the most powerful states.[16]

A fascinating French figure was Joseph-Pierre Proudhon (1809–65), whose thought passed through distinct phases, from favoring global utopian association to international functional federalism and eventually confederalism in world politics. Having started out in the 1840s as an anarchist, Proudhon had within twenty years begun to reexamine world order systematically in a study of war and peace in 1858, followed by his *Du Principe Fédératif* (1863) designed to forge instruments for the prevention of war through federalism. Thus, federalism was seen as the hand-maiden of functionalism, which in the rise and proliferation of public international unions (outlined in Paul Reinsch's book on the subject published in 1911) indicates the nature of European perspectives on IR in the nineteenth century.

By the turn of the century, however, the committee on a United States of Europe of the 1900 Paris Congress of Political Sciences had taken pains to reject a federal approach. Now the continental peace movement was, in the face of growing tension between European nations, turning away from federation just as British activists were moving toward it. It was in this atmosphere of increasing anxiety about the possibility of war and the cost of armament that the Tsar persuaded other monarchs to meet in a major conference at The Hague in 1899, to be followed by another in 1907. Contradictory expectations and explanations accompanied both, and everyone tried to capitalize on them to press his own views. Some saw them as the culmination of decades, even centuries, of gradual development of the rule of law in international relations. Others saw in The Hague meetings the assumption that since wars were bound to occur, their conduct needed to be better regulated.

At all events, there was an intensified interest in law and new theories about it. In 1899, T. E. Holland came out with a series of thoughtful studies in international law, as well as his *Letters on War and Neutrality*, which appeared over four decades starting in 1881. Sir Henry Sumner Maine, whose *Ancient Law in Relation to Modern Ideas* advanced the sociology of law, produced the second edition of his definitive work on international law in 1906. All of these represented the urgency as well as the anticipation of increased reliance upon law in the world of sovereign states. The reason for the sense of urgency lay in the opposite view of reliance: the state, in the form of the redefined and revivified nation, had to rely upon itself.

Nationalism and Aussenpolitik

As Marxism seemed unable to make good its threat to the social order and the peacemakers seemed equally incapable of elevating that order to the level of international cooperation, those who believed in force became more influential. Whether war was a probability or merely a possibility, prudent statesmen felt obliged to prepare for it, even if they did not believe it would really happen. Prussia led the way, stimulated early in the century by the idealistic nationalism of Johann Fichte, gradually shifting to Bismarck's "blood and iron" philosophy. *Realpolitik* became *Machtpolitik*. Foreign policy (*Aussenpolitik*) came more and more to be determined by the relationship of force between states.

The possibility of war and the threat to world order toward the end of the century revived interest in several countries in what was to become known as geopolitics. Anthropologists and geographers such as Friedrich Ratzel had shown certain connections between culture, national divisions, and migration on the one hand and topography, resources, position and climate on the other, without drawing from them any particular strategic implications. Then, three broad-gauged thinkers combined politics and strategy in a way not witnessed since the simpler days of Machiavelli. One was American, one British, and one Swedish, each assembling geographical information and interpreting it for foreign policy purposes. The first, Admiral Alfred T. Mahan, made explicit one of the principal assumptions that had guided American strategy since the promulgation of the Monroe Doctrine, namely that a state with predominant sea power could, if it chose to, blockade its rivals and dominate world politics. This paradigm of strategic thinking, set forth in Mahan's *The Influence of Sea Power upon History* (1890), was soon matched by a land school of strategy enunciated by Sir Halford MacKinder and others. Addressing the Royal Geographical Society in 1904 on "The geopolitical pivot of history," Mackinder spelled out his well-known "classic warning":[17]

> Who controls East Europe
> commands the Heartland;
>
> Who rules the Heartland
> commands the World Island;
>
> Who rules the World Island
> commands the World.

The term "geopolitics" had actually been coined by a Swede, the political scientist Rudolph Kjellen (1864–1922), who in describing a novel theoretical, organic system of government, influenced German thinking, particularly the man who was to turn geopolitics into a pseudo-science for Hitler – Karl Haushofer. It was Haushofer's influence which made geopolitics a factor in policy; other, more responsible students of the geographical impact upon politics were only brought into IR analysis later.

Toward a more systematic study

What about diplomacy? Was this an aspect of an alternative to power politics? It was generally not so regarded in the nineteenth century. Though not on a par with the great Callières, another renowned diplomat, Count Vincent Benedetti, drew upon his experience, particularly in unsuccessful negotiations, only to pass on useful lessons in technique in his *Studies in Diplomacy* in 1896. However, in another study ten years later, *The Practice of Diplomacy*, an American, John W. Foster, not only brought up to date the entire procedural dimension of the field but made some plausible new suggestions on the formulation and execution of foreign policy. In the words of Martin Wight, "The literature of the art of diplomacy, like that of the art of war, has always

combined history and analysis with practical advice";[18] unfortunately, it was advice not sufficient, if indeed it was applied at all,
to prevent a war in 1914. Yet, in discussing the development of
diplomatic theory, Nicolson asserts that

> in spite of dramatic periods when violence momentarily became
> more authoritative than reason, it is possible to recognize a
> distinct upward curve of progress . . . from the narrow concep-
> tion of exclusive tribal rights to the wider conception of inclusive
> common interests. . . .[19]

The first glimmerings of international relations as a discipline
had appeared with the publication of Reinsch's *World Politics at the
End of the Nineteenth Century* (1900). More a critique of imperialism
(including American) than an all-encompassing systematic treatment of the whole fabric of international affairs, the Wisconsin
political scientist nevertheless did deal with such topics as The
Hague Conference, popular opinion toward international questions, parties, and demands for policing the world. While the
political scientists assembled in Paris that year (as was to be the
case in the third decade of the twentieth century) were focusing
upon organization, Reinsch concentrated upon power. His work
suggests that a discipline of international relations had its real
beginnings in studies of imperialism, not in world order, as has so
often been suggested. In *Imperialism: a Study* (1905), J. A. Hobson
concluded that this general phenomenon could only be understood
through an analysis of capitalism as a whole, as a serious source of
friction between nations, as the Boer War had so recently demonstrated. To Hobson, capitalism did not need imperialism, whereas
Lenin and other Marxists argued that the two were inseparable. A
quite different framework was set forth by Norman Angell
between 1908 and 1914 in several editions of *The Great Illusion*,
which he contended was the assumption "that a nation's financial
and industrial stability, its security in commercial activity – in
short, its prosperity and well-being, depend upon its being able to
defend itself against the aggression of other nations."[20] He concluded that all this carries with it "the paradox that the more a
nation's wealth is protected the less secure does it become."[21]

Tracing the intellectual development of theory in international
relations must never be confined only to intellectuals, if by that

often-misapplied term is meant people who are not in the governmental sense "responsible" or accountable. For example, the famous memorandum of His Majesty's representative in Berlin, Eyre Crowe, constituted as thoughtful a piece of foreign policy analysis as one will find in the literature of the field.[22] In warning Whitehall in 1907 about the intentions and plans of the German decision-makers no longer restrained by Bismarckian statesmanship, he may have turned British foreign policy around. The balance of power, while certainly not abandoned, was given a new interpretation; instead of acting outside as the balancer, Britain now felt it more advisable to join with France and later Russia as a weight in the continental balance itself. Once committed, she could neither manipulate the system nor tip the scales at her convenience. But the purpose was still the same: to avoid a general war. It failed.

Even though the delegates to the renowned conferences in the Netherlands had devoted a high proportion of their time to the law of war and of neutrality in time of war, their meetings are generally known as The Hague Peace conferences. Yet the Algeciras Conference in 1906 had proved decisive in the realignment of the powers which produced war in 1914, just as the 1911 crisis had for a time made Agadir (on the west coast of Africa) the center of European diplomacy. Both events galvanized the peace movement to even more intensive activity. However menacing world politics had become, including the coming of the war itself, peace activists continued to propose remedies, not out of naïveté in all instances, but out of a well-intentioned conviction that if the proper kind of machinery for international cooperation could be created a war might be prevented. In 1908 the Universal Peace Congress adopted a "scheme for a complete Society of Nations, with a single executive as well as a legislative Council to supervise an international code and a court to apply it, and for the reduction of national armies to the minimum required for police purposes."[23]

In another domain, what may be regarded as the first professional journal in the field of international relations appeared in 1910. Published by the new Carnegie Endowment for International Peace, *International Conciliation* was for half a century to apply the highest academic standards in its editorial policy. It thereby created a professional norm (even though it was committed to a particular political goal) for the discipline that was to emerge after the war. The Endowment's founder, the great industrialist-philanthropist

Andrew Carnegie, had addressed a letter to the Universal Peace
Congress in 1904, urging somewhat optimistically that a union of
all the leading states renounce war and announce their intention of
enforcing this declaration. Nothing happened. In setting up a ten
million dollar endowment for peace, Carnegie ensured that the
income would be utilized for other socially useful purposes once
the problem of peace was solved, as he was confident it would be
within a relatively short time if only enough money were applied
to its solution. Naïve as this seems, it was a resonable expectation
for an industrial pragmatist of the prewar era.

The great burgeoning of analytical thought about world affairs
in the late nineteenth and first quarter of the twentieth century was
characteristic of the Western mind as it had developed since the
Dark Ages. But it also owed much to two of the most potent
forces of the nineteenth century – the industrial revolution and the
great surge of nationalism set free by the French Revolution and
the Napoleonic Wars. What made Western man "modern" was his
rejection of the traditional notion that what was, is now and always
will be. Thus his fate was in some part subject to his own efforts
to understand and reshape his environment. Western man through
the Renaissance, the Reformation, the rise of capitalism, the
Enlightenment and the Agrarian Revolution became ever more
competent, and therefore more confident, in understanding both
the physical and the social environments.

In the nineteenth century the industrial revolution had represented a quickening of pace in the application of the reasoning of
scientific method to the development of an empirical theory about
the physical world, so that its findings could be used for its
manipulation. Nature could be harnessed to man's purpose – at
least in part. The method that revealed the "secrets" of nature,
which were then applied in the form of the industrial revolution,
could also be used in the context of the social environment as well
as the physical environment. Bismarck had been one of the first to
use such notions in a comprehensive way when he initiated social
reforms. Others followed, including those who applied these
principles to relations among states. As the nineteenth century
progressed, three of the four great traditional afflictions of
humanity had become (at least so far as parts of Western Europe
and North America were concerned) amenable to societal control.
Famine could be banished by the application of science and capital

to agriculture. Pestilence could be defeated by public health pro-grams, public education, and investment in the engineering of the infrastructure of the new industrial cities. Poverty would be banished. The last great curse remained – war. By a logical progression, the application of scientific research and empirical findings to the physical environment first and then to the domestic social environment suggested that the *international* environment might also be subject to social engineering.

This sense of progress, of betterment, of pride was brutally interrupted by a calamity – the justly named Great War. Those very states, which had justified their world hegemony by their white man's burden, their duty to teach others how to live, their *mission civilisatrice*, their manifest destiny, used the tools of the industrial revolution to arm and supply great armies. They now found themselves mobilizing whole societies for years on end in a war that destroyed the Eurocentric world order. The industrial revolution produced the gun; the French Revolution and the ensuing flowering of nationalism motivated people to pull the trigger. This contrast with the confident and widespread belief in progress was devastating for some. For others it was a spur. If war was now too terrible to be allowed to happen again, it must be understood and then measures taken to control it. Peace was regarded then, as it is by many today, as the supreme task of those engaged in the analysis of international politics. To others, that task is to analyze the nature of power in the relations of states. These twin objectives were about to merge.

Although no effort had yet been made to create a separate discipline of international relations, four different threads which would be woven into its fabric began to form in the nineteenth century. One was the traditional pattern of diplomacy and of international law. A second was the idealistic tradition that com-bined with public activism in the peace movement. This would dominate the period of the first consensus in a new discipline in the early years following the Great War. In stark contrast stood the third, *Realpolitik*, which would come to dominate the period of second consensus following the Second World War. The fourth was Marxism which, except for the true believers, was for some time to play only a secondary role in the development of the discipline.

Ironically, the whole process was accelerated by the coming of the First World War. Within a year of the outbreak of hostilities, novel postwar proposals were being advanced. Hobson, for example, shifted from criticism of imperialism to a provocative pamphlet, *Toward International Government*, in which he advocated the eventual creation of a legislature entitled to utilize force against violators of international agreements. G. Lowes Dickinson went even further, proposing that an international army be empowered to maintain *internal* order, although he was later to conclude that a world state (or even the loosest federation that might be called a state) was not yet a serious political consideration. Because of his bellicose reputation, many are unaware of the early advocacy by Theodore Roosevelt of a "League of Peace," based upon the commitment of force by the Great Powers. Another American, Walter Lippman, wrote in *The Stakes of Diplomacy* in 1915 that any postwar organization could command what he called "a world patriotism" only if it were able to demonstrate its utility to its member-states, and nothing resembling a "Federation of Mankind" was in the offing. Nevertheless, the "supreme task of world politics" was "a satisfactory organization of mankind,"[24] which would develop gradually from a Western league.

In order to implement these ideas, new organizations sprang up in various western countries looking towards a lasting peace. Even before the war, the British League of Nations Society had been set up in 1913. The American League to Enforce Peace (1915) followed, with the *Organisation Centrale pour une Paix Durable* in the Netherlands (1916) and the French *Association de la Paix par le Droit*. In non-belligerent Sweden, one August Schevan went so far in promoting world law as to assert that existing states would be "stripped of sovereignty and independence, and transformed into subdivisions of humanity."[25] Few others agreed, though the Union for Democratic Control, established in London in 1914, actively supported the abolition of secret diplomacy, the renunciation of alliances, and the establishment of universal disarmament. Most agreed that an actual union of states was not required, but an organization of the powers was. The main question was how far sovereign states should go in restricting their own freedom of action. Increasingly, this was to turn on how far they could take their publics with them.

In a totally different context, one of the most significant works of the war years was Lenin's *Imperialism: The Highest Stage of*

Capitalism (1917), in which he argued that in the scramble for markets, the capitalist states would inevitably come to blows with one another as they turned their attention to undeveloped countries. Marx had addressed the nationalist phase of capitalism; now Lenin added the internationalist dimension. He felt that he was witnessing such a war, to be followed by proletarian revolts. Imperialism would be the final phase of capitalism.

A contrasting prophesy took the form, in terms of voting rights as well as a name, of *A League of Nations* (1917) by H. L. Brailsford. He proposed restricting membership in a Council to the Great Powers, who also would possess a larger vote than the smaller states in a legislative assembly and a court.[26] Another idea not generally expressed in the growing pro-league consensus came from Americans (perhaps not surprisingly in light of what was to happen later), whose League to Enforce Peace advocated provision for members' withdrawal. So many proposals had been advanced that by 1916 Randolph Bourne compiled his *Towards an Enduring Peace: A Symposium of Peace Proposals and Programs*, convinced that they represented the framework for a new world order.

An interdisciplinary experiment

The first of what might be termed "mainstream" IR (works dealing systematically with the entire world, taking into account insights from several disciplines) appeared during the war. Books or chapters were written by such economists as Greenwood of Leeds, political scientists as Buell of Harvard, international lawyers as Lawrence of Bristol, geographers as Bowman of Johns Hopkins and historians as Heatley of Edinburgh, whose *An Introduction to the Study of International Relations* (1916), rudimentary by later standards but nevertheless intellectually respectable, was years ahead of its time. Featuring chapters on war and peace since 1815 and on the causes of modern wars by two historians, one on international economic relations by an economist, and on international law by an international lawyer, this pioneering effort corresponded favorably with the consensus of principal topics that would emerge after the war. Even more striking from the perspective of an emergent discipline is the fact that this first real textbook was written at the suggestion of the British group that called itself the "Council for the Study of International Relations." Who constituted this Council and whatever happened to it has thus far unfortunately eluded us, as it would appear to constitute the first genuine effort to lay the groundwork for a truly multidisciplinary new field of study.

The growing importance of the public was reflected in writings of such leaders of the American establishment as the President of Columbia University, Nicholas Murray Butler, who argued in 1913 that "the rise in the world of a real public opinion . . . makes war increasingly difficult and increasingly repulsive,"[27] and former Secretary of State Elihu Root in his "Need of popular understanding of international law" in 1916. Before America entered the war, a few Britons were already trying to influence the course of public opinion about the world after the war; Graham Wallas even anticipated later thinkers by taking a psychological view of the world in his controversial *The Great Society* in 1917. In 1918, G. Lowes Dickinson developed his ideas in *The Choice before Us*, another clear indicator of the impact public opinion was expected to have upon the peace process once it took place. All of this set the stage for the American President's approach to the conduct of foreign policy based upon public understanding and acceptance of a "world safe for democracy."

Notes: Chapter 3

The authors wish to thank Professor Sir Harry Hinsley of Cambridge for the exceptional value of his book, *Power and the Pursuit of Peace*, for this chapter.

1 Karl Marx and Friedrich Engels, *Basic Writings on Politics and Philosophy* (Garden City, NY: Doubleday (Anchor Books), 1959), p. 245, xi.
2 Parkinson, *Philosophy of International Relations*, p. 87.
3 Shlomo Avineri, *Karl Marx on Colonialism and Modernization* (Garden City, NY: Doubleday, 1968), p. 4.
4 Cited by Avineri, ibid., p. 33.
5 Hinsley, *Power and the Pursuit of Peace*, p. 112.
6 F. Tonnies, *Community and Society*, trans. and ed. by Charles P. Loomis (London: Harper and Row, 1957), pp. 258–9. First published in 1887.
7 Hinsley, *Power and the Pursuit of Peace*, p. 106.
8 Parkinson, *Philosophy of IR*, p. 146.
9 ibid., p. 114.

10 ibid., p. 115.
11 The relationship in Europe, and to some extent in America, between public opinion, government, and the peace movement is thoroughly discussed by Hinsley in Chapter 7, esp. pp. 114–26.
12 Hinsley, *Power and the Pursuit of Peace*, p. 132.
13 Quoted in Hans J. Morgenthau and Kenneth W. Thompson (eds), *Principles and Problems of International Politics* (New York: Alfred A. Knopf, 1950), p. 53.
14 ibid., p.56.
15 Cited by Hinsley, in *Power and the Pursuit of Peace*, p. 134.
16 ibid., p. 135.
17 F. L. Schuman, *International Politics*, 4th edn. (New York: McGraw-Hill, 1948), p. 408. For perhaps the best summary of the long-term significance of Mackinder's ideas for students of IR, see Wight, Martin, *Power Politics*, ed. by Hedley Bull and Carsten Holbraad (New York: Penguin, 1978), pp. 72–7.
18 Wight, *Power Politics*, p. 161.
19 Harold Nicolson, *Diplomacy* (New York: Oxford University Press, 3rd edn, 1964), p. 17.
20 Norman Angell, *The Great Illusion: A Study of the Relation of Military Power in Nations to their Economic and Social Advantage* (London: Heinemann, 1910), p. 24.
21 ibid., p. 31.
22 "Memorandum by Sir Eyre Crowe on the present state of British Relations with France and Germany, January 1, 1907", *British Documents on the Origins of the War*, ed. by G. P. Gooch and H. Temperley (London: HMSO, 1928). The main sections are quoted in Fred Sondermann, David McLellan, and William C. Olson. *The Theory and Practice of International Relations*, 5th edn. (Englewood Cliffs, NJ: Prentice-Hall, 1979), pp. 119–22.
23 Hinsley, *Power and the Pursuit of Peace*, p. 143.
24 Cited by John Morton Blum (ed.) in *Public Philosopher: Selected Letters of Walter Lippmann* (New York: Ticknor and Fields, 1985), p. xxii.
25 Hinsley, *Power and the Pursuit of Peace*, p. 144.
26 ibid., p. 145.
27 Nicholas Murray Butler, *The International Mind: An argument for the Judicial Settlement of International Disputes* (New York: Charles Scribner's Sons, 1912), p. viii.

Further reading

Ashton, K. M. *The Industrial Revolution, 1760–1830*. London: Oxford University Press, 1948.
Carew-Hunt, R. H. *The Theory and Practice of Communism*. New York: Macmillan, 1945.
Hinsley, Sir Harry. *Power and the Pursuit of Peace: Theory and Practice in the*

History of Relations between States. Cambridge: Cambridge University Press, 1963.

Lenin, V. I. "Imperialism, the highest stage of capitalism," in *The Essentials of Lenin*, Vol. 1. London: Lawrence and Wishart, 1947.

Mahan, Admiral A. T. *The Influence of Sea Power on History, 1660–1783*. Boston: Little Brown, 1890.

Marx, Karl and Engels, Friedrich. [1848]. *Manifesto of the Communist Party*. New York: Rand School, 1919.

Sabine, G. H. *A History of Political Theory*. New York: Henry Holt, 1950.

Stanwick, H. M. *Builders of Peace: Ten Years' History of the Union of Democratic Control*. London: The Swarthmore Press, 1924.

Tonnies, Ferdinand. [1887]. *Community and Society* (trans. and ed. by Charles P. Loomis). New York: Harper and Row, 1957.

Weber, Max. [1904]. *The Protestant Ethic and the Spirit of Capitalism* (trans. Talcott Parsons). New York: Charles Scribner's Sons, 1958.

Webster, Charles K. *The Art and Practice of Diplomacy*. London: London School of Economics and Political Science, 1952.

Webster, Charles K. *The Study of International Politics*. London: H. Milford, 1921.

Whitney, Edson L. *The American Peace Society: A Centennial History*. Washington, DC: The American Peace Society, 1929.

4 The period of the first consensus: a quest for peace

> The vanquished might dread the prospect; the victors might welcome it, the neutrals might be divided in their sympathies; but almost all would have agreed, at that moment, that the termination of the Peace Conference would mark a greater epoch in the history of the world than the outbreak of the War. (Arnold J. Toynbee, *The World after the Peace Conference*)[1]

In assessing efforts to analyze, to understand, or even to change the relations between countries after the First World War, we must look – if only briefly – at the preparations for the Paris Peace Conference that followed it. By the time the Conference at Versailles got under way a wealth of material awaited possible (though by no means certain) use by the respective plenipotentiaries. Of particular utility was a report by several British authors, which Lord Phillimore submitted to the Foreign Office in March 1918. In the end, the treaty of peace contained, in addition to traditional terms of settlement which usually follow a war, provision for a formal postwar organization, which certainly could not have been created on short notice. In contrast to Kant's irrelevance at Vienna, there can be little doubt that the ideas of the peace movement, particularly societies promoting a postwar organization of states, at least indirectly affected the outcome at Paris. It was this novel feature of the peace settlement that had most to do with the development of the study of international relations: the League of Nations. And the individual who had most to do with adoption of the idea in the first place was the former President of the American Political Science Association, Woodrow Wilson. Again, in contrast to Vienna, he was the only world leader who could be called an intellectual with a formula for reordering the political universe. Ironically, he seemed to overlook the lessons of his own specialty, *Congressional Government* (1887), in losing the battle to bring his own country into the League.

For a while, the League system promised for the first time to organize all of international society through what might be called "global social engineering." Despite the unexpected defection of the United States and the absence of two other potentially Great Powers, Germany and Russia, the new configuration is often known as the "League system," even though the political process was not in fact altered all that much. Great Britain initially saw in the League an instrument for maintaining world peace, but gradually came to utilize it mainly to promote British foreign policy goals. Though far more skeptical, France was just as ready to make use of this unprecedented agency to serve its own national interests. The third European member, Italy, was so disillusioned and diplomatically, economically, and militarily weak that the purposes of her constitutional monarchy, soon supplanted by the world's first fascist dictatorship, scarcely mattered. Japan, courteous and cooperative to the letter, became disaffected as she observed other Powers' behavior. In striking contrast to Vienna, there was no Talleyrand for the defeated Power at Paris; Germany was kept down by the victors for as long as they saw it in their interest to do so. Excluded because of its communist system of government with its international revolutionary pronouncements and activity, the Soviet Union only joined in the new organization's work in the mid-1930s. Proceeding with their strategy and diplomacy outside the League, the Americans did play a crucial role in debt and reparations settlements and hosted two naval conferences, but remained, by choice, outside the principal arena. Wilson was gone.

Nevertheless, the "succession" states in East Central Europe and other weaker states saw distinct advantages in a system designed to protect them from larger potential predators. The Scandinavians, who after centuries of bitter rivalry were becoming a model of international organizational innovation, slipped readily into the League pattern. The Latin American states gradually acquired a sense of regionalization and solidarity, recognizing as did the Scandinavians that these values protect weaker states unable to assert their rights through military power, and some of their delegates became well-known champions of international law and order. Two large countries played a minor role, India because of

its status of relative dependency upon London, and China because
it continued to be rent by internal strife. What all of this meant in
terms of the political environment for scholarship was that, while
there was a certain fascination with the dream and to some degree
the realization of world organization, the overriding reality was
that Europe was still the epicenter of world politics. Its two
strongest states reverted to traditional diplomacy. The League
gradually came to be merely a function of the European balance of
power.

So "realist" a view was muted both in Britain and the United
States, however obvious it may have been on the continent and in
the years to come. Idealism – and in Britain even pacifism –
profoundly affected public opinion in both countries, influencing
the manner in which many political leaders now addressed world
affairs. At the same time, close observers recognized that, whatever
its form, the system had to deal with real problems, the solutions
to which often had to be sought outside the League machinery.
During what G. M. Gathorne-Hardy terms "the period of settlement," these included: the reparation and debt problems left over
from the war; security; the settlement of Eastern Europe; disarmament; the place of the USSR in world affairs; political isolation of
the United States; the economic crisis; and regional issues.[2] While
governments obviously held responsibility for dealing with these
questions, those that had been democratically elected could do so
only to the extent to which they enjoyed the support of their
respective electorates. No longer could the public be isolated.
Instead if solutions were to be found, it had to be educated, not
necessarily to one point of view but to the point of understanding
what was at stake.

Nor was educating diplomats all that easy. Recalling the experience of John Maynard Keynes in trying to teach the elements of
economics to statesmen at Versailles (an effort which failed),
Webster reflected upon both the source and object of much that
went into the early promotion of international studies in a
democracy:

It was useless for him to try and instruct statesmen while their
people were still in ignorance. One cannot help wondering
whether he would not have had a far greater influence on the

Treaty of Versailles if he had preached sooner in the market-place rather than to the Council of Four. We have, in fact, reached the age in politics when expert knowledge must be brought within the reach of the mass of the people if it is to have its full influence upon affairs.[3]

How to educate the public

"Reaching the masses" was the populist approach. A second was elitist. A better-informed public was the objective in both instances. As a result of informal talks during the Conference, the French, the British and the Americans agreed to create new private institutions for the purpose of raising the level of international understanding of opinion leaders in their respective countries. In London, what was to become the Royal Institute of International Affairs was established in order to "advance the sciences of international politics, economics and jurisprudence, and the study, classification and development of the literature in these subjects, to encourage and facilitate the scientific study of international questions. . . ."[4] In the United States, the Council on Foreign Relations was set up, not in the then relatively provincial national capital, but in New York City, the bastion of corporate and banking power. In retrospect, leaders of the Council recalled its origins and development in this way:

> Under the pressure of a public opinion which was impatient to be done with war-making, decisions had to be made in haste; and the minds of diplomats, generals, admirals, financiers, lawyers and technical experts were not sufficiently well furnished to enable them to function satisfactorily on critical issues at top speed. Realizing their own shortcomings, some of these men began to talk about a way of providing against such a state of things in the future.[5]

In a description of its "Program of Studies" in 1929, the Council's aim was stated as being "to develop, by scientific and impartial study, a better understanding of international problems, and an intelligent American foreign policy."[6] In both centers, there was a tacit expectation that *scientific* studies in IR would prevent the next war. But as Max Beloff would succinctly put it many years later, "it didn't work."[7]

In Paris similar efforts proved abortive. A somewhat comparable institution was established a few years later in Geneva, a French-speaking city of neutral Switzerland, the *Institut Universitaire des Hautes Etudes Internationales* (now the Graduate Institute of International Studies, the difference being that HEI was primarily an academic institution awarding degrees in international studies, not a public opinion forming base. Its location in the city of the League of Nations afforded it a special opportunity in the development of international studies by facilitating contacts between academics and practitioners from all over the world. The purpose was to train the international leaders of the future.

The populist approach was practiced in quite different ways, taking one form in Britain, another in the United States. The Union of Democratic Control was less interested in objective presentation of broad international affairs information to the British public than it was in getting parliament to assert more control over the actual conduct of foreign policy.[8] The aim of the Foreign Policy Association, on the other hand, was "to carry on research and educational activities to aid in the understanding and constructive development of American foreign policy."[9] Everything from dinner meetings to highly readable topical brochures were utilized to provide background for anyone in the United States who wanted to take part in its activities or subscribe to FPA services, dealing very little with either political branch of the government as such, at least in its early stages. No claim to being scientific was made.

All of these organizations, populist or elitist, played a crucial role in the development of IR insofar as they were performing independent research and "teaching" functions. In some ways, they were ahead of most universities, where any new discipline required time to take root if it was to be taken seriously. For that to happen, a literature of a distinct order would have to be produced. Meanwhile the peace societies, having appeared to gain so many of their nineteenth-century objectives through the establishment of the League, were for a time at least relatively quiescent, as were "cause" groups of various kinds. This would soon change in the United States as the World Court issue came to a head in Congress. Newspapers continued to perform their traditional though, for them, secondary role of chief educator in international affairs. It would be difficult to locate anything systematic or disciplinary in their reams of copy, though a few pundits like Walter Lippmann for many years set a high standard of journalistic analysis. Nevertheless, the views and perhaps even more importantly the moods of the people in democratic societies had become, as they had only threatened to do in the previous century, a real factor in shaping government decisions. In the words of Sir Harry Hinsley, looking back from the 1960s:

> Before 1914 it is almost impossible to find evidence that French or British or American public opinion ever acted as a deterrent to decisions in foreign policy, as opposed to being an incitement to the men who took them. It is almost equally impossible to show that French and British and American foreign policy have ever been free from the hampering effect of public opinion – if only from the hampering effect – since that date.[10]

A more scientific analysis of popular opinion is to be found in Almond's seminal study,[11] which made the crucial distinction between an informed attentive public and the rest of the body politic whose "moods" only created a climate of opinion.

This necessity to be sensitive to the will of the people, greatly encouraged by Wilson's popular war aim of "open covenants, openly arrived at," created what ambassadors and other foreign affairs professionals derisively, and liberal internationalists proudly, called "The New Diplomacy." Much as members of the diplomatic community deplored it, they could no longer ignore it. And, it must be added, much as the idealists longed for it, they were unable fully to achieve it. Even Wilson is said to have come around to "open covenants, secretly arrived at" during the protracted negotiations at Versailles. The implications for the way international relations were now to be studied were enormous. One of the leading chroniclers of IR describes how the problem of war would be handled:

> Various simplistic determinisms . . . among which economic determinism and the devil theory of war were probably the most fashionable, flourished. In a way the belief in the possibility of discovering *the* cause of war reflected the prevailing optimism;

for if the cause could be isolated, the cure could be prescribed
. . . the historian in this respect frequently had little more to
offer than the political scientist. The tremendous research effort
on war guilt seemed only to document the badness of the
diplomats and their system and to contribute little to understanding the causes of war and the conditions of peace.[12]

Yet the educational dimension was slow in being perceived; "past
experience seemed to have little to teach," and the old system "was
thought of as absolutely bad."[13] Precious little attention had been
given to analysis of the political functions, which even in a
reorganized system of states would still have to be performed.

How to teach the subject

To fill the vacuum, political scientists had two immediate options:
to concentrate, as they had sometimes done, upon form rather than
function, or to devise innovative ways of analyzing the political
process as it then operated. In the United States, the profession
tended to opt for the former, which allowed international organization to become the first focus of a new study or branch of an
older discipline. Some independent departments of international
relations were created. In the United Kingdom, the field's beginning can probably best be dated from the creation in 1919 at the
University College of Wales at Aberystwyth of the first academic
Chair in International Politics, named after Woodrow Wilson,
with Alfred Zimmern the first of several distinguished occupants.
Neither he, a classicist, nor his immediate successor, the diplomatic
historian C. K. Webster, were trained as political scientists, but
they were deeply aware of the charge implied in the Trust Deeds
defining "Political Science in its application to International Relations with special reference to the best means of promoting peace
between nations."[14]

When international relations emerged in university syllabi in the
United Kingdom, it was on its own, so to speak, not as a branch
of political science as was usually the case in the United States.
Indeed except for the London School of Economics and Political
Science, which antedated the war by many years, and possibly the
noted "PPE" (philosophy, politics, economics) degree at Oxford,

the discipline of political science as such tended to occupy a distinct place in British higher education *after* international relations did, not before. Across the Atlantic it was the other way around, which understandably created a certain tension between the two disciplines in the United States, which for some continues to rankle to this day. In light of all this, what can one say about the then respective capabilities of other recognized academic fields for studying international relations?

The contributing disciplines

The most logical place to begin is with law. Even today law faculties are the locus of whatever international studies there are in Latin America and, to a lesser degree, continental Europe. As a discipline, law reflected little attempt either to block or to nourish the new discipline, though of the thirteen books which may be regarded as the early mainstream IR texts, three were written by international lawyers, more than from any other discipline except history. Indeed the first comprehensive *Cumulative Book Index* (1922–28) grouped the literature in both fields together under the heading "International Law and Relations," a combination which was kept in practice until the *Index* of 1943–48 appeared a generation and a war later. Both the American, Elizabeth Read in her *International Law and International Relations* (1925), and the Briton, Pearce Higgins, Professor of International Law at Cambridge, in his *Studies in International Law and Relations* (1928), discussed the substance of international relations.

But legal methodology could not easily accommodate such earnest purposes as peace planning, internationalism, and certainly the growing force of pacifism. Indeed the legal profession tended to take pride in continuing to analyze international legal questions in its conventional manner, based upon cases, precedents, and procedures. In a striking exception, Higgins lectured in Illinois in 1927 on "Some difficulties in international relations" in which he observed that

> it will be appreciated that international relations are involved in difficulties of the greatest complexity and it follows that the conduct of international business demands that those who are

engaged in it should possess abilities of the highest order. For their success, statesmen and diplomatists should be able to rely on the intelligent understanding of those for whom they are acting, and this can only be acquired if their citizens will take the necessary trouble to make themselves acquainted with the problems which they were endeavoring to solve.[15]

In all fairness, it must be noted that by 1925 the periodic Conferences of Teachers of International Law (CTIL), created in 1911 as one of the earliest undertakings of the Carnegie Endowment, embraced "related subjects," which really meant international relations. The restriction of the agenda to law at CTIL's initial conference, which fell between the second Hague conference and Sarajevo, itself reveals the elementary fact that before the war the only place where the word "international" was likely to be found in curricula was in law schools. Their professors no more dealt with the balance of power, sabre-rattling, dollar diplomacy, or military strategy in their classes than did the agendas of the peace societies for re-ordering the relationships of nation-states.

All the same, the new discipline of international relations may be said to have sprung from law; had the element of international legal considerations been missing, its foundation would have lacked one of its sturdiest building blocks. Law was central to IR (though not *vice versa*). Holland's studies had been a reflection of the Hague legacy of regulating neutrality in war, not preventing it, but it was the eighth edition of William Hall's *Treatise on International Law* (1924) that came to be regarded even by those outside the field as its most reliable guide. In 1928, N. Politis produced his innovative *New Aspects of International Law*, shortly to be followed by a comprehensive survey of research on international law[16] since the wars by a scholar who was to become one of the philosophers of a new discipline, Quincy Wright of Chicago. This is only a sampling of the new literature; no less than 150 titles appear in the first Cumulative Index under "International Law and Relations," half of them explicitly on law (less than 50 are listed under "World Politics," most of them cross listings with the other category). In the United States, the legal approach dominated early writing in IR; in Britain, it was historical.

As for history itself, the compelling demands for public education, from the higher reaches of the ancient universities to editorial writers of all but the penny-press, would not be met by this most traditional of disciplines. Like law, history presumably carries no particular political purpose of its own (if it did it would no longer be regarded as history, but as polemics) yet *schools* of historians have almost always been divided for different political purposes and even practice different approaches to evidence. Nevertheless, there were well-established principles for the guidance of "objective" historians. In contrast, a historian felt obliged to observe in his inaugural address in 1923 for the new Chair in International Politics:

> There is no general acceptance of the principles of the study. Indeed, even if such principles had existed before the Great War, that event has so sapped the foundations of international order, and changed so remorselessly our conception of International Relations, that a recasting of our ideas would be necessary . . . no ordered and scientific body of knowledge did exist in 1914.[17]

Noting his freedom from restraint in setting new guidelines from among "the various lines of development suggested," Webster understandably – perhaps inevitably – chose modern history as his point of departure. The prevalent conceptual base for the teaching of international relations at Cambridge (where it was not extensive) and Oxford (where it was) has always been contemporary history, although more recent trends have been away from history, especially in the so-called "redbrick" and "green field" universities.

As a discipline, history was bound by its own methodogical canons; like law, this is what makes it a discipline in the first place. Historians generally have been reluctant to render judgements about government policies and actions until the record is in. Others, more determined to develop studies that would prevent the outbreak of another, even more terrible, war could not wait that long. In the fullness of time, historians could be counted upon generally to interpret what happened, if not always to agree exactly upon which events had occurred or why. They could hardly be expected to help *make* them happen – the very thought was unprofessional. Neither lawyers nor historians were future-oriented. The expertise of both had been relied upon heavily at Versailles; neither was programmed to institute a new order. As Fox has pointed out, historians (at least in the United States) were so preoccupied with reassessing the question of whether Germany was in fact guilty of starting the war that they had little or no interest in this new subject.[17] In Britain, however, a number of historians, notably Webster, Mowat and later Carr, made crucial contributions.

What then of the economists? Had not the most influential book to come out of the Peace Conference been John Maynard Keynes's *The Economic Consequences of the Peace* (1919)? While his 1931 book was to carry the title *Unemployment as a World Problem*, his mind did not turn to the larger disciplinary question of how to analyze and present international relations as an integrated field, probably because he did not think it could be done and possibly because he thought it would not have been worth the effort if it had. Other immediate postwar publications by economists reveal only a few works of general international scope, such as Michael Pavlovitch's *The Foundations of Imperialist Policy* (1922). Though in a sense interdisciplinary (economics, history, sociology and/or military science), these gave little evidence of interest in a new social science discipline to deal with international relations as a whole, only parts of it.

If the more traditional disciplines fell short of dealing comprehensively and systematically with international relations, others fell even shorter. Sociology was caught up in developing its own scientific methodology, which for many years apparently found in IR a subject with too many variables to be capable of scientific analysis, to say nothing of prediction. To be sure, 1926 saw the third edition of Tonnies' *Community and Society*, with a new introduction in which Pitirim Sorokin discusses not only Aquinas and Hegel, but Ibn Khaldun and Confucius as well.[19] Neither demography nor ethnology had yet demonstrated their relevance for understanding and analyzing international relations, despite the ethnic basis for most of the nationalist movements, which finally found expression at Versailles in the creation of the successor states and despite the contention which could be made that there had occurred the crowning triumph of the nation as the basis for the state system. To be sure, a few tentative steps had been taken by A. M. Carr-Saunders in *The Population Problem* (1922), but he was not at the time concerned with a discipline of IR. The same could be said of anthropology, but within a generation a few anthropologists were to take on a significant foreign policy-related role, at least in Washington.

Geography was destined to occupy a prominent place in IR, though in a quite different way from that in which the work of Mahan and MacKinder had proceeded. Sir Halford's own *Democratic Ideals and Reality: A Study of the Politics of Reconstruction* in 1919 revealed an interdisciplinary comprehension of the relation of the field to world politics, as did the work of Isaiah Bowman. Eight years after he produced *The New World: Problems in Political Geography*, Bowman wrote a modest general booklet entitled *International Relations* (1930), but it hardly takes its place in Appendix A as a mainstream text. In all fairness, it must be observed that two things were to occur which blunted geography's long-term involvement in any new discipline of international relations. One was the "bad name" later given the field by "geopolitics" as it developed in the hands of the Nazis. The other was a possibly related shift from a human, cultural, and political approach to a more scientific and thus more reputable physical geography, leaving political interpretation to others.

Understandably, the contribution of military science was a mixed one in the immediate post-Versailles years. On the one hand, pacifism was growing to the point where anything considered to be tainted with militarism was hardly given a hearing, certainly by those who felt that more careful analysis and understanding of interstate politics within the evolving League system would produce the solution of the whole problem of war itself. Contrary to this constraint was the undeniable fact that a great many things about strategy, tactics, logistics (and even lobbying!) had been learned from the war, the doubtful utility of gas warfare and the probable utility of air power, to name but two. The need to educate the public was not lost on military planners any more than it had been on peace planners, as was demonstrated by Major-General Sir George Aston's *The Study of War for Statesmen and Citizens* (1927), and by books by two other influential and widely read British analysts of military problems, B. H. (later Sir Basil) Liddell-Hart (1927) and Maj.-Gen. J. F. C. Fuller (1932), both of whom put their arguments in a broadly political context.

The psychological dimension was suggested by Harold Lasswell's *Propaganda Technique in the World War* (1927), though his book eight years later on personal insecurity as an outcome of international politics would prove more enduring. The sleeping giant of propaganda, discredited by the war, was yet to reawaken,

but it would only be a matter of time before it foreshadowed a
new sub-discipline: international communication theory. Except
for the work of C. E. Playne, Gustav LeBon (who had published
The Psychology of Peoples as early as 1899), and George Stratton in
Social Psychology of International Conduct (1929), psychological literature explicitly related to international relations was relatively
meager in the decade following the war.[19]

The emergence of a consensus

What of international relations itself? Was there any similarity in
the way their authors made use of this concept? Was there any
consistency in the manner in which they subdivided the subject-
matter? Did they come from several disciplines? If so, this suggests
the dimensions of a new discipline, or at least of what might be
called an "interdiscipline." As early as 1916, as we have seen, a
Council for the Study of International Relations published a series
of studies representing history, economics, law and journalism,
the first book to make use of the term which was eventually to
label the new discipline. The second was D. P. Heatley's *Diplomacy
and International Relations* (1919). This was followed at once by the
first to use it exclusively as a title, *International Relations* (1920) by
S. H. Allen, a former Kansas Supreme Court Judge; it proved
actually to be a well-organized treatise on international law.
Possibly the first academic text as such was *International Politics*,
published the same year by the British social philosopher, C.
Delisle Burns.

Of the many works on every conceivable aspect of international
affairs between the war and the demise of the League system in the
1930s, less than fifteen can be said to represent overall treatments
resembling textbooks of a discipline. Four were entitled *International Relations*, five others having that term as part of the title;
of the remaining three, two used "society" and three preferred
"politics." The authors were equally divided between British and
American. From these first efforts, certain generalizations can be
advanced about how the subject first came to be defined in a
mainstream literature dealing comprehensively with the world
system.

Although there was a surprisingly high degree of consensus,

there were differences of opinion on what should be included and, even more, excluded. For example, that old stand-by of the eighteenth and nineteenth centuries, the balance of power, was rarely mentioned in this new literature of the twentieth, and then often pejoratively. In general, politics, history, law, and organization were given primary attention, with little space usually alloted to psychological, sociological, demographic, and especially military factors. Economic considerations were usually brought in, though not in any consistent manner. Little attention was as yet being paid to the nature of the study and especially to the methodology of the field. A model or composite "table of contents" for an IR text of the fifteen years between the appearance of Heatley's book and the League's failure to stem Japanese aggression in Manchuria in 1931 might look something like this (the recapitulation is based upon fourteen textbooks or other comprehensive analyses, in Appendix A (see p. 183) with topics covered by two-thirds of more of the authors, listed in order of frequency):

    I The history of international relations (often termed "diplomatic history")
   II International organization
  III Economic aspects of world affairs
  IV International politics, including foreign policy
   V International law
  VI War and the causes of war
 VII Diplomacy
VIII The nation and nationalism
  IX Imperialism

To what extent was this literature "idealist internationalist?" The short answer is, "not much." All the authors possessed an international, as contrasted to a narrowly nationalistic, outlook. None of them thought for a moment that war as a human institution was over for good. To be sure, public opinion was now more important than ever before, but it served only to extend the political process, not to replace it. It is not an exaggeration to say that the new IR literature was designed to overcome some of the dubious assumptions and hopeful expectations of the idealists, widespread as their influence may seem to have been. The mainstream literature of the 1920s did not particularly reflect this paradigm, however much some of those outside the IR professional literature may have done so.

The organizational base

Several non-academic organizations came into being at this time as a result of the impulse for the systematic analysis of international relations or the promotion of peace in a responsible manner. In the United States, these efforts apparently sprang, partly at least, from a desire to compensate for what was regarded as the profound moral and political blunder of America's having declined, because of the nature of its constitutional structure, to become part of the League of Nations. In Britain, the principal effort was being made at Chatham House under the scholarly direction of Arnold J. Toynbee, who masterminded a colossal annual called *Survey of International Affairs*. The "sister house" to the Royal Institute, the US Council on Foreign Relations, also featured study groups and an annual survey, *The United States in Foreign Affairs*, all of which tended to concentrate upon American foreign policy in contrast to Toynbee's more universal approach. In 1931 the Council produced a survey (which unfortunately did not become a periodical one), *American Agencies Interested in International Relations*. Like Chatham House and its *International Affairs*, the Council published a learned quarterly journal, *Foreign Affairs*, which featured articles by world leaders and included exceptionally competent brief reviews, by such recognized scholars as Robert Gale Woolbert, of the rapidly growing literature in world politics and economics. However, these provided less a picture of an incipient academic discipline with an emerging body of theory than a reflection of the State Department's traditional regional – functional compartmentaliza-tion of the world. Little attention was given to whatever scant theoretical work may have appeared, nor to what might be termed disciplinary development. The object was to educate the business, financial, and legal elites, not academics, though some professorial members (often rapporteurs of study groups, such as in later years Kissinger and Zbigniew Brzezinski) could help educate this informed and presumably influential public.

In Boston, in 1931 the World Peace Foundation made a signal contribution to the development of the study in the form of a sweeping survey[20] of what was being taught in this field all over the country, to be matched two years later by a similar effort by Chatham House, *International Studies in Great Britain* by S. H. Bailey, a leading figure in promoting systematic studies. The Institute of International Education published some scholarly works, such as Parker T. Moon's *Syllabus on International Relations* (1925), but tended to concentrate upon student exchange. Founded in 1924 by Edward R. Murrow, who early in the Second World War was to become a renowned radio journalist ("This – is London"), IIE nevertheless did share with the then prevalent assumption that greater knowledge could only create deeper and broader understanding, which in turn could not but contribute to a more peaceful world. Eventually the Chatham House-CFR model would be adapted to informing various elites throughout the world, but at first the English-speaking countries were virtually alone in this kind of endeavor.

The first international conferences on IR

Two more institutions provided a place for the nurturing of ideas that contributed to developing the discipline. One has already been mentioned, the Conference of Teachers of International Law and Related Subjects, which published the works of some towering figures in the field: Manley O. Hudson (law), Pitman B. Potter (organization), Quincy Wright (foreign relations) and Nicholas J. Spykman (sociology), a number of whom wrote specifically on methods of teaching. The second was the International Institute of Intellectual Cooperation, set up in Paris under League auspices. Both of these represented attempts to analyze world affairs objectively as well as assessing how the subject was being taught. Among the more significant of the institute's efforts were the International Studies Conferences.

The first such gathering of experts on coordinating the work of institutions dedicated to "higher international studies" took place at the *Deutsche Hochschule für Politik* in Berlin in 1928. Among the delegations from Austria, France, Germany, Great Britain, Italy, The Netherlands, Switzerland and The United States, four institutional bases for analysis were represented:

1 Centers of study and discussion, such as those conducted at Chatham House.
2 Special courses, such as those taught at the Geneva School of International Studies or the Academy of International Law in the Hague.
3 Teaching institutes outside the University proper, such as the *Ecole libre des Sciences Politiques* in Paris or the Consular Academy in Vienna.
4 University faculties, such as the London School of Economics and Political Science or the faculties of political science at some Italian universities.

In an analysis based upon the work of the Sub-Committee of Experts and of the Annual Conference of Institutes for the Scientific Study of International Relations, Professor (later Sir) Alfred Zimmern of Oxford noted after the Paris conference four years later that:

> Anyone drawing up an university syllabus for the study of international relations will find himself on the horns of a dilemma. Either he will limit himself to the subject in its narrower, technical sense, or he will include studies which provide an indispensable foundation for the understanding of the nature, purpose and working of the machinery.[21]

If one chose the former, the result might be "profoundly dehumanizing," but if the latter he might be overwhelmed in trying to decide "where does the subject begin and end?"[22]

These important conferences continued to be held periodically until the outbreak of war in 1939, resuming in 1946, earnestly going over essentially the same ground. Each succeeding year did see more emphasis upon such specific issues as population, land utilization, and perfecting of the League machinery for peaceful settlement of disputes, and less upon the "scientific" organization of international studies as such. A definition of sorts did begin to take shape during consideration of and agreement upon an IR bibliography, but it was not conclusive. The 1929 conference in London passed no less than ten resolutions, covering everything from the designation of national centers, to an interlending library, to "the equivalence of degrees." For our purposes, Resolution IX would prove more practical, calling for a "meeting of teachers concerned with international studies for the purpose of discussing among other matters methods of teaching, relations and arrangement of subjects, relations of academic teaching and practical experience." Now they were getting down to business. In subsequent years, several such meetings were held, known in Britain as "the Bailey meetings," which in turn would eventually become the British International Studies Association.

The place of "idealist internationalism"

Although, as we have seen, mainstream literature did not necessarily represent the idealist internationalist approach, that perspective or bias was highly visible in other endeavors in the immediate postwar era. It clearly occupied the high ground of advocacy, though any distinction made or contradiction noted between scholarship and polemics would have been met with heated objection. Hopeful assumptions about the future of world affairs were prevalent in the writing of some educators of the period, notably in Zimmern's "The development of the international mind" (1925) and "Education for World Citizenship" (1931), "How to make the League of Nations known and to develop a spirit of international cooperation" (Institute for Intellectual Cooperation, 1927), and Ben Cherrington's *Methods of Teaching International Attitudes* (published doctoral dissertation, Teachers College, Columbia, 1934). Each of these highly motivated writers was perhaps trying to "make a point" more than primarily to make progress toward more scientific study. In one of his more lyrical expressions, for example, Zimmern said to a pre-University audience in 1924,

> For the world of our vision is no single field of waving grain, every ear like its fellow and blown the same way by the same breeze, but an infinitely diversified landscape, seen, as an airman would see it, from above, land and sea, city and country, cornland and pasture, orchard and forest, all placed at the service of man, of a humanity united in one great community of mutual understanding.[23]

Attitude outweighed analysis. Not only that. In approaching politics in the Greek sense of the term, Zimmern broadened hopelessly the range of what IR *should* encompass rather than endeavoring to narrow the definable and manageable dimensions of a discipline. Arguably, this actually set it back. Sixty years later, excessive eclecticism was still impeding rather than advancing the acceptance of the field as a true discipline. Nevertheless, these efforts did represent a sincere impulse of a significant body of those engaged in its early development and may well have led the way to the scholarly emergence of normative theory. Though the idealists did not see themselves as such (especially if by "idealist" one meant "unrealistic"), it was this feature, along with the popularity which IR teachers enjoyed in interpreting headlines or "current events," which drew criticism (or was it "envy"?) from many in the conventional disciplines. The critics were seldom themselves prepared to undertake the difficult task of rationalizing the process of examining world affairs as a whole. The new internationalists may have been guilty of ignoring the trees for the wood; the traditionalists' error was the reverse. Another related factor inhibiting legitimacy were "cause groups," which in their zeal for international change allowed ends to color means. A remarkable exception was the Foundation for the Advancement of the Social Sciences, located at the University of Denver and doubling as one of the first formal Departments of International Relations in the country.[24]

The early role of government and foundations

The state was slow to recognize the value of a comprehensive and objective approach to foreign affairs, which would in effect place its own sometimes narrow policies within a broader context. In Britain, the government appears at first to have resented the creation of a second source of information-in-depth at Chatham House, which incidentally might serve to provide the Opposition with ammunition with which to attack Whitehall's cherished aims. This sometimes awkward relationship between democracy and public affairs was as important in defining the nature of the new discipline as was the yearning for a peaceful world order. It helps to explain why in authoritarian states the study of international relations or foreign policy could only exist as an explanation and justification of state policy. It also sheds light on why IR, at least at first, only developed in a few democratic countries, where it could enjoy indirect government support without being subject to official control. Much more analysis of this dimension is needed.

While governments, foundations, and institutes for quite different reasons could stimulate the systematic study of international relations, the field had to find its home in the university. The academic dimension in Britain initially took the form of the Montague Burton Chairs in three Universities: the University College of Wales at Aberystwyth, the London School of Economics and Political Science, and Oxford, each held initially by scholars of high intellect and genuine commitment to the scientific study of world politics. In the United States, university activity took two forms: the first was obviously the gradual increment of courses, usually based in departments of political science, covering world politics, international relations, or some similar designation. The other was the establishment, at the rate of about two a decade as it turned out, of about a dozen non-governmental professional schools or centers for the training of diplomats and other hopefuls for international careers. Even though their primary function was seen to be training for the foreign service rather than contributing to the emerging field of international studies, their programs did represent a beginning of professionalism. Nothing like this has ever been tried in the UK, and most other countries set up governmental institutes for training young diplomats once they were appointed.

Another critical institutional base affecting the way in which IR developed was provided by philanthropic institutions, especially the Carnegie Endowment, the Rockefeller and later the Ford foundations. Their contribution should not always be regarded as an advance, especially in cases where scholars were tempted to trim their proposals to whims of foundation officers. Another dimension of philanthropic endeavor took the form of gifts of seminal current books on IR to libraries all over the country from the Carnegie Endowment, which later encouraged intercollegiate conferences of what were usually called "International Relations Clubs" (IRCs) featuring debates on crucial foreign policy issues of the day. Many a future diplomat, author, or professor of IR got his or her start through active participation in IRCs. On balance, the field could hardly have progressed as it did in this formative era without the assistance and, in many cases, wisdom of philanthropy.

Shifts in the balance of power in the wake of Japan's destructive challenge to the League system marked the beginning of world-wide disillusionment with that system. Other shocks were soon to follow. Inevitably they led to new approaches to thinking about world politics. They also led to a quickening of interest in the latest news from all over the world. The press, bored by dull League Assembly debates of plenipotentiaries from states for the most part minuscule in their weight in the balance of power, thrilled to the highly newsworthy shelling of Chinese cities by Tokyo's military forces on the offensive.

The effect of these striking events upon the orderly fostering of a scientific discipline was both destructive and salutary – destructive because they concentrated attention upon the short run and the spectacular, and salutary because they forced specialists to give more weight to power realities and their systematic analysis. As we shall now see, with the discipline beginning to mature, the consensual base of its innocent phase also began to erode. It would take a second world war for consensus to return. Then it would rest upon quite different intellectual foundations in a quite different world of politics.

Notes: Chapter 4

1 Arnold J. Toynbee, *The World after the Peace Conference* (London: Oxford University Press, 1926), p. 1.
2 G. M. Gathorne-Hardy, *A Short History of International Affairs 1920–1939*, 4th edn, (London: Oxford University Press, 1950), pp. 1–141. The "political isolation of the United States" was dropped somewhere between the first and fourth editions, probably because of the war debts question, and "the Islamic world" was substituted for "regional issues".
3 C. K. Webster, *The Study of International Politics* (Cardiff: University of Wales Press, 1923), p. 27.
4 *Handbook of Institutions for the Scientific Study of International Relations* (Paris: Institute of Intellectual Cooperation, 1929), pp. 68–9.
5 *The Council on Foreign Relations* (New York: CFR, January 1, 1947), p. 5. See also the *IIC Handbook*, p. 95 (see note 4 above).
6 *IIC Handbook*, p. 95.

7 Conversation with Olson, Reform Club, London, October 1987.

8 H. M. Stanwick, *Builders of Peace, being Ten Years' History of the Union of Democratic Control* (London: The Swarthmore Press, 1924), p. 23.

9 *IIC Handbook*, p. 96. This book's brief recapitulation of reports from all over the world is especially instructive in showing how the membership, dues, and activities' structure varied between the RIIA, the CFR, and the FPA. Both the "sister houses" had programs of studies, the FPA did not; the Council and Chatham House had a limited membership by invitation after formal nomination, whereas the Association was open to anyone who paid the $3 per year dues (more than 10,000 joined). Dues for the Council were $100 the same year, 1929.

10 Hinsley, *Power and the Pursuit of Peace*, p. 285.

11 See Almond, *The American People and Foreign Policy*, p. iii n.

12 W. T. R. Fox, *The American Study of International Relations* (Columbia, SC: Institute of International Studies, University of South Carolina, 1966), p. 5 n.

13 ibid., p. 11.

14 Webster, *International Politics*, p. 5.

15 Pearce Higgins, *Studies in International Law and Relations* (Cambridge: Cambridge University Press, 1928), p. 36.

16 Wright, Quincy. *Research in International Law since the World War* (Washington: Carnegie Endowment, Division of International Law, 1930).

17 Webster, *International Politics*, p. 4.

18 Fox, *The American Study of IR*, p. 4–5.

19 Tonnies, F. *Community and Society*, 3rd edn, 1926, p. vii.

20 Farrell Symons, *Courses in International Relations in American Colleges, 1930–31* (Boston: World Peace Foundation, 1931).

21 A. E. Zimmern, "Education in international relations: a critical survey", *Education Survey*, Geneva, League of Nations, III, 1, March 1932, p. 35.

22 ibid., p. 36.

23 A. E. Zimmern, "Education in international goodwill", *The Sixth Earl Grey Memorial Lecture* (Oxford: Oxford University Press, 1924), p. 14.

24 Ben M. Cherrington, *The Social Science Foundation of the University of Denver, 1926–1951: A Personal Reminiscence* (Denver, Colo: Social Science Foundation, 1973).

25 Once young diplomats enter the Department of State, they are now usually assigned for a period of intensive language study at the Foreign Service Institute, depending upon their country of assignment, and return routinely for this purpose from time to time.

78 'Then': the formative years

Further reading

Bailey, S. H. *International Studies in Great Britain*. London: Royal Institute of International Affairs, 1937.

Benns, F. Lee. *Europe since 1914 in its World Setting*, 8th edn. New York: Appleton-Century-Crofts, 1954.

Bracher, Karl Dietrich. *The Age of Ideologies: A History of Political Thought in the Twentieth Century* (trans. Ewald Owers). London: Weidenfeld and Nicolson, 1982.

Churchill, W. S. *The Aftermath, 1918–1928*. New York: Scribners, 1929.

Davis, John W. *et al. The Council on Foreign Relations: A Record of Twenty-Five Years*. New York: Council on Foreign Relations, 1947.

Fox, William T. R. *The American Study of International Relations*. Columbia, SC: University of South Carolina Press, for the Institute of International Studies, 1966.

Hall, William E. *A Treatise on International Law*, 8th edn. Oxford: Oxford University Press, 1924.

Hirschfeld, Charles (ed.). *Classics of Western Thought*. Vol. III, *The Modern World*. New York: Harcourt, Brace and World, 1964.

Keynes, John Maynard. *The Economic Consequences of the Peace*. New York: Harcourt, 1919.

Notter, Harley. *The Origins of the Foreign Policy of Woodrow Wilson*. Baltimore: The Johns Hopkins University Press, 1937.

Zimmern, Sir Alfred. "Education for world citizenship," *Problems of Peace*. 5th series for the Geneva Institute of International Relations. London: Oxford University Press, 1981.

Zimmern, Sir Alfred. "University teaching of international relations," *Proceedings 11th International Studies Conference* Paris: International Institute of Intellectual Cooperation, 1988.

5 The impact of the collapse of the League system

> The passage of another ten years was sufficient to see the commencement of a world war even more calamitous than its predecessor, and the attempt to avoid such a catastrophe had ended in apparently complete and disastrous failure. The main problem for us all must be to discover what went wrong. . . .
> (G. M. Gathorne-Hardy, *A Short History of International Affairs 1920–1939*)[1]

A time of change in international politics produced a change in ideas about the world. The first postwar decade had reflected an essential consensus in the mainstream literature because there was a certain degree of consensus in politics. The second decade produced no such consensus in the one because it was absent in the other. Hence, although a composite model from basic texts of the first decade of the discipline's formal growth could reasonably (if not very scientifically) be constructed, we were now confronted with a pattern of distinctions. Between collapse of the League system and extension of the European war to most of the world by 1941, there were almost as many conceptual frameworks as there were authors to explain what rapidly shifting events meant.

Conventional wisdom contended that idealist internationalist assumptions, having dominated early postwar thinking about world politics, were gradually replaced by realism as the League inexorably demonstrated its inability to cope with aggression. Neither paradigm was very often expressed in unadulterated form. Idealists had seen the League as an alternative to power politics; their challengers merely regarded the Assembly as another arena for its pursuit. Intellectually, realists lived in a world of states, accepting power as the principal currency of IR in place of the expectation of, and preparation for, peace. To them, international cooperation was possible only when it served the national interests of the participants; indeed, no form of international cooperation was imaginable save the balance of power. All this rested upon a conception of the nature of man that was conflictual, to cynics even bordering on evil. The one paradigm did not replace the other. Idealism struggled for acceptance even after it was apparent that the League experiment was failing. Realism simply became more convincing. To the degree to which the moods of public opinion and the pundits whose eye-catching tracts affected it are the criteria for judging prevailing thought, this duality is not difficult to demonstrate. But if the emerging professional or mainstream literature of international relations constitutes the test, then the proposition becomes, as we have seen, less easy to sustain. It strove for balance between the two perspectives.

The beginning of the end of consensus

The Japanese attack at Mukden took place in 1931, two years after the Wall Street crash and two years before Hitler became Chancellor. It is a convenient year of division in the development of ideas in IR. Obviously this is no accident, merely serving to illustrate a rather obvious feature of this new discipline: the direct impact of events in world politics, upon not only the relative emphasis respective authors gave to the same topics, but their assumptions as well. The same could be said of such disparate writers as Thucydides and Grotius, even more so of Machiavelli and Kant. Not surprisingly, the international law, organization and peace literature tended to remain at least implicitly hopeful, but writers in the sub-field of foreign policy, like history, were rarely anything but "realistic," never being taken up by those whose wishful thinking expected too much or even something fundamentally different in League politics. To such authorities the inadequacy of the League, far from causing a "sea change" in interpretation, was to some degree anticipated in their treatments. Of the dozen or so "mainstream" writers only Buell in 1929 went into a second or revised edition of *International Relations*, and he told the public a tale of woe rather than of hope. An entirely new set of writers entered the front line of analyzing IR.

As the literature developed, further breaks with tradition emerged, as fears and expectations of a new war were reflected in new titles. Yet mainstream texts continued to cover international institutions designed to prevent war, though less was claimed for them. Credit for "correcting" the naïveté of the literature of the League period was first to be bestowed upon a British diplomat–journalist–academic, Edward Hallett Carr, and later upon Hans Morgenthau, one of many driven out of Central Europe by Nazism who profoundly enriched American intellectual life. Actually, the realist phase had begun to surface years earlier. For example, the caution of most early post-Versailles IR specialists was only confirmed by Charles Hodges, who introduced a background text on world politics with these words:

> This endeavour has been cast along realistic lines . . . . To those who seek short cuts to the outlawry of war and to world peace in ready-made idealism, we commend the whole pageant of human progress as a struggle against human nature, successful only where leadership had proceeded slowly and painfully over the solid ground of prevailing world realities.[2]

This Hobbesian perspective appeared in print just *before* the multiple crisis that accompanied the shift from the optimistic 1920s to the forlorn 1930s. Hodges saw IR as the "apex" of the social sciences. In one sense, his treatment was consistent with the literature of the first decade, devoting even more space to international law and organization than most, but it was in an essentially realist context.

Putting aside specific country or regional studies and dozens of titles that concentrated upon the closely related fields of international law, history, foreign policy, international organization and especially peace, we can identify about forty titles in what we have termed "mainstream" IR from 1916 to the entrance of the United States into the Second World War. Even if by "idealist" we mean no more than stressing the efficacy of law and organization, only about half of these can be said to be even primarily idealistic in tone. The long-range effects of political events are rarely understood at the time they occur, particularly in the still relatively unfamiliar domain of international developments that challenge the very foundations of the existing order. So that while diplomats, reporters, and some pundits realized that something crucial was happening in Asia, academics tended to continue their painstaking efforts to develop, enhance, and especially to organize scientifically the teaching of the new discipline. Most of them concentrated, not on current events, but on continuing the efforts initiated more than a decade earlier, to all appearances undeterred and hardly discouraged by what was occurring on the new battlefields of actual interstate contact.

Defining the subject-matter

A landmark in these patient efforts, at least in Britain, was an extensive survey undertaken in 1933, under the chairmanship of Sir William (later Lord) Beveridge, by the British Co-ordinating Committee of Institutions for the Scientific Study of International Relations. The survey not only covered the entire range of student and adult education in the country at that time, but the study of international law and relations as such in universities as well, including a few "separate" Departments of International Relations. Objectivity in methodology and presentation seemed to be one of the keystones in the scientific approach, just as education was the key to creating an informed citizenry. In the words of the National Union of Students, "the function of a University is not only to produce highly trained specialists but people who are both highly trained specialists and 'good citizens'."[3]

The editor, S. H. Bailey, made it clear that, in this subject especially, there should be no trace of propaganda from the state. But just what was meant by "this subject?" Was this eminent committee now prepared to give definition to a new discipline? According to Bailey, this question could be considered from two viewpoints – the theoretical or ideal, and the practical or possible. On the theoretical side, it encompassed these subdivisions:

(a) International History – particularly diplomatic relations.
(b) Economics and the Theory of International Trade.
(c) The Structure of International Relations, or of the Great Society – a composite study of geographical, economic, social, psychological, ethical, political, and other factors influencing international conduct.
(d) Principles, history, philosophy and International Law, mainly public.

(e) Study of what has been called "the technique of peace," that is, growth, structure, and practice of both national and international institutions for the conduct of international relations.

Practical problems produced in the committee a consensus on several factors, notably the absence of uniformity in facilities for teaching history, economics and international law, the time-factor for IR students required to cope with an already overloaded undergraduate schedule, and the problem of whether the subject should be postgraduate, undergraduate or both. The generalization can probably be made that, whereas in the United States considerable intellectual effort was going into the preparation of textbooks analyzing the comprehensive field, the main effort in the UK was upon teaching, conferring about the nature of the subject, and deciding how universities could better accommodate it. The American writers taught, to be sure, just as the British teachers wrote, but the latter tended to make their mark through specialization, not overall treatment of problems on a global scale.

Within a few years after the Bailey survey, two American studies (1934, 1937) were completed under the competent eye of Edith Ware on all aspects of American IR studies and, indeed, activities. They were sponsored by a duly impressive "American National Committee on International Intellectual Cooperation," a veritable Who's Who of stateside world-minded intellectuals headed by Professor James T. Shotwell of Columbia and The Carnegie Endowment. In her 1937 preface, Edith Ware cited Secretary of State Cordell Hull's charge to the Third World Power Conference in Washington in 1936:

> You meet in a spirit of friendly cooperation with no thought of chauvinism or political jealousy . . . you also advance the cause of peace. And the cause of peace is the cause of civilization; religion, science, culture and social betterment only go forward in a world without war. . . .[4]

Hull asked, "Shall the brains of the world be used to lighten the burdens of man, or shall they be used for the grim purposes of war?" Ware's book did not answer the question, but in 1937 there was ample reason to wonder. Hundreds of pages were devoted to organizational activities on an international plane, from temperance societies to The American Tariff League, but with no more than twenty pages to the study of international relations in academic institutions, seven of which concentrated upon the several professional schools then in being or planned.

Though hardly definitive, certain of Ware's comments are instructive in bringing into the analysis of IR's growth insights from yet another new discipline: Education. Some of what she wrote fifty years ago is still true today:

> Educational theory and many other factors have contributed to break down the separatist character of the various disciplines. . . . In order to understand any one subject adequately, it has often been necessary to understand a great deal about one or more of the others. . . . Something approaching a new discipline has been created. . . .[5]

In light of this essentially educationist assessment, how were the political scientists and others, who were writing the textbooks for actual IR courses, now looking at the subject? The frequency of general texts remained about the same as in the earlier period. In apparent contrast to discussants in the British committee, however, consensus on what the student of IR should learn is much more difficult to find among their authors, most of whom were now Americans. Narrower, more specific treatments of world economics and politics became more commonplace. At least in the literature, the discipline of IR did not advance in ways that had been anticipated. Hitherto plausible certainties accompanying an incipient *science* of IR gave way to doubt, just as optimism gave way to pessimism in world politics. Indeed the literature of this middle period, particularly outside the mainstream on both sides of the Atlantic, may even be regarded as retrogressive. Consensus on what topics needed to be given major treatment gave way to novelty, challenge, and experimentation. Hence, while Ramsay Muir was still looking back to *The Political Consequences of the Great War* (1931), titles by responsible writers such as David Davies (*Suicide or Sanity?*), James T. Shotwell (*On the Rim of the Abyss*), and even Buell (*War Drums and Peace Plans*) contended for the reading public's attention. The cover of one book, an update of *The Great Illusion* of 1910, featured "Angell warns again!" This "apocalyptic" literature looked ahead to what seemed to be a growing probability of another major conflict. Concentration was no longer upon the system but upon its collapse. Just as would be the case a generation later in the American response to Vietnam, polemics often replaced scientific analysis. But this was not mainstream.[6]

Contrasts in the new mainstream literature

Although only six comprehensive texts appeared between The Mukden incident of 1931 and the Munich crisis of 1938, eight more were published by the time Japanese struck at Pearl Harbor three years later. Dominant among them were Frederick L. Schuman's *International Politics*, whose three editions in this second decade (1933, 1937, 1941) had many competitors. Yet while the term "mainstream" remains useful to describe those authors whose perspective was universal rather than regionally or functionally restricted, the tidy formulations of the previous, more optimistic decade gave way to a variety of interpretations that had little in common but their non-consensual realism and their scope.

To try now to extrapolate a "composite consensus" similar to what had readily emerged from the first decade would only demonstrate that it cannot really be done. Some revealing conclusions can nonetheless be drawn from the effort. First of all, the range of topics was extensive. Only four topics were dealt with by a majority of the authors, eight still regarding law as a key feature of international relations and six treating diplomatic history, the state system or power politics, and world order (mainly the League) as of major importance, with such headings as nationalism, economic factors, imperialism, and war also receiving emphasis. In contrast to this modest level of consensus, more than three times as many unique or dissimilar subjects were taken up in these texts than had been the case in the previous decade. Second, political scientists now dominated, even though writers continued to come from a number of disciplines. Third, all but three of the books were published in the United States, one of the others being a symposium of no less than thirteen writers from several countries on the faculty at Geneva. Several reasons in addition to specialization suggest themselves for this relative lack of general texts from Europe: first, except possibly in law, textbooks were customarily not used in university instruction; second, there was therefore little "market" as existed abundantly for US courses; third, there was no "publish or perish" culture in Europe; and, fourth, there was as yet no "critical mass" of competent scholars in the new discipline as was beginning to emerge in America and, to a lesser extent, in Britain. Finally, regarding the organization of the subdivisions of IR, although only four topics cited rated major attention by more than half of the authors, at least forty other subjects were set forth as separate chapters, including such disparate and often inconclusive examples as "The international aristocracy," "The dream of world unity," "The non-national pattern," and "The retreat of the vanquished." Regional topics were covered separately and in detail by three authors; their work anticipated a postwar rush to "area studies." In other words, there was little agreement on the components of a distinct discipline as the fragile new world order fell apart; indeed, in contrast to the participants in the Bailey conferences, most American textbook writers showed little interest in "the discipline" during what they increasingly implied would turn out to be a prewar decade. Why?

To find the answer to this, there is no better place to begin than with the decade's most successful author in the field, if the widespread adoption of Schuman's *International Politics* text in the United States is any guide (British students were reading international history, principally as set forth by the anti-Wilsonian, Gathorne-Hardy). In a "Preface for social scientists," Schuman argued that up until then international lawyers and historians had monopolized the study of international relations. Jurists had looked at the subject from the perspective of international public law. Historians treated world politics in a general way "by the usual word jugglery and the intellectual acrobatics habitually indulged in by those who conceive of social science as a vehicle for dispensing moral judgments."[7] In apparently ignoring any real interdisciplinary collaboration in approaching the subject, Schuman failed even to mention economists, geographers or others who presumably had something to contribute to an understanding of international relations. His approach was based upon what he termed "the new political science," not the old variety "circumscribed by barren legal and historical concepts" but one which showed that political science, as one of the social sciences, is concerned with the description and analysis of power in society – i.e. with those patterns of social contacts which are suggested by such words as rulers and ruled, command and obedience, domination and subordination, authority and allegiance.[8]

A new vocabulary would even be necessary along with novel ideas in order that political scientists might "escape from these frustrations," namely "the blind alley of legalism" and "elaborate fact gathering on a variety of topics which they are unable to put together into any unified scheme of interpretation."[9]

The methodological revolution, which thirty years later would provide both the methods and the language of an even newer political science, did indeed overcome these particular frustrations, but at the expense of producing frustrations of their own based upon excessive claims and a certain inability to communicate. In describing the Western State System (which he seemed to identify with "the whole state system of modern world society"), Schuman devoted as many chapters to "world anarchy" as to the rise of modern world society and world order combined, leaving a lonely final chapter for "toward tomorrow." Disorder hence replaced international law and organization in this scheme of things, a distinct departure from the previous decade.

Schuman's power-based analysis was countered by an economic base of power in *The Great Powers in World Politics* (1935) by a journalist named Frank Simonds teamed with a Yale professor, Brooks Emeny (who soon left academe to pursue the other educational target of the early theoretical practitioners, public opinion, as president of the Foreign Policy Association). Their study of international relations and economic nationalism frankly eliminated everything not a part of what was termed "the world that matters," fundamentally economic in nature and encompassing Western Europe, the United States and Japan. Here was indeed one of the first modern examples of international political economy, though it would be nearly fifty years before IPE would signify a growing point in the discipline. Full of maps and charts, this interpretation set forth the factors of national power and their relative standing among the contending states in Europe and East Asia, with the United States as "the third center of industrial power." By the time the student reached the relatively brief last

section, "Can peace be preserved?", he had every reason to doubt
it. If he wanted a differing interpretation published at about the
same time, his doubts could have a Marxist base, *World Politics
1918–1936*, by R. Palme Dutt, an Anglo-Indian, most of whose
work had been on India.

A new word now appeared in the literature, one which in time
would become very familiar: "theory," first in a long tome written
by a fellow political scientist whose roots in history were as strong
as Schuman's, Frank Russell of Berkeley. His *Theories of International
Relations* (1936), unsophisticated by later quantitative and
behavioral standards, must be regarded as a landmark contribution
to the discipline. As Russell put it:

> There is no book in any language, as far as I know, that attempts
> to present from the earliest times, and in the light of environ-
> mental influences, the more significant ideas, whatever their
> character or implications may be, that men have entertained
> concerning international relations.[10]

The only possible exception might be F. S. Marvin's *The Evolution
of World Peace* (1921); despite contributions by such distinguished
scholars as Toynbee on Hellenism and G. P. Gooch on the impact
of the French Revolution, however, the book must be regarded as
a polemic for what today might be called the peace paradigm. It
included, for example, a chapter by H. G. Wells entitled "An
apology for a world utopia," which only provided grist for future
realists' mills.

A second book in theory was less historical and more philosophical, Salvador de Madariaga's *Theory and Practice in International
Relations* (1937). Recalling his years in the League Secretariat in
Geneva, de Madariaga was struck by the contrast between what
people were thinking or saying about international relations and
what they, and particularly others in chancelleries throughout the
world, were actually doing. What did he have to say about theory?
Though perhaps not much in light of advanced analyses to be seen
later, he was nevertheless original and full of insight. As one
"temporarily taken away from his real vocation, that of a man of
thought, into the field of action," de Madariaga set forth a series of
theoretical propositions linking these two worlds (italics his):[11]

1 Obviously international relations is a form of politics . . .
2 Politics may be defined as *"all manifestations of life endowed with power to influence collective events . . ."*
3 "The State is based entirely on moral forces . . . much gnashing of teeth, and much disappointment, might have been avoided if people had realized that it is impossible to expect of a world community which is groping towards its State (with a capital *S*), that it should go further and rise higher and become more efficient than the state (with a small *s*) of the moral forces which compose it allows . . ."
4 The world community, like every other community, may be defined by "the solidarity which binds together all its members; *Solidarity may be defined as the interdependence between parts of a whole, without which the whole does not exist . . .*"
5 Sovereignty (from a moral, not a legal perspective) *"is a tendency, both primary and reactive, to consider or to assert the national will as the sole, or at least as the final determinant of action."*

To pursue the ideas of these four quite diverse writers more fully would be rewarding even today, but before returning to the literature of the time, let us see what was going on in another arena: the international conference.

Several shelves, both at Chatham House and at the headquarters of the Council on Foreign Relations, Harold Pratt House on 68th Street in New York, are filled with papers and verbatim reports (mostly in French) from the ISC (International Studies Conferences). The proceedings of one of the most fruitful of these, which took place in Prague about a year before the outbreak of the Second World War, were published in Paris under the title *University Teaching of International Relations*. Noting that other discussions of teaching IR had recently taken place (London, 1935, and Madrid, 1936), the rapporteur cited a "substantial consensus of agreement" on three propositions:[12]

> first, within the general mass of the social phenomena of the present-day world there is a distinguishable body of material which lends itself to separate study under the name of International Relations.

second,   it is desirable that this material should form the subject of teaching in Universities and institutions of University rank, and

third,   it is desirable also that such adjustments as may be necessary should be made in the academic framework to enable this teaching to take place under the best conditions.

As for sub-topics, Zimmern also ecumenically suggested that "the indispensable nucleus of the subject" was contained in political science, political economy, international law, geography, history, sociology and political and moral philosophy.[13] Some "nucleus"! He even asked whether other subjects should be included, namely psychology and in their more general aspects law, biology, geology, and demography, adding many questions about methodology and academic organization and winding up with a concern about ultimate values: "What is the good implicit in the notion of a peaceful solution? Is Peace an ultimate good? Or are there other values superior to it? If so, can they be defined and applied to the problem under review?"[14] These were considered the real questions, rather than the urgent practical issues that were soon to lead to the Munich conference of European statesmen, which split off German-speaking Sudetenland from the rest of Czechoslovakia and gave it to Hitler (neither Czechs nor teachers of international relations were invited). Nevertheless for four days, the professors discussed philosophy and pedagogy, including reports on the status of teaching international relations in several of the countries represented: Australia, Austria, Canada, Denmark, Netherlands, Norway, Romania, Switzerland, and Yugoslavia, with a "bulky volume" circulated to the Conferences by the American Coordinating Committee.

What is most striking in these reports is the consistent theme that, even though general formal acceptance of IR as a discipline or a separate department was yet to come, universities were at last becoming responsive, somewhat reluctantly within their existing faculties, to the insistently growing interest in world affairs and the need for its systematic study. Exchanges were exceptionally rich in both conceptualization and innovation, the first with respect to the nature, scope, and methodology of IR and the second with

how to organize instruction more effectively within a compart-
mentalized academic environment. In closing, the rapporteur
marked the relative progress of American effort and experience:

> The broad fact that emerged was that the study of international
> relations is very much more systematically developed in the
> Universities of the United States than in any other part of the
> world and that this development has taken place almost entirely
> since 1918. Even allowing for the great preponderance of the
> United States in the number and size of its University insti-
> tutions, no other country could show a volume of work in the
> academic field comparable. . . .[15]

One other statement at this last prewar conference is noteworthy,
coming as it did from a leading international economist, a New
Zealander, J. B. Condliffe:

> If I am not greatly mistaken, the academic discipline of econ-
> omics may have to undergo certain great changes in its leading
> conceptions. . . . We are, in fact, now facing a situation in which
> the balance of economic power has changed within each country,
> between countries, where the forms of economic organization
> are changing and where the whole problem must be re-stated.[16]

Carr

Shortly after the Prague conference ended two mainstream
books appeared that portended a new consensus. One was a
complex volume containing essays by no less than thirty-four
authors. The editors designed their book as one of the first truly
*inter*disciplinary (as contrasted to *multi*disciplinary) texts and not a
mere collection of individual papers by experts in different fields.[17]
While not designed as a text, the other was to have as much to do
with bringing about a shift in attitude as any other analysis in the
history of the discipline. Like others in this second decade, Carr's
*The Twenty-Years' Crisis 1919–1939: An Introduction to the Study of
International Relations* (1939) bore little resemblance to previous
mainstream books.

As a leader writer for *The Times*, Carr had been impressed by
the contradiction between how Hitler's successes were bringing
another war ever closer and how public opinion was expressing
itself in his country. He had spent years in the Foreign Office

before turning to journalism and was later to find himself, as occupant of the IR chair at Aberystwyth, a man with a triple vantage point. Consistent with the purposes of Chatham House (with which he had for years been closely associated) Carr defined what he meant by "the science of international politics." Discussing the "beginnings of a science," he observed that utopianism had occupied a place in the development of this new science not unlike that which had occurred earlier in the physical sciences, including medicine, that is, "the desire to cure the sickness of the body politic has given its impulse and its inspiration to political science,"[18] of which international politics is a part. Responding to a popular demand,

> It has been created to serve a purpose and has in this respect followed the pattern of other sciences. . . . The course of events after 1931 clearly revealed the inadequacy of pure aspiration as the basis for a science of international politics, and made it possible for the first time to embark on serious critical and analytical thought about international problems. Utopia and reality are two facets of science.[19]

There are other politico-intellectual phenomena that, Carr argued, must be understood before any attempt can be made to examine the crisis in actual international relations: free will or determination, theory related to practice, the intellectual and the bureaucrat, left versus right, and finally the dichotomy between ethics and politics. The last of these, along with utopianism versus realism, makes up a philosophical dimension of political outlook; collectively they go far towards delineating what today would be called a paradigm. With reference to the nature of a post-crisis international order, Carr asked whether the nation itself would continue to exist as the unit of power in such an order, concluding that one prediction could be made with some confidence, "the concept of sovereignty is likely to become in the future even more blurred and indistinct than it is at present"[20] (and, he might have added, more widespread).

Carr's significance lay in what Fox recently characterized as "four great virtues":

He relentlessly exposed the hollowness of the edifice of then prevailing Anglo-American "utopian" international thinking. He had a sense of the sweep of modern European history and was well-equipped to identify the salient changes which marked the passing of the European age in world politics. He was a pioneer in bringing the insights of Karl Mannheim and the sociology of knowledge to bear on the relation between thought and action in world politics. Finally, whether or not he always got the right answers, he asked very good questions.[21]

One of the wrong answers of this realist theoretician was his defense of appeasement in 1939.

After Carr and the relative dearth of mainstream literature in the depression decade, three basically conventional texts were published before the United States entered the Second World War following the attack on Pearl Harbor. Two of them were harbingers of the new realism. One, *Elements of International Relations* (1940) by Frederich Middlebush and Chesney Hill, warned against preoccupation with current events and the "blood and thunder" aspects of international affairs, resulting in the danger of superficiality, loss of a sense of perspective, and failure to grasp "fundamentals." The other represented the then best example of the "state of the art", Walter Sharp and Grayson Kirk's *Contemporary International Politics* (1940), which was

not designed to provide any simple or complete answer to these complicated and perplexing aspects of a new world that through infinite travail is struggling into being. It constitutes, rather, an attempt on the part of the authors to explore and examine those fundamental forces which in their view are most responsible for the motivation of foreign policies. . . . In our opinion, a functional interpretation of the interlocking factors of geography, population, race, nationalism, technology, economics, and government offers distinct advantages by comparison with any strictly chronological, regional, or country-by-country treatment of subject matter. Accordingly, we have in large part avoided the latter approach for the former.[22]

All of these authors were interdisciplinary realists, bringing in almost as many other ancillary disciplines, but from a foreign policy rather than the world society perspective of Zimmern. Where Zimmern was the consummate idealist, they represented the new mainstream pragmatism.

The third text was in the idealist tradition. *Foundations of Modern World Society* (1941) appeared before analyses grounded upon the war took over. In presenting what might be called a "welfare" approach to the subject, Linden Mander dealt with problems of health, crime, labor, conservation, population, minorities, and intellectual or religious cooperation, anticipating the non-state-centric perspective that was to emerge thirty years later. But should such an approach occupy a place in the mainstream literature? Yes, because toward the end of his book, the American political scientist finally (and one feels reluctantly) deals with war, sovereignty, security, and the "present war and the prospects for world order" (about which he remained essentially optimistic, if only in the long run).

Despite concentration upon social issues, Mander did not place IR in the context of the discipline of sociology as a British international lawyer was soon to do. Sociologists themselves were not yet writing mainstream IR texts and generally ventured into the field only marginally. There was one exception: Luther L. and Jessie Bernard had attempted an intellectually broad approach in their *Sociology and the Study of International Relations* (1934). Such writers as Karl Mannheim in *Man and Society in an Age of Reconstruction* (1940) and P. A. Sorokin in *Crisis of Our Age* (1941) dealt with world society, but hardly from a classical IR perspective. Aside from these studies, Janowski and Fagen's treatment of the international aspects of German social policies in 1937 and Theodore L. Stoddard's *Clashing Tides of Color* (1935) were among the few to suggest possible linkages.

As for other disciplines, some geographers gave an inkling of the role they were soon to play. Along with D. S. Whittlesey in *The Earth and the State* (1939), Richard Hartshorn analyzed the relationship between physical environment and political organization, as well as trying to lend theory to the field of geography. Even before that, in 1938, Charles Colby edited a book of essays by seven leading geographers (one of them French, Pierre Denis), *Geographic Aspects of International Relations*. Except for Colby, Samuel Van Valkenburg, and James Fairgrieve, most geographers dealt with countries, regions, or the planet as a whole, not interstate relations. In economics, analyses of particular problems increased in the 1930s, but only a few endeavored to cover the broad range of international affairs as had certain of the lawyers, political scientists and historians. The work of R. F. Harrod and Jacob Viner in international economics as such stand out, just as Sonia Z. Hyman, Lionel Robbins and H. B. Butler made notable contributions to an understanding of the relationships between economics, planning, peace, and world order. A monograph for the *British Journal of Psychology* by meteorologist L. F. Richardson[23] represented a pioneer effort at statistical analysis. The contributions of Gunnar Myrdal in demography and Tom H. Pear in psychology were beginning to be felt, representing a growing relevance of work in the cultural dimension. The famous *Open Letters* (1933) between Sigmund Freud and Albert Einstein, "Why war?" are still of interest,[24] as is Harold Lasswell's *World Politics and Personal Insecurity* (1935). In the passing flood of what we have chosen to call "apocalyptic" literature, G. D. H. Cole's *Guide through World Chaos* (1934), T. Ishimaru's *Next World War* (1937) and George Fielding Eliot's *Bombs Bursting in Air* (1939) added to the decade's store of controversial ideas but hardly to the discipline of IR as a science.

In the field of law, general treatises continued to enrich the literature in the mid-1930s before the fabric of law broke down, notably Hersch Lauterpacht's *The Function of Law in the International Community* (1933), Hans Kelsen's weighty *The Legal Process and International Order* (1935), and J. L. Brierly's compact *Law of Nations* (1936). There were others, but these qualify as classics. Note the terms "order" and "community," reflective of the same extra-legal concern later to be expressed by another international lawyer, Georg Schwarzenberger. The most respected international lawyers were neither narrow legalists nor parochial conventionalists, but reflected the longest tradition of scholarship about statecraft. So-called idealist internationalists had all but disappeared from law, if indeed any had ever really come from that discipline in the first place.

To give the impression that genuine idealists like Zimmern and especially Toynbee had been totally out of touch with the reality that writers such as Schuman and Carr had grasped would be grossly to mislead the contemporary student of international relations. In one respect, Toynbee was a realist ahead of his time in that he clearly foresaw the coming impact of what is today known as the "Third World" upon international politics. Zimmern anticipated the stress now being placed upon values by statesman and scholar alike. Both of them frequently exchanged views with Carr at Chatham House. The basic point is that each wrote within the political context of his times with what he regarded as scientific objectivity. What had changed were the times. The high degree of consensus in the literature of the 1916–31 phase reflected, with a certain degree of confidence, consensus in the world of politics itself. Now that was not so. Successive editions of Schuman do provide a linkage in that his way of subdividing the subject matter of IR resembles the early model, though his perspective is more akin to the coming stage of consensus based upon power. What is even more useful in terms of the development of the field is the way in which he interpreted shifts in the balance of power. His is the best example of what Fox means by undergraduate texts representing a "prism" through which their authors interpret a changing world.[25]

To summarize: in contrast to the literature of the first modern period of international relations as a discipline when there was agreement on the nature and scope of the subject among the authors of mainstream books, the decade between the basic challenges to the League system starting in 1931 and the extension of the European war to the entire world in 1941 was characterized by widely divergent approaches. The power approach of Schuman, the stress upon economic nationalism of Simonds and Emeny, the theoretical history of Russell, the Marxist critique of Dutt, the thought/action nexus of de Madariaga, the scientific definition of Carr, the interdisciplinary pragmatism of Brown and his colleagues, the functionalist perspective of Sharp and Kirk, and the welfare paradigm of Mander all stood in contrast to traditional descriptive expositions, and indeed from one another. Excessive attention to a new world order had been corrected. Truly interdisciplinary analysis, except possibly for recognition of the necessity to understand historical antecedents, had yet to be achieved by most experts. The essential place of economics had been understood by only a few, notably Simonds and Emeny. There was apparently little discussion even with those few economists, such as Harrod and Ellsworth, who were writing general texts on international economics, so that international political economy had its exponents mainly in the past in Smith, List, and Ricardo, or in a distant future which would once again stress international political economy. Similarly, only a few geographers such as Colby and Fairgrieve were attempting to apply the lessons of their well-established discipline to the issues of world politics. Sociologists were as yet dealing only with edges of the subject, and "macro-sociology" was a term to be invented only in the 1960s. Even the broad-gauged contributions of such international lawyers as Lauterpacht and Kelsen must be regarded as exceptions.

Hence, after a promising start, there had now to be real doubt whether the literature demonstrated any such thing as agreement in defining a discipline of international relations. Workers in the IR vineyard might well have taken a cue from their fellow social scientists; "what is economics?", it is asked, the answer being "what economists do." Clear progress had been made in the conferences and the surveys. No such doubt attended the need for it. The "power-shock" had destroyed the first consensus, but the second was yet to emerge. As in the case of the traditional glass, which is either half-full or half-empty depending upon how you look at it, doubters should remind themselves of just how little time had elapsed since the whole idea was first broached.

At this point (almost as if to clarify their thinking) the second of the world wars engulfed the planet. How did this affect the field? The war itself produced an even greater variety of approaches, initially the geopolitical perspective appropriate to a military phase, with many others to follow. Before we leave the interwar period, one other lesson needs to be noted. If we take Carr's definition of the phases in the development of science, both decades take a legitimate and logical place in the growth of the discipline, with the second providing a transition to a new consensus. The apparent contradiction between them may easily be overdrawn, as the return in the wake of Vietnam to some of the humane values which so concerned Zimmern and his colleagues in the wake of the carnage of the First World War would later serve to demonstrate.

Anticipating a new consensus

The "Cold War" did not initiate the new realism. It would be given a running start into the postwar era by a handful of wartime mainstream books, which managed to surface despite shortages of everything from paper to time to think. About a year after the so-called "phoney war" came to an abrupt end with the Nazi invasion of Denmark and Norway, one of the last mainstream texts to be written by an international lawyer, Schwarzenberger, was published in London: *Power Politics* (1941). Although he was later to deal extensively with the legal dimension in his *International Law and Totalitarian Lawlessness* (1944), Schwarzenberger now played down this aspect of the subject, sharing with Schuman a belief in the centrality of power. But it was another feature of *Power Politics*, implicit in its subtitle, *A Study of World Society*, which was more unusual and possibly more promising. Schwarzenberger contended that IR constituted "that branch of Sociology concerned with international society"[26] (the last two words will be recalled as the title of Brown's book in 1923: see Appendix A). Even the historical sociologist, Harry Elmer Barnes, had in 1930 avoided both the term "society" and its disciplinary implication for location of the subject matter in the halls of academe. In its actual organization, however, *Power Politics* proved to be fairly consistent both with mainstream treatment from Buell to Mowat in the period after Versailles and with Sharp and Kirk at the beginning of the Second World War. For Schwarzenberger, law, organization – and even morality – were essentially functions of power. Indeed, instead of citing Grotius as the "founder" of this new discipline (as might have been expected of an international lawyer) he designated Machiavelli.[27]

Several wartime authors contributed to the discipline's maturity. Based upon childhood experiences in Romania, wartime cooperation in shipping, and working for the League, David Mitrany looked beyond the fighting in developing functionalism as the basis for postwar planning. Hitler's war machine was still scoring successes when Robert Strausz-Hupé tried both to explain and to expose its reliance upon a deterministic view of geography; "even if geopolitics were simply the German blueprint for world conquest and nothing else, it would be worth studying," he wrote, "but it is far more than that . . . it remains a challenge to our conception of world policy."[28] A chapter entitled "Heartland and hokum" attacked the entire approach. Thorsten Kalijarvi, a scholar giving wartime service in the State Department, somewhat apologetically began his anthology, *Modern World Politics* (1943), with the question, "Why another book on international relations when the market is already filled with them?" His answer is sobering in the light of the later siren call of government and foundation research "honey-pots": at one of those times when "the scholar gladly tends to throw off his usual objectivity and detachment in order to preserve his country's stake in the present war," Kalijarvi felt compelled to provide a "detached" presentation of the background of world events.[29] A chapter on world organization concluded that "the elaborate machinery of the League could not, of itself, keep the peace if States were determined to go to war." His place in the field's development could be said to rest on assenting "in all modesty the distinction" of including military disruption, psychological warfare, espionage, treachery, and international secret organizations, unpleasant elements of international relations that could never again be ignored.

Another lasting contribution took the form of an interpretation of the military dimension differing from the dominant prewar theme of collective security as the means of guaranteeing peaceful change. Edward Mead Earle and his colleagues in *Makers of Modern Strategy* (1943) anticipated strategic studies as an integral element in IR. Their interpretation of great military thinkers of the past by prominent thinkers of the present (e.g., Ludendorf by Hans Speier, Jomini by Gordon Craig, Douhet by Margaret Sprout) represented a shift in thinking in the IR community from collective security to grand strategy. A Dutch sociologist turned political geographer, the first Director of the Yale Institute of International Studies (dubbed "The Power School" within the trade), Nicholas J. Spykman provided both another answer to, and a new expression of, geopolitics. His map-filled *Geography of the Peace* (1944), advancing a counter-theory to Haushofer's distortion of Mackinder's "Heartland Theory," the "Rimland Theory," followed his more influential volume, *America's Strategy in World Politics* (1942). Representing a logical outgrowth of Mahan's earlier idea of seapower based upon control of the coasts around the great ocean basins to the east and west of the Western hemisphere, this held great appeal for Pentagon postwar planners. Unfortunately for the development of IR, professional geographers after the war tended to drift toward physical geography, so that strategic thinking profited less from their expertise than might have been desirable; this was the price both disciplines may have paid for having become associated with a subject, or even a "pseudo-science," because of what Haushofer and Hitler had done with geopolitics.

As other and more reputable ideas encouraged by the war were finding their way into the literature, one author even added a new term to the language of politics, "the Super-Powers." Fox had every reason in 1944 to include the United Kingdom as well as America and Russia. This short but significant book opened with an apt quotation from the journalist Samuel Grafton relating to a cardinal principle of the emerging international order, "sovereign equality": "even after you give the squirrel a certificate which says he is quite as big as any elephant, he is still going to be smaller, and all the squirrels would know it and all the elephants will know it."[30]

Fox made no attempt to write a general text at any time in an illustrious career capped by his holding the Bryce Professorship in the History of International Relations at Columbia. The farsighted influence of his essay had already earned him a place in the history of "the field" (to his dying day, he declined to be drawn into any argument on whether IR is a discipline), even though it was perhaps one of the least of his manifold contributions as an original thinker, teacher and professional counsellor during four decades. Like Thucydides and Machiavelli, Fox described politics as it was; like other wartime writers he had little to say about international law and organization. If it now seems odd that he deemed it necessary to explain why he was writing "In defense of talking about power," remember that many other observers were now preparing for another postwar era in which, this time with active American participation, world cooperation would at last prove to be a viable alternative to power politics. It would be a recurring phenomenon, as Lasswell's insights should have made clear. To what extent would the new mainstream literature reflect this hopefulness?

Notes: Chapter 5

1 G. M. Gathorne-Hardy, *A Short History of International Affairs*, 4th edn, 1950, p. 503.
2 Charles Hodges, *The Background of International Relations. Our World Horizons: National and International* (New York: Wiley 1931), p. viii.
3 Cited in S. H. Bailey (ed.), *International Studies in Great Britain* (London: Oxford University Press, 1933), p. 22. This is the official report of the British Coordinating Committee carrying out its part of the June 1931 Copenhagen resolution of the Third Annual Conference of Institutions for the Scientific Study of International Relations.
4 Edith E. Ware (ed.), *The Study of International Relations in the United States: Survey for 1937* (New York: Columbia University Press, 1938), p. xii.
5 ibid., p. 114.
6 For a complete list of the texts surveyed for this contradictory phase, see Appendix B (p. 184).
7 F. L. Schuman, *International Politics*, p. xii.
8 ibid.
9 ibid.
10 F. M. Russell, *Theories of International Relations* (New York: D. Appleton–Century, 1936), p. vi.
11 Salvador de Madariaga, *Theory and Practice in International Relations* (Philadelphia: University of Pennsylvania Press, 1937), pp. 2–15.
12 Sir Alfred Zimmern (ed.), *University Teaching of International Relations* (Paris: International Institute of Intellectual Cooperation (League of Nations), 1939), p. 16.
13 ibid., p. 16.
14 ibid., p. 18.
15 ibid., pp. 332–3.
16 ibid., pp. 334–5.
17 Frances J. Brown, Charles Hodges and Joseph S. Roucek, *Contemporary World Politics: An Introduction to the Problems of International Relations* (London: Chapman and Hall, 1940), pp. viii–ix.
18 E. H. Carr, *The Twenty-Years' Crisis 1919–1939* (London: Macmillan, 1942; 5th printing), p. 5.
19 ibid., p. 9.
20 ibid., p. 230.
21 "E. H. Carr and political realism: vision and revision." *Review of International Studies* 11, 1, January 1985, p. 1.
22 *Sharp and Grayson, Contemporary International Politics* (New York: Farrar and Rinehart, 1940), pp. vii–viii.
23 L. F. Richardson, "Generalized foreign politics," *British Journal of Psychology*, Monograph Supplement No. 2 (Cambridge: 1939) Cited in Wright, pp. 413, 346.
24 Freud and Einstein, *Open Letters* (Paris: International Institute of Intellectual Cooperation, 1933).

25 Correspondence with Olson, July 1988.
26 Georg Schwarzenberger, *Power Politics*, 2nd edn, 1951, p. 8.
27 "Another potential threat to freedom of research arises from unwilling-ness of the many to accept disagreeable truth in good humour. The scientist in the field of international relations must be prepared to share the fate of the founder of his science. Machiavelli dared to describe the politics of the Renaissance as he saw them." ibid., p. 3.
28 R. Strausz-Hupé, *Geopolitics: The Struggle for Space and Power* (New York: Putnam, 1942), p. xii.
29 T. Kalijarvi, *Modern World Politics* (New York: Thomas Crowell Co., 1943), p. vii.
30 W. T. R. Fox, *The Super-Powers: the United States, Britain, and the Soviet Union: Their Responsibility for Peace* (Harcourt, Brace, 1944), p. 3. Grafton's sentence appeared in the New York *Post* on 23 November 1943.

Further reading

Bentwich, Norman D. *The Religious Foundations of Internationalism: A Study of International Relations through the Ages*. London: Allen & Unwin, 1933.

Brierly, Sir James L. *The Law of Nations*. 6th edn, Oxford: Clarendon Press, 1962.

Bull, Hedley. "International theory: the case for a classical approach," *World Politics*, 18, 3: 361–77 (April 1966).

Carr, Edward Hallett. *The Twenty-Years' Crisis 1919–1939: An Introduction to the Study of International Relations* (rev. edn). New York: St Martin's Press, 1966.

Earle, Edward Mead, Craig, Gordon and Gilbert, Felix (eds). *Makers of Modern Strategy*. Princeton, NJ: Princeton University Press, 1943.

Fox, W. T. R. *The Super-Powers*. New York: Harcourt, 1944.

Freud, Sigmund and Einstein, Albert, "Why war?" *Open Letters*. Paris: International Institute of Intellectual Cooperation, 1933.

Gathorne-Hardy, G. M. *A Short History of International Affairs 1920–1939*. 4th edn, London: Oxford University Press, for the Royal Institute of International Affairs, 1950.

Lasswell, Harold. *World Politics and Personal Insecurity*. New York: McGraw-Hill, 1935.

Lippmann, Walter. *The Good Society*. Boston: Little, Brown, 1937.

Spykman, Nicholas J. *Method of Approach to the Study of International Relations*. Washington: Conference of Teachers of International Law (CTIL), Vol. 5, 1933.

Strausz-Hupé, Robert. *Geopolitics: The Struggle for Space and Power*. New York: Putman, 1942.

Thompson, Kenneth W. *Masters of International Thought: Major Twentieth-Century Theorists and the World Crisis*. Baton Rouge, La. and London: Louisiana State University Press, 1980.

Ware, Edith E. *The Study of International Relations in the United States. Survey for 1934*. New York: Columbia University Press, 1934; *Survey for 1937*, published for the American National Committee for Intellectual Cooperation, 1938.

6 *The second consensus: the quest for power*

Rational political action consists in achieving the best possible reconciliation of the desirable and the possible. We ought therefore to attempt to order the blooming, buzzing confusion of world politics by collecting and arranging our data so that it helps us to understand the relatively fixed, the changing but uncontrollable, and manipulatable aspects of world politics. William T. R. Fox, "The Uses of International Relations Theory" in *Theoretical Aspects of International Relations*.[1]

The nuclear age that emerged from secrecy in the late summer of 1945 transformed the nature of world politics. Most of the world was exhausted. The usual new configuration of powers that follows wars differed this time in that there were now two giant states engaged almost at once in a confrontation. There was a second attempt at world organization, this time embracing all the victorious powers. Just as the 1919 peace settlement and the early promise of the League produced a literature dominated by international organization, nuclear weapons would give rise to strategic studies. Now the Cold War would take precedence, with its politico-strategic orientation serving to affect nearly every aspect of the study of international relations. Though it became more disciplined in terms of recognition of the need for more of what Thompson termed "rigor of analysis,"[2] it was also dominated more by power than by balance. It was a new consensus, but as before, it did not entirely replace the earlier one; both were state-centric.

However instructive they may have been, the contradictions of the Depression decade leading up to the war and its extension to most of the world in 1941 stood in stark contrast to the hopeful consensus of the relatively prosperous League period. A new, less optimistic level of consensus, anticipated by Schuman and Carr and buttressed by the experience of the war itself, was to be a consensus of power. A new breed of idealist internationalists nevertheless asserted themselves in an earnest outpouring of meetings, resolutions, pamphlets, organizations, and pledges of postwar cooperation. If the Charter of the new United Nations was in fact a realistic document,[3] this was not so understood by many of its most ardent and idealistic supporters. It was "realist" in that it provided for the mobilization of power collectively to face aggression, and it did this more effectively than had the Covenant of the League. In neither case did the problem lie in the document, but in its application. Shortly after the UN's founding, the rude awakening provided by Joseph Stalin's grimly ideological speech on 9 February 1946, reaffirming Marxist–Leninist predictions of inevitable confrontation with capitalism, convinced most observers that, far from being an alternative to power politics, the UN was destined to become its arena.

A new generation of analysis of IR

The centrality – if not the exclusivity – of power had already been stressed by the wartime mainstream writers. An important transitional anthology based upon Navy officer training courses in universities during the war, *Foundations of National Power* (1945) by Harold and Margaret Sprout, became the first widely used text of the postwar period, stressing national rather than collective security, though successive editions would move toward a more planetary perspective. In the preface to the second edition of his *Twenty-Years' Crisis* (1946), Carr wrote that, although he had altered nothing of substance, he had departed in two respects from his prewar thinking (actually, there were three, any reference to his controversial defense of the Munich deal now being omitted). One was that the "almost total neglect of the factor of power"[4] by others had now been overcome; he even acknowledged that his judgements in 1939 might have been "rather one-sided" in this regard, which confirms the findings above concerning the mainstream inter-war literature. The second change was even more interesting (and one wonders whether this would have been written at all had there been a third edition after the Cold War set in): his first edition "too readily and too complacently accepts the existing

nation-state, large or small, as the unit of international society."[5]
Here was the basis of what was later to be a new thrust in IR to
which major attention will be given in the following chapter – the
"world society" approach. The basic idea was that the unit of
analysis in IR should not be the state but, in the tradition of
Protagoras, man.

While casting his analysis in international societal terms, Schwarzenberger did not change his basic paradigm this far in his postwar
edition. Indeed he placed an entire new section on the economic,
social, educational, and other non-political programs of the UN
under the heading of "power politics in disguise." By now it was
evident that the old consensus based upon establishing the basis for
a cooperative world was not to be restored. Based upon power,
the die was cast for a new consensus, though it was within a decade
to face challenges which would come not from one but from many
different directions. In terms of a second consensus this may have
been an advance, but in interdisciplinary terms it must be seen as a
retreat because other disciplines, notably economics but also diplomatic history and geography, were to be given less emphasis. At
the same time, St Antony's college was created at Oxford, most of
the Fellows of which were historians well grounded in the economic, political and geographic realities of a particular part of the
world. Another thrust served to "skew" the way in which the
discipline grew, and that was an unstructured "paper triangle"
between academic entrepreneurs, the great foundations, and the
national security establishment. The principal effect, particularly
though not exclusively in the United States, was to stress regional
and strategic studies at the expense of universal and functional
perspectives.

At the same time, Chatham House reinvigorated its original dual
commitment to the systematic analysis of international affairs and
to public education, with the new Royal Institute series, "Looking
forward." *Power Politics* (No. 8) appeared in 1946. In it, Martin
Wight dealt with very broad concepts appropriate for responsible,
somewhat sophisticated citizens, such as law, geography, the
nation, freedom, science, trade, and "Britain and the World."
Especially in a revised and expanded form published in 1978, it is a
classic, rich in historical and philosophical insight; "What we mean
by power politics," wrote Wight, "came into existence when
medieval Christendom dissolved and the modern sovereign state

was born."[6] In discussing "Beyond power politics," he carried his perspective into the future:

> In the study of international politics we are dogged by the insistent problem, whether the relations between Powers are in fact more than "power politics" as the popular sense of the term, and whether they can become more. From one point of view, the central view, the central question is how far Powers can be said to have interest in common. . . . But the idea of common interest can never have much vitality if it is separated from the idea of common obligation.[7]

Wight argues that, although there had always been a theory of international relations asserting the primacy of such common ideas as law, right, and justice, the tradition of natural law as the basis of international law had now been "eclipsed by the new revolutionary creed of progress." But another tradition, that of the international community, though weakened by colonialism, had never completely faded and "still gleams faintly in the preamble of the Charter."[8] Yet Wight could not be optimistic. He took his place among the new realists creating a second consensus in the discipline.

Shortly after this Royal Institute study was published, a survey prepared for its sister house in New York by Kirk on the basis of six conferences of IR professors in every part of the United States provided a quite different basis for judgment. Though not a text, *The Study of International Relations* (1947) was perhaps the closest the Council on Foreign Relations ever came to emulating the Institute's initial objective of scientific analysis, or the *study* of IR along with the study of international affairs *qua* politics. Kirk found that prevailing opinion favored introducing a course of study with "a general survey of the field," covering:

1 The Nature and Operation of the State System
2 Factors which affect the Power of the State
3 International Position and Foreign Policies of the Great Powers
4 The History of Recent International Relations; and
5 The Building of a More Stable World Order.

Whereas Wight and Carr's contributions served to challenge old
paradigms and to raise the intellectual sights of a still relatively
new field, Kirk's contribution provided a kind of consensual
springboard into the second postwar era. The year following his
survey saw one of the most significant events in the history of the
field, inauguration of the journal *World Politics* by professors at the
Yale Institute of International Studies and others. It covered ground
that the Council's venerable and stately *Foreign Affairs* seemed
almost to disdain – the scholarly world of methodology, theory
and model-building, appealing to researchers and teachers in
academe more than to those in positions of power in banking,
government and industry.

Among the authors of the many texts that appeared after Kirk,
most undertook at least a brief review of "the study." IR was still
far from being a well-organized discipline, wrote Norman Palmer
and Howard Perkins of the University of Pennsylvania in *International
Relations* (1953). Having "emerged from its earlier status as
a poor relation of political science and history," it had been plagued
more recently by the "extreme" schools of utopianism and a
realism emphasizing "the virtual inevitability of war." IR is a very
inexact science, they concluded, "in fact, it is hardly a science at
all."[9] Palmer would later produce a number of significant historical
papers on the study of IR. Yet another pair of authors, Norman
Padelford and George Lincoln, began their book this way:

> Frances Bacon once spoke of Science as the "endless frontier."
> Today, the people of this country and other free nations are
> being increasingly impressed with the fact that international
> politics is a realm of endless frontier . . . our objective has been
> to stress those fundamental elements and foundational principles
> which . . . underlie the policies and actions of nations.[10]

The policy orientation was given further emphasis by Ernst Haas
and Allen Whiting, who argued in their text that

> the ends of foreign policy are qualitatively similar to ends
> implicit in any other field of politics. . . . The scheme of
> international affairs which emerges is thus a compendium of the
> ways in which shapers and conditioners of policy view their

mutual interrelations. . . . The methodological challenge of this approach has been severe.[11]

All seemed to agree that the field had now been established as a distinct, legitimate academic subject, but whether it was a "science" was another thing. Carr's utopian phase in the development of the science of international relations had long since come to an end. Others had joined him in the assult upon utopianism, notably the distinguished diplomat, George Kennan in *American Diplomacy, 1900–1950* (1951) and the realist theologian, Reinhold Niebuhr in *Moral Man and Immoral Society: A Study in Ethics and Politics* (1952). It now remained to be seen whether IR could move ahead into a more mature second phase in the tradition of other disciplines.

The answer was not long in coming. The terms "science" and "scientific," so dear to the early savants of Chatham House, again appeared, now on a somewhat higher level of sophistication. They had apparently meant hardly more than comprehensive, objective, and systematic analysis as an antidote to the self-serving, short-sighted propaganda of politicians, publicists and especially governments. To them, science could perhaps be seen as the contemporary historians' answer to a charge that their discipline constituted something of a contradiction in terms; true history would not be written accurately until all the evidence was in, which meant until the diplomatic archives were open. Readers of the *Survey of International Affairs* could not wait that long, so Toynbee and his small band of colleagues had to proceed as systematically as possible in the pursuit of the scientific study of international affairs with what they had. Wright was to point out that "international relations is a field extraordinarily difficult for science to enter."[12] That depends upon how "science" is defined. The Marxist paradigm, for example, seemed to move from a mastery of an understanding of the inevitability of historical forces, to predictability, to scientific certainty, all based upon an understanding of the politico-economic process that enabled true believers to claim to know what was coming. Carr had suggested more appropriate definitions, and Hans J. Morgenthau, the next major figure to employ the term "scientific," exerted an even stronger transforming influence.

In his first postwar contribution, *Scientific Man vs Power Politics* (1946), Morgenthau was engaged in "the search for the general

causes of which particular events are but outward manifestations."[13] It is these events that demonstrate the inability of contemporary society to understand and cope with political issues – a
"general decay in political thinking" represented most typically in
the conviction that science could solve all problems – so the
"purpose of this book is to show why this belief in the redeeming
powers of science is misplaced."[14]

This was not a rejection of science. "The Science of International
Politics" (Part I of *Principles and Problems in International Politics*
(1950), an anthology of classical essays, speeches, and documents
edited with a younger Chicago colleague, Kenneth W. Thompson)
represented an attempt to apply a more systematic method of
understanding to this science. The authors start with a frank
contrast between two schools of thought concerning the proper
content of the subject: the eclectic and the systematic. Representative of the first of these was the work of Zimmern; acknowledging
Zimmern's inter-war leadership of the field since his approach at
International Studies Conferences seemed to go unchallenged,
Morgenthau and Thompson stressed his "extreme vagueness," his
"unconcern with methodological problems," and his "aimless
humanitarianism."[15] The eclectic school combined all kinds of
disparate fields, apparently from agriculture to zoology, "seeing in
the qualifying adjective 'international' the common denominator
with which to transform this mass of unconnected material into
one field of international relations." Today this mélange has come
to be known as "international studies" in many institutions. The
second school, which they saw as dominant in institutions of
higher learning,

> applies a systematic principle of selection to the great mass of
> phenomena which transcend the frontiers of a particular nation
> and therefore fall in the general category of "international" . . .
> it finds that systematic principle in the power relations of
> sovereign states.[16]

As the essential subject matter of international politics was the
"struggle for power" the authors of *Principles and Problems* "touch
but lightly" on what previous writers had almost always given
major attention to in their analyses as being "no more than
marginal to the subject matter thus conceived." Here was an

opportunity to distinguish clearly between three terms more or less interchangeably employed to describe the field's scope: politics, relations, studies. Unhappily for any definition of a discipline, that opportunity was missed. The confused application of all three to the study of international affairs continues to plague the field.

Power politics as the core

Morgenthau's more influential and more lasting text, *Politics among Nations* (1948) has gone through six editions (one usefully edited by Thompson in 1986 after Morgenthau's death). Less openly "scientific" and more conventional (though in an unconventional manner) than the anthology, it concluded that the only real way to deal effectively with power is through the quality of diplomacy, a concept which led naturally to one of several novel approaches of the following decade: decision-making. Elaborating upon Carr, who had criticized utopianism in general terms, Morgenthau was explicit in attacking three equally ineffective kinds of international efforts to place limitations upon national power. After a classically brilliant interpretation of the first of these – the balance of power – he proceeded to show how uncertain, unrealistic, and inadequate it is. Then after noting the frequency with which some kind of world moral consensus is cited, he observed that "as for the influence of that system of supranational ethics upon the actors on the international scene, it is rather like the feeble rays, barely visible above the horizon of consciousness, of a sun which has already set."[17] Similarly, "a world public opinion restraining the international policies of national governments is a mere postulate; the reality of international affairs shows as yet hardly a trace of it."[18] Sometimes mistakenly accused of rejecting the place of moral force in politics (effectively corrected years later in his *Truth and Power* in 1970 as well as in the successive editions of *Politics among Nations*), Morgenthau actually merely insisted that its place be better understood. Universal morality – or internationalism – had lost out to "nationalistic universalism," as a tremendous force in world politics. As for any "psychological unity of the world which in the form of public opinion could or would ever restrain the holders of national power," he simply denied that it exists (except as a form of wishful thinking) because of the obstacle of nationalism. Morgenthau regarded international law as a third inadequate limitation on power, but again not in totally negative terms; his delineation of its proper legislative and judicial function is perhaps as good an introduction as can be found. His emphasis upon the central problem of enforceability clarifies what is obscured by both extremes on this issue: those who say "it isn't law if it can't be enforced" and those who appear to believe that, just because it is called "law", it can.

Possibly encouraged by this notable success, texts in international relations now began to proliferate, particularly in the United States. No less than eight appeared from 1954 to 1956.[19] While Morgenthau and Thompson's concentration upon power politics as the analytic core went generally uncontested, few of these emulated their model in regarding all else as "marginal." Indeed Fox may be right in characterizing Morgenthau as "the last prominent realist theoretician,"[20] for there remained a high and sometimes intense degree of commitment on the part of the American academic community to trying to create a viable world order. Just as their government's rejection of the League had generated a certain kind of ameliorative fervor after the First World War, the acceptance of international obligations, initially under the Charter but very soon within an "entangling alliance" called NATO, created a political climate in which mainstream IR texts flourished. What did they say and how did they say it?

The period of the second consensus

To define this period of essential agreement, just over twenty standard texts[21] of the realist period of 1945 to 1960 have been compared, including the 4th and 5th editions of the venerable Schuman, still one of the mostly widely used and popular of all books ever written on international relations. About twenty-five distinct topics were now put forth as constituting principal divisions of the subject-matter of IR. Actual chapter titles varied a great deal, though the areas of concern did not, so they are grouped under major substantive categories. Taking those covered by more than two-thirds of the authors and listing them in order of frequency, a composite consensual table of contents of texts during this prolific period might look something like this:

I Power Politics
II International Organization, the New World Order, and Peace
III Sovereignty and International Law
IV Strategic Studies
V Nationalism, Ideology and Propaganda
VI Foreign Policy Analysis
VII Imperialism or Colonialism
VIII Economic and Technological Issues

Regional topics, particularly in the context of the "Cold War," were given prominence by a majority (though less than two-thirds) of the authors. Population was given major attention. The study of IR as a discipline or at least separate field now occupied many a preface and even occasionally a substantive chapter. There were many different ways of approaching the same topic; consensus did not require absolute consistency.[22]

Three things stand out when this model table of contents is compared with that following the first World War:

1 There was now less emphasis upon diplomatic history, or "what caused the war?" topics.
2 Economics played a less prominent role in the analysis of international relations.
3 A preoccupation with power had replaced the concern for peaceful change.

Of the authors of these texts, only three were British, two of whom were refugees from Nazism. Where were the books by other successors from the country that had been responsible for more than half the mainstream works of the twenties? First of all, many of those works had been designed to educate the knowledge-able public, not teach students. Secondly, a textbook as such was rarely required by British teachers, whose course syllabi were based on extensive library reading lists and whose writing was more specialized than "IR." A third reason was, simply, the "market." Instead of writing "required texts", European authors had to persuade publishers that their books had appeal, not only for pundits of press and pulpit, but for the concerned general reader, including university and institute librarians. Not only that. These scholars were actively trying to define the discipline through international conferences. But the most notable attempt to do that came from one man, an American, and not through a textbook.

Quincy Wright's tour de force

What is still perhaps the prime (one writer calls it "majestic") intellectual achievement in the discipline's history, *The Study of International Relations*, was published in 1955. It grew out of several years of advanced seminars taught by Wright, who had completed his impressive two-volume *Study of War* thirteen years earlier.[23] Encyclopaedic in scope, almost Olympian in vision, this is in a class by itself, neither its depth nor its breadth ever having been approached by others' efforts to deal comprehensively with so ambitious a subject. Given "all this activity" (referring to the proliferation of textbooks, courses, and conferences on what is called "international relations"), the great sage impishly began, "there might seem to be little doubt that international relations exists. Yet there is some doubt on this point or, at least, on the sense in which it exists."[24] It is no exaggeration to say that in outlining his impressive tome, he then proceeded to deal fairly comprehensively with almost every conceivable sense in which IR might be said to exist.

Wright's opus is divided into five parts: the meaning of international relations, objectives in its study, practical analyses, theoretical analyses, and "toward a unified discipline" of IR, dealing with conceptions, approaches, form and the value of such a discipline. Successfully encompassing this vast range, Wright achieved what some of his Chicago colleagues implied was impossible: a combination of generic eclecticism with systematic rigor. Not all of them were convinced; for example, Harold Lasswell, in a basically sympathetic review in *World Politics*, concluded a year or so after its publication that "on the central theme there are grave reservations to be made" regarding the future of IR "as a discernible discipline."[25]

Nevertheless, Wright's long chapter on "the science of international relations" is far more sophisticated than what Toynbee tried to effect at Chatham House in the 1920s, to say nothing of being much more comprehensive than what Morgenthau had written twenty years later. In anticipating the next phase in the development of IR (which was to approximate to Carr's "second stage"), Wright shows how difficult it is to be truly scientific in any of the social sciences. Carr and Morgenthau had made no claim that anything approaching the capability to predict of physics, chemistry, or any of the pure sciences was at hand, nor did Wright.

What then is the scientific dimension of IR? To answer that, we must first delineate the criteria for a science. Although the primary criterion was the capacity to predict and control, others were critical: accuracy in observation, clarity in definition, measurability by reducing qualitative to quantitative differences, elimination of cultural and personal bias, concern for the consistency and simplicity of science as a whole, and the use of imagination in creating hypotheses. Perhaps only by the last of these could international relations be said to have "arrived." No wonder Wright went on to say that IR shares with all the social sciences difficulties in the application of scientific method!

In what sense then might IR be called a discipline? In citing the theoretical deficiencies of the field in 1968,[26] Harry Howe Ransom implied what some of the characteristics of a discipline ought to be: first of all, a distinct subject matter; secondly, agreed-upon abstractions or models; thirdly, concepts uniquely adapted to the analysis of international behavior; fourthly, a specialized vocabulary, with precise definitions; fifthly, standardized analytical methods allowing re-testing or replication of initial analysis; and finally, a central system for cataloging, evaluating, and communicating the state of research and its results. At that stage of the game, it must be conceded that this represents more of an agenda for change than a catalog of achievement in a field yet to reach full maturity, at least by the lofty standards set by Wright and Ransom. It was less a question of whether IR met their criteria than one of whether its subject-matter and available methodologies make it reasonably certain than it could. Among European scholars, these criteria were always important intellectually, but the question of whether IR is a discipline or not seemed to be important mainly as it represented an obstacle in university organization. In the United States, it was not well enough understood that criticisms levelled against international relations as a discipline could to some degree be levelled at other subjects just as well; for example, was not "political science" something of a contradiction in terms (especially as few if any in history made any claim to being a science, to say nothing of law)? As for economists, a great many from Smith and Marx onwards had indeed claimed a scientific status for economics, but one sees neither departments of economic science nor any scientific consensus that claims are supported by results. Unfortunately, there is one claim which, if ever made, would be greeted with derision, and that is that IR is a science.

A new round of conferences

At all events, C. A. W. Manning and Geoffrey Goodwin of the London School of Economics and Political Science renewed a practice going back to the 1920s in meeting with other IR scholars in various parts of the world. Concentration was upon the teaching of IR in Europe, although countries as distant and divergent as India and the United States participated. Two of the most valuable of these interchanges took place in 1950 and 1954.

The stated purpose of the first of these, which brought together eight countries, was to discuss "the more important views on the desirability, or otherwise, of making more general provision for the inclusion of International Relations, as an independent discipline, in the curriculum of University students."[27] This faced the issue head on. The General Rapporteur carefully analyzed why this was still a problem, citing four possible University responses to growing student interest in IR. The first was wholly negative, involving doubts concerning the subject itself: its very existence, its nature, its social value, its unitary character, its necessity, and even its "academic merits," to say nothing of technical feasibility and staffing problems. Most of these reservations could not only be answered but could be directed at other new subjects as well. A second response would simply give somewhat more attention in the curriculum to the international aspects of subjects already being taught, adding no new ones. A third involved grouping portions of modern history, economics, and political institutions under a distinctive category of "so-called" international studies. Finally, there could be genuine acceptance of a new independent discipline of IR. A generation later, IR, that most introspective of disciplines, would still be asking the same questions (and still getting the same unsatisfactory answers from university administrators).

The conference concluded that there was clearly a "widely felt need for the extension of the study and teaching of international relations." It had "not yet received due recognition," partly because of "structural differences" between universities in different countries. Turning to substance rather than form, it was agreed that what was needed now was "a greater comprehension of the structure and functioning of international society."[28] In other words, the discipline could not and should not ever try to separate itself from the political environment of which it was a part. IR could perform an important synthesizing role in overcoming the fragmentation of knowledge, an opportunity being stressed at the same time at Chicago by Wright and his colleagues; Jacob Viner, for example, not only offered international economics for budding economists but a special course for those in the Chicago IR program, probably the first in the country at the doctoral level.

Separate reports from five of the participating countries were filed. Only two, the United Kingdom and the United States, could demonstrate that progress had clearly been made toward an integrated discipline of IR. Several syllabi from universities in the UK were summarized; for example, at Aberdeen, a one-year course as a subsidiary subject for the MA encompassed the fields of international history (to 1939), public international law, international organization and, the "study of some contemporary international problems." Neither economics nor geography was required. Perhaps the most comprehensive syllabus was for the BSc (Econ.) at the University of London:

Part I   The Structure of International Society (two years, including several courses on theoretical and applied economics, political theory, and economic and political history)

Part II   The "specialism" of International Relations
    1.   International History
    2.   International Relations (general)
    3.   International Institutions
    4.5. Two of the following
       a.   International Law
       b.   International History
       c.   the problem of international peace and security

    d. philosophical and psychological aspects of International Affairs
    e. geographical and strategical aspects
    f. the interplay of politics at the domestic and international levels
    g. "either political or social theory, or an approved foreign language"

However, as Goodwin pointed out in his summation:

> There is no call to urge teachers of International Relations to agree on a uniform methodology, but perhaps the claims of the subject will gather strength if it can gain in unity and coherence by the development of a more systematized conceptual framework within which the constituent parts can form a better integrated and articulated whole. Such a development is the responsibility of teachers of the subject; it will not be furthered by extravagant doctrinal claims by one teacher or another but rather by a sensitive empiricism on the part of all. Then the very diversity of approach reflected in this note need not be regarded as a reproach but rather as a sign of growing vitality.[29]

In the United States, the professors from several conventional departments which made up the Yale Institute of International Studies provided what was probably the most prestigious International Relations masters – and doctoral – program in place at the time. Requirements were grouped very simply under five headings: diplomatic history, international politics, methods and instruments of control, international economics, and regional studies. Ironically, its highly selected graduates often found themselves teaching in the conventional Government department in the absence of a separate department specific to the discipline in which they had just been trained. While it mattered little to most, some (one of the present authors among them) felt that PhD-granting implied a mandate to promote separate departments to which graduates would logically be drawn in future years. Had the Yale Institute not been broken up, it might have advanced to this level of discipline-building. Instead, the field tended more and more to become an especially lively sub-field of political science, although in Britain the independent, interdisciplinary nature of IR was never in doubt.

The Paris conference, summarized in a volume in a UNESCO series entitled simply *International Relations*, carried out a 1954 General Conference resolution "to undertake surveys in some countries of the types of consensus and methods of instruction in the social sciences."[30] Contrasting experiences in Egypt, France, India, Mexico, Sweden, the United Kingdom, the United States, and Yugoslavia revealed the near-impossibility of discovering any consensus at all on any aspect of the inquiry, at least outside the Anglo-American world. For example, the spokesman from India, Dr A. Appadorai, reported that "little headway" had so far been made introducing IR "as an integrated subject" there, and that "such teaching of international relations as exists" is done in courses in history, economics, politics and law. In Yugoslavia, Professor Djordevié saw no sign that the existing "system of decentralized teaching of international relations" would become "concentrated into a common subject, having International Relations as its name." Though one French delegate, Professor V. J. Chevallier, optimistically asserted that "all that is required is to establish a meeting point, a crossroads, a place of assembly, a point of convergence for the several avenues of approach," a colleague was less sanguine. M. Vernant argued that as long as there was no possible liaison in studies between two *groups* of subjects (sociology, anthropology, psychology) and (history, law, economics), there was no way for French universities to set up "in a healthy form, the teaching of International Relations." In Egypt, Professor M. A. Yehia asserted that, even though there were numerous fully qualified teachers in "subdivisions of the field of study prescribed as international relations," the university system with its internal regulations did not permit an interested student to "follow a full course" in IR. Similarly, Dr Karl Birnbaum of Sweden admitted that the prospects of international relations achieving independent status in institutions there were "very poor." Even though in Mexico an Institute of High International Studies was established in 1952, "the truth is that, for advanced studies in the field of international affairs, the youth of Mexico have thereafter been, for the most part, obliged to go abroad." And so it went. It may be, as Arnold Wolfers and Laurence Martin suggested in *The Anglo-American Tradition in Foreign Affairs* in 1956, that the two countries shared world views not shared by the rest of the world. As we have seen, Grosser of the Institut de Science Politique in Paris ("Science Po"), argued in a paper[31] published that same year, that IR was in fact an American subject, and indeed it would be another generation before the field really took hold in France.

A contrast needs to be pointed out at this juncture between American academic programs and standard IR texts. As a degree subject, IR was almost invariably interdisciplinary, whereas textbooks tended to be state-centric, generally power-oriented, with emphasis upon foreign policy. Two reasons suggest themselves for this. First, in the absence of a department of international relations, a committed student interested in the subject took what he could in a political science department, where economics and other collateral disciplines were secondary if they were brought in at all. Second, textbooks were not only written for the most part *by* political scientists, but were designed primarily for use *in* a single political science course on international politics (which might or might not have been part of a broader major in IR), rather than as an introduction to the overall subject. But where Padelford and Lincoln had been explicit in making the distinction, conceiving of their book *International Politics* as covering only *part* of "international relations," the two terms tended to be employed interchangeably.[32] On the other hand, to Charles Merriam and his followers in "the Chicago school of political science," power was the *integrating* concept in municipal, national, and global politics. IR was simply a special case, just as to Frederick Sherwood Dunn (who was responsible for developing the Yale Institute to its one-time position of eminence), IR was "politics in the absence of central authority."[33] Could not one postulate that the difference is that political science is politics *within the context* of central authority?

One of the most informative interpretations of the stage at which IR had arrived in 1960 was a paper prepared by Annette Baker Fox and William T. R. Fox and first presented at NATO headquarters in Paris at "The Conference on International Relations in the University," and later published by the Institute of International Studies at the University of South Carolina. They predicted that "in the next decade some of the problems which have emerged in the United States will be seen as problems of the extended North American–West European–British Commonwealth family of scholars in international relations."[34] With the realist Max Beloff

of Oxford in the chair, twenty-five or so specialists such as Grosser
and J. B. Duroselle of France, Manning and P. A. Reynolds of
Britain, and Fox and Olson of the United States confronted
essentially the same issues as had earlier gatherings, but on a
narrower geographical base and one with strategic policy
undertones.

Contradictory conclusions can be drawn from these and other
postwar conferences. One was that there was an awareness of a
need in all the countries to develop and integrate the study as a
distinct field. The other was that only modest progress had been
made toward that end. Most degree programs were covered, not
by separate departments, but by teams or committees drawn from
the traditional disciplines, such as the long-standing program at
Pomona College in California. Given the unhurried nature of
change in universities, where doubts still remained as to whether
such an uncertain and contemporary subject belonged there at all,
this was not surprising. According to the old saying, war was too
important a subject to be left to the generals; it could now be said
that both peace and war were too important to be left out of
academe. It was this conviction that led President Dwight Eisenhower of Columbia University to invite Fox to establish an
"Institute of War and Peace Studies" in 1950. This served as a
reminder of the contribution IR might make to the prevention of
the next war (although in some other American contexts, it seemed
designed more to help *win* the next war). Indeed, some felt that IR
had become a "cold war subject." The stress on power politics as
yet rarely went that far, however, and the new consensus it
represented, at least the literature, was less a break with the first
consensus than a refinement of it.

To what degree did both texts and conferences reflect this second
consensus? Several features stand out when compared with the
field's first and second decades. First of all, the study of international relations itself now often introduced the subject, revealing
recognition or at least a consciousness of the degree to which IR
had matured as a discipline. Secondly, the neglect of power so
deplored by Carr and Morgenthau had been overcome. Indeed,
power had become the hallmark of the discipline, at least in
standard American texts. More attention was given to "international society" in Europe (where IR was certainly not a cold war
subject), as well as to the cultural dimension by such American

writers as Adda Bozeman in her *Politics and Culture in International History* (1960). Third, conventional diplomatic history was given less attention, possibly because the locus of the field had moved from historically minded Britain to an American academic environment dominated by political science. In the fourth place, despite six years of global war followed by the Cold War, major attention was still being given to the original key elements, international law and organization. Fifth, the distinct treatment of key regions and even countries stood out; indeed, "area studies" itself was becoming a kind of discipline, some professors (notably J. B. Duroselle of Paris) regarding a global perspective as being too broad to be handled in a systematic manner. By the same token, some even felt that continents were too vast for integrated analysis; at St Antony's, Oxford, for example, one American IR generalist found that everyone else seemed to be a country specialist and that his own interest in general theory was an unshared one. Finally, and possibly most important for an interdisciplinary perspective, economics was given less emphasis than in either earlier period. Texts were designed for courses in departments of political science where economics was regarded as belonging elsewhere. Majors and advanced degree programs did pay increasing attention to the economics component of IR, however, as did the international conferences. We perhaps need to note here that in the mother discipline of them all, history, so many tended to separate politics and economics that a new discipline, economic history, had to find its way into the academic firmament.

The dual challenge: behavioralism and quantification

An entirely new kind of literature was now beginning to present alternatives to mainstream thinking. It had been anticipated by the work of Harold Lasswell on the psychology of propaganda during the First World War and later by Otto Klineberg's notable "tensions project" for the Social Science Research Council in 1950. The following year saw both psychologist George Kisker's anthology, *World Tension* (1951), and Frederick S. Dunn writing in a similar vein as an international lawyer by training and now Director of the Yale Institute in his *War and the Minds of Men*, a title obviously influenced by Archibald MacLeish's famous preamble to the Constitution of UNESCO. But it was *Decision-Making as an Approach to the Study of International Politics* (Richard Snyder *et al*) in 1954 and *System and Process in International Politics* (Morton Kaplan) in 1957 that were the prime examples of a new phase in the development of the discipline. The first of these logically grew out of Morgenthau's reliance on the quality of diplomacy, the second from Quincy Wright's longing for a unified if not quite scientific discipline. Of possibly more lasting impact was *Man, the State and War*, by Kenneth Waltz (1959), in which he postulated that there were three "images" upon which answers to the timeless question, "where are the major causes of war to be found?",[35] have been based. The first, he argues, lies within man himself ("human behavior"), the second within separate states ("internal structure of states"), and the third within the state system ("international anarchy"). Although not a standard text, Waltz's book became a major influence in the teaching of IR for a period of a quarter century. The critical contribution of L. F. Richardson needs again to be noted here; in an important work, *Arms and Insecurity* (1960), which correlated armaments and the outbreak of war, the role of mathematics in economics led him to ask "whether mathematical language can also express the behavior of people in another situation where they act together in large groups, namely in relation to war."[36]

New standard texts continued to appear regularly, but their distinctive role in developing the field of study seemed now to have been played, particularly in elevating it from a level of explaining the latest headlines. We must turn elsewhere to find the growing points of the discipline, to discover what Klaus Knorr and James Rosenau were to call "contending approaches" to theory in IR. Fox contributed his still-useful *Theoretical Aspects of International Relations* in 1959. Part of the "fallout" group from the precipitous breakup of the Yale Institute, Knorr edited *The International System: Theoretical Essays* (1961) with Sidney Verba, drawing upon economics less than one seeking an interdisciplinary foundation might have expected to do. Similarly, Stanley Hoffmann's *Contemporary Theory in International Relations* (1960), was a well-regarded reader, stronger in philosophy, politics, and sociology than in economics. Two years later there finally appeared the long-awaited study of the nature of international society by Manning,[37] capping many years of intellectual stengthening of the conceptual foundations of the program of studies at LSE.

Developing trends in thought reveal once again that novel insights rarely totally replace old approaches. They overlap. Some demonstrate more validity, more utility, and more resilience than others. A few, like utopianism, disappear completely, (or almost completely, for there are always those for whom the silver lining is the only reality). Others, as Anne Fox has pointed out, are essentially new, such as dependency theory, which emerged with the creation of new states in the wake of the breaking up of colonial empires, and integration theory, which has emerged from the creation of the European Community.[38] Still others, saddened perhaps by the barrenness of intellectual squabbling, plead for greater tolerance and mutual advantage from advocates of contending approaches; as Robert North has constructively put it,

> As research scholars and would-be theorists in international relations we might all derive at least three useful lessons from the old fable about the blind man and the elephant. The first is that the elephant presumably existed; the second is that each of groping investigators, despite sensory and conceptual limitations, had his fingers on part of the reality; and the third is that if they had quieted the uproar and begun making comparisons, the blind men might – all of them – have moved considerably closer to the truth.[39]

At all events, the second definitional phase was now over. Many singular contributions to theory, often based upon challenges to a consensus based upon power, appeared. Partly in response to a need for a home for the expression of these ideas, the International Studies Association, dedicated to interdisciplinary advancement of almost any serious approach, was created in 1960, followed by national bodies such as the British International Studies Association some years later. Hence that year is a logical place to bring to a close any attempt to delineate sequentially the development of ideas. Now something quite different in the long-term development of the discipline was taking place. Basic alternatives to the power politics approach, as it had been set forth by Schuman, Carr, and Morgenthau and confirmed by many others, now demanded attention. The classical state-centric paradigm which had dominated the discipline since its inception was about to encounter the "world society" and "global village" approaches, as well as a growing concern with analytical method. A "paradigmatic debate" was about to take place.

The methodological revolt took two closely related forms, the behavioral and the quantitative approaches to political science. First, just as Marxism had challenged the basic system of political and economic power, behavioralism now challenged the accepted system of the analysis of power. With aggressive enthusiasm, the behavioralists adapted relevant methodologies and conclusions from psychology, anthropology, and sociology to the analysis of actors on the international stage. As Bruce Russett and Harvey Starr have observed,[40] deductive interpretations of politics such as the balance of power, man's search for the good life, or the class struggle were rejected in favor of more inductive definitions based upon scientific analysis of the actual behavior of human beings. Politics was defined in terms of *observable* "ranges of action and reaction" instead of more abstract impressions and concepts. Second, the use of mathematics, assisted if indeed not stimulated by the increasingly widespread availability of computers, greatly enhanced research capability throughout the social sciences. Like behavioralism, exponents of quantitative methodology tended to discredit older methodologies based upon historical and legal scholarship, partly because of the promise of results.

The behavioral and quantitative perspectives both promised for a time to engender an entirely new kind of scientific consensus. It featured what many regarded as excessive claims, particularly for predictive capability, and what to the uninitiated was a bewildering array of algebraic formulae. Neither in the end brought about such a consensus, but their contribution to the growth of the discipline was to be unmistakable, if not dominant. Debates such as those which erupted between the "classical" Hedley Bull of Oxford (who had developed his ideas while still at the Australian National University) and the "scientific" Morton Kaplan of Chicago served in the long run to stimulate even more than to divide. As Hamid Mowlana has put it, IR was now analytical rather than descriptive, "with new models based on systems, games, bargaining, decision-making procedures, and multifarious other methods of approach . . . the result has been to emphasize the tangible, the formal, and the measurable."[41] At the same time, terms like "post-behavioral-ism," "structuralism," and "neo-realism" signalled a return to classical theory in a new guise. IR would now enter a pluralist phase. This parallel existence of many approaches has appropriately been termed "the paradigmatic debate."[42] To that phase, in which the unified theory which Wright sought would be even more remote, we now turn.

Notes: Chapter 6

1 William T. R. Fox, "The uses of international relations theory," in *Theoretical Aspects of International Relations* (Notre Dame, Ind.: University of Notre Dame Press, 1959), p. 46.
2 "The internationalist's dilemma: relevance and rigor," *International Studies Quarterly*, 12, 2: 161–73, June 1968.
3 See esp. Chapter VII of the Charter of the United Nations, "Actions with respect to threats to the peace, breaches of the peace and acts of aggression".
4 Carr, 2nd edn. (New York: St Martin's Press, 1966), p. vii.
5 ibid., p. viii.
6 *Power Politics*, ed. by Hedley Bull and Carsten Holbraad (New York: Penguin, 1979), p. 25. Published for the Royal Institute of International Affairs in 1946, the original work came to only 68 pages and was presumably being expanded for later publication when Wight died in 1972, the editors completing the work from his drafts and notes.
7 ibid., p. 289.
8 ibid., p. 291.
9 Palmer and Perkins, *International Relations: The World Community in Transition* (Boston: Houghton Mifflin, 1953), p. 6.
10 N. J. Padelford and G. A. Lincoln, *International Politics: Foundations of International Relations* (New York: Macmillan, 1954), p. v.
11 E. Haas and A. Whiting, *Dynamics of International Relations* (New York: McGraw-Hill, 1956), p. vii, considered by Fox as perhaps the best among the standard texts in providing a distinct contribution to the field (correspondence with Olson, July 1988).
12 Wright, *Study of International Relations*, p. 115.
13 Morgenthau, *Scientific Man vs Power Politics* (Chicago: The University of Chicago Press, 1946), p. v.
14 ibid., p. vi.
15 Morgenthau with Thompson, *Principles and Problems in International Politics*, pp. 18–19.
16 ibid., p. vii.
17 Morgenthau, *Politics among Nations*, p. 195.
18 ibid., p. 206.

19 See Appendix C (p. 186).

20 Correspondence with Olson, July 1988.

21 See Appendix C (p. 186).

22 Of numerous commentaries on texts one stands out, Rosenau's "Of syllabi, texts, students, and scholarship in international relations: some data and interpretations on the state of a burgeoning field," *World Politics*, XXIX, 2: 263–340 January, 1977. Also particularly useful is Kenneth Boulding's review article on several current texts in *The Journal of Conflict Resolution*, VIII, 1: 65–71, March 1964.

23 Quincy Wright, *Study of War* (Chicago: University of Chicago Press, 1942), 2 vols.

24 Quincy Wright, *Study of IR*, p. vii.

25 H. D. Lasswell, "Some reflections on the study of international relations," *World Politics*, VIII, 4: 562, July 1956.

26 Harry Howe Ransom, "International relations," *Journal of Politics*, 30, 2: 369, May 1968.

27 Geoffrey L. Goodwin (ed.). *The University Teaching of International Relations* (Oxford: Blackwell, 1951), p. 5.

28 ibid., p. 36.

29 ibid., p. 126.

30 Manning, C. A. W., *International Relations* (Paris: UNESCO, 1954), p. 5.

31 "L'étude des relations internationales, specialité américaine?", *Revue Française de Science Politique*, VI, 3: 634–51, July–September 1956.

32 Quincy Wright, *Study of IR*, is particularly useful in defining this distinction (p. ix), as is Schwarzenberger, *Power Politics* (p. 23–5).

33 Cited by W. T. R. Fox, "Growing points in the study of international relations," address at the University of Southern California, 1 October 1966, reproduced in Fox, *The American Study of International Relations*, p. 100.

34 W. T. R. and Annette Baker Fox, "The Teaching of International Relations in the United States" ibid., p. 33.

35 K. Waltz, *Man, the State and War* (New York and London: Columbia University Press, 1959), p. 36.

36 L. F. Richardson, "*Arms and Insecurity. A Mathematical Study of the Causes and Origins of War*, ed. by. Nicholas Rashersky and Ernesto Trucco (Pittsburgh, Pa: The Boxwood Press, 1960), p. xvii.

37 C. A. W. Manning, *The Nature of International Society* (London: G. Bell and Sons, 1962).

38 Correspondence with Olson, July 1988.

39 "Research pluralism and the international elephant", in Klaus Knorr and James N. Rosenau (eds), *Contending Approaches to International Politics* (Princeton, NJ: Princeton University Press, 1969), p. 218.

40 Bruce Russett and Harvey Starr, *World Politics: A Menu for Choice* (San Francisco: W. H. Freeman, 1981), pp. 3–41.

41 Hamid Mowlana, *Global Information and World Communication: New*

Frontiers in International Relations (White Plains, NY: Longman, 1986), p. 177.
42 Part I of Margot Light and A. J. R. Groom (eds), *International Relations: A Handbook of Current Theory* (Littleton, Colo: Lynne Rienner, 1985); see esp. Michael Banks, "The inter-paradigm debate," pp. 7–20 plus references.

Further reading

Alger, Chadwick. "International relations," in the *International Encyclopedia of the Social Sciences*, Vol. 8, pp. 60–8. The Macmillan Company and the Free Press, 1968. David Sills (ed.).

Deutsch, Karl W. *Political Community at the International Level: Problems of Definition and Measurement*. Garden City, NY: Doubleday, 1954.

Dunn, Frederick Sherwood. *War and the Minds of Men*. New York: Council on Foreign Relations, 1950.

Fox, Annette Baker and Fox, William T. R. "International politics," *International Encyclopedia of the Social Sciences*, Vol. 8, pp. 50–60 + brief bibliography. The Macmillan Company and the Free Press, 1968, David Sills (ed.).

Fox, W. T. R. (ed.). *Theoretical Aspects of International Relations*. Notre Dame, Ind: University of Notre Dame Press, 1959.

Herz, John. *Political Realism and Political Idealism: A Study in Theories and Realities*. Chicago: University of Chicago Press, 1951.

Harrison, Horace V. (ed.). *The Role of Theory in International Relations*. Princeton, NJ: Van Nostrand, 1964.

Kisker, George (ed.). *World Tension*. New York: Prentice–Hall, 1951.

Klineberg, Otto. *Tensions Affecting International Understanding*. Social Science Research Council, New York, Bulletin No. 62. New York: SSRC, 1950.

Lasswell, Harold. "Some reflections on the study of international relations," *World Politics*, VIII, 4: 560–5, July 1956.

Lijphart, Arend (ed.). *World Politics: The Writings of Theorists and Practitioners, Classical and Modern*. Boston: Allyn and Bacon, 1966.

Manning, C. A. W. *The University Teaching of Social Sciences: International Relations*. Paris: UNESCO, 1954.

May, Mark A. *A Social Psychology of War and Peace*. New Haven, Conn: Yale University Press, 1943.

Mathison, Trygve. *Methodology in the Study of International Relations*. New York: Macmillan, 1959.

Morgenthau, Hans J. *Scientific Man versus Power Politics*. Chicago: University of Chicago Press, 1946.

Morgenthau, Hans J. and Kenneth W. Thompson. *Principles and Problems in International Relations* (selected readings). New York: Knopf, 1950.

Richardson, Lewis F. *Statistics of Deadly Quarrels*. Pittsburgh, Pa: Boxwood, 1960.

Snyder, Richard C., Bruck, H. W. and Sapin, Burton (eds). *Foreign Policy Decision-Making: an Approach to the Study of International Politics*. New York: Free Press, 1962, a revised Version of *Decision-Making as an Approach to the Study of International Politics* in the Foreign Policy Analysis Series (Vol. 3) of the Princeton University Organizational Behaviour Section, 1954.

Waltz, Kenneth N. *Man, the State, and War*. New York: Columbia University Press, 1959.

Woodward, Sir Ernest L. *The Study of International Relations at a University*. Oxford: Oxford University Press, 1945.

Wright, Quincy. *A Study of War*, 2 vols rev. edn. Chicago: University of Chicago Press, 1942.

Wright, Quincy. *The Study of International Relations*. New York: Appleton-Century-Crofts, 1955.

Appendix A

Books on general international relations, 1916–31 (in order of date of publication)

Greenwood, Arthur with Grant, A. J., Hughes, J. D., Kerr, P. H., and Urquhart, F. *Introduction to the Study of International Relations*. London: Macmillan, 1916.

Heatley, David P. *Diplomacy and the Study of International Relations*. Oxford: The Clarendon Press, 1919.

Lawrence, T. J. *The Society of Nations, its Past, Present, and Possible Future*. New York: Oxford University Press, 1919.

Burns, C. Delisle. *International Politics*. London: Methuen, 1920.

Allen, S. H. *International Relations*. Princeton, NJ: Princeton University Press, 1920.

Bryce, James (Lord). *International Relations*. London: Macmillan, 1922.

Gibbons, Herbert A. *Introduction to World Politics*. New York: Macmillan, 1922.

Walsh, Edmund (ed.). *History and Nature of International Relations*. New York: Macmillan, 1922.

Brown, Phillip. *International Society: Its Nature and Interests*. New York: Macmillan, 1923.

Moon, Parker T. *Syllabus on International Relations*. New York: Macmillan, 1925.

*Potter, Pitman B. *This World of Nations: Foundations, Institutions, Practices*. New York: Macmillan, 1929.

Barnes, Harry Elmer. *World Politics and Modern Civilization*. New York: Knopf, 1930.

Mowat, R. B. *International Relations*. London: Rivington, 1931.

Hodges, Charles. *Background of International Relations*. New York: Wiley, 1931.

★ The "Sir Alfred Zimmern" collection of books on international relations was donated by Dr Potter to the Library of the American University, Washington DC, when he became Professor there after leaving the Secretariat of the League of Nations in Geneva.

Appendix B

General IR works of the 1932–44 period (in order of date of publication)

*Bailey, S. H. *The Framework of International Society*. London: Longmans, Green, 1932.

*Morley, Felix. *The Society of Nations*. Washington: The Brookings Institution, 1932.

Schuman, Frederick L. *International Politics. An Introduction to the Western State System*. New York: McGraw-Hill, 1933, 1937 (successive editions carried different sub-titles 1941*et seq*).

Lasswell, Harold. *World Politics and Personal Insecurity*. New York: McGraw-Hill, 1935.

Simonds, Frank and Emeny, Brooks. *The Great Powers in World Politics*: *International Relations and Economic Nationalism*. New York: The American Book Co., 1935.

Russell, Frank M. *Theories of International Relations*. New York: Appleton-Century Co., 1936.

Dutt, R. Palme. *World Politics 1918–1936*. New York: Random House, 1936.

Hauser, Henri. *Economie et Diplomatie: Les Conditions Nouvelles de la Politique Etranger*. Paris: Librairie du Recueil Sirey, 1937.

Mantoux, Paul (and others at the Geneva Institute of Higher International Studies). *The World in Crisis*. New York: Longmans, Green, 1938.

Brown, James F., Hodges, Charles, and Roucek, Joseph S. (eds). *Contemporary World Politics*. New York: Wiley, 1939.

Carr, Edward Hallett. *The Twenty-Years' Crisis 1919–1939: An Introduction to the Study of International Relations*. London: Macmillan, 1939.

Maxwell, Bertram W. *International Relations*. New York: Thomas Y. Crowell, 1939.

Middlebush, Frederick A. and Hill, Chesney. *Elements of International Relations*. New York: McGraw-Hill, 1940.

Sharp, Walter R. and Kirk, Grayson. *Contemporary International Politics*. New York: Farrar and Rinehart, 1940.

Schwarzenberger, Georg. *Power Politics: An Introduction to the Study of International Relations and Post-War Planning*. London: Cape, 1941 (also published by Praeger in New York as *Power Politics, a study of International Society*).

Mander, Linden A. *Foundations of Modern World Society*. Stanford, Calif.: Stanford University Press, 1941.
Kalijarvi, Thorsten V. and associates. *Modern World Politics*. New York: Thomas Y. Crowell, 1943.

* Bailey and Morley could well have been included in the "consensus" period, as they were no doubt written before the League system collapse had become fully apparent. Schuman's text, on the other hand, clearly perceived the fundamental changes that were taking place in world politics at this time.

Appendix C

"Mainstream" texts during the second consensus 1945–62 (in order of date of publication)

Sprout, Harold and Sprout, Margaret (eds). *Foundations of National Power.* Princeton, NJ: Princeton University Press, 1945.

Wight, Martin. *Power Politics.* London: Royal Institute of International Affairs, 1946 ("Looking Forward" series, No. 8).

Morgenthau, Hans J. *Politics among Nations: The Struggle for Power and Peace.* New York: Knopf, 1948.

Schuman, Frederick L. *International Politics,* the destiny of Western State System, 4th edn. New York: McGraw-Hill, 1948.

Strausz-Hupé, Robert and Possony, Stefan T. *International Relations.* New York: McGraw-Hill, 1950.

Schwarzenberger, Georg. *Power Politics.* 2nd edn, London and Toronto: Cape, 1951.

Huszar, George B. and de Grazia, Alfred Jr. *An Outline of International Relations.* New York: Barnes and Noble, 1951.

Friedman, Wolfgang. *An Introduction to World Politics.* New York: McGraw-Hill, 1951.

Schuman, F. L. *International Politics:* the Western State System in Transition. 5th edn. New York: McGraw-Hill, 1953.

Palmer, Norman and Perkins, Howard C. *International Relations: The World Community in Transition.* Boston: Houghton Mifflin, 1954.

Hill, Norman. *Contemporary World Politics.* New York: Harper and Row, 1954.

Padelford, Norman J. and Lincoln, George A. *International Politics.* New York: Macmillan, 1954.

Schleicher, Charles P. *Introduction to International Relations.* New York: Prentice-Hall, 1954.

Ball, Margaret and Killough, Hugh B. *International Relations.* New York: The Ronald Press, 1956.

Haas, Ernst B. and Whiting, Allen S. *Dynamics of International Relations.* New York: McGraw-Hill, 1956.

Lerche, Charles O. *Principles of International Politics.* New York: Oxford University Press, 1956.

Mills, Lennox A. and McLaughlin, Charles H. *World Politics in Transition.* New York: Henry Holt, 1956.

Van Dyke, Vernon. *International Politics*. New York: Appleton–Century–Crofts, 1957.

Hartman, Frederick. *The Relations of Nations*. New York: Macmillan, 1957.

Schuman, Frederick L. *International Politics and the World Community*, 6th edn. New York: Mcgraw-HIll, 1958.

Organski, A. F. K. *World Politics*. New York: Knopf, 1958.

Herz, John. *International Politics in the Atomic Age*. New York: Columbia University Press, 1959.

Manning, C.A.W. *The Nature of International Society*. London; G. Bell and Sons, 1962.

PART TWO

'Now': contending paradigms

7 A pause for reflection

Ambiguity in 'international relations' is not to be imputed to the inadequacy of our concepts: it is an integral part of reality itself. (Raymond Aron)[1]

The first part of this book ended with the intellectual dominance of realism over the academic study of IR being such as to constitute a consensus – at least in so far as the English-speaking world was concerned. This consensus included many practitioners and journalists, so that there was a mutual reinforcing element which in effect precluded any real debate on fundamentals between academics and practitioners. The sole major exception was the Indian academic and political scene, where the philosophy and practice of non-alignment was a powerful balancing factor. Elsewhere there was, during the 1940s and into the 1950s, consensus in the English-speaking world. Viewed from the perspective of the beginning of the last decade of this century such a consensus seems in itself to be an anomaly, for we now have at least three intellectual traditions in full flood. Moreover, IR in the English-speaking world has been greatly influenced since by conceptual approaches that are not indigenous to it and there is the promise of a greater globalization of the subject in terms of approach and substance. However, for the moment we, too, do have an element of consensus in that there is general acknowledgement of the existence of three intellectual traditions in approaches to IR. The burden of this part of the book is to explain how we have gone from a consensus on one approach to three salient, competing and mutually influential conceptual frameworks.

Changes in approach are not usually immediate, wholehearted or effective. Indeed, anomalies are rarely so overwhelming and blindingly obvious that scholars are willing to jettison their intellectual baggage in order to re-equip themselves with a new set, which happens to be conveniently waiting, complete and convincing, ready for an instant switch. Normally it takes time and is the outcome of a messy and confused process. Although realism achieved an acknowledged salience, nevertheless in the 1950s anomalies begin to disturb that remarkable state of intellectual cohesion. Some were red herrings in so far as the intellectual development of the field was concerned, such as behaviouralism, since it became evident eventually, but not until after a fierce intellectual debate characterized by many intemperate *ad hominem* exchanges, that behaviouralism was more a question of methodological proclivities than one of conceptual differences. 'Color it Morgenthau' was the title of a highly influential conference paper,[2] which pointed out, in an authoritative manner, that most 'behavioural' research was firmly embedded in the realist framework. Other developments were not red herrings but, although identifying anomalies in realism, they did not propose dispensing with it as a framework, in part because they were only concerned with aspects of the framework and in part because there was no convincing alternative readily available. Now we acknowledge two more frameworks to add to that of realism.

Banks and Groom have sketched the outlines of these frameworks,[3] which correspond to Rosenau's notion of the state-centric, multi-centric and global-centric approaches to world politics[4] and to the three approaches identified by Kal Holsti in his recent essay, *The Dividing Discipline*, as the classical tradition, the world or global society model and the dependency/world capitalist-system theories.[5] But to arrive at the current triumvirate involved great travail as realism was challenged but not eclipsed. There has been, and continues to be, an exciting intellectual debate as the mould of realism has been broken and the world society and structuralist approaches have been sketched out and their ancient intellectual provenances explored. In many subjects there is a well-trodden and well-marked path across the field to the uncertainties of the frontiers of knowledge. In IR there is no such path, but a milling around in a field, the dimensions and shape of which are not known or are in dispute. We are not solving a puzzle with shapes of a fixed character and a final picture that is known to exist, we are struggling with a problem in which the shape of the pieces is not clear and it is not known whether they can constitute a final picture. Indeed, different pieces (of empirical data) suggest different pictures (or conceptual frameworks). IR is, therefore, both exasperating and exciting. It is exasperating because there is no conceptual consensus, but also, thereby, exciting, since the search for a new conceptual framework is currently exercising the minds of some of the most talented scholars in IR.

There have been three decades of debate and, more profitably, of discussion since the heyday of realism. The purpose of this part of the book is to point to benchmarks in this literature and, in particular, to examine the way in which the world society framework evolved and structuralism came back into the mainstream. Both englobe a rich variety of different emphases and concerns, but they are readily differentiated from each other and from realism even if there is a mutual influence. Moreover, as the conceptual triumvirate emerged, the disciplinary balance between the twin centres of Britain and the United States altered.

Until the 1950s Britain and the United States were the 'Big Two' in intellectual and disciplinary terms where IR was flourishing. There was a separate and isolated Marxist tradition, virtually forgotten but for a few in the Western academic world who mostly ridiculed and despised it. Thereafter, mirroring events in the political world, the relationship between Britain and the United States was by now asymmetrical. In the terminology of Wallerstein, Britain was moving from the centre towards a semiperiphery status. In Britain major contributions to the conceptualization of world society were made by Mitrany and Burton, although neither was born in Britain and both were controversial figures there, unrecognized, indeed denigrated, by the British academic establishment. In the realist vein, Martin Wight achieved almost a cult status as much of his teaching as for his writing, and Hedley Bull (like Burton an Australian) made his mark with *éclat* in defence of the traditional approach and, more conventionally, in continuing the Wight tradition. But, for the most part, it was a matter of getting on the American bandwagon or getting nowhere. Moreover, like the Marxist tradition before it, structuralism did not take firm root in the British intellectual climate. Mitrany, Burton and Bull were the only British-based scholars to make an academic impact of note beyond Britain, and they did this chiefly through their participation in the academic discourse in the USA.

The reasons for this are not difficult to discern. In the United States the number of scholars and students, the demand for textbooks and monographs, the market for journals and an academic structure based on the 'publish or perish' syndrome, all contributed to the growing asymmetry. Moreover, the state and foundations offered patronage to scholars in the United States undreamed of in Britain. Indeed, British scholars would hardly have known how to put such resources to good use. The United States was a super power in more than one sense, but one with an insular mentality. As Holsti has demonstrated in *The Dividing Discipline*, the profession in the United States has been less open to outside influences over the last three decades than previously.[6] For those in the periphery, it was necessary, and a struggle, to get access to the discipline through the centre.

It was, happily, a different story in the structuralist paradigm. Here the intellectual thrust came as much from Scandinavia, Germany, and above all from Latin America, as from the United States. Not unnaturally conceptions of the periphery were often and fruitfully conceived in the periphery, but surprisingly (given the theory), they were taken up by some in the centre both in the United States and even, of late, in Britain. The intellectual dominance, and isolation, of the United States now seems to be less acute as we enter the 1990s than it was. IR, as a discipline, is bidding fair to being not only worldwide, through the medium of English, but truly global. Perhaps by the end of the century this will be achieved as more exchanges take place within regions, language and culture groups, as in Europe, and between regions, especially between Japan, North America, Latin America and Europe, both East and West. Nor can major centres in China, India, Korea and Australasia be ignored. And while some regions have a proclivity for a particular approach this is rarely to the complete exclusion of the others. Moreover, it is difficult to avoid a suspicion that new frameworks are in the making and old ones are being reformulated as was the case in the last decade with neorealism. We shall allow ourselves a cautious speculation in our final chapter, but we have a feeling that a consideration of IR at the turn of the century may have a distinctly changed air about it from that which follows.

Our present task is to take us from consensus to consensus – from the domination of realism to the uneasy cohabitation of three conceptual frameworks: that is, realism, world society approaches and structuralism. We shall do this first by attending to the breaking of the mould of realism and then by an analysis of the emergence, and a statement of the tenets of, world society approaches. The chronological evolution of thought, at least in the Anglo-American mainstream, brings us thereafter to the third intellectual tradition in its current guise – structuralism. But the realists, too, became enamoured by notions of structuralism, so that chapters on 'Breaking the mould', 'World society approaches' and 'Structuralism' will be followed by one on 'Realism resurgent?'. We shall then look at the implications of the three frameworks for that topic which more than any other gave rise to our discipline – 'Conflict and war' – as well as others, before essaying the 'Future imperfectly'.

Notes: Chapter 7

1 Raymond Aron, Peace and War: *A Theory of International Relations* (London: Weidenfield & Nicolson, 1966), p. 7.
2 John Handelman, Michael O'Leary, John Vasquez and William Coplin, 'Color it Morgenthau', ISA Conference Paper, 1973 (mimeo.).
3 Michael Banks, 'The inter-paradigm debate', in Margot Light and A. J. R. Groom (eds), *International Relations: A Handbook of Current Theory* (London: Pinter, 1985) and A. J. R. Groom, 'Paradigms in conflict', *Review of International Studies*, April 1988.
4 James N. Rosenau, in the introduction to Ray Maghroori and Bennett Romberg (eds), *Globalism versus Realism* (Boulder, Colo: Westview, 1982), p. 3.
5 K. J. Holsti, *The Dividing Discipline* (London: Allen & Unwin, 1987), p. 22. See also Hayward R. Alker Jr and Thomas J. Biersteker, 'The dialectics of world order: Notes for a future archaeologist of international savoir faire', *International Studies Quarterly*, 28, 2, 1984.
6 Holsti, *The Dividing Discipline*, pp. 105–7.

Further reading

Alker, Hayward J. Jr and Biersteker, Thomas J., 'The dialectics of world order: Notes for a future archaeologist of international savoir faire', *International Studies Quarterly*, 28, 2, 1984.
Holsti, K. J., *The Dividing Discipline*. London: Allen and Unwin, 1987.
Light, Margot and Groom, A. J. R. (eds). *International Relations: A Handbook of Current Theory*. London: Frances Pinter, 1985.
Maghroori, Roy and Romberg, Bennett (eds). *Globalism versus Realism*. Boulder, Colo: Westview, 1982.

8 Breaking the mould

a new theory . . . is seldom or never just an increment to what is already known. Its assimilation requires the reconstruction of prior theory and the re-evaluation of prior fact, an intrinsically revolutionary process that is seldom completed by a single man and never overnight. (Thomas Kuhn).[1]

The emerging agenda

The consensus on the conceptual mould of realism was not shattered by a single revolutionary insight. Rather, as the axioms of power politics were found to be incomplete or wanting, it became necessary to think in terms of the reform of realism or, failing that, of its replacement. Indeed, Morgenthau, himself, had lamented the decline, in the postwar world, of the conditions most propitious for the proper working of the balance of power – a view echoed cogently by Inis Claude.[2] But the very axioms of power politics were challenged by John Burton[3] and later, from the perspective of political theory, by Charles Beitz and empirically, in a behaviouralist mode, by John Vasquez.[4] By then an agenda had emerged, which gave emphasis to the questions of the degree of state-centricity in the contemporary world and that of the pervasiveness of power politics.

Various writers began to edge away from the state as the basic unit of analysis. Among these were systems theorists, such as Morton Kaplan and David Easton, and writers in comparative politics, such as Gabriel Almond, all of whom had a significant influence.[5] However, they did not stray far from a state-centric framework. For Easton and Almond it was a question of 'states conceived as systems' within which processes were of fundamental importance and interest, while the fertile mind of Morton Kaplan explored a 'system of states' – the international system – in terms of the traditional concerns of power politics, such as the balance of power.

Karl Deutsch, in his innovative work on integration,[6] was looking towards the creation of a state, and in his formulation of a cybernetic model he gave us new insights into how a state might work.[7] But Deutsch also pointed to some nagging anomalies in the realist framework. Peace in the form of a security community did not, he discovered, require a Leviathan, but could be just as efficaciously found, if not more so, through a pluralistic framework involving not only governments but other elites and even the masses. In addition, cybernetics suggested a move from 'power', based on instinct and drives, to 'steering' based on feedback processes, which could be applied to *any* social organization. Deutsch therefore opened the way to the challenge to the state as *the* unit of analysis and this challenge was taken up with alacrity by Burton, who also latched on to the movement from power to steering and applied it to the theory of non-alignment and, later, to problem-solving.

Burton's challenge to state-centricity and realism was not the first to make a mark. David Mitrany, like Burton a seasoned practitioner as well as an influential academic, had, between the wars and during his war years in the Foreign Office, looked to functional solutions for the creation of a 'working peace system.'[8] With its emphasis on transactions, security by association and the obsolete and dangerous nature of the existing state system, Mitrany's work again became a focus of interest. These ideas did not find particularly fertile ground in Britain, but they were more fructuous in the United States and contributed to the flowering of the neofunctionalist school. But indigenous writers there, such as James Rosenau, were also beginning to challenge the state-centricity of realism.

Rosenau edged away from the state, but gingerly. He wrote of penetrated societies, linkage politics and foreign policy as an issue area straining to the limit the very notion of IR in its traditional state-centric mode.[9] While Rosenau described world society and formulated schema for its investigation, it was not until relatively late that he embraced it as a conceptual framework. His approach was incremental and had less impact for that reason. Even the idea of an issue area, later much developed by Mansbach and Vasquez,[10] was initially conceived in the context of the comparative study of the foreign policy of states. However, it made greater sense when thought of as a system of transactions relating to a particular issue which was the concern of a heterogenous group of actors, drawn from many levels, whose relations could be both conflictual and cooperative. In the United States it was Keohane and Nye, in their early work,[11] who crystallised this approach. However, in neither Britain nor the United States did salient books emerge to fulfil the role of those of Carr, Schwarzenberger and Morgenthau for realism. Only Mitrany's essay *A Working Peace System* approached this status. Nevertheless, an agenda had emerged that clustered around two principal themes – the unit of analysis and the nature of transactions that formed the substance of international relations and, therefore, the study of IR.

The principal unit of analysis for both realists and idealists was the state. Indeed, the nature of the state and inter-state relations in an environment of anarchy were the justification for the separate status of IR as a discipline. The debate in the 1960s and 1970s concerned the appropriateness of the state to explain sufficiently that which was deemed important in international relations. Are states only affected primarily by what they themselves do and is only what they do important? In the ensuing discussion many other units of analysis were proposed, which reflected doubts regarding the state-centricity of contemporary world society. Behaviouralism in the social sciences generally had its impact on political science and IR, leading *inter alia* to consideration of the individual as the prime unit of analysis. But individuals interact in a framework, so transactions, processes and structure are all relevant. Is process, in the form of transactions, and the resultant structure, which then acts as a constraint upon transactions and socialises individuals and groups, the key? Is the contemporary world such that its interdependencies need to be seen as a single unit of analysis, broken down perhaps into issue areas, regimes or questions? And, if so, should we go beyond the confines of the world society approach to embrace a structuralist notion of the single world system – capitalism – with its centre, semi-periphery and periphery? And what is the role of the state, and of class, in such a conception?

Whatever the answer the unit of analysis chosen has a significant impact upon the level of analysis at which research is focused. Waltz, in his *Man, the State and War*[12] and David Singer in a justly famous article,[13] had focused attention on this issue. Traditionalists asserted that the international level was the proper one for IR because states interacted there in the full plenitude of their power and the political processes, due to the international anarchy, were different in kind from national politics. Others responded that states were not always 'in charge', nor were they always coherent units, and therefore non-state actors, whether operating internationally (e.g. World Health Organization) or transnationally (e.g. Amnesty International), were relevant. Moreover, the nature of the state, and its form, varied and this affected policies. Or should we concentrate on the individual? Was Morgenthau wrong to ascribe a drive to dominate to all individuals, but right to identify drives as important, as Burton was later to do with his universal human needs? Or, at the other end of the spectrum, is an ever-contracting and increasingly polluted and overcrowded 'Spaceship Earth' to be our principal concern? And if it is to be all, or some of these potential units and levels of analysis, how can they be melded together to achieve our goal – a parsimonious explanation of as great a part of the relevant data as possible – especially when whatever level or unit we choose goes a long way towards defining what is relevant?

The second item on the agenda concerned the degree to which all politics is, by nature, power politics. While acknowledging that power politics is common, the world society approach denies that it is ubiquitous. Moreover, it defines politics broadly to include the process whereby values are allocated and roles assigned in a wide variety of dimensions such as the economic, social and cultural systems. This process may be characterized by varying degrees of legitimation, and the interaction and movement between power politics and legitimized processes is complicated and not easy to predict. Should we start from the notion of a harmoniously working, non-coercive, legitimized society – a healthy political system – and seek to understand why it works, or should we concentrate on breakdown, especially when its consequences may be global nuclear war? And what is the relationship between the two? Furthermore, what is the import of such phenomena being evident in every social system – economic, social, cultural and the like? Is the political system something special? Or a chimera? Or a process *within* other systems and thus not separable from them? The agenda, whether concerning units and levels of analysis or the character and form of processes, was broad and exciting. It is to the literature that we must now turn, beginning with the emergence of anomalies that chafed the edges of the realist consensus.

Power politics in question

In his great work codifying the principles of political realism, Hans Morgenthau lays emphasis on the concepts of power, interest, imperialism and the balance of power, all of which later became the object of discussion and challenge. For many realists, power was conceived in terms of capabilities – especially military capabilities. Such capabilities are, of course, amenable to measurement and thus a hierarchy of Powers could be established, which would facilitate the prediction of outcomes and perhaps render actual physical conflict unnecessary. Unfortunately relative capabilities are not a reliable indication of likely outcome. Big states can and do lose small wars: Britain and France lost at Suez, the United States in Vietnam and the Soviet Union in Afghanistan. Power is thus better seen as a relational concept. It is the ability successfully to impose or resist change at a given time in given circumstances against the will of other actors. Capabilities are important in this, but not necessarily and solely determining. This renders doubtful Morgenthau's notion of the struggle for power. As Charles McClelland remarked, 'How can anyone struggle for a relational property – a quality of a relationship?'[14] And the term 'interest' is equally subjective. No one has ever produced an undisputed set of national, class or other interests, certainly not as Morgenthau would have them, that is, defined in terms of power. And even if we were all agreed, it would not necessarily mean that we were correct, but only that there was a consensus, since there is no objective way of telling if we are right. Nevertheless, Morgenthau went on to argue that if we pursue interest in terms of power, imperialism will result. Schumpeter had put the argument forcefully – 'Imperialism is the objectless disposition on the part of a state to unlimited forcible expansion.'[15] This disposition has its origin in warlike instincts and the quest, usually by military means, to create a state to embody a nationalist movement. Thereafter, power politics are the order of the day in international relations whereby 'To take the field was a matter of course, the reasons for doing so were of subordinate importance. *Created by wars that required it, the machine now created the wars it required.* A will for broad conquest without tangible limits, for the capture of positions that were manifestly untenable – this was typical imperialism.'[16] But the Schumpeter-Morgenthau thesis on imperialism was not the only one. Hobson and Lenin had already had their different words to say on the relationship between capitalism and imperialism. Others emphasized the strategic and cultural motivations or the haphazard ways in which imperialism occurred. Imperialism, in the form of structures of domination, is now once again a central item on the agenda in the structuralists' framework.

The balance of power was perhaps the lynch-pin of the realist framework. As a concept its utility is diminished by the many meanings that have been attributed to it.[17] However, the two dominant meanings are those of a homeostatic equilibrium and a balance of power in favour of the status quo Powers. It is also not clear whether a balance of power will emerge automatically or whether it is a prescription. In effect, most writers, including Morgenthau, see it as a prescription. Thus, if the great Powers are in antagonistic competition, Hobbes's state of nature will ensue, with political life being 'nasty, poor, brutish, solitary and short'. Each great Power wishes to impose its own world order, which will act as a constraint on all the others. Napoleonic France was a case in point. However, if a Power is unable to do this it will cooperate with others in order to prevent the most likely dominant state from succeeding in its ambition – hence the balance of power. It is a system predicated on conflict and managed through a degree of cooperation. But this management requires accurate information available to all, a comprehension of and willingness to operate agreed rules of the game, and tactical flexibility – a tall order. Even then, limited wars, as in the Crimea or Korea, may have to be fought to avoid general wars, and the system works only to preserve the role and status of the great Powers. If it is necessary to partition Poland or reassign colonies in the interest of great Power stability, then so be it. Morgenthau himself expressed concern about the system in that it is uncertain in its measurement of relative power capabilities, unreal, since the aim is superiority rather than cooperation, and inadequate, because it depends on a value consensus reflected in an understanding of, and belief in, the rules of a game that no longer exists in a more rigidly ideological

second half of the twentieth century. Morgenthau wished, therefore, to diminish the impact of these deficiencies, because he set
little store by collective security or world government and had
no desire to see the world relapse into a Hobbesian nuclear
nightmare.[18]

In a beautifully written book Inis Claude likewise expressed his
concern at the inadequacies of the realists' prescriptions for the
management of power in international relations.

> The crucial fact about the human situation . . . may be simply
> and starkly expressed: Mankind stands in grave danger of
> irreparable self-mutilation or substantial self-destruction. The
> circumstances which underlie this perilous condition may be
> succinctly described: Humanity is divided into basic units called
> states; some of these units possess the awesome capacity to
> destroy others. Once this power is unleashed, there is the high
> probability of a competitive struggle which may draw the whole
> world into its devastating vortex . . . the march of military
> technology is so rapid that it is no longer premature to contem-
> plate the danger of the annihilation of the human race . . . This
> catastrophe may not occur. In principle, it is doubtless avoidable.
> But the hard fact is that humanity has developed no means for
> providing reasonable assurance, let alone confident certainty,
> that it *will* be avoided.[19]

The balance of power, for reasons that Morgenthau had enunciated, was found wanting in such a context. Moreover,

> all the fundamental tendencies affecting the political realm in
> recent generations run counter to the requirements of a workable
> system of balance of power. There is nothing to indicate that the
> global setting is likely to become more, rather than less, appro-
> priate to the operation of a balance system . . . today, the balance
> of power system exists by default.[20]

But the alternatives as Claude saw them – collective security and
world government – were no less flawed. Thus realism was found
wanting as a prescription to its own identification of the problem
of our time. But that was not the end of it: John Burton was
arguing that change, not power, was the central concern.

Burton's work has gone through several metamorphoses. In the 1960s it was concerned with a challenge to the orthodoxy of power politics. Burton argued that neither men nor states were inherently aggressive.[21] Conflict arose out of change. Change, for all actors, was an environmental factor as well as an internal one. In the domain of power politics change was always likely to lead to violent conflict, because its incidence on the interests of the actors would differ and those who were less well off as a result of change would resist it. Conflict with potential beneficiaries would ensue. But this was not always the case and Burton called for an analysis of 'what stimulates passive or non-passive responses, what types of change can be absorbed, what values can be traded, and what types of change provoke aggressive responses.'[22] He rejected the idea that the balance of power could manage change, since it could not absorb systemic change. For example, the growth of nationalism in the nineteenth and twentieth centuries had disturbing implications for practically all of the major Powers of 1914 regarding their continuing political viability. The parameters of the nineteenth century system were thus breached and sooner or later the system would collapse under the strain of systemic change. The question was only 'how?' and 'when?'. Burton (and Karl Deutsch) thus began to look to cybernetics and the concept of steering as a means of non-cataclysmic change which, for Burton, led him to explore further the nature of non-alignment as a policy and the possibilities of controlled communication.[23] With power politics now being questioned in a sustained manner the way was open for a wider debate on the emerging agenda.

Systems thinking

Movements away from the realist consensus occurred along two principal axes – the relaxation of assumptions about the state-centricity of the world and about the pervasive nature of power politics. We shall proceed along the spectrum of declining state-centricity. As for the centrality of power politics, no one can deny its presence in the contemporary world, but the question is the degree, and effects, of its incidence, and its relationship with legitimized politics. Legitimacy is a notion that can be associated with both state-related and non-state-centric perspectives. However, for the sake of convenience, our discussion will follow the spectrum of declining state-centricity without wishing thereby to imply that the question of the relationship between power politics and legitimized politics is secondary. It is not.

In 1957 Morton Kaplan published his *System and Process in International Politics*.[24] The book was important because it brought the notion of system into the mainstream of IR and was thereby instrumental in opening the gates of the field to insights, frameworks and methods from sociology, comparative politics, biology, cybernetics, mathematics and beyond to the philsophy of science. New developments often come late to IR – behaviouralism is a contemporary case in point. Historically, the notion of balance entered the lexicon of diplomacy at the time of the Italian city states, later than in science and other social fields. 'Balance' has permeated and impregnated our thought ever since. The notion of system is analogous – coming from science, biology and engineering – but it is now part not only of the behavioural sciences but also of our everyday thought patterns. 'Feedback', an important notion in systems terminology, was esoteric jargon thirty years ago; it is now common parlance. Kaplan rightly called his book heuristic and eclectic, but in opening these gates to a new world it was also influential – 'system' and 'process' were notions that were taken up with alacrity. As for the detail, Kaplan's studies of six different international systems have had less impact partly because of their normative nature.[25] Subsequent debates on the relative stability of multi- and bi-polar systems of the balance of power call to mind medieval disputes regarding the number of angels who can stand on the head of a pin. Perhaps it is not a question of numbers of actors so much as their continuing viability that is the key to stability.

One of the most frustrating aspects of IR is the absence of a settled meaning to an agreed terminology – and so it is with systems. There is also the dichotomy between objective and subjective phenomena, which reveals itself in the difference between general systems theory and systems analysis. Kenneth Boulding, in a celebrated article, has observed:

General Systems Theory is the skeleton of science in the sense that it aims to provide a framework or structure of systems on which to hang the flesh and blood of particular disciplines and particular subject matters in an orderly and coherent corpus of knowledge.[26]

In other words, the implication is that all science, indeed the world, is organized along systemic lines with systemic properties that can be revealed by assiduous research. We are back seemingly in the metaphysical world familiar to IR scholars through natural and divine law. Charles McClelland, on the other hand, has a much more subjective notion:

> Any system is a structure that is perceived by its observers to have elements in interaction or relationships and some identifiable boundaries that separate it from its environment.[27]

Clearly, in this instance systems are a mental construct, a mechanism for ordering data according to the interests and concerns of the observer. Systems analysis is thus a convenience whereby if one set of transactions 'works' for the observer's purpose it will be retained or, if not, it will be dispensed with and another set chosen. It is not a question here of some grandiose 'skeleton of science' that has an objective reality waiting to be revealed that will, *nolens volens*, follow its prescribed pattern of behaviour, thereby affecting outcomes, whether it is perceived or not.

But what is a system? It is a set of patterned interactions in which behaviour has a rhyme and a reason so that at some level of abstraction general statements can be made about it. Without this belief social science would have to shut up shop. Pattern, however, implies duration and interactions imply structure. Systems, then, are not entirely a matter for the free-floating imagination of the observer. Systems also have boundaries as the world is not a single system. There may be systems at the world level in various dimensions, but there are also sub-systems and sub-sub-systems after the manner of a Chinese box. The boundaries of these systems are marked by significant discontinuities in either the quantity or quality of transactions. Such boundaries are, of course, subject to change as transaction flows vary, but it is a matter of dispute about the extent to which they will vary.

Those writers influenced by Talcott Parsons point to a proclivity towards pattern maintenance in which the structures of a system, and its normative rules that have evolved, combine to set in motion homeostatic processes.[28] In other words, we are stuck with what we have got. Others have a far more dynamic view of systems persistence, evolution, collapse and revolution as the work of Burton, Easton and Chalmers Johnson attests. In other words, what we get is in some measure what we deserve to get. Systems thinking in the Parsonian mode also carried with it some notion of an intra-systemic harmony of interests in that there is a mutually supporting role differentiation – tasks are functional for the maintenance of the pattern of the system. It is as though everything was for the best in the best of all possible worlds. But conflicts can also be conceived in systemic terms, particularly if systemic boundaries, in terms of valued transactions flows, are at variance with, hampered or disrupted by state boundaries. Dropping bombs on people, too, can be considered a patterned interaction. However, many theorists in political science latched on to systems thinking as a way of explaining political development, by which they meant how the developed state – and its political system – reflected consensus and harmony. The standard of pattern maintenance, integration and the like was thus set for 'developing' countries and world society to emulate. The conservative nature, indeed, the arrogance – and the failure – of this approach have been well catalogued.

'Systems thinking is holistic thinking', wrote Richard Smith Beal and then went on to explain the import of this:

> The principle of holism asserts that social reality, to be understood adequately, should be apprehended as a complete, assembled and integrated ensemble. An holistic understanding is vital because (1) the whole is always something different from the mere sum of the parts, (2) parts assume novel properties as a function of their inclusion in the whole, (3) interactive effects modify parts in conjunction in ways undetectable when the parts are disjoined, and (4) the union of the parts is, after all, the most interesting phenomenon because its reality is most unequivocal. In effect the principle of holism is committed to the idea that many phenomena are simply indivisible. To fragment a given phenomenon, even for the sake of scientific inquiry, is equivalent to losing the rich delineation among the components which made the entity so interesting in the first place.[29]

This idea was uncontroversial among systems thinkers. But what was the whole to be? Easton settled upon the political system of a state, and Johnson on a social system, while Burton and Mitrany laid greater emphasis on transaction systems which were not necessarily state-centric. Moreover, was the international system a system of states or, as in Burton's conception, a world society?

David Easton's work was undoubtedly innovative, because he was able to come to terms with this maelstrom of systems ideas and apply his conception of them, with insight and care, to political phenomena in a way that made its impact not only in political science but also on IR. Easton went to considerable trouble before he finally rejected the idea of natural systems as a basis for his research,[30] and he came to the conclusion that 'We can simplify problems of analysis enormously, without violating the empirical data in any way, by postulating that any set of variables selected for description and explanation may be considered a system of behaviour'.[31] Which set we choose depends upon our interests, but Easton would doubtless agree that it behoves us always to be alive to the implications of our choice. Easton's choice fell upon the political system, which he did not differentiate from a state. However, he did, like the structural-functionalists in sociology and comparative politics, take interactions as the basic unit of analysis as opposed to political structures, which he saw as secondary.[32] Later approaches in this tradition embodied a greater concern for structural constraints.

Easton had to come to terms with the idea of a political system. He commented that 'In its broadest context the study of political life, as contrasted with economic, religious, or other aspects of life, can be described as a set of social interactions on the part of individuals and groups.'[33] One wonders what a social interaction is that differentiates it from other aspects of life. The comment is not flippant, for it raises the question of whether there is a political system, as such, or merely a political process within other systems whereby in each system there can be what Easton called the authoritative allocation of values.[34]

Burton approached this problem in a different manner, which could suggest ways of looking beyond the state as a political system. He suggests that we should map all kinds of transactions in world society:

trade flows, tourist movements, aircraft flights, population
movements and transactions in ideas, cultures, languages and
religions, traffic flows within towns and social interactions
within village communities . . . The map of this society would
appear like millions of cobwebs superimposed upon one another,
covering the whole globe, some with stronger strands than
others representing more numerous transactions, some concentrated in small areas, and some thinly stretched over extensive
areas.[35]

Such systems have relations with each other.

They are linked functionally . . . They are linked also by reason
of shared unit, and sometimes have shared values. This is
particularly so of social systems: the same people belong in
different roles to many systems. *Linked systems* create clusters
that tend to be concentrated geographically: communication,
trading and other systems tend to be linked and to form societies.
The areas covered by these societies are determined by the
frequencies of social interactions amongst units within the systems comprising them . . . Linked systems tend to consolidate
into administrative units, and this is the case in industry no less
than in social life. There are *administrative systems* including
parliaments, cabinets and civil services, and others in industry
and finance, that restrain the free interaction of systems. These
administrative systems, unlike others, do tend to be confined to
conventionalized geographical boundaries that include major
clusters of systems . . . they have power to control the interaction of systems within given areas, thus limiting the consequence
of change.
    Once consolidated and accepted by other clusters, linked
systems and their administrative controls acquire an identity and
a legitimized status within their environment . . . It would be
misleading, however, to regard these concentrations as systems.
This may have been the case in a past age when each was
relatively self-contained and isolated: the transaction points of
systems tended to be within the boundaries of the linked
systems. But this is no longer the case.
    States are better regarded as the resultant of the interacting
behaviour of systems. Regarding them as systems does not draw

attention to the way in which boundaries disturb transaction flows and prejudices in advance an analysis of the role of States in world society. This approach of systems is a departure from that which has been customary when applied to politics. Systems in the Eastonian analysis, for example, are uniformly of the type described here as 'administrative': that is they are structured, with defined inputs and supports. In reality, systems are not frequently of this kind, and the assumption that they are so would seem to be a carry-over from traditional thinking that regarded States as entities, and moreover, the only actors in World Society. It is not intended to imply that States are no longer significant; on the contrary, their role and range of activities has increased, but it is a role in relation to systems. World society is perhaps best analysed by considering systems first, and then the role of States, which is the reverse of a traditional approach.[36]

There are a number of points to be made in this context. The 'world society' and 'political science' conceptions of Burton and Easton are evidently very different sorts of systems. Burton relates to the international functionalism of Mitrany, which clearly goes beyond the state, whereas Easton is state-centric, but with an emphasis on transactions rather than structure. It is difficult to have Easton 'writ large' at the global level since it is not easy to identify his variables in that context, because what Burton would call 'administrative boundaries' get in the way, whereas Burton's conception arises out of, and is well fitted for, the investigation of world society. In both cases, however, judgement had to be held in abeyance because there was no proper empirical test of either conception. The influence of these notions was not subsequently great in the study of world society because Easton is irrelevant and Burton's cobweb model has never been properly tested empirically except indirectly by Mansbach, Ferguson and Lampert[37] and in Burton's problem-solving workshops.[38]

How does the question of change, which has always been a central issue in IR and which is often a matter of peace and war in international relations, relate to the Eastonian framework? Easton relaxes the Parsonian notion of homeostatic pattern maintenance and, by implication, the equilibrium systems of the balance of power. He writes:

Maintenance is weighted with the notion of salvaging the existing pattern of relationships and directs attention to their preservation. Persistence signalizes the importance of considering, not any particular structure or pattern, but rather the very life processes of a system themselves. In this sense a system may persist even though everything else associated with it changes continuously and radically. The idea of systems persistence extends far beyond that of systems maintenance; it is oriented toward exploring change as well as stability, both of which may be interpreted as alternative avenues for coping with stress.[39]

Although the Eastonian analysis is firmly esconced in one level of analysis, nevertheless, as Mansbach and Vasquez pointed out,

> it moves the analysis of global politics away from conceptions of power and security and toward the assumption that demands for value satisfaction through global decision making must be at the heart of any theory, and must be the central process that awaits explanation . . . and toward still more basic questions of how dissatisfaction is generated and the processes that respond to it, including the creation of new actors and the disappearance of old ones.[40]

At this point Chalmers Johnson's treatment of *Revolutionary Change*[41] is apposite, since he makes change his central theme and sees it in an Eastonian framework.

Johnson argues that when limited change occurs social systems may be able to cope within their homeostatic capability. But what if this capability is inadequate? It is then up to the leadership to undertake structural change and value adjustment to resynchronize the system. Indeed, this 'may occur without disturbing a homeostatic equilibrium so long as the value structure and the environment *change in synchronization with each other* . . . A social system can change its structure and still remain equilibrated.'[42] Of course, not all leaderships will be farsighted enough, able or willing to do this in an appropriate manner and so the dissynchronized system is ripe for revolutionary change in ways that need not concern us here. What is important is that systems' change, in whatever its shape and form, is the very stuff of international relations and, although Johnson, Burton and, to a lesser extent, Easton have addressed this problem, many of the Parsonian sociologists who influenced systems thinking did not do so. It is for reasons such as this, and the rejection of the idea of natural systems, at least as a research problem, that general systems theory and Parsonian sociology have not proved to be the 'skeleton of science' as Boulding had hoped. However, Burton, Johnson and Easton have shown that systems analysis is worth taking further. Other systemic approaches have also had an influence upon the evolution of the world society model. In particular, we need to consider other state-related approaches, such as the work of Almond in comparative politics, Deutsch in cybernetics and Rosenau in his issue area formulation before broaching integration theory. Then we shall come to 'world society' proper in the next chapter.

Comparative politics

Some thirty years ago comparative politics seemed to be in a much livelier state of intellectual ferment than IR. This was due to the assimilation of structural–functional ideas culled from anthropologists and sociologists. In the broadest sense systems thinking, whether of the structural–functional, cybernetic or Eastonian variety, seemed to offer a tool for comparison. Put simply, all societies, indeed all organizations, need to perform various functions – at least to a minimum level – if they are to survive. There is, of course, no necessary implication that they should survive. Lists of functions varied, but the fundamental ideas were similar. A unit must be able to communicate with, and receive messages from, its social and ecological environment; it must be able to integrate its sub-units so that it can act as a whole; it must be able to generate a modicum of loyalty – of 'we-feeling'; and finally, it must be able to set goals so that it can put its other attributes to purposeful use, which implies that it has a memory in the form of values and preferences drawn from past experience. These are a necessary requirement for survival at some, perhaps limited, level of cohesion, whether for a village in the highlands of Papua New Guinea, London or the USA. *How* these functions will be performed will vary from setting to setting. In other words, structures and forms may vary, but functional prerequisites for survival remain constant and, as such, constitute a standard for comparison. As Rosenau has remarked,

> Until structural–functional analysis was made part of the conceptual equipment of the field, the most salient dimensions of political systems were their unique characteristics and there seemed little reason to engage in comparison, except perhaps to show how different governmental forms give rise to dissimilar consequences . . . Structural–functional analysis lifted sights to a higher level of generalization and put all political systems on an analytic par. Thereafter, tracing differences was much less exhilarating than probing for functional equivalents . . .[43]

Gabriel Almond was an acknowledged 'prober in chief'.

Almond replaced terms such as state, powers, offices, institutions, public opinion and citizenship training with political system, functions, roles, structures, political culture and political socialization.[44] But Almond aspired to more than a cosmetic change. He wished to go beyond parliaments and the like to '*all of the structures in their political aspects*, including undifferentiated structures like kinship and lineage, status and caste groups, as well as anomic phenomena like riots . . .'[45] But then he drew back from this 'world society' type philosophy by a restrictive definition of the political system: for example,

> While we can say that the religious organization and the social stratification of a society influence the political system, we would not say that they are part of it. Only when a religious group makes claims upon the political system through religious authorities, or through specialized structures . . . do the intermittent political actions of the clergy, or the regular action of the specialized religio-political structures, become part of the political system.[46]

Nevertheless, all political systems have things in common – political structure, the same functions, substantial multifunctionality, and a mix between modernity and tradition.[47] This led Almond to propose his famous functional categories for comparison: Input functions of (1) Political socialization and recruitment, (2) Interest articulation, (3) Interest aggregation, and (4) Political communication. These were followed by the response of government in Output functions: (5) Rule-making, (6) Rule application and (7) Rule adjudication.[48]

For Almond the political system was something special. He acknowledged that the 'political system is not the only system that makes rules and enforces them' but, nevertheless, 'The political authorities, and only they, have some generally accepted right to utilize coercion and command obedience based upon it.'[49] The analysis is still state-centric since, despite an acknowledged concentration on interactions, the emphasis is on *the* political system rather than the political *process* of the authoritative allocation of values within any system. To move further would require due acknowledgement that political *systems* do not exist (except perhaps in the sense in which Burton describes them above), but political *processes* or *functions* are ubiquitous in family, firm, economic system or whatever. Almond and his colleagues were not prepared to look beyond the state-by-another-name. Charles Tilly has pointed out that comparative analysis requires the identification of boundaries, but adds,

> The boundaries need not be geographic; they may separate different groups of people who are scattered or mingled in space. The means may be arbitrary, permitting the political scientist to analyze *any* local population as a 'political system' in something like the manner that an ecologist designates any localized set of organisms and their environment as an 'ecosystem'. Or the means may derive from some theory of the social bond, using common language, degree of contact with a particular metropolis, or some such criterion to separate one nation, political system or society from another. In that case, the investigator has a special obligation: he must actually use that criterion to bound his units.

What have political scientists done in practice? For the most part, they have sneaked back to the state. They have treated the people and the territory subject to the control of a particular state as the basic unit to be compared with similar units elsewhere . . . The procedure is convenient and even justifiable. But it has the disadvantage of begging most of the questions which induced comparative political analysts to turn away from the state in the first place.[50]

But the work of Almond and his colleagues did have an important influence by bringing structural–functionalism as a means of comparison, potentially between all organizations, to the forefront in political science and IR. The notion of the functional requirements for survival and the importance of interactions were further strengthened by the cybernetic approach.

The cybernetic approach

The cybernetic approach is most frequently, and rightly, associated with the work of Karl Deutsch. Like Almond and Easton, Deutsch put the emphasis on interactions but, ultimately, did not stray far from state-centricity, although the implications for further movement in that direction were implicit in his work. It is, however, important not to forget and to acknowledge fully the second dimension of the world society approach – the movement away from the realist's conception of power politics. As Deutsch put it, 'It might be profitable to look upon government somewhat less as a problem of power and somewhat more as a problem of steering . . . steering is decisively a matter of communication'.[51] Deutsch devoted his justly renowned *The Nerves of Government* to this seminal idea.

Deutsch brought into the mainstream of political science and IR a new *Weltanschauung* from science and engineering – cybernetics:

the systematic study of communication and control in organizations of all kinds . . . Essentially it represents a shift in the center of interest from drives to steering, and from instincts to systems of decisions, regulation, and control, including the noncyclical aspects of such systems . . . In other words, the viewpoint of cybernetics suggests that all organizations are alike in certain fundamental characteristics and that every organization is held together by communication . . . It is communication, that is, the ability to transmit messages and to react to them, that makes organizations . . .[52]

Thus, as with general systems thinking and more especially structural–functionalism, we are given a tantalising means for comparison of all social entities that may have the potential for enabling us to broach the study of world society. Deutsch, however, restricts himself to government, which he likens to the nervous system of the body.

We can simplify Deutsch's categories in the decision-making process in the following manner, and they can be applied to any decision from whether or not to have a cup of coffee or to go to war. First, there must be a stimulus, which can arise endogenously or exogenously. In the coffee example it could be because I see it is 11 a.m., which is coffee time (exogenous), or because I have given a lecture and have a dry throat and mouth (endogenous). Next, I have to be able to interpret these stimuli by reference to past experience, so that I can give a useful meaning to them. I realize that I am thirsty and need a drink. Then I have to examine my priorities regarding means of slaking my thirst – a good claret? a cup of coffee? former Indian Prime Minister Desai's morning elixir? – and consider their opportunity cost in time, money, convenience and the like. Perhaps that claret would go down better over dinner tonight and so I end up by deciding to go to the common room for a cup of coffee. This is my output or response to my perceived input or stimulus. I have perceived and assessed subjectively the nature of the input and I have made a judgement in the light of my hierarchy of values and current priorities in the context of my perception of the operating environment. However, an output does not necessarily lead to the desired outcome. I find that there is no coffee in the common room because the coffee lady has stayed at home because she is ill. The operating environment is not what I thought it was and the negative feedback tells me to try again. I repeat the process and 'satisfice' by feeding twenty pence into a machine in the corridor, which dispenses a coloured liquid that resembles coffee about as much as the ersatz coffee essence which I dimly remember from the war years.

This simple schema could be applied to any decision; Deutsch's contribution was to spell it out and to suggest that we need to give great attention to each aspect and to their interrelationship. Are we picking up relevant information from the environment? How efficient is our costing procedure and identification of alternatives from our past experience? Do we have a realistic assessment of the operating environment? Above all, are we learning from, and steering according to, our feedback mechanisms? It is from negative feedback that we learn to do things better. This feedback may simply indicate the need for a minor adjustment of method to achieve a given end, say tea rather than coffee for the mid-morning drink, or it may indicate that we should re-formulate our goals, for example, to drink less or fewer stimulants. Without feedback, any social unit will drift – ultimately to catastrophe.

Cybernetics is, then, the science of control and communication, of decision-making and interactions. Deutsch, in applying the framework to government, indicated that which was necessary to avoid breakdown – the precise monitoring of accurate negative feedback and a timely ability to take corrective measures.[53] He put the emphasis on processes rather than outcomes, that is, on the domestic environment rather than the operating environment. However, as he acknowledged, they are part and parcel of the same phenomenon.

Further consideration enhances significantly Deutsch's contribution, for it sheds some light on our second dimension – the movement away from power politics. Imagine more than one actor as well as myself, say the coffee lady who, sensibly, stayed at home because she had 'flu. Her action caused me negative feedback and steering from common room coffee to corridor machine coffee. This adjustment, and that of the coffee lady, who stayed at home because of the 'flu, were legitimized because the behaviour of both of us was based on criteria fully and knowingly acceptable to us both. But what if I had felt that the coffee lady was skiving and reported her to her supervisor, who had demanded that she return to work immediately on pain of dismissal? And what if the coffee lady refused, citing her doctor's advice, and, upon dismissal, appealed to an industrial relations tribunal with the support of her trades union? Clearly we are now in a system of power politics. Rather than steer or adjust to the negative feedback engendered by her illness, I tried to force the burden of adjustment on to her. She must come and make my coffee, 'flu or no 'flu. Power, therefore, in the Deutschian formulation is the ability to thrust the burden of adjustment on the environment, that is, on others, by not responding to negative feedback. This notion of steering had a significant influence on Burton in his study of non-alignment as a policy and in the adoption of problem-solving techniques. More generally, it helps us to conceptualize better both power and legitimized politics in the same framework and thereby brings us closer to the real world. But Deutsch's framework is entirely a conceptual one whose potentialities have not been put fully to the test in an empirical framework. However, his contribution did enable us to think about the nature of government and the relationship between power politics and legitimized politics in a new way. Moreover, it was not the only seminal contribution that Deutsch had to offer.

Deutsch was one of the first in IR to undertake empirical work following the canons of behaviouralism and he inspired others to do so as well. Indeed, this inspiration, and the work that ensued, is an important part of his legacy. In *Nationalism and Social Communication* and his *Political Community and the North Atlantic Area*, Deutsch demonstrated the virtues of his transactional approach.[54] Neither states nor security communities were henceforth necessarily to be seen as the creatures of coercion. International relations and intranational relations could be conceived fundamentally as collaborative processes. Thus, as Donald Puchala points out, the findings of integration studies in the 1950s and 1960s, inspired and led by Deutsch among others, knocked a sizeable hole in the realist paradigm and did so with the force of empirical research at hand. Orthodoxy was brought into question in a manner that led to theories of transnational relations and interdependence and to a greater prominence being given to international political economy and to negotiating theory as applied to international relations.[55]

While Deutsch might rightly be seen as the 'father' of transactional analysis, he did offer a counter-intuitive finding that the level of interdependence was declining in the contemporary world. This ran flat against the assertions of the world society school. Although Deutsch found that national self-preoccupation was becoming more intensive and extensive in the contemporary world, as Oran Young pointed out,

This argument does not *necessarily* imply that there has been no increase in absolute terms in the level of interdependence in the world system. It does suggest, however, that a far more striking and important development is an increase in the ratio of interdependencies within component units to interdependencies characteristic of the world system as a whole.[56]

Young found this 'a provocative and important argument', but one subject to several important criticisms:

> First, it is severely restricted by the tacit assumption that nation-states are the only important actors in world politics . . . Secondly, Deutsch's argument is based upon a rather narrow and selective range of indicators of interdependence in the world system . . . Thirdly, Deutsch frequently (though not always) focuses on indicators of interdependence that are primarily associated with the development of co-operative activities across national boundaries . . . Fourthly, there is a certain deceptiveness in Deutsch's general emphasis on percentatges and ratios, especially when coupled with his focus on iterative transactions as indicators of interdependence . . . Fifthly, there are some tricky methodological issues that plague efforts to determine the level of interdependence in the world system in empirical terms.[57]

Young, for these reasons and others, like many in the world society approach, argues 'that the level of interdependence in the world system has risen sharply in the contemporary period' in terms of sensitivity to events elsewhere, the revolutionary expansion of the physical possibilities for interdependence, their relative ease of accessibility and the 'contemporary revolution in military technology . . . [which] has produced a qualitative shift in the patterns of interdependence among the component units of the world system'.[58] This would, indeed, be hard to gainsay.[59]

In a stimulating *Festschrift* for Deutsch, *From National Development to Global Community*, his colleagues and students paid him the compliment not only of praising him (and there is every justification for that) but also of criticising him. One area in which this was the case concerns his ideas on social mobilization and political development.[60] His approach melded ideas previously gleaned from his studies of nationalism and political community with concerns in comparative politics regarding political modernization. The general idea is a captivating one. As traditional societies unravel under the impact of modernizing forces, often the more capitalistic organization of agriculture, then a rootless class of landless peasants are created bereft of organizing structures in most dimensions. They are thus ready to be assimilated into modern culture economically, socially and politically. This culture is, of course, much more homogeneous than its traditional predecessors. If mobilization and assimilation within a modern state structure proceed *pari passu*, then there is likely to be stability and 'political development'. Indeed, at a wider level it might even lead to the 'end of ideology' as all industrial societies grow more alike. We could envisage, therefore, the makings of a single world society.[61] However, there are significant reasons to question the central thrust of the argument, especially since ethnic politics are now a major phenomenon in both developed and developing societies (for different reasons). Rather than a homogenising world society we seem to be seeing a growth of interdependence *and* diversity. It is a fundamental task of our time, for scholar and practitioner alike, to come to terms with this in both analytical understanding and practical institution building – a task more likely to be fructuous in the world society paradigm than any other. However, that is a task for the future – a global task – and so are the implications of Deutsch's work, but our concern is primarily IR. By now, however, the innovations of Deutsch, Burton, Easton, Almond, Kaplan and others needed to be considered in the context of the traditional confines of the subject.

Foreign policy analysis (FPA)

One of the traditional concerns of IR is the analysis of foreign policy. However, ever since Snyder, Bruck and Sapin[62] broke the mould in their new conception of foreign policy decision-making, the study of foreign policy has been in a confused state. Does it concern formal state-to-state relations and, if so, is it confined to Foreign Offices or does it include other Ministries, which may have their own foreign policy? And what of the foreign policy of state enterprises or chartered bodies such as nationalized industries or the BBC? Again, private bodies have foreign policies that are of significant import for official foreign policy: for example, the TUC in the ILO. Transnational bodies, whether non-profit making, such as Amnesty International, or profit-making, such as ICI, are far from being irrelevant. Transgovernmental alliances between, say, Ministries of Agriculture in the EC, further complicate the analysis. And who controls and coordinates all this? Is it in fact controllable? Where is foreign policy? Has it merged into external relations and transnational ties? Yet courses are still taught in it, often as if nothing has happened.

For the realist, these questions present no great problem since his conception of the world is state-centric and power political. His interests suggest a fairly traditional and circumscribed notion of foreign policy, sometimes to be summed up as 'high politics', which is central to his concerns. In the world society framework, foreign policy is conceived as part of external relations, broadly defined, whereas structuralists give less emphasis to actors and therefore, for them, the question is less acute, since states and governments are often seen as being under the control or guiding influence of other actors or subject to powerful structural constraints. Nevertheless, FPA is a core element in the IR curriculum.

Snyder, Bruck and Sapin produced a checklist of factors and actors involved in the formulation of foreign policy. Their work attracted a great deal of interest but not much follow-up,[63] although the research of Michael Brecher has a flavour of their approach.[64] Karl Deutsch's advocacy of a cybernetic approach, however, continues to exert a powerful influence,[65] as does the legacy from the Sprouts' examination of the man–milieu relationship.[66] The psychological aspects of decision-making were given particular prominence by Kenneth Boulding in The Image.[67] These strands began to be pulled together by various authors, of whom three were particularly salient – Joseph Frankel in Britain and James Rosenau, followed later by Graham Allison, in the United States. Frankel's contribution was plain and straightforward, for which many were grateful.[68] Rosenau, however, has a remarkable ability to stimulate debate. His reader, International Politics and Foreign Policy,[69] has been, since its first edition, and remains, a staple part of the literature. But Rosenau in his pursuit of The Scientific Study of Foreign Policy has delved into its domestic sources, its comparison, the convergence of national and international systems and adaptation – all to stimulating effect.[70] But the field of FPA has been marked by less cumulative effect than might be expected, a matter put right to some extent, at least in decision-making, by Graham Allison in his The Essence of Decision.[71]

Allison applied three different conceptions of decision-making to US policy-making in the Cuban missile crisis: that of the rational actor, organizational processes and bureaucratic politics.

Each threw a different light upon that process, thereby suggesting that there is no 'royal road' to understanding. The rational actor model can be given short shrift. In an ideal formulation it assumes that actors will strive to maximize values that are hierarchically organized and not contradictory. The actor will consider the full range of options before choosing, and the decision will be rapidly, faithfully and completely implemented: that is, proposive acts by unified governments will be comprehensively implemented in the spirit in which they were intended. Quite simply this approach does not correspond with behaviour. Governments are rarely coherent, hierarchical or maximizing. Moreover, information is often inadequate, either through its paucity or overabundance, analysis is costly and time-consuming, and the criteria of choice are, at best, fuzzy. This suggests that organizational processes, in which governments 'satisfice', in Herbert Simon's phrase, are nearer the mark more of the time.

Braybrooke and Lindblom[72] have coined an inelegant, but surprisingly retentive phrase, 'disjointed incrementalism', to describe the processes of government. Foreign policy, they suggest, is carried forward by an endless sequence of small moves. 'Micro experts' push paper from their in-trays to their out-trays, or into the waste-paper basket, with scant consideration, or knowledge of the larger policy framework within which they are acting. Their aims are essentially neutral: to keep the wheels turning so that they do not stop in their own patch, and to avoid known pitfalls rather than to seek positive goals. Uncertainty is minimized in the short run and the long run is at a discount. Organizations break down problems into parts that they can manage and which correspond to their internal structure rather than make the organization match the problem. The files rule. There is control at the micro level, but not overall. Major change is therefore usually exogenously induced, rare, and out of control. It can be catastrophic for the organization. What holds things together in the normal course of events is shared values and socialization into a conventional wisdom. It is drift in the same direction rather than control. Only when the drift looks like going beyond the bounds of the bearable do top decision-makers step in, and then their hands are tied because the range of options has usually been foreclosed, and they have, in effect, little real choice. They can seek either to push out the bonds of the bearable, but this is frequently painful, or, more frequently, to steer back towards the mainstream. In short, top decision-makers are herdsmen looking for lost sheep rather than leaders. They themselves have little time to think; they can only react and rush from one crisis to the next. Policy is a retrospective rationalization rather than a guiding goal and a set of acts designed to achieve that goal in a controlled environment. It is for historians to 'make sense' of chaos and drift, and to give it order.

Morton Halperin has expanded upon Allison's third category, that of bureaucratic politics.[73] This approach suggests that problems are not treated on their merits but according to whether they will advance or impede the interests and self-image of the actor considering them. 'Where you stand depends on where you sit', that is, location in a bureaucracy will determine reaction to an issue, at least to a significant extent.

All this is not to suggest that rational action never occurs – ironically it may be more likely to do so in a crisis when normal decision-making practices may be in abeyance. Nor does it rule out the possibility that governments can set clear goals and pursue them single mindedly, as occurred in Britain's attempt to join the EEC, or that a leader can stamp her values willy-nilly not only on government, but on society at large, as Mrs Thatcher has done. But these tend to be exceptions rather than the rule. In large complex Western liberal democracies the suggestion is that Parliaments reign but do not rule. Government is a loose confederation of like-minded, semi-autonomous bureaucracies. A twice-weekly Cabinet meeting, for perhaps thirty-five weeks of the year, of more than twenty people, lasting two hours or so, barely has time for mutual greetings and the rubber-stamping of departmental briefs let alone control of an administration, particularly if, as in the United States, the separation of powers is built into the system. Government, in short, is like a dinosaur: it has an enormous weighty body (the bureaucracy), and a very small brain. And where does this leave FPA? In the doldrums, it would appear, since there has been little new of note for more than a decade.

For a long time attempts were made, chiefly by scholars in the United States, to develop the comparative study of foreign policy. Rosenau was one of the instigators of this and McGowan and Kegley have doggedly struggled to give substance to the idea, and in particular its quantitative aspects.[74] However, the approach has not fulfilled its promise. But there are intriguing questions to be addressed. Do super Powers have problems in common, as super Powers? Does it make sense to consider middle Powers as a viable category, and in what circumstances, or to what effect? What are the modalities of being a pariah state, a divided state or a mini-state? The literature is slowly coming into existence.[75]

At the other end of the spectrum the psychological and sociological aspects of foreign policy-making continue to exert a fascination. Works by de Rivera, Jervis and Janis,[76] together with those of psycho-historians, hold their place for the insights revealed. Of particular and recent interest, and of some significance is the work of Robert Axelrod on the *Evolution of Cooperation*.[77] Axelrod highlights the significance of discounting whereby players who weight the future heavily may play cooperatively even in the prisoner's dilemma game. Too often, in the past, IR specialists have discounted the learning process engendered by repetition. Power politics may pay in the short run, and leaders may choose to indulge in it for that reason, thereby leaving their successors to rue their shortsightedness. However, events are rarely, if ever, completely discrete and isolated, so that there is always a long run, although that after a nuclear war does not bear contemplation. Since in the long run cooperative strategies may pay, perhaps FPA should put greater emphasis on the long-term aspects than hitherto – Axelrod's approach is a suggestive one. Consideration needs also to be given to how best the fruits of FPA, and IR more generally, can be brought to the attention of decision-makers. Neither the British (arms length) nor American (in–outers) practice seems to be ideal.[78]

Over the decades the instruments of foreign policy have changed and require analysis. Diplomacy is no longer what it was in Harold Nicolson's day.[79] In particular, multilateral and conference diplomacy have become much more commonplace[80] and the social composition and training requirements of diplomats have been evolving too.[81] Crises and crisis management are other permanent fixtures on the FPA agenda, although, after a fructuous period in the 1960s and 1970s, little of great moment has been forthcoming recently.[82] Perhaps the most useful formulation of FPA has been that of issue areas, since it places traditional concerns of foreign policy in a context of declining state-centricity.

James Rosenau's important contribution to the discussion

included the notions of a penetrated society, linkage politics and foreign policy as an issue area.[83] Rosenau was not the only writer to give attention to the permeability of the state; John Herz and Andrew Scott were others.[84] While Rosenau's conception of foreign policy as an issue area did not immediately evoke a response, the notion of issue areas was given a new lease of life by Mansbach and Vasquez in the early 1980s. They suggest that the distinction between domestic and international politics is confusing, and should be dropped, and that issues which may involve either domestic or international politics, or both, are not necessarily, indeed not often, characterized by power politics.

Mansbach and Vasquez offer what in effect is a world society paradigm, although they call it an issue paradigm.[85] They make four assumptions:

(1) Actors in global politics may consist of any individual or group that is able to contend for the disposition of a political stake.
(2) The fundamental causal processes that govern political interaction are the same regardless of whether contention occurs between or within groups. A single theory of politics, domestic and global, is therefore possible.
(3) Politics can be defined as the authoritative allocation of values through the resolution of issues . . .
(4) The shape of political contention is a function of three general factors – the characteristics of the issues on the agenda, the pattern of friendship–hostility among contending actors, and the nature of the institutional context in which allocation decisions must be made.[86]

The issue is the unit of analysis and it determines the actors, since they are not ascribed but coalesce as a function of the issue, as well as the level of analysis. Of central interest is the nature of the transactions concerning the issue – whether they are conflictful or cooperative.[87] We have in fact arrived at a world paradigm quite distinct from realism on at least two crucial dimensions: those of state centricity and power politics. This was a framework compatible with another major area of research that blossomed in the late 1950s and 1960s, namely integration theory.

Integration theory

The anarchical society of classical political theory and the realists implies some measure of integration, as indeed does any form of organized activity at whatever the level.[88] Integration has two complementary aspects: it is a state of affairs and a process. A state of affairs implies criteria setting a standard which, if met, constitutes integration. As a process there is movement towards (or away from in the case of disintegration) collective action based upon consensual values for the achievement of common goals, in which the parties have long-term expectations of mutually compatible and acceptable behaviour. The process is self-maintaining and, unlike imperialism which is an enforced integration, it is not based on coercion. Since no actor exists in total isolation, integration is ubiquitous.

While a state of global integration is not an important characteristic of world society in so far as realism is concerned, the conscious process of integration in Europe in the decades after the Second World War, and theorizing about it, provided a major challenge to the prevailing orthodoxies of the 1950s.[89] The process of decolonization, too, focused attention on integration, whether within states, such as India or Nigeria, or between states, as in the West Indies or West Africa. The mixed record suggests that insufficient attention was given to processes of disintegration from unitary states towards autonomy, federation, devolution, association or secession, despite the prevalence of disintegration in both the developed and developing worlds.

At the other end of the scale, the contemporary world is often described as 'one world' or a 'shrinking world'. This is not inaccurate: 'one world' problems abound, such as population, food, environment, development, women . . .[90] The shrinking world is reflected in the prodigious movement and interdependence of goods, services, ideas and people. How can and should such developments be conceptualized? The literature is heavily weighted in favour of certain integration theories – in particular neofunctionalism, regionalism and federalism – to the neglect of other approaches such as anarchism, cooperation or harmonization. Moreover, disintegration has only recently been taken seriously as something other than an anomaly or a pathological state.

The literature on integration can conveniently be placed into

three categories: that which has, as its essential function, to take
advantage of opportunities, or deal with problems, within the
ambit of the existing state system; that which envisages the
rebuilding of the existing state system; and that which goes beyond
or escapes from either the existing or a refurbished state system.[91]

Within the existing state system there is a variety of ways in
which a greater degree of integration can be sought without
substantial structural impact. At the lowest level, *cooperation*
involves an agreement to undertake a specific task without any
thought of task expansion or spillover into other areas. Where
there is a process of continuous adjustment by governments,
through a process of intensive consultation within an international
institution designed to serve important goals that can only be
achieved together, then *coordination* results, while *harmonization*
involves the joint setting of standards and goals, again, frequently,
in an institutional framework. However, this is not usually the
case in parallel national action, where complementary or compatible legislation and practices are instituted separately by different
actors in order to reduce the impact of frontiers. *Association*, on the
other hand, is usually more formal and has greater structural
implications. Paradoxically, it can enable both integration and
separation to be pursued at the same time, promoting integration
in certain domains, but restricting it in others, thereby denying the
'functional imperative' of task expansion and spillover. Donald
Puchala has suggested that an amalgam of these processes can form
a *Concordance System*.[92] In such a system governments remain
important actors, but so do actors from the subnational, transnational and supranational arenas. However, there is no fixed
relationship between such actors in terms of hierarchy or the like.
Nevertheless, there is a strong institutional framework and
bureaucracy concerned with and reflecting 'ordered, standardised,
planned, efficient problem-solving in relations'.[93] But this need not
be done centrally, nor is it necessarily obligatory. Attitudes of the
actors tend to be pragmatic and characterized by a high degree of
mutual sensitivity and responsiveness, with a willingness to
acknowledge, and act to promote, the greater good of the whole.
Moreover, a concordance system depends, for its successful operation, upon a large degree of popular support – a permissive
climate. However, the concordance system, and the 'menu' set out
above, does not lead to an irrevocable derogation of sovereignty.

Regionalism, however, is a hybrid, which may stay within the bounds of the existing state structure (its conception in the UN Charter) or become the embryo for a new state system. Region is a geographical concept and the doctrine of regionalism implies that geographical variables are a prime influence on behaviour. While the notion of region may be helpful in individual dimensions such as transport, it does not appear to be the great organizing principle when considering multidimensional phenomena. This much is evident from Bruce Russett's work.[94] The subject has not excited much comment for some time but there are signs of a renewed interest.[95]

Neo-functionalism, as a means to regional integration, goes beyond the conception of regionalism enshrined in the UN Charter in its implications for sovereignty, especially in the context of a regional or putative federal body coming to possess authority over national sub-systems, function by function. The end-goal of neo-functionalism is in fact a federation.[96] We have now gone beyond the confines of the existing state system into the realm of rebuilding the state system in a new form, in which the former units are arranged or otherwise changed so that they no longer have the attributes of sovereign independence. The establishment of federations is a case in point. In *federalism* the stress is upon a constitutional instrument setting out the relationship and competence of the federal and local bodies within a defined territorial area. *Consociation*, which may have greater relevance in the contemporary world, avoids the creation of strong central institutions in an endeavour to encourage joint and consensual decision-making, avoiding any possibility of the tyranny of the majority. It is appropriate for units with cleavages such as language, religion or ethnicity, which nevertheless wish to establish or maintain an element of political unity. This can be achieved by establishing a 'grand coalition' of representatives of the segments, each of which in effect maintains a veto. Although consociation is more typical within states, such as Switzerland, it is relevant between states, for example, in the European context.

The neofunctionalists undoubtedly owe much to Ernst Haas. Influenced by Mitrany, but aspiring to a more rigorous methodology, he pioneered the American study of European integration[97] before expressing doubts about the whole neofunctionalist enterprise.[98] Nevertheless, the impetus to the study of integration that

Haas's work provided must be handsomely acknowledged.[99] But the neofunctionalists' day is over because too much of their theorizing was dependent on an unusual period in Western Europe. Their reliance on the 'functional imperative' as an analytical tool, and by practitioners as the driving force for integration, was misplaced because it was too simplistic. Puchala's notion of concordance embracing diversity in a collectivity better describes the present European experience and may continue to do so after 1992.[100]

Neofunctionalism has been called a strategy for 'federalism by instalments'. The literature on federalism, which includes classics such as that by Sir Kenneth Wheare,[101] is voluminous. But constitution-building has, of late, been innovative more in the form of consociation as Lijphart's work attests.[102] Consociation, rather than federalism, may be able better to respond to a felt need for flexible arrangements which can reflect diversity. So, too, may collective goods[103] and some types of regime. This literature, however, and the theories to be found in it, does not go beyond the state system. The theories have implications for the sovereignty of participating states, but they are still state-centric in that their purpose is primarily to rebuild the state-system on a new and more appropriate basis. Some theories, however, specifically aim to go beyond the state system.

The informality, diversity and flexibility of *networks* are well suited to the growth and decline of systems of transactions and the need for intensely responsive institutional arrangements. Complex interdependence may give rise to *regimes* with sufficient flexibility to involve both state and non-state actors. At the extreme, mutual dependences without institutionalization of a formal kind are a form of *anarchy* which is usually only relevant at the micro-level. The centrality of the state system thus tends to be circumvented and possibly subverted – but not by direct confrontation. Typical of this tendency is *functionalism*.

The literature going beyond the state system received an excellent impulse from the pioneering, and more recent work of Karl Deutsch.[104] Anthony Judge, however, is less well-known, but his contribution has seminal elements that ought to have a wider dissemination, especially the thought-provoking symposium that he organized on the *Open Society of the Future*.[105]

Disintegration involves a process whereby units of a whole

assert themselves politically: for example, in multi-ethnic states where regions seek territorial separatism ranging from autonomy to independence.[106] The Soviet Union is now becoming a case in point. The negative connotation associated with the term disintegration is unfortunate, but 'building down' has no inherent positive or negative value. Furthermore, integration and disintegration are both significant phenomena in contemporary world society and they reflect the need to find diversity in collectivities. Theories of disintegration are thus to be taken seriously, because they address the important question of why separate groups persist and collective identities, in defiance of class or state, emerge, persist or resurge, becoming politically salient.

While much thinking about disintegration has been the obverse of theories of integration and cohesion or indirect approaches to disintegration or separatism, direct theories of disintegration have their intellectual forebear in the study of nationalism.[107] However, the two main primary or direct approaches of the last decade are internal colonialism and ethnicity.[108]

Internal colonialism, as developed by Hechter[109] and others, suggests that the very essence of politicized regional or ethnic assertiveness lies in the relationship between the political–economic–cultural centre and the periphery of a modern state. The fusion of ethnic differentiation with regional inequality renders disintegration almost unavoidable. Yet separatist tendencies on the part of rich territories also exist, so clearly internal colonialism cannot explain all separatisms. A far larger, but more disparate, group is formed by the proponents of ethnicity, which includes the early critics of the nation-building thesis such as Connor and Enloe, students of nationalism such as A. D. Smith and the proponents of consociationalism and of control. The cultural thrust of their argument is that ethnic identity alone is sufficient to lead to political assertiveness and militant separatism even without inequality or dominance. On the other hand, extended struggles for separation on the part of groups of a non-ethnic character have been motivated by extreme levels of inequality and discrimination. Thus both internal colonialism and ethnicity are relevant, since neither alone provides a complete explanation.

IR has a traditional bias against non-state actors, and the issue of disintegration and non-state nationalist movements has been seen as part of the subject only with difficulty. Yet ethnic politics, indeed identity studies, whether of an ethnic, individual, gender or national nature, are of increasing significance in contemporary world society and meat fit for IR scholars. An interesting example is Alexis Heraclides' study of the *International Dimension of Secessionist Movements* and the project of Gunnar Nielsson.[110] But this takes us into the speculative element of the final chapter.

For the time being we can now observe how the mould of realism has, for some, been dented and, for others, been shattered. Whether it be the state-centricity of the contemporary world or the pervasiveness of power politics the issue has been joined. While most scholars clung, perhaps hesitantly, to the axioms of realism, others were prepared to venture on the perilous enterprise of the exploration of world society. It is to their fortunes that our attention must now be turned.

Notes: Chapter 8

1 Thomas Kuhn, *The Structure of Scientific Revolutions* (Chicago: University of Chicago Press, Second Edition, enlarged, 1970), p. 7.
2 Inis L. Claude, *Power and International Relations* (New York: Random House, 1962).
3 J. W. Burton, *International Relations* (London: Cambridge University Press, 1967).
4 Charles R. Beitz, *Political Theory and International Relations* (Princeton, NJ: Princeton University Press, 1977), and John A. Vasquez, *The Power of Power Politics* (London: Frances Pinter, 1983).
5 Morton Kaplan, *System and Process in International Politics* (New York: Wiley, 1957); David Easton, *A Framework for Political Analysis* (Englewood Cliffs, NJ: Prentice-Hall, 1965); David Easton, *A System Analysis of Political Life* (London: University of Chicago Press, 1979); Gabriel A. Almond and James S. Coleman (eds), *The Politics of Developing Areas* (Princeton, NJ: Princeton University Press, 1960); Gabriel A. Almond and G. Bingham Powell Sr, (eds), *Comparative Politics* (Boston: Little, Brown, 1966).
6 Karl W. Deutsch, *Nationalism and Social Communication* (London: MIT Press, 1966), Karl W. Deutsch *et al., Political Community and the North Atlantic Area* (Princeton, NJ: Princeton University Press, 1957).
7 Karl W. Deutsch, *The Nerves of Government* (London: Collier–Macmillan, 1963).
8 David Mitrany, *A Working Peace System* (Chicago: Quadrangle, 1966).
9 James N. Rosenau (ed.), *The Domestic Sources of Foreign Policy* (New York: Free Press, 1967); Rosenau, *The Scientific Study of Foreign Policy* (London: Frances Pinter, 1980); Rosenau (ed.), *Comparing Foreign*

Policies (New York: Wiley, 1974); Rosenau (ed.), *Linkage Politics* (New York: Free Press, 1969).

10 Richard W. Mansbach and John A. Vasquez, *In Search of Theory* (New York: Columbia University Press, 1981).

11 Robert O. Keohane and Joseph S. Nye Jr (eds), *Transnational Relations and World Politics* (London: Harvard University Press, 1971).

12 Kenneth N. Waltz, *Man, the State and War* (New York: Columbia University Press, 1959).

13 J. David Singer, 'The level of analysis problem in international relations', in Klaus Knorr and Sidney Verba (eds), *The International System* (Princeton, NJ: Princeton University Press, 1961).

14 Charles McClelland, *Theory and the International System* (London: Collier–Macmillan, 1966), p. 84.

15 Joseph A. Schumpeter, *Imperialism and Social Classes* (Oxford: Blackwell, 1951), p. 7.

16 ibid., p. 33.

17 Ernst B. Haas, 'The balance of power: prescription, concept or propaganda?' *World Politics*, July 1953.

18 See especially Hans J. Morgenthau, *Politics among Nations* (New York: Knopf, 1959), 2nd revised and enlarged edition, Chapter XIV.

19 Claude, *Power and IR*, pp. 3–4.

20 ibid., pp. 92–3.

21 Burton, *International Relations*.

22 ibid., p. 54.

23 See J. W. Burton, *Conflict and Communication* (London: Macmillan, 1969).

24 Kaplan, *System and Process*.

25 ibid., Chapter 2.

26 K. E. Boulding: 'General systems theory: the skeleton of science', *General Systems*, Vol. 1, 1956, p. 17, quoted in J. W. Burton, *Systems, States, Diplomacy and Rules* (London: Cambridge University Press, 1968).

27 McClelland, *Theory and the International System*, p. 20.

28 Parsons stresses that four functional prerequisites must be performed if societal equilibrium is to be maintained: (1) Pattern maintenance, which is the ability of a system to ensure the reproduction of its own basic patterns, values and norms; (2) Adaptation to the changing environment; (3) Goal attainment; (4) Integration of the various functions and sub-systems into a coherent whole. For Parsons it is important to maintain such an equilibrium.

29 Richard Smith Beal, 'Theoretical innovations in systems theory in international relations', in K. P. Mishra and Richard Smith Beal (eds), *International Relations Theory* (New Delhi: Vikas, 1980), p. 83.

30 Easton, *A Framework*, pp. 26 ff.

31 ibid., p. 30.

32 ibid., p. 49.

33 ibid., p. 49.

34 Easton discusses this in David Easton, *The Political System* (New

York, Knopf, 1953), pp. 130 ff., and Easton, *A Framework*, pp. 50 ff.

35 J. W. Burton, *Systems, States*, p. 8.

36 ibid., pp. 8–10.

37 Richard W. Mansbach, Yale H. Ferguson and Donald E. Lampert, *The Web of World Politics* (Englewood Cliffs, NJ: Prentice-Hall, 1976).

38 See Burton, *Conflict and Communication*, and Edward E. Azar and John W. Burton (eds), *International Conflict Resolution* (Brighton: Harvester, 1986).

39 Easton, *A Framework*, p. 88.

40 Mansbach and Vasquez, *In Search of Theory*, p. 29.

41 Chalmers Johnson, *Revolutionary Change* (London: Longman, 1983).

42 ibid., pp. 57–8.

43 James N. Rosenau, *The Scientific Study of Foreign Policy* (London: Pinter, 1980), pp. 71–2.

44 Almond and Coleman, *The Politics of Developing Areas*, pp. 34–6.

45 ibid., p. 8.

46 ibid., p. 9.

47 ibid., p. 11.

48 ibid., p. 17.

49 Almond and Powell, *Comparative Politics*, p. 18.

50 Charles Tilly (ed.), *The Formation of Nation States in Western Europe* (Princeton, NJ: Princeton University Press, 1975), p. 618.

51 Deutsch, *The Nerves of Government*, p. 9.

52 ibid., pp. 76–7.

53 ibid., pp. 221 ff.

54 See note 6.

55 Donald J. Puchala: 'Integration theory and the study of international relations', in Richard L. Merritt and Bruce M. Russett (eds), *From National Development to Global Community* (London: Allen & Unwin, 1981), p. 148.

56 Oran Young: 'Interdependencies in world politics', in R. Maghroori and B. Romberg (eds), *Globalism Versus Realism* (Boulder, Colo: Westview, 1982), p. 60.

57 ibid., pp. 60–3.

58 ibid., pp. 64–5.

59 Peter Katzenstein has presented empirical evidence to suggest that 'international transactions are beginning again to approach or surpass the high points which they had reached in the early twentieth century'. Peter Katzenstein: 'International interdependence: Some long-term trends and recent changes', *International Organization*, Autumn 1975: 1033.

60 Karl Deutsch, 'Social mobilization and political development', *American Political Science Review*, September 1961.

61 For an explanation of Deutsch's approach and some criticisms of it, see the articles in his *Festschrift* by William J. Foltz and Michael C. Hudson, in Richard L. Merritt and Bruce M. Russett (eds), *From*

National Development to Global Community (London: Allen & Unwin, 1981).

62 R. C. Snyder, H. W. Bruch and B. Sapin, *Foreign Policy Decision-Making* (New York: Free Press, 1962), earlier versions of which circulated in the mid-1950s.

63 G. D. Paige, *The Korean Decision* (New York: Free Press, 1968) is a notable exception.

64 Michael Brecher, *Decisions in Israel's Foreign Policy* (London: Oxford University Press, 1975).

65 A. V. S. de Reuck and Julie Knight (eds), *Conflict in Society* (London: J. & A. Churchill, 1966). John Steinbruner, *The Cybernetic Theory of Decision* (Princeton, NJ: Princeton University Press, 1976).

66 Harold and Margaret Sprout, *Man-Milieu Relationship Hypotheses in the Context of International Politics* (Princeton, NJ: Center of International Studies, Princeton University, 1956).

67 Kenneth Boulding, *The Image* (Ann Arbor, Mich.: University of Michigan Press, 1961).

68 Joseph Frankel, *The Making of Foreign Policy* (London: Oxford University Press, 1963).

69 James N. Rosenau (ed), *International Politics and Foreign Policy* (New York: Free Press, 1961, 1969).

70 James N. Rosenau, *The Scientific Study of Foreign Policy; The Domestic Sources of Foreign Policy; The Study of Political Adaptation* (London: Frances Pinter, 1980); *Comparing Foreign Policies; Linkage Politics*.

71 Graham Allison, *The Essence of Decision* (Boston: Little, Brown, 1971).

72 David Braybrooke and Charles Lindblom, *The Strategy of Decision* (New York: Free Press, 1970).

73 Morton H. Halperin, *Bureaucratic Politics and Foreign Policy* (Washington: Brookings, 1974).

74 Pat McGowan (ed.), *The Sage International Yearbook of Foreign Policy Studies* (Beverly Hills, Calif.: Sage); numerous volumes including some edited with Charles Kegley.

75 M. R. Singer, *Weak States in a World of Powers* (New York: Free Press, 1972); Michael Handel, *Weak States in the International System* (London: Frank Cass, 1981); Christor Jonsson, *Superpower* (London: Pinter, 1984); Carsten Holbraad, *Middle Powers in International Politics* (New York: St Martin's Press, 1984); Sheila Harden, *Small is Dangerous* (New York: St Martin's Press, 1985).

76 J. De Rivera, *The Pyschological Dimension of Foreign Policy* (Columbus, Ohio: Charles E. Merrill, 1968); Robert Jervis, *The Logic of Images in International Relations* (Princeton, NJ: Princeton University Press, 1970); Robert Jervis, *Perception and Misperception in International Politics* (Princeton, NJ: Princeton University Press, 1976); I. L. Janis, *Victims of Grouthink* (Boston: Houghton Mifflin, 1982).

77 Robert Axelrod, *The Evolution of Cooperation* (New York: Basic Books, 1984).

78 Robert Rothstein, *Planning, Prediction and Policy Making in Foreign*

Affairs (Boston: Little, Brown, 1972); Lincoln P. Bloomfield, *The Foreign Policy Process* (Englewood Cliffs, NJ: Prentice-Hall, 1982); A. J. R. Groom: 'Academics and practitioners', in Michael H. Banks (ed.), *Conflict in World Society* (Brighton: Wheatsheaf, 1984) p. 8.

79 Harold Nicolson, *Diplomacy* (London: Oxford University Press, 1963).

80 Paul Taylor and A. J. R. Groom (eds), *Global Issues in the United Nations' System* (London: Macmillan, 1989).

81 Robert Boardman and A. J. R. Groom (eds), *The Management of Britain's External Relations* (London: Macmillan, 1973).

82 Charles Hermann (ed.), *International Crises* (New York: Free Press, 1972); Coral Bell, *The Conventions of Crisis* (London: Oxford University Press, 1971); Daniel Frei (ed.), *International Crises and Crisis Management* (Farnborough: Saxon House, 1978).

83 See Rosenau's collected papers in a trilogy published by Frances Pinter in London including *The Scientific Study of Foreign Policy* (1980), *The Study of Political Adaptation* (1980), *The Study of Global Interdependence* (1980).

84 John H. Herz, *International Politics in the Atomic Age* (New York: Columbia University Press, 1962) and Andrew M. Scott, *The Revolution in Statecraft* (Durham, NC: Duke University Press, 1962).

85 Mansbach and Vasquez, *In Search of Theory*.

86 ibid., pp. 68–9.

87 In an earlier work Mansbach and colleagues came up with the astonishing finding, 'The more conflictful the behaviour, the less the state-centric model can explain; the more cooperative the behaviour, the more the state-centric model can explain!' Mansbach, Ferguson and Lampert, *The Web of World Politics*, p. 278.

88 See A. J. R. Groom and Alexis Heraclides, 'Integration and disintegration', in Margot Light and A. J. R. Groom (eds), *International Relations: A Handbook of Current Theory* (London: Frances Pinter, 1985), on which this section draws liberally.

89 See Donald Puchala, in Richard L. Merritt and Bruce M. Russett, *From National Development*.

90 See Paul Taylor and A. J. R. Groom (eds), *Global Issues*.

91 This framework is that used in A. J. R. Groom and Paul Taylor (eds), *Frameworks for International Cooperation* (London: Pinter, 1990). This volume contains a chapter on each of the approaches mentioned, with appropriate reference to the literature.

92 Donald J. Puchala, 'Of blind men, elephants and international integration', in M. Smith, R. Little and M. Shackleton (eds), *Perspectives on World Politics* (London: Croom Helm, 1981), pp. 238 ff.

93 ibid., p. 240.

94 Bruce N. Russett, *International Regions and the International System* (Westport, Conn: Greenwood, 1975).

95 See, for example, Maurice Bertrand: 'Some reflections on reform of the United Nations', in Paul Taylor and A. J. R. Groom (eds), *International Institutions at Work* (London: Pinter, 1988).

96 For an overview, see A. J. R. Groom, 'Neofunctionalism: A case of mistaken identity', *Political Science*, July 1978.
97 Ernst Haas, *The Uniting of Europe* (London: Stevens, 1958).
98 Ernst Haas, *The Obsolescence of Regional Integration Theory* (Berkeley, Calif.: University of California, Institute of International Studies, 1976).
99 See Leon Lindberg, *The Political Dynamics of European Economic Integration* (Stanford, Calif.: Stanford University Press, 1963); Leon Lindberg and S. Scheingold, *Europe's Would-Be Polity* (Englewood Cliffs, NJ: Prentice-Hall, 1970); Lindberg and Scheingold (eds), *Regional Integration* (Cambridge, Mass.: Harvard University Press, 1971).
100 See Puchala, in Smith *et al.* (eds), *Perspectives on World Politics* and A. J. R. Groom, 'Europe: A case of collective amnesia', *Australian Outlook*, April 1989.
101 Kenneth Wheare, *Federal Government* (London: Greenwood, 1980). See also A. H. Birch: 'Approaches to the study of federalism', *Political Studies*, XIV, 1, 1966.
102 Arend Lijphart, *Democracy in Plural Societies* (New Haven, Conn.: Yale University Press, 1980); 'Consociational democracy', *World Politics* XXI, 2, 1969; 'Consociation and federation', *Canadian Journal of Political Science*, XXII, 3, 1979.
103 See John Gerard Ruggie, 'Collective goods and future international collaboration', *American Political Science Review*, LXVI, 3, 1972; Bruce M. Russett and J. Sullivan, 'Collective goods and international organization', *International Organization*, XXV, 4; Mancur Olsen, *The Logic of Collective Action* (Cambridge, Mass.: Harvard University Press, 1971).
104 Karl Deutsch, *Nationalism and Social Communication*; Deutsch, *Nationalism and its Alternatives* (New York: Knopf, 1969); Deutsch *et al.*, *Political Community and the North Atlantic Area*.
105 *Open Society of the Future* (Brussels: Union of International Associations, 1973); A. J. N. Judge, 'The world network of organisations', *International Associations*, 24, 1, 1972; A. J. N. Judge, in Paul Taylor and A. J. R. Groom (eds), *International Organization* (London: Frances Pinter, 1978); A. J. N. Judge in A. J. R. Groom and Paul Taylor (eds), *Functionalism* (London: University of London Press, 1975).
106 Our understanding and awareness of this literature owes much to the work of Alexis Heraclides.
107 See A. D. Smith, *The Ethnic Revival in the Modern World* (Cambridge: Cambridge University Press, 1981); Smith *Nationalism in the Twentieth Century* (Oxford: Martin Robertson, 1979); Smith *State and Nation in the Third World* (Brighton: Wheatsheaf, 1983).
108 See A. H. Birch, 'Minority nationalist movements and theories of political integration' *World Politics*, XXX, 3, 1978, for a useful summary.
109 Michael Hechter, *Internal Colonialism* (London: Routledge & Kegan Paul, 1975).

110 Alexis Heraclides, *The International Dimension of Secessionist Movements* (London: Frank Cass, 1990). Neilsson's project is still under way but working papers are in circulation. See 'Sobre los conceptos de etnicidad, nacion y estado' (On the concepts of ethnicity, nation and state), in Alfonso Perez–Agote (ed.), *Sociologia del Nacionalismo* (Vitoria: University of Basque Country Press, 1989).

Further reading

Allison, Graham. *The Essence of Decision*. Boston: Little, Brown, 1971.

Almond, Gabriel A. and Powell, G. Bingham Sr (eds). *Comparative Politics*. Boston: Little, Brown, 1966.

Beitz, Charles R. *Political Theory and International Relations*. Princeton, NJ: Princeton University Press, 1977.

Burton, J. W. *International Relations*. London: Cambridge University Press, 1965.

Claude, Inis L. *Power and International Relations*. New York: Random House, 1962.

Deutsch, Karl W. *Nationalism and Social Communication*. London: MIT Press, 1966.

Deutsch, Karl W. *The Nerves of Government*. London: Collier–Macmillan, 1963.

Easton, David. *A Framework for Political Analysis*. Englewood Cliffs, NJ: Prentice-Hall, 1965.

Groom, A. J. R. and Taylor, Paul (eds). *Frameworks for International Cooperation*. London: Pinter, 1990.

Johnson, Chalmers. *Revolutionary Change*. London: Longman, 1983.

Kaplan, Morton. *System and Process in International Politics*. New York: Wiley, 1957.

Keohane, Robert O. and Nye, Joseph S. Jr (eds). *Transnational Relations and World Politics*. London: Harvard University Press, 1971.

McClelland, Charles. *Theory and the International System*. London: Collier–Macmillan, 1966.

Mitrany, David. *A Working Peace System*. Chicago: Quadrangle, 1966.

Rosenau, James N. *The Scientific Study of Foreign Policy*. London: Frances Pinter, 1980.

Rosenau, James N. (ed.): *International Politics and Foreign Policy*. New York: Free Press, 1969.

Smith, Michael; Little, Richard and Shackleton, Michael (eds). *Perspectives on World Politics*. London: Croom Helm, 1981.

Snyder, Richard C. *et al*. *Foreign Policy Decision-Making*. New York: Free Press, 1962.

Vasquez, John A. *The Power of Power Politics*. London: Frances Pinter, 1983.

Waltz, Kenneth N. *Man, the State and War*. New York: Columbia University Press, 1959.

9 *World society approaches*

> To conceive of societies as confederal, overlapping, intersecting networks rather than as simple totalities complicates theory.
> (Michael Mann)[1]

Two of the most important forebears of international relations as a discipline were international law and diplomatic history. International law, as an organic element of the state system, is likely to be important as long as the state system functions. Indeed, it may outlast that system by becoming the legal component of various world society approaches or transnational regimes. Moreover, international law can be seen in many guises. For example, the Austinian notion that law is the sovereign's command and is only law so long as it is backed by an effective sanction fits well into the realists' schema. And the historical derivation of international law must not be forgotten: it arose out of the Christian Commonwealth of Europe and was imposed by the rising European Powers on the rest of the world, whether they liked it or not. It reflected European values of Christianity and Capitalism – the prevailing social and economic system – and it became a world system through Colonialism and, where necessary, through Coercion – the four 'Cs'. While international law tends to reflect the values and the interests of the great Powers of the past, this is not entirely or always so. International law can also arise out of a jural community reflecting genuinely shared values and be based upon reciprocity, convenience, coordination or a high degree of normative consensus. Then law is not coercive, but consensual. As such it is a good predictor of behaviour because it reflects behavioural patterns emanating from freely shared values. Where no such consensus exists, where the dispute is over basic values rather than within a consensus on values, law tends to become a weapon of propaganda to be used by those who benefit from the status quo against those who wish to change it to reflect different value systems and conceptions of world order. It acts then not as a constraint or a guide to and predictor of behaviour, but as a normative stick with which to beat an adversary.

The international lawyers, who played such an important and fructuous role in fashioning the great consensus in IR in the first decade of our discipline, and before, viewed law as a positive reflection of the progressive elements of free democratic nation-states associating themselves in a League of Nations to create a better international community. Law would henceforth reflect a genuine jural community rather than the power of states, and as such the need for sanctions would be rare. The goal was to build an international community based on collective security, in a manner similar to that of national communities. We have seen how, in political relationships, they failed and realism returned to rule the roost. But they did not fail in economic and social matters – the functional dimensions – as the Bruce Report on those aspects of the League's activities attested in a clear and forthright manner. Thus there were lessons to be learned from both the successes and the failures of the League, as we shall see in the discussion of functionalism as a prescriptive approach to world order and as a description of world society. But what of the second great intellectual forebear of IR as a discipline – diplomatic or international history?

In a sense we have law and history with us always, because any sort of order implies some form of law and it is rare indeed for there to be no hint of a collective memory. But what we choose from that memory is influenced by what we are trying to do as well as having its influence on our goals. We use history for a purpose, but in part history shapes what that purpose will be. There can be realist history or structuralist history, for all history is selective. Many of the early holders of chairs in IR were historians, especially in Britain, and their attitude to their old calling was ambivalent, because diplomatic history tended to be imbued with the tenets of realism, and was thus out of focus with the new spirit of the times, both in terms of philosophy and method, for example, the desire to be 'scientific'. However, old methods prevailed and the intellectual and methodological baggage of the new discipline was, in its first decades, clearly reflective of its legal and historical forebears – but not entirely so, as the names of Lewis Richardson and Quincy Wright suggest, and these were both concerned with central aspects of the new field, that is, the study of war. One other name comes to mind in this context, that of Arnold Toynbee, for long a stalwart of Chatham House and a historian of civilizations. Both of his historical fortes, that of contemporary international history and the study of the grand sweep of civilization, are part of IR 'now' and they are not restricted to any particular framework or paradigm. On the contrary, they are prominent in all aspects of the subject. Among the new school of realists Robert Gilpin has a strong sense of international history and in the United States the 'revisionist' school of historians of the Cold War had the merit of being instrumental, with others, in bringing structuralist ideas once again into the mainstream of Anglo-American thought. But a Toynbeean grand sweep of history can be found in the work of George Modelski, Immanual Wallerstein and Michael Mann, all of whom bear consideration, and it is to Mann that we turn in this chapter. He is one of several British and American historians who have, in the last decade, given IR a historical perspective, beyond the minutiae of the diplomatic historian, to our great benefit. Mann's position fits as well into the world society approach as any other and it is to him, therefore, that we turn first before considering other world society approaches – those of Mitrany's functionalism, the *IO* network, global approaches and Burton's world society framework.

The domination of Europe as a process

Modelski, Wallerstein and Mann are all concerned with the rise of the Eurocentric world, not so much as a chronology of a particular set of human beings, but as a social process. Mann's views are set out in the first volume of a longer study that is still being written.[2] However, in his history of power to AD 1760, Mann gives us the central thrust of his argument.

Mann's approach stems from two statements, of which the first is that 'Societies are constituted of multiple overlapping and intersecting sociospatial networks of power.'[3] Societies are therefore neither unitary, nor social systems, nor totalities.

Because there is no whole, social relations cannot be reduced 'ultimately', 'in the last instance', to some systemic property of it – like the 'mode of material production', or the 'cultural' or 'normative system', or the 'form of military organization'. . . . Because there is no social system, there is no 'evolutionary' process within it. Because humanity is not divided into a series of bounded totalities, 'diffusion' of social organization does not occur between them. Because there is no totality, individuals are not constrained in their behaviour by 'social structure as a whole', and so it is not helpful to make a distinction between 'social action' and 'social structure'.[4]

Mann, unlike many of his fellow sociologists and others, does not conceive of society as an 'unproblematic, unitary totality', nor does he take politics or states as the 'society' or unit of analysis. He puts it bluntly: 'I would abolish the concept of "society" altogether.'[5]

Mann's second position accounts for societies, their structure and their history 'in terms of the interrelations of . . . the four sources of social power: ideological, economic, military, and political relationships'[6] He goes on to state that,

These are (1) overlapping networks of social interaction, not dimensions, levels, or factors of a single social totality . . . (2) They are also organizations, institutional means of attaining human goals. Their primacy comes not from the strength of human desires for ideological, economic, military or political satisfaction but from the particular organizational means each possesses to attain human goals, whatever these may be . . . The central problems concern organization, control, logistics, communication – the capacity to organize and control people, materials, and territories, and the development of this capacity throughout history. The four sources of social power offer alternative organizational means of social control. In various times and places each has offered enhanced capacity for organization that has enabled the form of its organization to dictate for a time the form of societies at large.[7]

Mann does not conceive of this as a smooth process, but one in which there are spurts or breakthroughs that engender major structural transformation. Although these may be cumulative, they 'are not part of a single immanent process'.[8]

Mann's conception encourages us to look upon world society as a loose-fitting confederation of cross-cutting networks of interaction. This, in his view, characterizes the contemporary world as much as the past. Whereas in the past such networks were at most worldwide in that they touched upon several major regions of the world, now it could be argued that of his four principal networks some are broaching a global extent and so we are approaching a totality for the first time. However, for the time being, few would dissent from Mann's assertion that the 'boundaries and capacities of these networks do not coincide. Some networks have greater capacity for organizing intensive and extensive, authoritative and diffused, social cooperation than others'[9] – hence the four separate sources of social power: networks of ideological, economic, military and political power. They are neither co-terminate nor is any one of them predominant in any permanent manner. We are tempted to dally in some of the glories of Mann's historical analysis as he shows how one, another or several of his networks lie at the basis of a historical spurt or breakthrough, but that is not the purpose of our book, fascinating though it would be. However, we cannot leave Mann's work without returning, with him, to the four sources of power, each of which is 'capable in decisive "world-historical moments" of generally reorganizing social life . . .'[10]

For Mann, ideological power has two distinct meanings:

First it offers a *transcendent* vision of social authority. It unites human beings by claiming that they possess ultimately meaningful, often divinely granted, common qualities . . . The second means of ideological power is what I called *immanence*, the strengthening of the internal morale of some existing social group by giving it a sense of ultimate significance and meaning in the cosmos, by reinforcing its normative solidarity, and by giving it common ritual and aesthetic practices.[11]

Economic power likewise has two components, the first of which involves cooperation (often coercive) in the exploitation of nature to produce goods and the second concerns commerce and consumption. The means of military power are what Mann calls 'concentrated coercion'[12] whereas the 'first means of *political power* is *territorial centralization*'.[13] But Mann maintains that 'autonomous state powers are precarious' because:

human societies are not unitary systems but varying conglomerations of multiple, overlapping, intersecting networks of
power. But where state powers are enhanced, then 'societies'
become more unitary, more bounded, more separated out from
one another, and more structured internally.

Additionally, their interrelations raise a second means of
political power, *geopolitical diplomacy*. No known state has yet
managed to control all relations travelling across its boundaries,
and so much social power has always remained 'transnational'
. . . But an increase in territorial centralization also increases
orderly diplomatic activity . . . Where centralization is proceeding in more than one neighbouring territorial area, a regulated
multistate system will develop.[14]

We are back in the familiar territory of IR as traditionally defined.
And Mann does not baulk at the question of change and what
'types of power configuration have pioneered jumps in world-
historical collective social development'.[15] He suggests that there
are two:

1 *Empires of domination* combined military concentrated coercion
with an attempt at state territorial centralization and geopolitical
hegemony. So they also combined intensive authoritative
powers along the narrow routes of penetration of which an army
was capable, with weaker, but still authoritative and far more
extensive, power wielded over the whole empire and neighbouring clients by its central state. The principal reorganizing role is
here played by a mixture of military and political power, with
the former predominating. 2 In *multi-power-actor civilizations*,
decentralized power actors competed with one another within
an overall framework of normative regulation. Here extensive
powers were diffuse, belonging to the overall culture rather than
to any authoritative power organization. Intensive powers were
possessed by a variety of small, local power actors, sometimes
states in a multistate civilization, sometimes military elites,
sometimes classes and fractions of classes, usually a mixture of
all of these. The predominant reorganizing forces were here
economic and ideological, though in varied combinations and
often with political and geopolitical help.[16]

The relevance of Mann's observation is clear and cheering, at least to those in the world society approaches who point frequently to the fundamental problems of the contemporary world such as nuclear war, ecology, the global economic divide, racism and the like, and the need for change. But they oscillate between the world and the individual as the unit of analysis. Mann's second model suggests that a spurt or a breakthrough is possible while encompassing both of these units. An empire of domination or the attempt to achieve one is not necessary to achieve a breakthrough. There are other ways. Where it will come from, Mann can only hint. He suggests that as a power centre develops it tends to lift its neighbours, 'who learn its power techniques but adapt them to their different social and geographical circumstances'[17] – often less confined and constrained circumstances. Here the interplay of the four sources of power may have greater scope and something new may be generated. Where it might be now, Mann does not surmise, but a modish view would be to suggest Asia and particularly East Asia, although South Asia and the Islamic world may yet be the locus of the next historical surprise. In the past the movement has been, largely fortuitously, westward. But what is to the west depends greatly on where you are!

Michael Mann's first volume ends in 1760, which is late enough to bring it within the purview of IR as usually defined – it is, after all, the heyday of the balance of power. But his work and that of other historical sociologists has led us back to vistas that we cannot and should not ignore. Indeed, some would argue that our subject is as much the political sociology of world society as it is anything else more narrowly or differently defined. However, historical sociologists differ among themselves and the sweep of history can be seen in economic or more purely political terms, as we shall see. It is because Mann puts the emphasis on the changing interactions of four different forms of social power, which overlap and intertwine, but do not coalesce into a coherent whole, that he sets a suitable historical backcloth to approaches to world society from within IR that share some of these same characteristics.

Functionalism

International functionalism as an approach to world order owes much to the work of David Mitrany. Mitrany was, of course, one of many writers in this approach, but his work has achieved such a salience that we can take it as an exemplar – perhaps an extreme one – much in the manner that Morgenthau's *Politics among Nations* is taken as an exemplar of realism. In addition, we must bear in mind that Mitrany was also a practical man of affairs in journalism, business and international organization as well as in transatlantic academic life. We are concerned with a short essay entitled *A Working Peace System*[18] that grew out of Mitrany's practical experience in his native Balkans and his role in a Foreign Office think-tank on the future of international organization during the Second World War. It was republished in 1966, whereafter Mitrany's conceptions again excited interest.[19] The style is an oldfashioned British one of the short succinct essay, distilling the wisdom of a lifetime, and written in exquisite prose.[20]

Mitrany sought to devise a strategy to create and sustain a 'working peace system'.[21] He was not offering a panacea for world government, the idea of which is completely alien to his thought. His premise was that form should follow function, so that the institutional element would reflect and promote the activity being performed without any constitutional hindrance and, in particular, without attempting to organize the activity around state actors or state boundaries.

But not any system of transactions is appropriate, according to the proponents of functionalism. Only those systems that reflect human needs and maximize welfare are truly functionalist, because they have not been 'corrupted' by state actors pursuing state and institutional values at the expense of human values. Indeed, it is precisely because the state is unable to guarantee such basic needs as security and the maximization of welfare, as evidenced by the world wars and the great depression, that functional institutions are needed. In a functional institution, problems will be dealt with in an open participatory manner by the relevant experts and concerned public on the basis of the best technical knowledge, and felt needs, free from the pressures of power politics and state chancelleries. Gradually, as more activities are organized along such lines, a working peace system will evolve, bringing people together in a positive manner to resolve problems and maximize welfare, rather than keep them fearfully and miserably apart.

To achieve such a working peace system, state sovereignty and national loyalties will not be attacked frontally but will be rendered harmless and obsolete, to the extent that they have no continuing functional rationale, by the growth of other institutions based on systems of transactions that maximize welfare. To this extent the state will 'wither away'. For Mitrany the starting point lies in the economic and social welfare sphere. This is thought to be separate from the power-ridden high politics of interstate relations. Individuals, peoples, groups, and even in some circumstances governments, will be working together to solve their common problems and maximize welfare. Gradually they will develop a sense of community, and common interests will arise out of interests previously held in common.

This will take place through a twofold learning process of task expansion and spillover in which cooperation will deepen in existing areas and spread to new domains. As such cooperative habits are established and nurtured, and when a realization of the benefits of such cooperation becomes more widespread, power politics will be tamed and then transformed. After individuals and groups join the diverse functional bodies, the institutions of the state are held to lose their salience and significance and cross-national ties will develop, which will be both instrumental and attitudinal. The greater the number and diversity of ties the less likely is war to occur, since any war is likely to disrupt such ties and thereby diminish welfare. War will quickly be rejected as a policy of cutting off the nose to spite the face. Thus, instead of separate states, the repositories of loyalty and inefficient sources of welfare, crashing into one another like balls on a billiard table, the world will evolve towards a myriad of actors concerned with a variety of topics organized along lines best suited for the management of matters of common concern to the parties involved. In short, it will no longer resemble the billiard ball analogy, but that of a cobweb.

Scientists, businessmen, students, workers and the like will develop their functional loyalties in addition to, and then instead of, their national loyalties. Moreover, superordinate goals will be identified and sought after, goals which, while desired by all, can only be attained through cooperation. The achievement and enjoyment of such goals will buttress peace and form an important element in the working peace system. In time, the barriers to relationships caused by state boundaries and loyalties will be circumvented and lifted, and welfare, participation and peace will be maximized. Security will depend not upon deterrence and threat systems, but will arise out of association, that is, through playing roles in systems of transactions that are valued and valuable to all the parties concerned on the basis of criteria acceptable to them. In short, it will be a working peace system.

The functionalist approach purports to be both a description and a prescription. It claims to describe aspects of contemporary world society in which there is a variety of effective actors besides states and in which levels of analysis are clearly intertwined. Moreover, while government has got bigger and has penetrated into many new facets of the activities of groups and individuals, it has also become functionalized. Departments, boards, ministries go their own way with little coordination or control. Government is no longer monolithic, but is made up of semi-independent, functionally based components. As a prescription the belief is that functional organization will bring about a working peace system, that it should facilitate the participation of all those relevant, and that it will maximize welfare by dealing with activities on the basis of expert advice on the merits of the question, and not in a context of the pursuit of power interests.

The goals of the functionalist approach – peace, welfare and participation – have been questioned much less than the practicability of its prescription for achieving them. The success of such a working peace system is heavily dependent on the learning process. It is abundantly evident that the learning and spread of cooperative habits through task expansion and spillover are far from being automatic. Indeed, the very separation of tasks that the functionalists propose has proved in some cases to be more of a hindrance to the learning of cooperative habits than an inducement to their achievement. It has also been argued many times that welfare relations and the economic and social sphere can be, and often are, highly political in the power politics sense. But the functionalist, by modifying rather than abandoning his argument, can still make his point. If, instead of beginning his functionalist endeavours in the economic and social welfare sectors, from which he hopes that they will begin to circumscribe and tame power politics, he starts from an area of legitimized politics, then his argument may still be valid, since he can seek to promote a learning process in which legitimized politics begin to efface power politics irrespective of the type of system (economic, cultural or whatever).

The functionalist would be unwise to surmise that a functionally organized world would be a conflict-free world. Conflict, after all, is endemic in the sense that separate decision-making centres are likely to embark upon incompatible policies. This phenomenon can arise, presumably, irrespective of whether the actors concerned are functional institutions, actors within them, or states. The relevant question concerns reactions when these incompatibilities have been recognized by the parties concerned. Are there appropriate and legitimized mechanisms available for handling the conflict, for steering in a cybernetic sense, or will parties persist in their courses, the one trying to impose the burden of change on the other? The functionalist asserts that institutional flexibilities, participatory decision-making and cross-cutting ties augur well for the development of legitimized conflict-handling mechanisms. A functionally organized world society would not eliminate conflict, but it would act as a prophylactic and possibly alter the form of conflict, by putting the stress more on non-violent forms of coercive activity.

Functionalism and imperialism in modern guise are, almost by definition, incompatible, since functional institutions are claimed to be system-wide, participatory and maximizing of general welfare, and thus unlikely vehicles for exploitation. Such functionalist prescriptions are, however, more appropriate for relations within the developed world, with their countervailing institutions, than in the relations between the developed and developing worlds. Yet, more organization in the functionalist mode, which is genuinely participatory and concerned with the welfare of all, might reduce the degree of exploitation of the Third World by the developed countries.

The functionalist is hard pressed to justify his faith in the notion of technical decision-making by experts on the merits of the question. First, he has to provide for the desired degree of participation by non-expert actors in the system. Secondly, a question can be decided on its technical merits only if there is a prior consensus on the values to be applied in deciding upon what constitutes merit. Corrupting political pressures may be kept at bay once the rules of the game have been decided upon: technical expert decision-making may then hold sway. But what if a functional institution, and relations between such institutions, is not based upon a value consensus? We are back to power politics. Functional institutions may facilitate the legitimization of the decision-making process and relationships, but it cannot guarantee this.

The transfer of loyalties from outmoded, power-maximizing state institutions to welfare-maximizing functional institutions is also an open question. Humankind is well known for its proclivity to bite the hand that feeds it. Empirical evidence is not clear about the relationship between affective ties and the satisfaction of utilitarian needs. Thus, even if a functional institution maximizes welfare and is fully participatory, there is no guarantee that it will attract the sort of loyalty that presently resides with national entities, the more so since such affective ties will be dissipated among a range of institutions. Once again, therefore, the central role of the learning process, and the functionalist's sanguinity in regard to it, comes to the fore. Yet is is precisely this learning process that the neofunctionalists latched on to when surveying the tenets of functionalism in their search for an explanation of integration, and particularly of Western European integration.

The differences between functionalists and neofunctionalists are marked. The neofunctionalists' unit of analysis is the state, and not a system of transactions, and their approach is teleological – a single decision-making centre for a newly integrated territorially based unit. Functionalists abhor such regional integration, in the form of state-building, unless it is based on coterminal systems of transactions, which in Europe, and elsewhere, is not the case. Thus, while the interests of both may coincide when restricted to a single functional dimension, such as the European Coal and Steel Community, they diverge radically in a multi-dimensional analysis. Functionalism, in Mitrany's conception, is a way to a world society that is beyond the state system, rather than an attempt to rebuild it on a regional basis. It is not a theory in any strict sense, but an argument pointing to a possible way to a better world. Rather than being a panacea, it is a sense of direction reflecting a set of (liberal) values. And the alternatives have been found wanting in the achievement of its goals of peace, welfare and participation. Mitrany is more a forerunner of Burton than of Haas and the neofunctionalists. But, before we turn to Burton, we must consider other related approaches – transactionalism and complex interdependence on the one hand and world order modelling on the other. Joseph Nye, who is a leading exponent of the former, came to it from his well-known studies of regional integration in East Africa and elsewhere. Indeed, as a major contributor to their development, Nye was thoroughly imbued with neofunctionalist ideas. In his early work with Robert Keohane the emphasis was put on the transnational aspects of neofunctionalism rather than the state rebuilding aspects.

The International Organization (IO) *network*

The reference to the journal *International Organization* should not be taken to imply that there is a school within world society approaches that is advocating the virtues of international institutions. This is not the case. Rather, for nearly two decades, *IO* has been the vehicle for a *coterie* or network of scholars to express their ideas and publish their research. Their contribution has been highly influential, clever and of an impressive standard, as well as agenda setting, as befits the work of those climbing into the leadership of the profession in the United States. Although they do not form a school, they are aware of, and respect, each others' work and have put *IO* to good use. But they are also part of the insularity of the IR profession in the United States to which Holsti referred so tellingly in *The Dividing Discipline*.[22]

One of the great contributions that this network has made has been to investigate notions of transnationalism, complex interdependence and regimes. They have done so with an eye to our two dimensions of state-centricity and power politics.[23] And they have been careful to undertake accompanying empirical work. To generalize, Keohane, Nye, Krasner and others are fully aware of the arguments regarding declining state-centricity and the changing nature and means of power politics, which they certainly do not consider as ubiquitous. They see the need to explain these phenomena, but they approach them from the perspectives of state-centricity and power politics. Mitrany, Burton, Mansbach and Vasquez approach the phenomena from the perspective of world society and legitimized politics. It is as though each is regarding the same phenomena from opposite ends of the telescope. The emphases differ considerably, but there is much in common. The special issue of *IO* on transnational relations, edited by Keohane and Nye, is a case in point.

Transnational Relations and World Politics is an impressive work.[24] Keohane and Nye commissioned a number of studies on a variety of areas involving different actors such as multinational enterprises, transnational revolutionary movements, the Ford Foundation and the Roman Catholic Church. They focused on what they anticipated would be

> five major effects of transnational interactions and organizations, all with direct or indirect consequences for mutual sensitivity and thereby for interstate politics . . . (1) attitude changes, (2) international pluralism, (3) increases in constraints on states through dependence and interdependence, (4) increases in the ability of certain governments to influence others, and (5) the emergence of autonomous actors with private foreign policies that may deliberately oppose or impinge on state policies.[25]

In their conclusion the editors reject the realists' idea that the state-centric model can *grosso modo* accommodate transnational relations simply because, in direct confrontation with transnational actors, governments prevail and that transnational relations, which have always existed, do not affect significantly the great issues of security, status and war.[26] They go on to state that:

> In summary, we believe that the essays in this volume support our contention that the state-centric paradigm provides an inadequate basis for the study of changing world politics. Transnational actors sometimes prevail over governments. These 'losses' by governments can often be attributed to the rising costs of unilateral government action in the face of transnational relations. For a state-centric theory this is represented as 'environment'. But it is theoretically inadequate to use the exogenous variables of the environment to account for outcomes in the interaction of various actors in world politics. State-centric theories are not very good at explaining such outcomes because they do not describe the complex patterns of

coalitions between different types of actors . . . We hope that our 'world politics paradigm' will help to redirect attention toward the substance of international politics, in which the major theoretical as well as practical questions can be found, and away from the relatively unenlightening application of subtle reasoning or sophisticated methodology to problems that have been narrowly defined by a limited theoretical outlook or the wrong units of analysis . . . The 'world politics paradigm' does not provide scholars with an instant revelation, but it does provide them with at least one path toward relevance.[27]

It was a path that Keohane and Nye trod with circumspection, as *Power and Interdependence* revealed.[28]

Keohane and Nye refer, by interdependence, 'to situations characterized by reciprocal effects among countries or among actors in different countries'.[29] Such situations do not always result in mutual benefit, since 'Our perspective implies that interdependent relationships will always involve costs, since interdependence restricts autonomy: but it is impossible to specify a priori whether the benefits of a relationship will outweigh the costs.'[30] It may be that everyone will gain, but not in what they perceive as an equal or equitable manner, and so there may be 'distributional conflict'.[31] This distributional conflict is likely to be structured by the relative degrees of sensitivity and vulnerability of the parties concerned. Sensitivity involves the speed and the extent to which changes in one country entail costly changes in another. Vulnerability concerns the relative availability and cost of alternatives to having to accept the burdens imposed by the sensitivity of the second country. If the effects of changes in one country are immediate, great and costly for the second country, and there is no alternative available, then that country may be at a disadvantage vis-à-vis its interdependent partner. Of course such disadvantages could be nullified by the initial country avoiding the damaging change – steering in Deutsch and Burton's terminology in an example of legitimized politics – or by attempting to cope with the costly effects jointly in a problem-solving manner. On the other hand, the initiating country could thrust the burden of change on its partner by refusing to change in a power response. Keohane and Nye give greater attention to the latter. If 'Power can be thought of as the ability of an actor to get others to do something they otherwise would not do (and at an acceptable cost to the actor) . . . [and] can also be conceived in terms of control over outcomes . . .'[32], then complex interdependence is an interesting concept to be explored along the power politics' spectrum.

The notion of complex interdependence, which Keohane and Nye rightly see as challenging the precepts of realism, conceives of 'a world in which actors other than states participate directly in world politics, in which a clear hierarchy of issues does not exist, and in which force is an ineffective instrument of policy'.[33] However, distributional conflict can still exist so that power politics in forms other than force can be prevalent, although its presence in one issue area does not necessarily presage its spread to, or its presence in, other areas. If the balance of power conceives of cooperation in a world of conflict, complex interdependence depicts conflict in a world of cooperation. The case studies in which Keohane and Nye explore distributional conflict concern complex interdependence in oceans and monetary policy involving the United States in its relationships with Canada and Australia. The case studies are not entirely apposite because, although they concern issue areas, they nevertheless create parameters for their analysis by bringing in the 'United States', 'Canada', and 'Australia'. Thus the study had a predeliction towards power politics and state-centricity – the all-pervasive influence of which it purported to deny. A way of thinking that might avoid this tendency is to think in terms of regimes – a subject to which the *IO* network paid considerable attention.

Stephen Krasner was the editor of the special issue of *IO* devoted to regimes.[34] His definition of regimes has been widely accepted. Regimes are:

> sets of implicit or explicit principles, norms, rules, and decision-making procedures around which actors' expectations converge in a given area of international relations. Principles are beliefs of fact, causation, and rectitude. Norms are standards of behavior defined in terms of rights and obligations. Rules are specific prescriptions or proscriptions for action. Decision-making procedures are prevailing practices for making and implementing collective choice.[35]

Regimes, of course, are not new phenomena. They have a nine-teenth-century ring about them, either of a colonial nature, as in the case of European Powers supervising the finances of some unfortunate debtor government or establishing an international enclave or, more benignly, international public unions for the standardization of weights and measures and the like. In their modern guise they can be construed to bear a strong resemblance to Mansbach and Vasquez's issue areas, Burton's systems and Mitrany's functional bodies.

Regimes can come into being in various ways. Some may emerge spontaneously, as a perception of common interest and interdependence grows, others may be arrived at by negotiation, particularly when an important issue is in a state of flux, but some may be imposed by a hegemonic actor or group of actors. However, regimes do not exist in themselves; they have to be perceived to exist. Moreover, once in existence they can wax, wane, transform themselves or collapse. But usually they are evolutionary phenomena, although they can be overthrown, or even created, in a revolutionary manner. And they can proceed in various ways, ranging from loose coordination to a single policy.[36]

In a particularly perceptive essay in the *IO* volume, Donald Puchala and Raymond Hopkins stress several features, including their subjective nature, in which 'participants' understandings, expectations or convictions about legitimate, appropriate or moral behavior' are important.[37] As we have seen, their decision-making processes can vary considerably, as can the standing of actors who range from governments, including bureaucratic units and individuals therein, to international, transnational and subnational organizations. Puchala and Hopkins also point out that 'a regime exists in every substantive issue-area in international relations where there is discernibly patterned behavior'.[38] We are, in other words, back in the systems framework so characteristic of world society approaches. And the transactions in the system may be under the tight coercive control of a hegemon or emanate from the voluntary consensus of all the participants characteristic of legitimized politics.

Puchala and Hopkins invite us to consider various characteristics of regimes – whether they are specific or diffuse, formal or informal, given to evolutionary or revolutionary change (after the manner of Chalmers Johnson) – and to note their distributive bias,

since they generally favour the interests of the strong, particularly
if they are imposed by a hegemon. But in the latter case they may
be shortlived.[39] Nevertheless, a hegemon does not have to impose
a harsh coercive regime, it can also act in a benign manner by
providing an appreciated collective good for the benefit of the
regime as a whole, itself included. On any account, regimes exist,
they are not overly state-centric, or necessarily power political,
and they form a significant phenomenon in world society.[40]
Frequently they outlive the particular concatenation of events that
led to their gestation and go on, often *faute de mieux*, providing a
guiding framework when there are no obvious reasons that they
should continue to do so. Perhaps, as Punchala and Hopkins point
out, it is because they 'mediate behavior largely by constraining
unilateral adventurousness or obduracy . . . and during transitions
of power'. Compliance with the rules and procedures of a regime
'depends largely upon the consensus or acquiescence of participants
. . . Usually it is self-interest, broadly perceived, that motivates
compliance.'[41] But that self-interest, being broadly perceived, can
also include notions of community interest, otherwise the regime
may have difficulty in surviving.

If we accept that the world is interdependent in a complex
manner then regime theory is a useful way of coming to terms
with it, because it can accommodate a wide range of actors in a
transactional framework, enabling us to investigate empirically
process and structure in an open-minded way. There is no a priori
reason why a regime should be state-centric and power political –
or the converse to a lesser or greater extent. The burden is on us to
find out how and why this may be so and how and why it may or
may not change. Complex interdependence may expand the
capacity of actors to play power politics with each other but it may
also, and perhaps more so, lessen their desire to do so. Regime
theory is, therefore, a useful tool for our understanding of world
society. But it is not the only one. Regimes may be worldwide,
but they are not global.

Global approaches

In some ways, it is only in the last thirty years that we have had global politics in international relations. Before that, issues may have been worldwide, but they were not truly global. The Second World War is a case in point. The increasing globalization of some aspects of world politics has given added impetus to global approaches far more sophisticated than previous schema for world government, which were often the pipe-dreams of well-meaning international lawyers. The global approach can refer to questions such as nuclear annihilation or the global ecosystem, but it can also take us back to the individual.

In the early 1970s a new *genre* of intellectual exercise captured the imagination of the attentive public in IR – global modelling. The Report of the Club of Rome, entitled *Limits to Growth*,[42] reached some highly disturbing, if subsequently very contested, conclusions:

1 If the present growth trends in world population, industrialization, pollution, food production, and resource depletion continue unchanged, the limits to growth on this planet will be reached sometime within the next one hundred years. The most probable result will be a rather sudden and uncontrollable decline in both population and industrial capacity.

2 It is possible to alter these growth trends and to establish a condition of ecological and economic stability that is sustainable far into the future. The state of global equilibrium could be designed so that the basic material needs of each person on earth are satisfied and each person has an equal opportunity to realize his individual human potential.

3 If the world's people decide to strive for this second outcome rather than the first, the sooner they begin working to attain it, the greater will be their chances of success.

   These conclusions are so far-reaching and raise so many questions for further study that we are quite frankly overwhelmed by the enormity of the job that must be done.[43]

Several other models were to follow, often using sophisticated modelling techniques, and their results were in some cases contradictory. Moreover, there was 'the relative lack of *explicit* political and social content [which] is widely recognized by modelers as a weakness'.[44] However, some political figures did come together in various commissions[45] to give a practical politicians' input to discussion of this range of issues.

In the narrower perspective of IR literature the greatest impact has been the World Order Models Project (WOMP). Since the initial meeting in New Delhi in 1968 many studies have been published. WOMPers seek to relate their starting point – world peace and security – to a new, but classic, agenda of issues. The issues concern problems of ecological balance, population, basic needs, such as food, and unbalanced development, but they come down to some classic questions of political life – equity, participation and justice – without which there can be no peace and security. Like Mitrany and Burton, WOMPers see the existing state system as part of the problem, and their vocation is to be radical in changing it. As in the Club of Rome report, there is a context of emergency and the perspective is globalist. They are not seeking the 'fixes' of technocratic futurism, but 'comprehensive value realization'[46] for all, but first and foremost for the oppressed. They accept the challenge of doing away with the 'avoidable evils'[47] of hunger, war, repression and environmental decay. In short, they see their task as threefold:

(1) a *diagnostic/prognostic* task of describing present world order conditions and trends, (2) a *modeling* task of designing preferred futures, and (3) a *prescriptive* task of mapping a transition process, including concrete steps and an overall strategy.[48]

Their critics contend that they may know where they want to go, and why, but they do not know how to get there. Nevertheless, we shall not find out without trying. Moreover, setting goals has an important benefit for the mundane affairs of day-to-day politics: preferred future worlds, likely future worlds and undesirable future worlds, as distant models, may give a hint in response to the question 'how do I go about today's work in such a manner as to make the first more likely and last less so?' Moreover, modelling of ideal types can be very heuristic in requiring us to specify independent variables which we might not have wished, or thought, otherwise to consider.

Andrew Scott would probably share these sentiments. His

Dynamics of Interdependence is a thoughtful and provocative book, not hysterical in tone, but frightening in implications.[49] It has long been evident that we are broaching the problems of the twenty-first century with the tools of the nineteenth century. Whereas in the past scientific and technical change, and its implications, may have proceeded at a rate that did not outstrip the rate of adjustment of political, social, economic and cultural mores, ideas, institutions and processes, this is manifestly no longer the case. Moreover, as Scott points out, some global problems did exist in the past but they were largely unperceived, and the more devastating for that reason: for example, deforestation of lands around the Mediterranean.

Scott (like Wallerstein) makes much of Braudel's history of the Mediterranean world, in which Braudel works at three levels, that of geographical time and social time which set slow-moving apurposive processes within which there is individual time during which princes and politicians enter on to the stage.[50] But their role is circumscribed by these deeper processes, even though they may have been unaware of it. The long-term processes of change are not the stuff of politicians' daily fare. Harold Wilson is reputed to have remarked that a week is a long time in politics. Scott notes that 'Before a process can attract much attention it must be dramatized by some discrete event, or its rate of change per unit must climb over a high threshold.'[51] We must, therefore, Scott suggests, look for them now and, with the help of the global modellers, we shall not have any great difficulty in finding them. But Scott remains pessimistic:

> The smaller problems are being dealt with, often by a 'techno-logical fix', but the larger problems are being merely survived, and their rate of accumulation is ominous. Actors have fashioned a game neatly rigged against themselves.[52]

The global approaches we have considered have all had a strong orientation towards action. They share a sense of a worsening predicament about which something must be done if catastrophe is to be avoided. And it is difficult to remain sanguine in the face of this *oeuvre*. Thus the call to action is clear, but it is not our present function. We have been endeavouring to set out three conceptual frameworks in contemporary IR literature. We have charted the questioning of the realist consensus and we have, in this chapter, explored some world society approaches. We turn now to a statement of a world society approach, drawn from the writings of John Burton and a group of scholars associated with him mainly, but not exclusively, in Britain.

Burton's 'World Society' approach – a statement

We have the benefit of hindsight. In his magisterial survey of the field in 1955 Quincy Wright exhibited an enviable degree of foresight:

> It is not only the nations [to] which *international relations* seeks to relate. Varied types of groups – nations, states, governments, peoples, regions, alliances, confederations, interntional organiz- ations, even industrial organizations, cultural organizations, reli- gious organizations – must be dealt with in the study of international relations, if the treatment is to be realistic . . . Is not the subject matter of *international relations* really the history, organization, law, economy, culture, and processes of world community? Should we not conceive of the human race as a community which, while divided into numerous geographic, functional, cultural, racial political, economic, and other sub- groups, is becoming integrated into a society with the progress of technology and the growth of population bringing the mem- bers of all sub-groups into closer and closer contact with one another?[53]

Such sentiments express the rationale of world society approaches. The formulation of one variant of this theme owes much to the thought and influence of John Burton. But there can be other formulations, with differing emphases, since the approach has neither an official nor a consensual credo. Moreover, it lacks a salient text like Morgenthau's *Politics among Nations*,[54] perhaps because of its complexity. However, the approach does have some shared characteristics.

In the first place, the role of states is treated as an empirical question rather than as being axiomatic.[55] States may, on signifi- cant occasions, be the most important actors, but this is not necessarily so. Nor are state boundaries necessarily the fundamental dividing line between intrastate consensus and interstate anarchy. Intrastate relations can be anarchical and interstate relations highly consensual. States are not alone in having effective means of self-help and the self-arrogated right to make use of them. Moreover, important systems of transactions, both qualitatively and quantitatively, both of a coercive and a legitimized nature, transcend state boundaries in ways that are not amenable, actually or potentially, to governmental control, even as a 'gatekeeper'. Furthermore, states themselves, and especially their governments, frequently do not act as cohesive, hierarchically organized, well-integrated units commanding the full loyalty of their citizens. Indeed, government departments may frequently be at odds with each other, and even seek alliances with like-minded departments of other governments in a network of transgovernmental relationships such as can be seen between Treasuries, Defence Ministries and Foreign Offices in NATO countries or similar phenomena in organizational settings such as the European Community. Moreover, non-governmental organizations (NGOs) can play an important world role, and even intergovernmental institutions can, usually through their secretariats, have an impact that escapes the control of their member-states. Greenpeace, Amnesty International, Bob Geldof and Band Aid, the International Olympic Committee, and the World Council of Churches – to name a random selection – illustrate, in contemporary world politics, the active and frequently independent role of NGOs and many of them operate in an aterritorial manner. So, too, do many multinational corporations, whose ability to mobilize financial, technical and human resources may rival or surpass that of many governments. A range of such actors can come together to form a regime that thereafter acts as a constraint on their behaviour. In short, the state is a penetrated society. It can be *a* nodal point, *an* actor, *a* potential gatekeeper, but when and the extent to which it is so must be an empirical question and cannot be assumed.

But if the state is not necessarily a basic unit of analysis, what can take its place? In the world society model the emphasis is put on transactions, so that the notion of system – a set of patterned interactions – is the basic unit of analysis. In this approach the level of analysis is not crucial (interstate, intrastate, individual), nor is the status of actors. To analyse a phenomenon, it may be necessary to include the activities of actors as widely disparate as a particular individual and the UN Security Council. Since an adequate explanation cannot be given at one particular level, say interstate relations, it is necessary to go beyond that level. By mapping transactions related to a particular phenomenon, and determining where marked discontinuities occur, both qualitatively and quantitatively, a systems analysis emerges. Such systems develop properties that have a durable and independent existence (as, in their different ways, regime theorists, structural-functionalists and general systems theorists would argue), but the world society approach is, in general terms, a systems approach, which does not necessarily imply farreaching normative consideration or 'deep structure'. It can be conceived mainly in descriptive terms, although it frequently goes beyond this and develops a strong normative orientation, as in WOMP or in Burton's concern with legitimacy.[56] Yet if international relations goes beyond the interstate system, where does it stop? Does world society include everything? Surely not, for then it would be of little use.

The starting point in the world society framework is a question, a problem or a phenomenon to be explained, and the approach to it is the mapping of transactions in a systemic framework. This gives an added dimension to the conceptualization of social science. Confining the analysis to one level, such as the interstate, is too constraining, and so is a limitation to one facet of behaviour, be it economic, legal, sociological, or political. Interdisciplinary research, therefore, became fashionable because few questions, problems or phenomena are exclusively, say, economic or could reasonably be treated as such. Hybrids came to the fore, or reappeared, such as political anthropology, political psychology, political sociology or political economy, throughout the social sciences. Interdisciplinary research teams and centres were established. But the results were often disappointing. The reason for this lay frequently in the non-cumulative nature of the work of members of the team: an economist would look at the problem from the perspective and within the paradigm of economics, and others likewise from their differing paradigms. These paradigms were not easily made compatible and therefore interdisciplinary research did not cohere – it lacked a discipline.

A solution to this problem is to reverse the process of proceeding from a discipline to a problem by making the problem, question

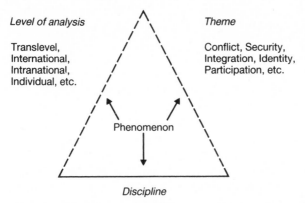

Figure 9.1

or phenomenon itself the starting point. And the choice of starting point is clearly impregnated with normative implications. However, themes such as conflict, security, integration, participation, identity and the like cut across both levels of analysis and academic disciplines. Conflict, for example, has economic, legal, psychological and other disciplinary dimensions. It manifests itself at different levels between individuals, between states, in industry and across all these levels. But conflict (and the other themes) also has a coherence of its own, so that, whatever the idiosyncracies of level and discipline, general statements can usefully be made. The problem, question or phenomenon in the world society framework is located within, and acts as the fulcrum of, three dimensions – level of analysis, discipline and theme (Fig. 9.1), to which some would add a fourth – basic human needs such as food, shelter, propagation, stability of response, affection and self-actualization.

Besides suggesting that the world is increasingly non-state-centric in character, adherents of world society approaches suggest that man is not driven primarily by an instinct to dominate. Thus aggressive behaviour at all levels results usually from other factors, notably as a learned response in certain environmental conditions. Peace, in the sense of being more than the mere absence of overt violence, is therefore possible. Indeed, transactions in any social system can be located on a spectrum between a pole of power politics and one of legitimized politics.

Realists view all politics as being necessarily power politics. Even ostensibly cooperative relations are merely 'power politics in disguise', in Schwarzenberger's phrase, because there are inevitably asymmetries in relationships that can be manipulated, a view echoed later by Keohane and Nye. Since the parties know this, they take it into account even in the 'cooperative' behaviour. Thus realists do not view transactions within the purview of international relations as being situated on a spectrum between power politics and legitimized politics. In so doing they limit themselves unnecessarily, since some degree of legitimization must always exist as it is difficult to coerce most of the people most of the time. Moreover, the idea of a continuum between a pole of power and a pole of legitimacy, rather than the realist's usual sharp distinction between intrastate and interstate politics, may be a more accurate reflection of the empirical world even in a Cold War. Prescriptions based on such a sharp distinction could therefore give rise to self-defeating policies. However, the notion of a continuum requires a criterion by which the transactions can be situated along it. This is the degree of acceptability of the transaction to all the parties concerned. The parties concerned are determined by their potential capability and likely willingness to 'spoil' a given set of transactions. If a transaction is acceptable then it is legitimized, if it is not, then it is situated towards the power end of the spectrum.

The operational definition of what is acceptable is a matter for the researcher, and it is a function of the problem in which he is interested. As a rule of thumb, a legitimized relationship is one in which the behaviour of the actor is based on criteria fully and freely acceptable to it without coercion, either overt, latent or structural. The essential element is not overt behaviour, but motivation. Motivation, that is acceptance by an actor of the criteria on which its behaviour is based, can only be free and without coercion if, among other things such as a low opportunity cost whenever the behaviour is rejected, the actor has 'perfect knowledge' of the range of possibilities. Without that knowledge the actor may be the victim of structural violence. Of course,

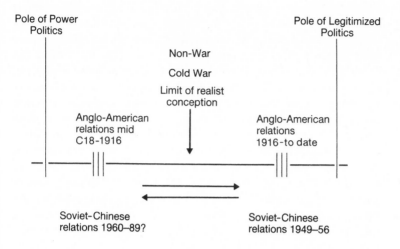

Figure 9.2

transactions rarely fall at either extreme end of the spectrum. At the power end the example of Rome and Carthage, the Nazis and European Jewry or Pol Pot are, happily, not the usual case, while at the legitimized end of the spectrum the Bible refers to a 'peace that passeth all understanding'. However, transactions can cluster consistently towards one or other end of the spectrum. Consider Franco-German relations from 1870–1950 at the power end or, towards the other end, Nordic country relations. The realist, however, would deny that the spectrum could venture much further from the power pole than a situation of non-war or Cold War. The conception in world society approaches, on the other hand, envisages the full spectrum and tries to account for a basic shift along it. Why, for example, have Anglo-American relations had such a shift towards the pole of legitimized politics since 1916 or Soviet-Chinese relations moved in the contrary direction? (Fig. 9.2).

A degree of power or legitimacy is simply a label to indicate the nature of a transaction. Because power relations tend to be dramatic and traumatic they monopolize the attention, but without the all-pervasive fabric of legitimization there is little chance of a stable social order. Moreover, even theorists who see the struggle for power as being universal in time and space usually accept some socialization of this instinct in the form of a limited degree of consent. Their rationalization of legitimized relationships ultimately depends on a truism, or they are excluded by definition.

The world society model acknowledges that the political function may be perceived in power terms, but it does not allow that this need necessarily be so. The reasons for this lie in a different conception of the nature of man. Behaviour is a rational response to the environment as the actor sees it, so that changing the environment can elicit different, more cooperative behaviour from that postulated by the realists. It is the old story of the predominance of either nature or nurture. The realist points to the ground rules being set by the former and the world society analyst sees them as a function of the latter.

This statement of *a* conception of the world society approach can act as a navigation point through the debates, discussions, confusions and controversies of the last three decades. It reflects the views of Burton and his colleagues, but Burton himself is now a somewhat erstwhile advocate of the world society framework. For him, the solution is to go back to the individual as the unit of analysis, since in his view, paradoxically, we can only reach global processes through the needs of the individual.

Needs theory

Burton is not the only scholar to return to the individual as a unit for the analysis of international relations and world society. Waltz, in *Man, the State and War*,[57] devoted part of his analysis to such theories and, in a well known paper, Sidney Verba drew our attention to assumptions and theories about individual decision-making in models of the international system.[58] More recently, Chadwick Alger has given much thought to innovative and exciting ways of bridging the micro and the macro in IR research.[59] Alger quotes Singer and Galtung to the effect, in Singer's case, that 'no theory which ignores the single person is scientifically adequate or morally defensible'[60] and, in Galtung's, that the empowerment of *all* people in world affairs through 'a plurality of revolutions at the micro level' is desirable.[61] Alger argues, with Galtung, that people have a right to know how they are affected by and affect others, through their involvement in world systems. This involves breaking with the state as the unit of analysis and the removal of constraints to the conduct of 'foreign policy' by all manner of local groups.

> From this perspective, research would extend beyond studying the individual as object and instead contribute to activate the individual as subject, or as purposeful actor.[62]

To some degree the 'Green' movement, stressing cultural identity, self-reliance, social justice and ecological balance, is a practical response moving in that direction.[63] Alger advocates a synthesis of research and practice between the student of world society and activists. He admits that it will not be easy, but 'What is particularly significant is the growing ties between research and action on global relations and research and action on human development in local contexts.'[64] In this, it is easy to see why Alger quotes Burton with approval.

For Burton the basic principles of the needs approach are:

1 there are certain human needs and desires that are specific and universal;
2 these *will* be satisfied, even at the cost of social disruption and personal disorientation;
3 some structures and institutions that have evolved over time, as a result of differentiation of power and of socialization do not necessarily, either in the short or the long term, reflect these needs and desires and frequently frustrate them;
4 disruptive behaviour is the consequence of interaction between the pursuit of human needs and the institutional framework created by power differentiation.

Thus 'the individual must be the unit of analysis, because it is individual human needs that ultimately have to be catered for in the interests of public policy at all levels'.[65]

Moreover, 'We are asserting that if there were to be discovered a definite set of human needs on the basis of which societies could be harmonious, major methodological problems in behavioural sciences and in policy-making would be avoided. If there were agreement as to human needs then there would be a logical starting point of behavioural analysis for there would be a scientific basis for determining goals.'[66]

It is a view shared by others.[67] The starting point is that the individual is adopted as the basic unit of analysis for all of social science from individual psychology to the study of world society. While institutions of all types at all levels and in all dimensions have a considerable effect, outcomes, it is argued, are significantly related to individuals acting as individuals out of role and in nature. In the hoary argument over whether nature or nurture 'maketh man', Burton comes down heavily in favour of nature. Moreover, since individual behaviour is fundamentally grounded in an unchanging nature then social science knowledge can be objective and constitute a set of navigation points for practitioners.

Burton, with others, points to the 'genetic drive to learn'[68] about a set of universal basic human needs 'such as stimulus, security, identity, consistency of response and the need for control by the person of his/her environment as a means of pursuing these needs'.[69] Since these drives are of a genetic origin, then they will be pursued come what may. The only constraints are 'values attached to relationships'.[70] If institutions obstruct the fulfilment of such needs, then conflict will result. However, the individual will prevail, for even if one, or many, are crushed others will (because they will have to) pursue similar goods. However, conflict is not inevitable, because the needs being pursued are not necessarily in short supply.

Everyone can be stimulated, secure, have a sense of identity and the like, although there is no guarantee of this in practice. Security, for example, can be defined so that it is thought by others to engender insecurity for them, whereupon conflict will ensue. But it can also be defined in such a way that it does not threaten others. The same can be said of identity, participation, development and other similar basic needs. Indeed, it is the job of the practitioner to ensure that basic needs are fulfilled in such a manner that conflict does not ensue, and Burton suggests the process of problem-solving to ensure that dysfunctional policies are changed.,

Basing himself on a number of needs theorists, Burton stresses Sites's notion that 'The individual's most fundamental drive [is] . . . to attempt to control his environment in order to meet his needs'[71] whether by societally acceptable means or otherwise. If society is not able to offer the individual acceptable relationships, then there will be no constraints on the forms of the pursuit of needs. If society offers relationships cherished by the individual, he or she will not prejudice them by anti-societal behaviour. The individual and his or her needs therefore provide 'objectively determined guides to policy – bases on which goals and policies could be assessed and predictions made as to success or self-defeating consequences'.[72] However, some groups and individuals are likely to engage in the defence of privileges that they feel can be rendered secure in the short term. But society, and especially world society in a nuclear age, may thereby find itself jeopardized in the long term in a possible clash between the inexorable pursuit of individual needs and a tenacious role defence in a world vulnerable to breakdown.

Such a controversial but potentially important argument requires examination. For example, are there genetically based universal needs? While needs theorists have offered some empirical data, Burton quotes Sites to the effect that such hard empirical data is unnecessary:

In using the need concept we must ever be conscious that we are operating at an abstract conceptual level and that in the last analysis the actual basis of the need is tied up with certain psycho-physiological processes which are in interaction with the environment and which are not at this point in our scientific development directly observable. The fact that these processes are not directly observable, however, should not prevent us from working with the need concept if it allows us better to understand and to explain human activity. (The atom was conceptualised long before it was 'observed'.) That is, if we observe certain kinds of activity (or lack of activity) in behaviour which we need to account for, and can do so with the use of certain concepts which do not do violence to other things we know and which are consistent with other data which cause us

to think in the same direction, there is no reason why we should
not do so. We can always admit we are wrong.[73]

Abduction is after all a respectable way of establishing causes from
effects. Burton follows Peirce in arguing that the hypothesis is an
end in itself: it is the hypothesis and the process through which it
is derived (abduction or retroduction), that is all-important, rather
than its falsification. But we still need to see this process demonstrated and in this Burton and other needs theorists are not as
forthcoming as they might be.

In short, we seem to be back to wisdom – perhaps even to
idealism, to deduction, to prescription and to the proof-of-the-
pudding test. If a hypothesis works to the best of our knowledge
after due care in application and observation, we will accept it as a
basis for explanation and prescription. And if it works others will
accept it too. But there will be feedback, for wisdom is not
immutable. Moreover, in the absence of wisdom, conventional
wisdom changes. Perhaps the basic needs currently in fashion are
not universal: this matters little if they give the analyst a rich
explanatory and predictory tool, enabling him thereby blithely to
treat them as a paradigm on which 'normal science' for practitioners can be based. Nevertheless, not all problems can be so
easily put aside.

In embracing so wholeheartedly the case of 'nature', Burton and
needs theorists may well have played down overly the role of
'nurture'. Even if there are basic universal human needs genetically
implanted, which act as the motor for learning and an explanation
of behaviour, their expression takes place in a social environment.
The social environment differs for each individual and the experience of the search for the fulfilment of basic needs feeds back into
a specific environment – that of each individual and group. While
society may not be able, in the last resort, to mould man so as to
turn him from his basic needs, it can engage in a dialogue with an
individual and influence substantially the way in which those needs
will manifest themselves. Moreover, society is not homogeneous.
Basic needs therefore are mediated by culture – *different* cultures.
The process of mediation may make the end result significantly
different in terms of concrete expression. Thus, even if the starting
point is universality, the end point is heterogeneity. This makes
things difficult for the practitioner – for he is dealing with the

heterogeneous concrete manifestation of basic universal human needs. For him it is no great consolation to know that there was universality before culture and nurture got to work to present him with his daily fare of very different looking problems. Difficulties in the operationalization of the needs approach therefore face the practitioner. Here, however, Burton has been especially innovative in his development of 'controlled communication' and 'problem-solving' and through problem-solving techniques the cultural factors can receive their proper due.[74]

Are we thus back to what has been considered traditionally as 'the proper study of mankind', namely 'humans'? This is not a view that all advocates of the world society approach would accept, at least not in Burton's formulation. World society approaches are non-state centric, on that there is agreement, and some form of systems or issue approach has been the most favoured unit of analysis, with stress on the importance of processes and interactions. Nevertheless, while the structuralists have made both realists and world society analysts more aware of structural factors, Burton and others have argued that structures may be a part of the problem in the sense of denying basic human needs. It is an individual's relationship with the environment that is crucial in determining behaviour and outcomes, which takes us back to the question of legitimacy and power politics. For some 'the relationship' is therefore the most appropriate unit of analysis.[75]

Cogito ergo sum was Descartes' famous formulation. 'I relate, therefore I am' might be a reformulation appropriate to the world society approach, particularly in Britain. Although, as Mitchell points out, 'relationship' can have many meanings, in the world society context it is usually considered as an exchange, transaction or interaction, which may give rise to the sense of belonging to the same set.[76] Within such a set relations are legitimized both in terms of transactions and distribution of roles. Role differentiation may involve inequalities, but not a sense of inequity. The relationship and role structure is freely and non-coercively accepted as 'right' in full knowledge of the circumstances. Difficulties arise when either the transactions or the role distribution are not considered to be 'right', or if actors extraneous to the system intrude upon it coercively or if some actors are likewise excluded. Then power politics ensues because one or other party has refused to steer, in a Deutschian sense, by putting the burden of adjustment on others.

To do this is to deny the legitimacy of a relationship but it is the 'values attached to relationships', as Burton has argued, that provide stability in society. If a relationship is denied it is, in this sense, a denial of worth to the individual or group, who may begin therefore to feel absolved of societal restraint. The business of politics, at any level – family or firm, system or state – is thus to promote the degree of legitimacy by responding to basic needs. Even for those sceptical of claims to universality, the fulfilment of basic needs makes a reasonable set of navigation points for a harmonious society. Failure to do so is to invite endless confrontation. Conflict may be endemic, but particular conflicts can be resolved, even protracted deep-seated conflicts, in a self-sustaining manner. They will be so resolved when the degree of legitimization of relationships is high, or so the conflict researchers in the world society paradigm assert, not without reason.[77] And Burton's basic needs are a good starting point for legitimacy.

Mitchell points to a difference between what we might call the 'British world society' and the 'American or *IO* complex interdependence' approaches in that:

> the world society approach begins by assuming that legitimised relationships should be regarded as a 'norm', in both a statistical and a prescriptive sense. In other words, in contemporary global society it is usual to find networks of relationships that are accepted by those involved and are thus both functional for the elements interacting, and self-supporting because of the mutually recognised benefits conferred by the transactions involved. The legitimised relationship is the norm, in the sense that the sheer number of such relationships far outweighs non-legitimised relationships involving power and coercion.[78]

It is thus power politics that requires explanation. The *IO* network seems to start from the other end of the stick: the question is why power politics and state-centricity do not prevail. Both acknowledge the existence of a power-legitimacy dimension and a state-centric-non-state-centric dimension, and assume that behaviour falls permanently at neither pole but oscillates between them. Nevertheless, the starting-point distorts perception of the spectrum – from either end – and this also colours prescription. As Mitchell comments:

the world society approach also posits that legitimised relationships are the norm in a prescriptive sense; that is to say, the search for peace and a harmonious global society can best begin by rejecting the conception that stability and absence of violence can most surely be assured by the use of threats, coercion and deterrence. These are the very signs that existing relationships are non-legitimised and will inevitably lead to further conflict and violence so that their continued use will inevitably be counter-productive. What is needed is a search for ways of changing existing coercive relationships into those acceptable to elements involved. This would remove the need for threat systems to ensure continuation, or 'stability', to use the polite euphemism. In the best of all possible worlds, relationships would be entirely legitimised and durable because of this fact. (As can be seen, there is a strong infusion of anarchist assumptions in the world society approach.)[79]

It is not an argument saying that the world will be 'good' when the world is good. Degrees of legitimacy can be measured. Burton has suggested ways in which legitimacy can be enhanced and procedures for achieving this. But they are in no sense a panacea.[80]

In short, realism seems to be too simple and stark, and it may be wrong. World society approaches are complex and confused, and not yet quite right. But what of structuralism?

Notes: Chapter 9

1 Michael Mann, *The Sources of Social Power*, Vol. 1 (Cambridge: Cambridge University Press), p. 17.
2 Michael Mann, *The Sources of Social Power*, Vol. 1.
3 ibid., p. 1 (italics deleted).
4 ibid., pp. 1–2.
5 ibid., p. 2.
6 ibid., p. 2 (italics deleted).
7 ibid., pp. 2–3 (italics deleted).
8 ibid., p. 3.
9 ibid., p. 27.
10 ibid., p. 518.
11 ibid., p. 519.
12 ibid., p. 520.
13 ibid., p. 521.

14 ibid., pp. 521–2.
15 ibid., p. 531.
16 ibid., pp. 533–4.
17 ibid., p. 539.
18 David Mitrany, *A Working Peace System* (Chicago: Quadrangle, 1966).
19 See David Mitrany, *The Functional Theory of Politics* (London: Martin Robertson, 1975); A. J. R. Groom and Paul Taylor (eds), *Functionalism Theory and Practice in International Relations* (London: University of London Press, 1975).
20 Mitrany was a Romanian who went to LSE as a postgraduate student in 1912. Among other things he was the foreign leaderwriter for the *Manchester Guardian* in the great days of C. P. Scott, and was a part of the interwar Bloomsbury set. He served on the Board of Unilever from the end of the Second World War until his death in 1975, aged 87, although latterly in an honorary capacity. See his autobiographical note in Mitrany, *Functional Theory*.
21 The paragraphs that follow draw upon A. J. R. Groom, 'Neofunctionalism: A case of mistaken identity', *Political Science*, 30, 1, 1978.
22 K. J. Holsti, *The Dividing Discipline* (London: Allen & Unwin, 1987).
23 See Chapter 8.
24 Robert O. Keohane and Joseph S. Nye Jr (eds), *Transnational Relations and World Politics* (London: Harvard University Press, 1971).
25 ibid., p. xvii.
26 ibid., p. 371.
27 ibid., p. 386.
28 Robert O. Keohane and Joseph S. Nye Jr, *Power and Interdependence* (Boston: Little, Brown, 1977).
29 ibid., p. 8.
30 ibid., p. 9.
31 ibid., p. 10.
32 ibid., p. 12.
33 ibid., p. 24.
34 *International Organization*, Spring 1982.
35 Stephen Krasner, *International Organization*, Spring 1982.
36 Ernst B. Haas, 'Why collaborate? Issue linkage and international regimes', *World Politics*, April 1988.
37 Donald J. Puchala and Raymond F. Hopkins, 'International regimes: lessons from inductive analysis', *International Organization*, Spring 1982, p. 246.
38 ibid., p. 247.
39 ibid., pp. 248ff.
40 Stephen Haggard and Beth A. Simmons (in 'Theories of international regimes', *International Organization*, Summer 1987) suggest that there are four 'families' of regime: structural, game-theoretic, functional and cognitive (p. 498). 'Most structural, game-theoretic, and functional theories of regimes are state-centred, presuming unified rational actors, even if the assumption is relaxed to gain explanatory leverage' (p. 499). Haggard and Simmons argue that the cognitivists have a 'radically

different research program. Focusing on the intersubjective meaning structures that bind actors together, they necessarily see a looser fit between structural constraints, interests, and choices. Where functional theories see regimes as more or less efficient responses to fixed needs, cognitive theories see them as conditioned by ideology and consensual knowledge and evolving as actors learn' (p. 499).

41 Puchala and Hopkins, *International Organization*, Spring 1982, p. 271.
42 Donella H. Meadows *et al.*, *The Limits to Growth* (London: Pan, 1974).
43 ibid., pp. 23–4.
44 Barry B. Hughes, 'World models: the bases of difference', *International Studies Quarterly*, March 1985, p. 81. In this useful survey of models, Barry Hughes points to two important world views that underpin world models and futures studies – those of political economy and of political ecology.
45 Such as the Brandt and Palme Commissions. The Brandt Commission, *North South* (London: Pan, 1980) and *Common Crisis* (London: Pan, 1983). The Palme Commission, *Common Security* (London: Pan, 1982).
46 Richard Falk and Samual S. Kim, 'World order studies and the world system', in William R. Thompson (ed.), *Contending Approaches to World System Analysis* (London: Sage, 1983), p. 207.
47 ibid., p. 208.
48 ibid., p. 211.
49 Andrew M. Scott, *The Dynamics of Interdependence* (London: University of North Carolina Press, 1982).
50 ibid., p. 42.
51 ibid., p. 44.
52 ibid., p. 60.
53 Quincy Wright, *The Study of International Relations* (New York: Appleton–Century–Crofts, 1955), p. 6.
54 Hans J. Morgenthau, *Politics among Nations* (New York: Knopf, 1959).
55 The following paragraphs are drawn from A. J. R. Groom, 'Paradigms in conflict', *Review of International Studies*, April 1988.
56 Burton first set out his conception of world society in three works: J. W. Burton, *Systems, States, Diplomacy, and Rulers* (London: Cambridge University Press, 1968); *World Society* (London: Cambridge University Press, 1972) and, with A. J. R. Groom, C. R. Mitchell and A. V. S. de Reuck, *The Study of World Society: A London Perspective* (Pittsburgh: International Studies Association, Monograph No. 1, 1974). His more recent views stressing the role of the individual as the basic unit of analysis can be found in *Deviance, Terrorism and War* (Oxford: Martin Robertson, 1979); *Dear Survivors* (London: Frances Pinter, 1983) and *Global Conflict* (Brighton: Wheatsheaf, 1984). For a brief overview, see his 'World society and human needs', in Margot Light and A. J. R. Groom, *International Relations* (London: Frances Pinter, 1985).
57 Kenneth Waltz, *Man, the State and War* (New York: Columbia University Press, 1950), p. 60.
58 Sidney Verba, 'Assumptions of rationality and non-rationality in models of the international system', in Klaus Knorr and Sidney Verba

220   *'Now': contending paradigms*

(eds), *The International System* (Princeton, NJ: Princeton University Press, 1961).
59 Chadwick Alger, 'Bridging the micro and the macro in international relations research', *Alternatives*, Winter 1984–5.
60 ibid., p. 324.
61 ibid., pp. 324–5. See Johan Galtung, *The True Worlds* (New York: Free Press, 1980).
62 *Alternatives*, Winter 1984–5, p. 325.
63 ibid., p. 335. Alger quotes the Swedish economists Friberg and Hettne, who neatly characterise 'Blue' (market, liberal, capitalist) and 'Red' (state socialism, planning) as well.
64 ibid., p. 342.
65 John Burton, *Dear Survivors*, p. 216.
66 Burton, *Deviance*, p. 63.
67 The following paragraphs draw upon A. J. R. Groom, 'Academics and practitioners: towards a happier relationship?', in Michael Banks (ed.), *Conflict in World Society* (Brighton: Wheatsheaf, 1984) – a *Festschrift* for John Burton.
68 Burton, *Dear Survivors*, p. 34.
69 ibid., p. 16.
70 ibid.
71 ibid., p. 35.
72 ibid., p. 36.
73 Paul Sites, quoted in Burton, *Deviance*, pp. 66–7.
74 See J. W. Burton, *Conflict and Communication* (London: Macmillan, 1969), and Edward E. Azar and John W. Burton (eds), *International Conflict Resolution* (Brighton: Harvester, 1986). For a recent discussion of the technique see J. W. Burton, *Resolving Deep-Rooted Conflict* (Lanham, Mass: University Press of America, 1987).
75 C. R. Mitchell: 'World society as cobweb', in Banks (ed.), *Conflict in World Society*, pp. 64 ff.
76 ibid., pp. 65–7.
77 See A. J. R. Groom, *Paradigms*.
78 Mitchell, *op. cit.*, p. 71.
79 ibid.
80 Burton, Deep-Rooted Conflict *op. cit.*

Further reading

Banks, Michael, (ed.). *Conflict in World Society*. Brighton: Wheatsheaf, 1984.
Burton, J. W., *World Society*. London: Cambridge University Press, 1972.
Burton, J. W., *Deviance, Terrorism and War*. Oxford: Martin Robertson, 1979.
Groom, A. J. R. and Taylor, Paul (eds). *Functionalism: Theory and Practice in International Relations*. London: University of London Press, 1975.

Keohane, Robert O. and Nye, Joseph S. Jr, *Power and Interdependence.* Boston: Little, Brown, 1977.

Mann, Michael, *The Sources of Social Power.* Cambridge: Cambridge University Press, 1986.

Meadows, Donella H. *et al. The Limits of Growth.* London: Pan, 1974.

Mitrany, David. *The Functional Theory of Politics.* London: Martin Robertson, 1975.

Thompson, William R. (ed.). *Contending Approaches to World System Analysis.* London: Sage, 1983.

10 Structural approaches to international relations

> The spread of capitalism is of fundamental importance to the consolidation of a novel world system from the sixteenth century onwards. Both capitalism and industrialism have decisively influenced the rise of nation-states, but the nation-state system cannot be reductively explained in terms of their existence. The modern world has been shaped through the intersection of capitalism, industrialism and the nation-state system. (Anthony Giddens)[1]

Structural approaches to international relations have had but a fitful recognition in Western universities until recently. International relations has therefore been incomplete as a discipline. Fortunately, during the last two decades that matter has begun to be put right. It is the burden of this chapter to chart attempts to achieve this goal. Moreover, as in the realist or world society approaches, we are able to call upon classical formulations in political philosophy, and in particular Marx, as a starting-point and guide in coming to terms with structure. Nevertheless, until recently the advocacy of any form of structuralism was a passport to exclusion from the mainstream in the Anglo-American study of IR.

In some ways the first approach to IR as an academic study in modern times was structuralist. The great debate on imperialism in the late nineteenth century and the early decades of this century marks the advent of the discipline. But, apart from Hobson, it was a debate that had its intellectual roots in Central and Eastern Europe and was somewhat alien to the intellectual climate of the English-speaking world. Moreover, it was an approach that later became associated with a particular state – the USSR – which was treated as a diplomatic pariah, and it lay at the basis of a political doctrine – Marxism–Leninism – which was feared, denigrated and reviled by Western elites. Structural approaches, especially those of a Marxist derivation or ethos as well as those of a geopolitical nature, were, for the most part, beyond the pale in the Anglo-American tradition as the discipline became established.

There are many structural approaches to IR. Moreover, structuralism, as an approach, does not originate in IR. On the contrary, it has flowered in French and German thought to an extent far greater than in the Anglo-American traditions that have governed IR as a discipline. If one name is to be associated with structuralist thought as being seminal for social science as a whole it is that of Claude Levi-Strauss, a name not often to be found on IR reading lists. But Levi-Strauss's work is not irrelevant, for in having an applicability for all social science it has one thereby for IR. Considerations of structure take us back to the epistemological division between a methodological individualism which, if everything is reduced to units, does not easily give rise to explanation, and holism, with its emphasis on autonomous laws. The one is a denial of social science, since it questions the feasibility of general statements about behaviour, as much as the other is its affirmation. Structural approaches are holistic. But structural approaches are vulnerable to the charge that they are thus deterministic, being 'laws', and absolutist to a significant extent, because there is only one all-pervading structure. Certainly structural approaches bring an element of grand theory to IR.[2]

The use of the term structuralist in IR is confusing. It evokes overtones of French-inspired grand theory, frequently it alludes to a more overt structuralism in the Marxist tradition, referring to the social relations of production, the world economic order and the role of the state therein, or again, it may reflect a concern with political structure. Behind the many stipulative definitions lies a hint of some conception of grand theory and this is not necessarily linked to any political position of left or right, although its emphasis on structure as opposed to actors does suggest some kind of 'anti-humanism'.[3] While structuralists give us new insights by asking questions different from those of other approaches, they do have a wide range of varying emphases among themselves in their approach to IR. We shall attempt to simplify this, albeit in a crude manner, by concentrating first on economic theories derived largely from the Marxist tradition, then on political theories and the debate between the advocates of economic or political underpinnings of structure, before considering the extent to which the geopolitical approach can be considered usefully in a structural light.

In each of these three categories of structural approach – economic, political and geopolitical – there is an element in common. Structure is independent of the actors within it. It is autonomous. While structure is affected by the activities of actors within it, nevertheless the structure has a significant, indeed perhaps a determining effect on the behaviour of actors and the outcome of social processes. An emphasis must be given to the whole, since this has an impact greater than the sum of its parts. It must therefore be taken into consideration in any empirical theory of behaviour at whatever level. As Richard Little puts it,

> Structuralists assume that human behaviour cannot be understood simply by examining individual motivation and intention because, when aggregated, human behaviour precipitates structures of which the individuals may be unaware. By analogy, when people walk across a field, they may unintentionally create a path. Others subsequently follow the path and in doing so 'reproduce' the path. The process of reproduction, however, is neither conscious nor intentional.[4]

Structure thus takes on a life of its own and becomes a social fact that moulds future behaviour so that individuals (or states) find it difficult either to escape from such constraints or to create new ones more to their liking.

This simple notion is now clearly acknowledged in the other two principal paradigms in IR. The structural realists or neorealists, as we shall see, have rediscovered the structuralist wheel, or at least its terminology. Even Morgenthau himself, while formulating his six principles of political realism from an actor's perspective, did consider the structure of the international diplomatic system and regretted the movement from multipolarity to bipolarity in the postwar period. Systems thinkers, for their part, came easily to thinking in terms of wholes since it is implicit in the very nature of their basic unit of analysis and endeavour. The resurgence of structuralism has had the happy effect of inducing them to consider more carefully the durable aspects of systems' structures. More generally, structuralists have had recently a significant impact upon the conceptual, empirical and prescriptive agendas and discourse to the extent that we are all to some degree impregnated with structuralist ideas. The interdependence of politics and economics is now widely recognized, if not enough by economists, and theories of *dependencia* and centre–periphery models have a cogency and relevance for the understanding of contemporary international relations. Wallerstein and Modelski, among others, have postulated a single world system that emerged in the fifteenth century and which continues to this day, thereby bringing to the forefront not only structural factors but also a heightened awareness of the need for historical depth.

In the last chapter we have already noted the importance of historical sociology for contemporary IR, by referring to the work of Michael Mann. We shall, in considering both economic and political structural approaches to IR, make reference to the work of structural historians. These historians give salience to the very long-term evolution of the world system, to the rise and fall of successive international orders and the waves in economics and war at the heart of the world system.[5] What is the driving force at a particular time – economics, political factors or culture – is a matter of fierce debate, but it is a debate about emphasis, because few structural historians would advocate one factor to the exclusion of others. We shall consider this debate, using the writings of Wallerstein and Modelski as exemplars.

Structural approaches, by nature of their emphasis, force us to think in grand terms. But the application of structural thought to economic, political, historical or cultural issues incites controversy, because it is difficult to be authoritative in demonstrating the play of grand theory in day-to-day events and processes and in the behaviour of actors. What, at one level, seems to be plausible is difficult to discern in the minutiae of daily life and, given the practical and pragmatic turn of mind of practitioners and most academics in IR, this constitutes an additional barrier to the proper consideration of structural approaches to the field. Why, then, and how, is IR beginning to give structural factors their due?

One starting point is the intellectual effervescence generated by post-behaviouralism in the United States and in parts of Europe, notably the Federal Republic of Germany and Scandinavia. Associated with this was the revisionist school of international historians of the Cold War and US foreign policy. This leads us into a consideration of the Marxist tradition of structural analysis, which takes capitalism as the basic structure. In contrast to the centre–periphery and *dependencia* theorists and the world-system approach of Wallerstein and his colleagues, Modelski espouses an analysis of long cycles, which is primarily political, not economic, in orientation. The debate is then joined about the relationship between economic and political factors in the world system. But it is not the only approach to world structure. The long-standing geopolitical tradition has its contemporary formulation in the work of those studying ecopolitics, such as the Sprouts, and the notion of lateral pressure developed by Choucri and North, which has been taken up by Ashley.

The new revolution in political science

'The new revolution in political science' was the title of a magister-ial presidential address by David Easton to the American Political Science Association in September 1969.[6] In it Easton urged his colleagues to come to terms with the post-behavioural revolution. Post-behaviouralists sought to go beyond the arid and hopeless quest for a value-free, positivistic social science to recognize that social scientists are not political eunuchs, but political actors, and that they should take cognisance of this. 'Its battle cries are *relevance and action*', Easton reported. Moreover, it is 'future oriented'.[7] Easton then proceeded to spell out the credo of post-behaviouralism:

> It is more important to be relevant and meaningful for contem-porary urgent social problems than to be sophisticated in the tools of investigation . . . Behavioral science conceals an ideol-ogy of empirical conservatism. To confine oneself exclusively to the description and analysis of facts is to hamper the understand-ing of these same facts in their broadest context. As a result empirical political science must lend its support to the mainten-ance of the very factual conditions it explores. It unwittingly purveys an ideology of social conservatism tempered by modest incremental change . . . The task . . . is . . . to help political science reach out to the real needs of mankind in a time of crisis . . . Science cannot be and never has been evaluatively neutral

. . . Hence to understand the limits of our knowledge we need to be aware of the value premises on which it stands and the alternatives for which this knowledge could be used . . . To know is to bear the responsibility for acting and to act is to engage in reshaping society . . . Contemplative science was a product of the nineteenth century when a broader moral agreement was shared. Action science of necessity reflects the contemporary conflict in society over ideals and this must permeate and color the whole research enterprise itself . . . Politicization of the professions is inescapable as well as desirable.[8]

Easton himself went a considerable way towards espousing this credo, and the line of thought takes us directly to critical theory with its strong criticism of positivism. But the jump was not immediate.

The intellectual effervescence of post-behaviouralism reflected the political and social context in the USA at the time. The Vietnam War, the revolt of the black community, nuclear issues, radical politics on the campus and abroad, May 1968 in Paris, were the context in which a new generation of scholars in the United States and on the Continent of Europe sought to lend their science and intellect to the building of a better world. The entry onto the political stage of a considerable number of third world states and the consequent placing of development issues high on the international agenda were instrumental in sparking an academic interest in the political and economic issues of development. By the late 1960s comparative politics and political development had lost some of their intellectual cutting edge and were losing salience to *dependencia* studies. The theories of *dependencia* integrated political analysis into an economic framework and, for the first time, a major academic thrust in Western IR came not from Britain or the USA, but from Latin America. Quickly the nature of capitalism became central to the analysis and, while dependency studies continued to be fuelled by third world scholars joined by their intellectual followers in Britain, North America and on the Continent, such studies were only partial theories of international political economy. Wallerstein, inspired by the ideas of Braudel, took the argument further by taking the capitalist world system from the late fifteenth century as his unit of analysis. The post-behavioural revolution had started a process that led to a metamorphosis of the intellectual agenda. There was now a structuralist world-system approach to rival world society conceptions (discussed in Chapter 9). Moreover, the structural realists or neorealists likewise began to give serious consideration to structural variables, but of a political nature, and in the case of Modelski, to do so in the same historical context as Wallerstein.

While the agenda was thus broadened and given great historical depth, the post-behavioural spirit of critical thought also broached a traditional area of IR – that of foreign policy, and in particular that of US foreign policy in the twentieth century, the policy of the principal Power of capitalism, the hegemon in the world-system be it conceived economically or politically. Most of the radical writers conceived the world system in economic terms. They saw US policy from Wilsonian internationalism to beyond the Vietnam War as being one to make the world safe for capitalism, and in particular American capitalism, if necessary at the expense of the old declining imperialist Powers. While conservative historians could agree on this central thrust of US policy, the radicals went on to express their conviction that capitalism was necessarily imperialistic and exploitative. Thus, many of the ills of the world could be laid at America's door. Particular attention by radical historians has been paid to US policy in negotiating the postwar political and economic framework after the two world wars.[9] In this, the United States was deemed largely to have been successful in achieving its aims after the Second World War, even at the cost of provoking the Cold War. And the imperialist system that the US successfully set in place continues to this day, working for the benefit of the rich at the expense of the poor. For the radical historians the deepening North–South problem is evidence enough of the plausibility of their thesis. Ironically, two of the most cogent and well-written statements of the radical case, even after due (but unnecessary) allowance has been made for bias, selective perception or the setting up of straw men, are made by writers in strong disagreement with the radical thesis. Robert Tucker's *The Radical Left and American Foreign Policy* and Benjamin Cohen's *The Question of Imperialism* are important contributions to the debate.[10]

For Tucker the core of the radical historians' approach lies in their unwillingness to see the growth to, and conduct of, world power by the United States in terms other than economic:

> The essence of the radical critique is not simply that America is aggressive and imperialistic but that it is so out of an institutional necessity . . . the institutional structure of American capitalism . . . [11]

As Harry Magdoff has so simply and starkly put it,

> Imperialism is not a matter of choice for a capitalist society; it is the way of life of such a society. [12]

Aggressive expansion cannot be explained by security needs, chance or the machinations of a bureaucracy, since these are all subservient to the capitalist imperative.

> America's expansion – the drive to pacify and to integrate the global environment under American leadership and control – must be understood primarily as the outcome of forces generated by American capitalism. [13]

This, Tucker sees as central to the radical analysis. It is a national policy driven by a transnational economic and social structure. Politics was merely the instrument of this drive. Tucker does not deny that 'America's economic war aim was to save capitalism at home and abroad', as Kolko put it, but he does question the assertion that this was the sole or overriding war aim. [14] For Tucker, political and security questions have an autonomous validity and they are not necessarily subservient to economic questions. Moreover, with Cohen, and like Hobson before him, Tucker rejects the notion that imperialism is a necessary and organic part of capitalism.

Cohen's thesis is that, although trade, investment and raw materials in third world countries are important to developed countries, they are not necessary for the developed countries and therefore, contrary to the radical thesis, economic imperialism is not an inevitable concomitant of capitalism: [15]

As important as trade and investment connections may be for the rich, they are not decisive.[16]

They may be important for particular firms, sectors or countries, but they are not a structural requirement for the system as a whole:

> They are simply a convenience – the path of least resistance to profits, prosperity, and growth. Of course, even convenience may be sufficient excuse to take advantage of the poor countries – to distort their growth and exploit them.[17]

Thus, Tucker and Cohen are not inclined to make a difference in degree become a difference in kind. Their argument is not to deny some aspects of the radical case – US policy was to make the world safe for (American) capitalism, which could exploit the third world – but these were not organic to, or necessary for, capitalism. This can be seen in their acceptance of Magdoff's thesis:

> But the reality of imperialism goes far beyond the immediate interest of this or that investor: the underlying purpose is nothing less than keeping as much as possible of the world open for trade and investment by the giant multinational corporations . . . When all these factors are taken into account, it will be seen that attempts to explain isolated actions in 'bookkeeping' terms make no sense . . . the killing and destruction in Vietnam and the expenditure of vast sums of money are not balanced in the eyes of US policy makers against profitable business opportunities in Vietnam; rather they are weighed according to the judgement of military and political leaders on what is necessary to control and influence Asia, and especially Southeast Asia, in order to keep the entire area within the imperialist system in general, and within the United States sphere of influence in particular.[18]

But for Cohen and Tucker this sphere was as much a politico-security sphere as an economic one.[19] Indeed, it was an integrated whole of the three elements.

One aspect of the radical critique that should not be ignored is the Leninist one of the imperial rivalry of the major capitalist Powers that Fred Halliday argues is still with us:

Inter-imperialist conflict lay at the origins of both the First and Second World Wars, and despite its displacement from the primacy which, until 1941, it occupied in world politics, and despite US predominance, it has continued to fuel major international tensions in the post-war epoch. After two decades of relative harmony, emphasis on the increased level of conflict between major capitalist states began to be noticeable from the late 1960s onwards, as the rivalry between the USA on the one side, and Europe and Japan on the other, gathered force. It was an emphasis found in the analyses of both left and right.[20]

Radical historians are not alone in noticing the degree to which the USA took Britain's economic place in Latin America, the Middle East and Near East, and not always in the most gentle of manners. The Marshall Plan was, of course, warmly welcomed by Western European governments and most of their people, but it did give US business a red carpet *entrée* into the European economy and it was only in the 1970s that a dependent relationship began to become an interdependent one in Atlantic terms. It still remains to become so to all parties' satisfaction across the Pacific. Rival blocs are not unthinkable as protectionism grows apace. What was the 'engine of growth' could become the 'apple of discord', to mix the metaphors. It is clear, therefore, that the Leninist thesis of inter-capitalist competition has both advocates and relevance today. Since the structuralist approach owes much to its Marxist–Leninist heritage, it is to that heritage that we now turn.

The Marxist heritage

As Tony Thorndike pointed out in an insightful essay,

> In International Relations, Marxism is primarily treated as an *ideology* in the formation of the foreign policies of particular states . . .[21]

Happily those bad old days are behind us. No student of IR would now deny the importance both of structural approaches and of the historic and present debt such approaches owe to the Marxist tradition. Marx argued that the superstructure of political and social ideas, institutions, and, indeed, social consciousness, was a reflection of and derived from the substructure of economic and production relations. In our time, and that of Marx, these relations are, to a lesser or greater degree, capitalistic. In such a situation the state and its servants are deemed to act in defence, and to further the interests, of the capitalist ruling class. But these interests are not immutable: they evolve. Nor are they always complementary within the capitalist class. Moreover, mistakes can be, and are, made. Nevertheless, while a state may have a degree of relative autonomy, it is not the starting point for fundamental analysis. The unit of analysis is class.[22] At the world level, capitalism is seen to be a progressive force because it is instrumental in the downfall of feudalism and it will itself succumb to its own internal contradictions as the proletariat overthrow the bourgeoisie to establish a socialist, and later a communist classless society. Capitalism, therefore, has its uses as an engine of change. But for the most part Marx concentrated on class relations within state and societal structures. It was Lenin, among others, who added a global dimension by postulating that imperialism was organic to, and the highest stage of, capitalism. Imperialism, too, had its contradictions between the imperial Powers each seeking to establish a single monopoly position in all aspects of the global economic system. Their global struggle was the death-knell of capitalism. Again there was a sense of progress, of stages on the way to a different and better world. However, more recently this sense of movement, indeed progress, has been challenged by *dependencia* and world-system theorists, who see a much more static system in which the present world is witnessing a greater accentuation of different levels of development and of exploitation. Indeed, the system has been stable structurally for five hundred years. In short, they are far less sanguine than Marx and Lenin about the degree and rapidity of progress that the contradictions of capitalism are likely to engender.

We have seen how in the late nineteenth and early twentieth centuries the debate on imperialism revitalized the Marxist tradition and provided one basis for the academic study of international relations. This tradition was ignored until the 1970s in so far as the mainstream of IR in Western academia is concerned. A new interest in economic theories of IR, which reflect the Marxist heritage, came not only from the revisionist historians but more centrally from scholars in Latin America, whose principal concerns were the causes of underdevelopment and the processes of development of what came to be known as the 'third world'. They came to the conclusion that structural considerations were of great moment in this and, in particular, the nature of capitalism as a global structure. As they articulated their ideas in theories of *dependencia*, they were absorbed into the mainstream of IR by scholars whose intellectual awareness had been heightened by the tenets of post-behaviouralism and the need to understand the post-colonial world and its concerns. Thus IR returned to its roots, or one aspect thereof: capitalism as a structure.

Capitalism as a structure

We have mentioned earlier those Marxists who saw historical evolution in teleological terms with an inevitable progress towards communism. For them, as for Marx himself, the spread of capitalism was to be welcomed as a movement towards that goal. Others, however, are not so sanguine. Paul Baran, in his *Political Economy of Growth*,[23] argued that the developing countries were not just 'behind' in this forward movement, but different in kind from developed capitalist countries. They needed, therefore, to be considered separately as fitting into capitalism in a different and especially disadvantaged way. Starting from different premises, a group of Latin American economists working for the UN Economic Commission for Latin America (ECLA), led by Raoul Prebisch, began to come to not dissimilar conclusions. In his clear and helpful survey on development and dependency Chris Brown suggests a threefold division of the literature: that is, *dependencia*, centre-periphery analysis and world-system analysis, which we shall adopt.[24]

ECLA analysts soon came to question the conventional wisdom of development theory in the 1950s and to suggest that the lack of development was due not only to deficiencies or mistaken policies in the developing countries themselves but, more important, to the terms of trade that, after the boom of the Second World War and the Korean War, were moving against exporters of primary products. This was a long-term trend, the remedy for which was deemed to be import substitution in which protected industries would be set up locally to obviate the need for so many increasingly expensive imports (in terms of their costs in exports necessary to finance the imports). The strategy of import substitution did not resolve the problem and writers in the *dependencia* school suggested that this was so for a number of reasons:

> because the internal market for consumer goods is too limited and the nature of demand is determined by elite tastes oriented to the products of the developed world and because it tends to be based on capital-intensive industries, which have low employment effects and therefore do little to create demand. Moreover, it is based on imported capital goods, components and materials which, therefore, does little to assist the balance of payments and may even cause crises, and it increases dependence on multinational capital and on foreign technology. [25]

The remedy, the *dependencia* school suggested, would have to be found elsewhere in the context of centre–periphery relations. It was not just a question of economic relations, which had been the main concern of the ECLA and *dependencia* analysts, but the structure within which these relations was embedded.

Andre Gunder Frank stresses the centre–periphery relationship or, in his terms, the metropolis–satellite structure of the capitalist system, both now and in the past. The metropolis exploits the satellite, a process which started in Latin America with the Spanish and Portuguese conquests, and it keeps the surplus, which is then used to develop the metropolis. Development in the satellite is thus hindered and choked so that there is the 'development of underdevelopment' in the satellite. This is a wilful process in contrast to the notion of 'undevelopment' – the state of affairs before capitalist penetration occurred. Frank notes that when the metropolis was cut off from the satellite, as in the case of Latin America in the World Wars or when, as with Japan, no metropolis existed, the development of underdevelopment ceased, and genuine development began. However, Frank's analysis needs to come to terms with the autonomous development in the periphery of NICs (newly industrializing countries) and a new stage in the international division of labour whereby MNCs invest and establish manufacturing subsidiaries in third world countries. Nevertheless, in Frank's view the problem was structural and so, therefore, would have to be the solution. Other writers laid different emphases, for example Emmanuel and Amin,[26] but the trend was clear: the issue of development was leading to a questioning of structure, and especially centre–periphery relations. But centre–periphery relations were not only an economic phenomenon, they could be seen as a multidimensional form of contemporary imperialism. Johan Galtung saw them as such.[27]

Galtung is concerned about centre–periphery relations both within and between states. These relations constitute, in their ensemble, a modern form of imperialism. The centre of a state in the developed world draws into it 'the best' of society, not only in terms of the fruits of industry, but cultural institutions, advanced hospitals and the like, which are supported by the wider society but enjoyed in a disproportionate manner by the centre. In Britain the south-east of England compared with the 'Celtic fringe' is a vivid illustration of this. But the same phenomenon exists in 'third world' countries, for example, the relationship of Nairobi to the rest of Kenya. In addition, the developed world as a whole acts as a global centre with the third world as its periphery. The IMF and World Bank are in Washington; the UN Specialized Agencies in Geneva, Vienna, Paris, Rome; the commodity and financial markets in London, New York and Tokyo; third world students and scholars flock to universities in Europe and North America, some of the best of them to remain there; young artists, whether musicians, dancers or painters can only 'make it' in London, Paris, Vienna or New York, and not in Australia, New Zealand, South Africa or Latin America; 'colonial cringe', whether justified or not, still exists even in such developed 'Western' parts of the periphery. But why do not the peripheries of the world unite so that they may escape from the debilitating exploitation of their centres? This is because the periphery in the centre part of the world is better off than the periphery in a peripheral country. The relative position of the centre's periphery is different from the absolute periphery. An unemployed Welsh miner can still enjoy his cup of tea in part because of the absolute peripheral status of tea pickers in Sri Lanka. Why then does the centre of the periphery not break its subservience to the centre of the developed world? Because by acting as a transmission belt from the global periphery to the global centre, it receives privileges so that its children can go to British schools and universities, its sick to British private hospitals, and its money is invested in British property as a bolt hole if ever a real revolution occurs in the periphery. The centre of the periphery is bought off; it is a collaborator. And frequently it develops a 'poor white' mentality, as we see in the classic cases of Israel and South Africa. Such is Galtung's conception, and he relates it to what he calls the five elements of imperialism – the economic, the political, the military, communications and the cultural elements. Moreover, such a situation is likely to be most stable if there is a lack of status disequilibrium, that is, if those who are advantaged are so across the board, and likewise for the disadvantaged. Trouble occurs when an actor is in a mixed situation, for then the disequilibrium creates a motive for change to even up the disadvantaged dimensions. The point had not escaped Marx.

This view of centre–periphery relations has a high degree of plausibility, when considered *grosso modo*, since it explains how there is an equilibriating harmony of interests in the context of a global conflict of interests, but the world is not quite as simple as that. Grand conceptions, such as centre–periphery or world-system, certainly shed light on global peaks and troughs, but most people live on less demanding terrain. There is, therefore, the problem of 'Bridging the micro and the macro in IR research', to cite the title of an insightful article on this subject by Chadwick Alger.[28] Alger has pointed to the city as a unit of analysis for transnational ties and provided a wealth of empirical research in this context. Moreover, the state cannot be entirely dismissed even when centre–periphery relations in the economic domain are considered. We may not live in a state-centric world as the realist conceives it, but neither the world society nor structuralist approach would suggest that, analytically, we live in an entirely state-less world. Indeed, Peter Evans has rightly suggested, with due caveats, that it is not always so that increasing transnational ties necessarily have 'a debilitating effect on the Third World state as an institution and social actor'.[29] Indeed, in some circumstances they may, paradoxically, strengthen the state. We have, therefore, a dilemma in that grand conceptions may have an intrinsic and intuitive plausibility, but there are many anomalous situations to be explained. How many exceptions must there be before they no longer 'prove the rule'? This is an epistemological question that need not concern us more than to note it in passing now, but it is one that cannot always be ignored when considering conceptual frameworks, paradigms or units of analysis as grand as the capitalist world-system of the last half-millennia, as conceived by Immanuel Wallerstein, to which we now turn.

The *oeuvre* of Wallerstein must surely be among the most talked about, the most quoted – and the least read in their totality – in the Marxist tradition since those of the master himself. Wallerstein says that the world-systems perspective was inspired by five rejections. The first was a denial of a single or multidisciplinary approach. Secondly, the state was rejected as a primary unit of analysis and the 'state–society antinomy was a misleading premise for enquiry'. Political action was seen as being 'inside *all* social action'. Thirdly, there was a rejection of both cyclical and evolutionary theories of history.

> Instead, insofar as any historical system existed, there were within it repetitive patterns (cycles), for as long as the particular system existed. But all such social systems were historically time bound because the cycles reflected contradictory internal thrusts that led to and accounted for the inherent structural stresses (trends) that eventually caused the disintegration or structural transformation of the historical system as a whole.

The fourth rejection was that of the notion of the sequential development of comparable subunits, because 'The dynamic of the system not only was the sum of all the forces contained in it but also affected all its zones at every moment'.[30] The final rejection was that of 'formulating concepts as essences rather than as processes'.[31] Thus Wallerstein had cleared the decks ready for his thesis.

Wallerstein's basic unit of analysis is the world-system, or, to be more precise, the contemporary world-system of capitalism, which began with the establishment of a capitalist world-economy, without the accompaniment of a world-empire, about 1500. The world economy is:

> a single division of labor within which are located multiple cultures . . . but which has no overarching political culture. Without a political structure to redistribute the appropriated surplus, the surplus can only be redistributed via the 'market', however frequently states located within the world-economy

intervene to distort the market. Hence the mode of production
is capitalist.

A capitalist mode is one in which production is for exchange;
that is, it is determined by its profitability on a market in which
each buyer wishes to buy cheap (and therefore that which is, in
the long run, most efficiently produced and marketed) but in
which each seller wishes to sell dear (and therefore is concerned
that the efficiencies of others are not permitted to reduce his
sales).[32]

Let us note in passing that Modelski would assert that, although
there was no world-empire in the cycles of the world system, there
was most certainly an efficacious global political structure – a
subject to which we shall return. Since Wallerstein does not accept
this he is surprised that the new world-economy did not collapse,
as similar such economies had before, when sub-systems drifted
away because there was no political authority to arrest the drift and
impose and maintain the unity in the form of a world-empire.
However, once surviving, it aroused three questions in Wallerstein's mind: those of its genesis, once consolidated that of its
modus operandi, and its secular trends.[33]

Wallerstein argues that feudal Eruope had ' "exhausted its potential" in its great socioeconomic spurt of 1100–1250'. The real
income of the ruling states was falling, due to the rising of real
wages caused by demographic disasters, peasant revolts and the
internecine warfare of the ruling strata.[34] There was no world-
empire to stop the rot.

> Instead there was a sort of creative leap of the imagination on
> the part of the ruling strata. It involved trying an alternative
> mode of surplus appropriation, that of the market, to see
> whether it might serve to restore the declining real income of
> the ruling groups. This involved geographical expansion, spatial
> economic specialization, the rise of the 'absolutist' state – in
> short, the creation of a capitalist world-economy.
>
> The genesis of capitalism was not in the triumph of a new
> group, the urban burghers, over the landed feudal nobility.
> Rather it should be seen as the reconversion of seignior into
> capitalist producer, an essential *continuity* of ruling families.
> Furthermore, it worked magnificently . . . [35]

It should be noted that in his work Wallerstein goes into detailed historical analysis, but not always without controversy.

The *modus operandi* of the system revolved around two struggles – between bourgeoisie and proletariat, and between core and periphery.

> The genius, if you will, of the capitalist system, is the interweaving of these two channels of exploitation which overlap but are not identical and create the political and cultural complexities (and obscurities) of the system. Among other things, it has made it possible to respond to the politico-economic pressures of cyclical economic crises by rearranging spatial hierarchies without significantly impairing class hierarchies.[36]

This it has done by outward expansion for, unlike in Modelski's conception, Wallerstein's world-economy grew piecemeal and it did not become truly global, in all its aspects, until after 1917. However, there is within this expansion a cycle of repression (necessary to enable the maintenance of unequal distribution) becoming more costly, and 'reform', to make that cost less onerous. A little of the surplus is used to 'buy off' the rising class, but this can then result in 'depriving the top strata of a prize high enough to be worth struggling for. This is the "failure of nerve" that is setting in'.[37] This may lead to changes within the core, Holland giving way to Britain, movement from periphery to semi-periphery, core to semi-periphery or the reverse: that is, the spatial dimension acts as a stabilizing factor for the class dimension. But eventually that may not be enough, and in the fullness of time – a long time, Wallerstein insists – the capitalist world-economy will give way to a socialist world government.[38]

Wallerstein lays particular stress on the semi-periphery as a factor likely to enable the smooth running of the world-economy. While repression by state forces has its efficacious uses and there is a 'pervasiveness of an ideological commitment to the system as a whole' by 'the staff or cadres of the system . . . [i]t is the normal condition . . . to have a three-layered structure [core, semi-periphery, periphery]. When and if this ceases to be the case, the world-system disintegrates'.[39] The semi-periphery countries are given a cut of the surplus to prevent revolt, but they are denied political rights to make them 'constantly vulnerable to confiscatory measures whenever their economic profits become sufficiently swollen so that they might begin to create for themselves military might'.[40] They are a political device to stop polarization, rather than an economic necessity. The semi-periphery is both exploiter and exploited. The state is one means by which reallocations within the core, semi-periphery or periphery or between them can take place. It can interfere in the market in such a way as to deflect normal market forces and secure a non-market rate of exploitation or distribution of surplus.[41] But there is not always agreement as to how this should be done, its extent and in favour of whom, among the bourgeois world class and their attendant states.[42] They may use states to intervene for the smooth functioning of the system in the general class interest, or they may use the state to steal a march on their 'class colleagues'. And beyond states there are cultural communities that have a potential to muddy the waters, since 'the formation and disintegration of cultural communities do form a fundamental set of processes in their own right . . .'[43]

As Giddens has pointed out, 'for Wallerstein the existence of separate states seems to be a largely historical residue of the fact that capitalism came into being within a pre-formed state system'.[44] In Wallerstein's conception states are there to be used or not, as the case may be, usually to meet the functional needs of the system. Indeed, there are strong functional elements of a sociological not Mitranian kind in Wallerstein's thought.

Wallerstein's position is a very clear-cut one in the Marxist debate between those who argue that the core–periphery division of labour of the capitalist world-economy leads to unequal exchange relations in favour of the core and others who 'argue that relations of production (class relations) precede economic exchange, making class relations the determinate social relation of world capitalism'.[45] The latter is the classical position in a debate that we have broached before – it is a debate about whether to emphasize class relations within societies or exploitation between core and periphery. It also raised the question of the relationship between the two struggles. Bergesen argues that since most of the global means of production are under the control of the core, this makes 'the core–periphery relation a class relation rather than an unequal exchange relation'[46] – at least in its essence. But Waller- stein's thought makes it difficult to square the circle in this way. His emphasis is on the spatial aspects of exploitation – the physically separate core and periphery – which could lead him to be more regionally or even state-oriented than he is wont to admit. As James Lee Ray argues,

> Ultimately, Wallerstein emphasises relations among states as the essence of capitalism to the point where he concludes that the 'class relations of production' *within* states are all but entirely irrelevant. 'Even if every nation in the world were to permit only state ownership of the means of production, the world-system would still be a capitalist system' . . . For Marx, socialism can be achieved when the working class within a state overthrows the capitalist ruling class within that state; for Wallerstein, socialism can be achieved only if the domination of the world-system by core states and competition among all states in general are terminated by a socialist world government.[47]

And this will be a long time, given the strong proclivities that Wallerstein identifies for systems maintenance. Wallerstein's emphasis on the core and core states, therefore, suggests that politics is important and that the world-system may not only have an economic rationale or logic but also the makings of a political logic as well – as is Modelski's contention. It is also easy to see why so many Marxists reject Wallerstein's work. Chris Brown has commented that 'Although Wallerstein uses much of the language of Marxism his notions are actually very unmarxist in their denial of 'progress', their stress on distribution/exchange rather than production, and their lack of interest in the law of value.'[48]

The plenitude of nuclear weapons (and other weapons of mass destruction), capable of destroying the world as we know it, is, of course, a powerful balancing factor on the side of an important political logic. The inability and inappropriateness of market forces to deal effectively with the 'green' agenda and other 'one world' problems also point to the imperative for political intervention. Moreover, exploitation gives rise to a contested distribution that is, in its nature, political, although its substance may be economic. In addition, the distribution of resources and the inequalities that arise therefrom again suggests a spatial and political factor. It also suggests that neither an economic nor a political theory of structure alone is likely to be as rich as an integrated theory of both. As Zolberg has remarked,

> In an analysis of global transformation, it depends very much on the investigator's starting point whether culture or social structure, politics or economics, is considered causally dominant. That starting point itself is dictated by the investigator's inclination toward one or the other intellectual tradition, by his position in contemporary political controversies, or merely by his field of academic specialization.[49]

The emergence, and now perhaps the demise, of the world system of states and the growth of alternative world political structures, as well as that of capitalism, is an empirical phenomenon the explanation of which is worthy of the intellectual heavyweights of structuralism. Wallerstein has made a start but so, too, in a more political conception of global structure, has Modelski.

Long cycles in a global structure

The existence of long cycles in politics, economics and civilization has been postulated, rejected and disputed in the literature for generations. Our own time is no exception, and just as Wallerstein has become pre-eminent in the economic field so have George Modelski and his associates in the political field. It is, therefore, to Modelski's work that we can turn to get the essence and flavour of this approach.[50] His is a major enterprise, but he is careful in his claims and in his presentation. He does not force us to 'take it or leave it', or exhort us to jump on the bandwagon – there is no intellectual bullying – rather we are led, gently but persuasively, to consider the notion of a world system in ways that previously have been unfamiliar. Modelski's argument captures the imagination. It is not exclusive, since it includes economic and cultural elements as well as the political, although the latter clearly dominate. For this reason, and his concern with governance in an anarchical society with emphasis on the concomitant prevalence of power politics, Modelski is clearly in the realist tradition. But his starting point is structure, or at least the last five centuries of world history at the global level, so he fully merits (if that is the right word) the appellation of a structural realist.

World-system approaches, such as those of Modelski and Wallerstein, have several characteristics in common.[51]. They acknowledge the existence of a single world system, on a global basis, for the last five centuries, which has political, economic and cultural components at the global level. They cannot agree on which component dominates or on the interaction between the components – the debate about which we shall discuss later. Nevertheless, there is a consensus that a fruitful starting point, and basic framework, is the notion of a world system. It is within this framework, or so it is contended, that other phenomena are likely to fall into place. Their importance is not minimized, but put into a historico-structural perspective. That perspective is no blind structure: it is enlivened by cycles as the processes of life manifest themselves. Such cyclical processes have, by their very nature, a predictive capacity. In short, there is the essential 'holism' of the structural approach: historically, in the sense of a major portion of recorded human history, in terms of dimension, be it political, economic or cultural, and in approach, since the traditional boundaries of discipline are set aside in a new fusion. And this is important, as Thompson points out:

> World system analysis emphasizes structures and processes that, while not altogether ignored in the past, have never received adequate and integrated attention. To the extent that world system arguments prove to be well supported by the evidence, a respectable proportion of social science knowledge will require considerable revision. In the process, our understanding of world history will undergo equally extensive revision . . . Finally, the potential of world system analyses for reintegrating a large number of frustratingly separate fields of study and levels of analysis is unusually promising.[52]

The stakes are indeed high.

Modelski's starting point is the long cycle.

> Long cycles offer a new perspective on world politics. They permit the careful exploration of the ways in which world wars have recurred, and lead states such as Britain and the United

States have succeeded each other in an orderly manner. They draw attention to the fact that great wars and leading powers were also linked to waves of major innovations, such as the age of discoveries or the industrial revolution, that have made the modern world what it is. They help cultivate a long-term outlook on international affairs . . . Long cycles are, in the first place, a conservative process of repetition . . . [but they] are more than mere repetition. Upon close analysis, they are revealed as dynamic phenomena, part and parcel of the rise of modernity. They embody evolutionary development through strategic innovations. That is why this analysis also supports the notion that long cycles are a progressive process of learning.[53]

The interaction between political and economic factors is an important element in Modelski's thought, which thus differs markedly from Wallerstein's in this regard. In their respective explanations of the world system, Modelski gives politics a primacy whereas Wallerstein gives capitalism a near exclusivity. As Modelski explains,

The long cycle is the process of change in the structure of politics at the global level; its essence has been the rise of nation-states to a position of world leadership and the competition that has followed. Running in tandem with it over the past five hundred years has also been the process of emergence, and subsequent decline, of lead economies. While the rise of world powers has been central to world politics, and the formation of lead economies has been fundamental to world economics, the relationship of these two processes to each other, . . . has rarely been subject to sustained analysis . . . [T]hese two basic processes . . . may be seen as linked in terms of a model of 'alternating innovations' wherein, at the global level, generation-long periods of fundamental political innovation alternate with those of change in the industrial structure, bringing about fundamental shifts in the economy. The coordinating mechanism seems to reside in the sustained movements in prices known as the Kondratieff waves.[54]

Modelski denies

the notion of international anarchy, meaning literally the absence of government, or established order, in international relations . . . what is amazing is the degree of structure created by leadership . . . and the continuity in that process going back for so many centuries.

Nor is the notion of self-help any more enlightening . . . in actual fact the characteristic pattern of world leadership has been the capacity for the organization of consensus and the elaboration of coalitions . . . the reality is of an increasing division of labor between the producers and the consumers of global order.[55]

On these grounds Modelski has cast doubt over the very foundations of the realist world – anarchy, separateness, self-help and, as we shall see in Kenneth Waltz's neorealist conception, no functional differentiation.

Modelski's rejection of anarchy stems from his acknowledgement of a 'global political system', which 'is the topmost political structure of the world'.

It is topmost because it is concerned with the longest-range problems of world organisation: the definition and clarification of global problems and of the action (or inaction) that may be appropriate in relation to them. But what it gains in elevation and perspective it loses in terms of being in touch with 'realities' at the grass roots. It needs to penetrate the layers of regional and national organisation before it reaches the true grit of the local level.[56]

Within this 'topmost political structure' leadership is exercised by a particular Power, thus providing a link with the 'true grit of the local level'.

World leadership . . . refers to the structural arrangement for resolving the most pressing problems of world politics. Obviously it is not world government because it is a structure marked by high improvization, intermittency, and crisis management. It is not a differentiated global institution but rather a set of functions performed by a nation-state that by dint of the right qualifications finds itself at the right moment doing the right things at the right place. But such a nation-state does not

rule the world (or other nation-states) in an imperial manner nor
exercise 'world-wide domination'; rather, it orders aspects of
global problems in a manner at the time regarded as legitimate.
We need also to distinguish world leadership from hegemony by
using the criteria of common interest and legitimacy. When a
leading state acts in the public interest and its actions are thought
legitimate, then its behavior cannot be described as hegemonial.
On the other hand, we need not assume that nation-states in
positions of world leadership can never act other than in the
common interest or legitimately. All we do is not to adopt an
initial presumption of hegemonial, that is, in the classical style,
tyrannical, behavior.[57]

There is both legitimized and non-legitimized role differentiation
and with it legitimized and power politics – a concern shared with
the world society approach.
In Modelski's conception:

> Leadership cannot be viewed solely or primarily as a display of
> power or a manifestation of superiority; it must be seen more
> essentially as the accomplishment of essential services that give
> impetus and example to the global polity and, eventually, to the
> entire world system. What are these services? They are, in
> respect of global politics: (i) agenda formation, (ii) mobilisation,
> (iii) decision-making, (iv) administration, and (v) innovation.[58]

Agenda formation 'concerns the clarification and definition of
global problems and the assignment of priorities'. It is thus 'a
function of knowledge and values, and is the product of debates'.[59]
Mobilization refers to the ability to build a coalition of support for
the existing global system, whereas decision-making arises out of
the ability to prevail in a systemic war and thus make 'a basic
decision about the political direction of the global system for a
significant period ahead'. This decision needs to be administered
and an 'active economy is a basic precondition for such administration'. Innovation, by definition, is unpredictable, but what
Modelski has in mind is

> Britain launching the Industrial Revolution, that moved and
> reorganised the world and achieved more than a strictly political

transformation. Without this kind of basic innovation, linked to leadership, and amounting in essence to the exercise of a teaching role, the world would have been short of evolutionary potential.[60]

The changing balance between legitimized and power politics is what Modelski identifies as the long cycle, of which in the present world system there have been five, with the following Powers exercising world leadership: Portugal (sixteenth century), the Netherlands (seventeenth century), Britain (eighteenth century), Britain again (nineteenth century) and now the United States (twentieth century). Portugal established the system, although Venice could be considered a forerunner, and, like its successors, it went through the long cycle.

> [E]ach contains the same characteristic sequence of events: a *global war*; a worldwide struggle of major proportions and consequences; an era of political and economic consolidation *(world power)*; a mid-course period of political unsettlement and possible innovation (delegitimation); and a final sequence of rivalry and competitive disruption (deconcentration), setting the stage for another global conflict.[61]

That there were serious rivals for such a position of world leadership, and Spain, France, Germany and the Soviet Union immediately spring to mind, Modelski readily admits, but they did not ultimately prevail because they lacked, in masterful plenitude, the capacities necessary for the task. These are:

(i) a secure platform from which to observe and debate the state of the world system and its problems – an insular position has traditionally proved the most advantageous; (ii) a society capable of coalitioning, that is coherent and stable, hence worth aligning with, but one that is also open to the world and pluralistic in its internal arrangements, i.e. accustomed to the politics of coalition – an open-democratic predisposition has proved helpful in the past; (iii) a political system with effective forces for global reach (particularly at sea and in the air) at its disposal – traditional sea-powers have been strikingly successful here; (iv) an economy that is of world significance in its lead industries and foreign trade; and (v) capacity to innovate and respond to emerging world problems – a secret ingredient whose precise make-up is hard to know in advance. As this list makes abundantly clear, leadership in this context does not bestow upon its holders the licence to govern other national states or to intervene in their domestic or local politics.[62]

But what of economics? A 'lead economy' is an important requirement for political leadership. Modelski has a clear idea of what constitutes a 'lead economy':

> we emphasise not size (as it might be indexed by area, population, or GNP) but those indicators that bear on status as 'active zone': the creation of leading sectors and the relative size of the industrial economy, and participation in world trade, both qualitatively (in goods of the leading sectors) and quantitatively (in shares of world trade or of foreign investment) . . . [T]he linkage between world power and lead economy is not really surprising. A lead economy requires the political stability and international protection afforded by the services of the quality and the dimensions afforded by the world power. Each world power has been, in its time, the area of the greatest security of rights and entitlements, and of lowest transaction costs and superior global information services, and therefore also most frequently, the economy of refuge. On the other hand, world power is also costly and cannot be maintained without the support of an active and growing economy. Operations of global reach and global wars in particular cannot be conducted on the cheap. Hence a lead economy built upon a global flow of activities becomes a sine qua non of world power . . . The basic relationship is that of the world power providing, among its range of political goods/services and through its own international economic policies and its initiatives in global arrangements, the political basis for global economic relations.[63]

But Modelski bids us note that 'The significance of the world powers has not been in their size but in their capacity to accomplish global functions'.[64] And it is this ability to fulfil *global* functions that resolves the apparent anomaly whereby the world leader might not necessarily be the principal regional Power. Indeed, until the United States, that was never the case. But the leader could survive in its region *and* perform global functions, whereas rivals might have the edge at the regional level, often through sheer size, but they were found wanting in comparative global capacities. Nineteenth-century Britain and France are a case in point.

Modelski gives a principal, but not the predominant place to economics in a symbiotic relationship between the political and economic systems. But what is the basis of this linkage? Is there a cycle of general expansion and a slowing down in both systems, or is there an alternance between political growth and economic explansion. Modelski favours the latter, because it is likely to be simple and require less coordination. Moreover, it 'would seem to offer an automatic manner of self-regulation, politics coming into play to deal with problems created by economics, or those economic [problems] progress has left unresolved and economics, in its turn, attending to the social system laid to waste by periods of excessive devotion to politics'. And the coordination and synchronization is achieved through 'the value system conceived in a broad fashion'.

> The value system monitors, reflects, and adjusts the social priorities; and the price system as a whole reflects not just the state of particular markets but also the value judgements of the whole society. Thus the price system becomes one proxy for the value system . . .

However simplisticly, this at least enables some handle to be obtained on world culture, a notion the importance of which Modelski acknowledges but finds difficult to accommodate in his framework. Prices are linked to values, which in turn are grounded in culture, which is also tied to 'the political–ideological priority system as expressed in demand for the political goods/services of order and justice'.

> It could be, therefore, that both global politics and global economics 'listen to the same drummer': coordinated by the same value-price-priority system, both being affected by, and both responding to, the same movements in social valuations.[65]

This explains Modelski's interest in Kondratieff cycles of prices, in which Kondratieff identified long-term movements of prices of thirty years' length. Modelski attempts to match these with his century-long world leadership cycles, not with unmitigated success. Nevertheless, despite this, and the more general difficulty of operationalizing and incorporating the notion of world culture in his framework, Modelski's schema has a plausible ring. He can provide convincing examples and explain sensibly counter-examples. His work has an authentically intuitive rightness to it in its grand lines.

Modelski's schema not only inspires the historical imagination by shedding a pale and fitful light where there was little before, it also alerts us to our current predicament. We seem, as we would expect, to be in the period of the delegitimation of the world leadership of the United States, both politically and economically.

> If present trends continue, and in the absence of significant political innovation, we would expect in the decades ahead increased fragmentation leading up to the period of deconcentration marked by severe competition among the major powers and declining attention to the common interest.

However, Modelski is quick to point out that this is so only if we assume the 'constancy' of the modern world system, a constancy which 'may indeed need to be questioned'.[66] Modelski alludes to transnationalism and the sorts of considerations that are important in the world society approach discussed in Chapter 9. We can go even further: as the half millennium since the establishment of the modern world system out of feudalism is coming towards its end so too may be that system. Ironically, there are now many qualities of contemporary world society that evoke aspects of the medieval world as state-centricity declines in a world that is, nevertheless, plainly an ordered world. The segments seem to be changing – from states? to systems? to what? Will there be a single world system segmented not on states, as Modelski has it at present, but on something else? The world society approaches would suggest a variety of possible segmentations, and Modelski is alive to this as well because:

one conceivable development could be *the differentiation of a so-far-undifferentiated role of world leadership* into several more special-ised components, with different countries devoting themselves to different functional areas, aspects of economic or cultural leadership, and elements of the strategic-political spectrum. Such an arrangement would, however, give rise to new and possibly quite difficult problems of co-ordination.

An alternative, and possibly more interesting, development might take the form of new kinds of *coalition-building*. Whereas the experience of world leadership to date refers only to single countries, in the future that role could be explicitly shared by a coalition . . . Inventing new forms of co-operation has been a hallmark of world leadership, and such novel arrangements are required particularly urgently in respect of nuclear weapons. These might well prove to be the most promising avenues of contemporary political innovation.[67]

And it is not only nuclear weapons, important as they are, but other elements of the 'green agenda'. Such a collaboration may be emerging if a leadership role is assumed by the EC in concert with the USA and in association with Japan, the USSR, China, India and Brazil, all of whom have their respective spheres of influence and specific strengths and specialities.

This points to the need for a fusion of political, economic and cultural factors. Modelski has explained a linkage between political and economic factors, but he is noticeably unconvincing on incorporating cultural factors. Wallerstein and the Marxist tradition give undisputed pride of place to economic structure. Yet there has been little debate between these two opposing conceptions. There has been a vigorous affirmation of position by the leading advo-cates of the two approaches, but beyond that little more than a dialogue of the deaf or an intellectual turning away of one from the other rather than a joining of debate. Perhaps this is understand-able, since such grand theories, while attractive, exciting and seductive, are weak on prescription for the affairs of today or tomorrow, and such issues are, for most of us, our daily lot. This is not to deny the wealth of detailed historical evidence sifted by both Wallerstein and Modelski, but history is, perforce, personal and selective – it is a plausible fairy tale. In effect, it reinforces rather than closes an argument, which lends it an intriguing fascination – in a sense you cannot lose! But historical argument is more than a charade. It can provide context to current events and point us in new directions. In this Modelski and his colleagues, although they have, until now, had less prominence in the field, may provide us with greater contextual relevance and point to more exciting vistas, precisely because of the fusion between political, economic and cultural factors. Equally to the point is their ability to broaden their horizon from the axioms of power politics to a conception of legitimized politics. Long cycles can be managed in concert through cooperation – or is this merely wishful thinking? Can capitalism evolve or must it be destroyed? Is a global war 'inevitable' no matter how catastrophic it might be? It cannot be gainsaid that those who study global structures, be they economic or political, are relevant. But these structures can also be conceived in other ways. It is to the geopolitical and geoecological conception of structure that we now turn.

Geopolitics

In Chapter 3 mention was made of geopolitical theorists who were prominent in the years when IR was coming to the point of being an academic discipline. Mackinder had a great intellectual influence and Alfred Thayer Mahan an enormous practical influence and popularity in Britain, the United States and Germany. Ironically, the Briton was the theorist of land power, while the American that of sea power, when the United States was still principally a continent in the making. But geopolitics also flourished on the Continent of Europe. The Swedish scholar, Rudolf Kjellen, and the German geographer, Friedrich Ratzel, both made noteworthy contributions, as did Yves Lacoste and the *Herodote* group in France.[68] Geopolitics at that time was concerned with the 'science' of the development and configuration of states, 'an expression of Social Darwinism and imperialist rivalry' or a strategic doctrine with normative implications.[69] Moreover, there is an element of holism, since Parker defines geopolitics as 'the study of the international scene from a spatial or geocentric viewpoint, the understanding of the whole – what Ritter called *Ganzheit* – being its ultimate object and justification'.[70] But it was the practical application of geopolitical analysis that led to a dramatic decline in the respectability of geopolitics, although analysts such as Nicholas Spykman continued to write in geopolitical terms and the wartime 'grand strategists' were also largely practitioners in the same *genre*. The occasion of the 'downfall' of geopolitics was its use by Nazi geographers, especially Professor Haushofer's school at Munich, in an attempt to provide a scientific rationale for Hitler's claim that the German *Volk* had need of *Lebensraum* (living space) in central and eastern Europe, giving them the scientific justification to create a new international order in the course of Hitler's *Drang nach Osten* (drive to the East). The terrible consequences of this policy did no good for the respectability, academic or otherwise, of geopolitics.

The approach did not really surface again until Harold and Margaret Sprout began to take a serious theoretical interest in the 'man–milieu' relationship. They circulated an essay in 1956, which elicited a wide and interested response.[71] A decade later they published *The Ecological Perspective in Human Affairs*, which surveyed a range of geopolitical themes, from environmental determinism to environmental possibilism, and brought attention to the interaction between the psychological environment and the operational environment in determining outcome.[72] The approach had similarities with that which Deutsch was developing in *The Nerves of Government*.[73] They succeeded not only in giving back the topic some respectability and reinserting it in the mainstream of discussion, but also in making a significant contribution to it. The work of the Club of Rome and the WOMP school, discussed in Chapter 9, was also instrumental in the climb back to respectability. At the present time the geopolitical approach has a clear structural emphasis, if we consider the work of Robert North, Nazli Choucri and Richard Ashley on 'lateral pressure'.[74] And it is to Ashley, who has built upon the work of North and Choucri and extended it into the area of critical theory, that we shall pay particular attention.

Ashley's *The Political Economy of War and Peace* is a young man's book, brimming with ideas, reflecting wide, if eclectic reading, strongly reminiscent, in its spirit, of the work of the young Galtung two decades previously (see note 27). It rambles, it is badly written, but it is, nevertheless, clear in its argument and its concern. Like Choucri and North, Ashley presents an empirical analysis as an exemplification of his approach – in his case that of the United States, Soviet Union and China locked in a security *problématique*, while Choucri and North concentrated on the decades before the Great War. Ashley adopts the Choucri–North notion of lateral pressure – a notion not alien to the ideas of Gilpin, Modelski and Wallerstein on the process by which expansion occurs. However, lateral pressure has specific roots in the interrelationship between growth in population, the economy and technology, which results in external expansion. Growth in any of the three induces the proclivity for like movement in the other two. But this may not be possible on the basis of the existing resource base. Can enough food be grown for a rising population, can the economy sustain it, is there a technological fix? Does the size of the market give the economies of scale for a technological breakthrough? The pressure is on to expand, and this lateral expansion quickly becomes politicized both within the expanding society, because it is seen as a justified pursuit of a better life, and externally, because it may run up against similar 'legitimate' tendencies on the part of others, either in bilateral confrontation or a multilateral balance of power system. Choucri and North show how these long-term processes of lateral expansion shed light on the structural aspects of the conflictual relations between the European great Powers between 1870 and 1914. Ashley examines the dynamics of rivalry in the context of China, the USA and the USSR in recent decades until 1980. While Ashley is aware that blind rivalry is not the necessary outcome, since there are possibilities for upgrading the common interest, it is the most common outcome. In attempts to rise above this, he takes his readers into the realm of critical theory. But, in the meantime, 'The progression from growth through rivalry to balance of power, then, is a creative progression, and what it creates and recreates is the modern security *problématique*', to this day from the 'dawn of absolutism' in Europe.[75] And this is because 'lateral pressure represents a generic, timeless social process, potentially evidenced by all living systems at all levels . . .'[76] But it is a dangerous process, because 'in a finite world of finite resources, its expansion cannot go on forever. War and conquest are among the mechanisms of its transformation once the limits of its growth are reached, approached, or become too costly to overcome . . . This logic applies so long as technical rationality prevails.'[77] Lateral pressure can create what has now become, potentially, a structure of doom.

In the preface to his book Ashley warns us that his 'is a story of human beings behaving quite rationally to gain and extend mastery over nature and creating an irrational global state of nature that masters humans and threatens their destruction'. Moreover, 'humankind is caught in the most tragic of traps . . . the trap is made through a long, cumulative history of false technical-rational solutions, and . . . the search for technical-rational solutions can never set us free'.[78] Hence the need ' "to get out of" this restrictive grammar of thought'[79] and this by means not of technical rationality but 'rationality proper'.[80]

> [A] technical-rational grammar of thought tends to conceive of life as consisting of so many more or less discrete problem situations; and problem situations are defined in terms of certain given purposes or needs, certain obstacles to or limits on the realization or satisfaction of these, and certain means by which the obstacles and limits can or might be overcome. Accordingly, such a grammar tends to take for granted hence disregard those slowly changing aspects of life that, relative to immediate purposes or needs, are too costly to manipulate. It tends also to leave unquestioned the boundaries of the immediate problem, how obstacles and limits might be given form by choices and actions in other sectors of life, and how attempts to solve the immediate problem might reverberate through time and impact upon other sectors. Most importantly, it takes purposes and needs for granted.[81]

For Ashley 'rationality proper' – or critical theory – can take us beyond this. We will then no longer need to pretend that we are 'in control', by making false puzzles out of real problems in order to make them amenable to technical-rational solutions, the long-run logic and cumulation of which are potentially of disastrous consequences.

> Where technical rationality seeks to focus knowledge and skills on specific, bounded problem situations, rationality proper starts from the premise that knowledge and skills so focussed are not and cannot be autonomous of the historical processes giving the problem situation its manifest form. The task within rationality proper is to begin with the specific problem situation and attempt to 'import' the larger historical reality within it. This

attempt is made, not by invoking the assumption that there exists some fixed, final, and potentially knowable structure predominating over the whole of reality, but through the attempt to engage, criticize, and synthesize competing vantage points associated with other aspects of reality as these do or might relate to the specific problem situation . . . rationality proper embeds and subordinates technical rationality within a richer logic . . . [82]

The relationship with the environment is no longer zero sum – conquer or submit – in a way that disenfranchises creative thought. Rather it must be one of critical engagement. It must be based on the realization that we are not freely autonomous in relation to our environment, but we are an integral part of it. But the relationship is one of continuous, constructive and critical engagement in order to transform it. And we must remember and take into account that the whole is always greater than the sum of the parts. Robert Cox, in summarizing the basic premises of critical theory, ends with the following propositions:

The framework for action changes over time and a principal goal of critical theory is to understand these changes; this framework has the form of an historical structure, a particular combination of thought patterns, natural conditions and human institutions which has a certain coherence among its elements. These structures do not determine people's actions in any mechanical sense but constitute the context of habits, pressures, expectations and constraints within which action takes place; . . . [this] is to be viewed, not from the top in terms of the requisites for its equilibrium or reproduction . . . but rather from the bottom or from outside in terms of the conflicts which arise within it and open the possibility of its transformation. [83]

The road has been long from Easton's summary of post-behaviouralism to Cox's of critical theory. But we are the better for having made the journey. IR now gives a more appropriate recognition to, and has a more proper appreciation of not only structural factors but also the need for historical depth and breadth. This is not the history of the inconsequential detail, but that of the appropriate timescale, so that we can appreciate properly the full implications of structure. Moreover, whatever the intrinsic merits of the approaches heretofore reviewed, they do collectively have the singular effect of causing those who feel more comfortable in other traditions, be it realism or world society, to take greater cognisance of structural factors than had hitherto been their wont. But too much of anything may be no good thing, and this applies to structural analysis as well. Even if the structure is treated genuinely as being autonomous, process cannot be ignored. Moreover, we must beware of an intellectual backlash. Once having been recognized as important and taken into consideration, structure may be discounted since it is slow to change and can thus be taken as given – and, being given, then forgotten. This is a danger, particularly when in the business of normal science, technical rationality or when exploring an 'island of theory'. One of the important functions of critical theory is to make us aware of such potentialities and able better to overcome them. We must know ourselves and how to better ourselves.

Since the end of the dominance of traditional realism as the framework of IR theory and the wealth of 'normal science' to which it gave rise, there has been a great intellectual ferment, drawing on long-standing intellectual traditions, which has stimulated two different conceptual frameworks: world society and structuralism. While neither of these frameworks is complete, nor accepted on a consensual basis even by their respective adherents – although sometimes there is harmony, even if there is never unison – the time for normal science is upon us again to explore, in a more detailed fashion, these frameworks so that they can be filled out and refined. This, anyway, is the lot of most scholars most of the time, and it can be done better in the knowledge of the larger frameworks. These frameworks, however, are not timeless and unchanging – they evolve – and particularly when they are faced with a formidable challenge such as realism has been by world society and structural approaches. Individuals are not wont to change their *Weltanschauung* at the mere suggestion of an anomaly, particularly if what is offered as a replacement is also riddled with anomalies. Realism has been under challenge and realists have in the 1980s been resurgent.

Notes: Chapter 10

1 Anthony Giddens, *The Nation-State and Violence* (Cambridge: Polity Press, 1985), p. 4.
2 See Quentin Skinner (ed.), *The Return of Grand Theory in the Human Sciences* (Cambridge: Cambridge University Press, 1985).
3 I am grateful to my colleague Chris Brown for this point.
4 Richard Little, 'Structuralism and neo-realism', in Margot Light and A. J. R. Groom (eds), *International Relations: A Handbook of Current Theory* (London: Frances Pinter, 1985), p.76.
5 See Joshua Goldstein, *Long Cycles: Prosperity and War in the Modern Age* (London: Yale University Press, 1988), p. 289.
6 David Easton, 'The new revolution in political science', *American Political Science Review*, December 1969.
7 ibid., p. 1051.
8 ibid., p. 1052.
9 On the First World War, see N. Gordon Levin Jr, *Woodrow Wilson and World Politics* (New York: Oxford University Press, 1968) and Arno J. Mayer, *Politics and Diplomacy of Peacemaking* (London: Weidenfeld and Nicolson, 1968). On the later period, other important works besides those mentioned in the text include Gabriel Kolko, *The Roots of American Foreign Policy* (Boston: Beacon, 1969) and W. Appleman Williams, *The Tragedy of American Diplomacy* (New York: Dell, 1972).
10 Robert W. Tucker, *The Radical Left and American Foreign Policy* (London: Johns Hopkins Press, 1971) and Benjamin D. Cohen, *The Question of Imperialism* (London: Weidenfeld and Nicolson, 1980).
11 Tucker, *The Radical Left*, p. 12.
12 Harry Magdoff, *The Age of Imperialism* (London: Monthly Review Press, 1969), p. 26.
13 Tucker, *The Radical Left*, p. 71.
14 ibid., pp. 94–5. See also Joyce Kolko and Gabriel Kolko, *The Limits of Power* (London: Harper and Row, 1972), p. 2.
15 Cohen, *The Question of Imperialism*, p. 132.
16 ibid., p. 134. Cohen's data, like that of Magdoff, who argues to the contrary, is from the period until the late 1960s.
17 ibid., p. 141.
18 Magdoff, *The Age of Imperialism*, pp. 14–15.
19 Cohen, *The Question of Imperialism*, pp. 250–1.
20 Fred Halliday, *The Making of the Second Cold War* (London: Verso, 1983), pp. 174–5.
21 Tony Thorndike, 'The revolutionary approach: the Marxist perspective', in Trevor Taylor (ed.), *Approaches and Theory in International Relations* (London: Longman, 1978), p. 57.
22 See Anthony Brewer, *Marxist Theories of Imperialism* (London: Routledge & Kegan Paul, 1980), pp. 14–15.
23 Paul Baran, *The Political Economy of Growth* (New York: Monthly Review Press, 1957).

24 Chris Brown, 'Development and dependency', in Margot Light and A. J. R. Groom (eds), *International Relations*, p. 63. A good survey of the theorists is Anthony Brewer, *Marxist Theories*, and a judicious selection of their writings can be found in Michael Smith, Richard Little and Michael Shackleton (eds), *Perspectives in World Politics* (London: Croom Helm, 1981).
25 Brown, 'Development and dependency', in Light and Groom (eds), *International Relations*, pp. 63–4.
26 See Brewer, *Marxist Theories*, for summaries of their positions.
27 Galtung developed a penchant for writing articles entitled 'A structural theory of . . .' which included aggression, imperialism and integration. They can be found in his collected essays: Johan Galtung, *Essays in Peace Research* (Copenhagen: Christian Ejlers, 1975–9), five volumes.
28 Chadwick F. Alger, 'Bridging the micro and the macro in International Relations research', *Alternatives*, Winter 1984–5.
29 Peter B. Evans, 'Transnational linkages and the economic role of the state', in Peter B. Evans, Dietrich Rueschemeyer and Theda Skocpol (eds), *Bringing the State Back In* (Cambridge: Cambridge University Press, 1985).
30 Immanuel Wallerstein, 'An agenda for world-system analysis', in William R. Thompson (ed.), *Contending Approaches to World System Analysis* (London: Sage, 1983), p. 300.
31 ibid., p. 301.
32 Immanuel Wallerstein, *The Capitalist World Economy* (London: Cambridge University Press, 1979), p. 159.
33 ibid., pp. 160–1.
34 ibid., p. 161.
35 ibid.
36 ibid., p. 162.
37 ibid., p. 163.
38 ibid., p. 164.
39 Immanuel Wallerstein, 'The rise and future demise of the world capitalist system', in Michael Smith *et al.*, *Perspectives in World Politics*, p. 376.
40 ibid., p. 376.
41 Wallerstein, *Capitalist World Economy*, pp. 223, 274–5.
42 ibid., p. 277.
43 Terence K. Hopkins, Immanuel Wallerstein *et al.*, *World System Analysis Theory and Methodology* (London: Sage, 1982), p. 43.
44 Anthony Giddens, *The Nation-State and Violence* (Cambridge: Polity Press, 1985), p. 167.
45 Albert Bergesen, 'The class structure of the world-system', in W. R. Thompson (ed.), *Contending Approaches*, p. 43.
46 ibid., p. 50.
47 James Lee Ray, 'The "world-system" and the global political system', in Pat McGowan and Charles W. Kegley Jr (eds), *Foreign Policy and the Modern World-System* (London: Sage, 1983), p. 19.
48 Chris Brown, private communication, 12 November 1988.

49 Aristide R. Zolberg, 'Origins of the modern world system', *World Politics*, January 1981, pp. 275–6.
50 See George Modelski, *Long Cycles in World Politics* (London: Macmillan, 1987) for an overall statement of his position. Several volumes of empirical data are now appearing, by Modelski and others. Modelski's ideas were first put into general currency in a series of articles: George Modelski, 'The long cycle of global politics and the nation-state', *Comparative Studies in Society and History*, April 1978; George Modelski, 'Long cycles, Kondratieffs, alternating innovations and their implications for U.S. foreign policy', in C. W. Kegley Jr and P. J. McGowan (eds), *The Political Economy of Foreign Policy Behavior* (Beverly Hills, Calif.: Sage, 1981); George Modelski, 'Long cycles and the strategy of United States international economic policy', in W. P. Avery and D. P. Rapkin (eds), *America in a Changing World Political Economy* (New York: Longman, 1982); George Modelski, 'Long cycles of World Leadership', in William R. Thompson, *Contending Approaches*. The Thompson volume does for world-system analysis what Robert Keohane (ed.), *Neorealism and its Critics* (New York: Columbia University Press, 1986) does for structural realism or neorealism. Each is an essential *vade mecum* for the respective debates.
51 William R. Thompson (ed.), *Contending Approaches*, pp. 8ff.
52 ibid., p. 11.
53 Modelski, *Long Cycles in World Politics*, pp. 1–2.
54 Modelski, in W. P. Avery and D. P. Rapkin (eds), *America in a Changing World Political Economy*, p. 97.
55 Modelski in W. R. Thompson (ed.), *Contending Approaches*, pp. 121–2.
56 Modelski, *Long Cycles in World Politics*, p. 9.
57 Modelski in W. P. Avery and D. P. Rapkin (eds), *America in a Changing World Political Economy*, p. 98.
58 Modelski, *Long Cycles in World Politics*, p. 14.
59 ibid.
60 ibid., p. 15.
61 Modelski, in W. P. Avery and D. P. Rapkin (eds), *America in a Changing World Political Economy*, p. 100.
62 Modelski, *Long Cycles in World Politics*, p. 16.
63 Modelski in W. P. Avery and D. P. Rapkin (eds), *America in a Changing World Political Economy*, pp. 104–5.
64 ibid., p. 106.
65 ibid., p. 109.
66 Modelski in W. R. Thompson (ed.), *Contending Approaches*, p. 136.
67 Modelski, *Long Cycles in World Politics*, pp. 232–3.
68 For an excellent summary, see a review article by Oyvind Osterud, 'The uses and abuses of geopolitics', *Journal of Peace Research*, June 1988, and especially one of the books reviewed, Geoffrey Parker, *Western Geopolitical Thought in the Twentieth Century* (London: Croom Helm, 1985).
69 Osterud, ibid., p. 191
70 Quoted in ibid., p. 192.

71 Harold and Margaret Sprout, *Man–Milieu Relationship Hypotheses in the Context of International Politics* (Princeton, NJ: Center of International Studies, Princeton University, 1956).
72 Harold and Margaret Sprout, *The Ecological Perspective in Human Affairs* (Princeton, NJ: Princeton University Press, 1965).
73 Karl Deutsch, *The Nerves of Government* (New York: Free Press, 1963).
74 Nazli Choucri and Robert C. North, *Nations in Conflict: National Growth and International Violence* (San Francisco: W. H. Freeman, 1975) and Richard K. Ashley, *The Political Economy of War and Peace* (London: Frances Pinter, 1980).
75 Ashley, *Political Economy*, p. 47, italics deleted.
76 ibid., p. 248.
77 ibid., p. 255, italics deleted.
78 ibid., p. xii.
79 ibid., p. 207.
80 ibid., p. 208.
81 ibid., p. 210.
82 ibid., pp. 216–7, italics deleted.
83 Robert W. Cox, 'Social forces, states and world orders', in Keohane (ed.), *Neorealism and its Critics*, p. 217.

Further reading

Ashley, Richard K. *The Political Economy of War and Peace*. London: Frances Pinter, 1980.
Brewer, Anthony. *Marxist Theories of Imperialism*. London: Routledge and Kegan Paul, 1980.
Wallerstein, Immanuel. *The Capitalist World Economy*. London: Cambridge University Press, 1979.
Modelski, George. *Long Cycles in World Politics*. London: Macmillan, 1987.
Sprout, Harold and Sprout, Margaret. *The Ecological Perspective in Human Affairs*. Princeton, NJ: Princeton University Press, 1965.

11   *Realism resurgent?*

States undoubtedly act with a certain autonomy. (Robert Cox)[1]

International relations, as an academic subject, has exhibited signs of both stability (or is it stagnation?) and change ('progress', for some) in its intellectual development. For more than seven decades some approaches to the subject have always found their adherents, and this despite challenges to such conceptions, their refutation and 'revolutions' in thought leading to new conceptions. Individuals may progress and change, intellectual fashions come and go, but the discipline merely seems to accrete new ideas in a non-discriminatory manner. In this context it is hardly surprising that there has been a resurgence of interest in realism, notwithstanding the strong criticisms of it contained in the world society and structuralist approaches. There is an almost tribal loyalty to certain approaches which become embedded in particular academic institutions and whose intellectual leaders become semi- cult figures. This phenomenon is not in any sense confined to realism, but the resurgence of realism in the late 1970s and 1980s provides a striking example of it. It has taken the guise of structural realism or neo-realism.[2]

Structural realism or neo-realism

Kenneth Waltz's monograph on the *Theory of International Politics*[3] has generated a great deal of academic interest in the United States, to the extent that it has become almost the basis of a cottage industry. It is thereby worthy of some consideration here, but Robert Gilpin's *War and Change in World Politics*[4] is a more sophisticated study in the same genre of neo-realism because it has a dynamic aspect, and thus a growth potential, which is lacking in Waltz. Both Waltz and Gilpin have what is, in essence, a 'sub-system dominant' view of structure (however much Waltz may deny this and – understandably – dislike the term) and so theirs is not a full-blooded structural approach. However, by concentrating on these two writers initially, before exploring further the new realist literature, we hope to purvey the essence of the debate surrounding the resurgence of realism.

The *Theory of International Politics* is a quirkish and eclectic essay that, in relatively short compass and an easy style, reviews the contribution of various writers such as Hobson, Lenin, Rosecrance, Hoffmann and Kaplan, takes a controversial position on the stability of bipolar and multipolar systems of the balance of power, and purports to present a structural theory of international politics. It has attracted attention more perhaps for the robust manner in which Waltz expresses his views than for their originality or insight. The book has a rumbustiousness about it, which, with the new interest being shown in structural approaches in IR and the social sciences more generally, has given it a greater salience than might otherwise have been expected. At one level Waltz's theme, like that of political realists generally, is a big one: how to create order and tame anarchy, that is, to enhance stability in an anarchical society.[5]

Waltz starts in a conventional manner, familiar from that of the systems' theories discussed in Chapter 8. International politics can be considered from the point of view of the actor or unit (the reductionist position) or from that of the system as a whole. A system is a set of interacting units, which in this case are states. The structure of the system acts as a constraint on actors and is autonomous for the individual actor, but not for the actors as a whole. In short, the whole is as great as, but not greater than the sum of the parts, since any change in the structure is likely to come from the activity of units or actors having systemic implications rather than from the autonomous role of the system vis-à-vis the actors individually or collectively. Thus, in this sense, Waltz is not a full blown structuralist. Joseph Nye has commented that 'Waltz's own assignment of characteristics to the systemic or unit levels seems odd' because it assigns 'everything except the distribution of capabilities to the unit level', including demographic trends, trans-national flows and nuclear technology notwithstanding their 'system-wide' effects.[6] For Waltz:

> To define a structure requires ignoring how units relate with one another (how they interact) and concentrating on how they stand

in relation to one another (how they are arranged or positioned). Interactions . . . take place at the level of units. How units stand in relation to one another . . . is not a property of the units. The arrangement of units is a property of the system.

By leaving aside the personality of actors, their behavior, and their interactions, one arrives at a purely positional picture of society. Three propositions follow from this. First, structures may endure while personality, behavior, and interactions vary widely. Structure is sharply distinguished from actions and interactions. Second, a structural definition applies to realms of widely different substance so long as the arrangement of parts is similar. Third, because this is so, theories developed for one realm may with some modification be applicable to other realms as well.[7] . . .

A domestic political structure is thus defined, first, according to the principle by which it is ordered; second, by specifications of the functions of formally differentiated units; and third, by the distribution of capabilities across those units . . . The three-part definition of structure includes only what is required to show how the units of the system are positioned or arranged.[8] . . .

The states that are the units of international-political systems are not formally differentiated by the functions they perform. Anarchy entails relations of coordination among a system's units, and that implies their sameness. The second term [formally differentiated units] is not needed in defining international-political structure, because so long as anarchy endures, states remain like units. International structures vary only through a change of organising principle or, failing that, through variations in the capabilities of units.[9]

The notion that no functional differentiation of states exists has attracted criticism, which is hardly surprising given the literature precisely on this topic, such as that on the role and functions of middle Powers, super Powers and all manner, shape and form of 'hegemons'. Switzerland, for example, has specific differentiated international functions. It is the neutral base for international humanitarian and financial functions. John Ruggie, who is generally quite favourably disposed towards Waltz, suggests that the failure to acknowledge functional differentiation has quite profound implications because it means that the dimension of change is missing from Waltz's conception.[10] Structural change is of abiding interest to any structuralist, but Waltz emphasizes stability, not change, since he argues that the single major change in several centuries has been the move from multipolarity to bipolarity after the Second World War. This, he sees, as being a change bringing a fundamental enhancement of stability. As Ruggie points out,

> The problem with Waltz's posture is that, in any social system, structural change itself ultimately has no source *other than* unit-level processes . . . Waltz's theory of 'society' contains only a reproductive logic, but no transformational logic.[11]

To this extent Waltz is not a full-blown structuralist, despite his aspirations, since structures are not seen as being autonomous and systems are sub-system dominant. They are autonomous from the point of view of individual units for most of the time, but even then, not for all of the time, since units can bring about structural change. This takes us back to the 'good old-fashioned' state-centricity and power politics of traditional realism from which Waltz has strayed, in reality, but little. After all, the balance of power, Waltz's fundamental structural notion, is equally crucial for Morgenthau, even if the latter deplored bipolarity as much as the former has welcomed it.

Waltz has no doubts about the state-centricity of the contemporary and past world:

> States are the units whose interactions form the structure of international-political systems. They will long remain so . . . States are alike in the tasks they face, though not in their abilities to perform them.[12]

These abilities vary with power which 'is estimated by comparing the capabilities of a number of units'.[13] The situation, Waltz frequently points out, is like a market. Individual firms, or states, by their activity create, willy-nilly, a structure, the market or system, which thereafter constrains them. However, by changing their activities in such a way that changes in capabilities occur, they are at the same time bringing about a variation in the structure. The system is sub-system dominant. Waltz suggests that changes *in* systems are relatively easy to achieve, but he concedes that, though possible, changes of systems are hard to imagine.[14] In part, this is because Waltz is himself a reductionist owing to his 'understanding of system structures as only *constraining* the agency of preexisting states, rather than . . . as *generating* state agents themselves . . . system structures cannot generate agents if they are reduced to the property of agents in the first place'.[15]

Waltz acknowledges that states 'differ vastly in their capabilities' and that 'Out of such differences something of a division of labor develops'. However, this is 'slight in comparison with the highly articulated division of labor within them'.[16] They are thus separate, alike and alone, in an anarchic situation where war is likely.[17] In classical realist style they then resort to the balance of power on the basis of their differing capabilities. It is not necessary here to rehearse again the discussion of whether states are coherent, integrated units, capable of acting in a maximizing rational manner on the basis of a fungible notion of power. Waltz's critics, many of whom are well-disposed towards him, have raised such issues in this context, which were discussed in a previous chapter.[18] However, since the balance of power is so crucial to Waltz's ideas of structure, his rather special views of its nature are worthy of consideration.

Waltz suggests that a bipolar system is stable because both actors know the ropes and can have a proper basis of accurate information on which, in a rational manner, to manage their relationship. They are likely, therefore, to be vigilant since they know what the danger is and from whom and whence it comes. In a multipolar system the waters are much more likely to be muddied. There is no proper basis of accurate information regarding capabilities, actual or potential alliances and the likelihood of their implementation. This induces instability, born of the fear engendered by uncertainty. The danger can arise from a greater variety and number of sources about which less is known. Happily, according to Waltz, the contemporary world remains in the bipolar state into which it had emerged after the Second World War and the degree of interdependence between the two super Powers is low, which causes him to be sanguine about stability, because control is thereby facilitated. However, Gilpin has pointed out that vigilance does not always characterize a bipolar situation, as in the case of

Sparta and Athens. Moreover, while a multipolar system of roughly equal Powers may be prone to violence, it does not necessarily lead to the collapse of a system, whereas there is another meaning of instability in this context.

> This is the propensity in a system under particular sets of conditions for relatively small causes to lead to disproportionately large effects . . . One of the most likely disturbing factors is entry of a newly powerful state into the system, either because of steady growth of a state in the system or because of entry into the system of a peripheral power . . . It is easier for a multipolar system to make the necessary adjustment.[19]

This question is not without point in contemporary international relations, as Dr Kissinger acknowledged when he tried to refashion a multipolar balance of Western Europe, Japan and China in addition to the postwar super Powers. Gilpin also disagrees with Waltz's 'assertion that wars are caused by uncertainty and miscalculation'. On the contrary, 'it is perceived certainty of gain that most frequently causes nations to go to war . . .'[20] Thus,

> Both bipolar and multipolar structures contain elements of instability . . . the most important factor for the process of international political change is not the static distribution of power in the system (bipolar or multipolar) but the dynamics of power relationships over time. It is the differential or uneven growth of power among states in a system that encourages efforts by certain states to change the system in order to enhance their own interests or to make more secure those interests threatened by their oligopolistic rivals. In both bipolar and multipolar structures, changes in relative power among the principal actors in the system are precursors of international political change.[21]

This is the essence of Gilpin's version of structural realism, to which we shall return later. However, it is relevant at this point also to bear in mind another factor likely to bring about systemic change in both bipolar and multipolar systems: that is, the declining viability of existing actors due either to exogenous or endogenous factors. A case in point was the vulnerability of most actors in the nineteenth century to nationalism, as the subsequent collapse of the Austro-Hungarian, Ottoman, French and British Empires attests. The present difficulties in the Soviet Union and potential problems in the USA suggest that this destabilizing factor has far from run its course.

For Waltz, however, the nineteenth century, and the two preceding centuries, were stable. The only change has been the emergence, of late, of a bipolar system to which Waltz sees no challengers. Nye comments,

> this portrayal of history . . . leaves an enormous number of important changes unaccounted for, and lends credence to the charge that it is too static. There are so few strands in the web of Waltz's theoretical net that even very big fish slip through it.

Nye also comments that it is odd to consider a situation in which the super Powers (and others, we might add) can destroy themselves and the world as we know it in a matter of minutes or hours, as not being one of interdependence. However, Waltz does reject utterly the interdependence argument.[22] It is for reasons such as these that we began by suggesting that Waltz's essay was quirkish. But despite this and the existence of a more balanced exposition of structural realism by Gilpin, to which we shall shortly turn, Waltz's work has excited the discipline of IR in the United States. Most of the criticisms reviewed so far have been conceived and couched within the realist tradition: that could not be said of those of Richard Ashley.

In the 'Poverty of neorealism', Ashley refers to an 'orrery of errors',[23] some of which have already been mentioned. In a passage that illustrates well Easton's analysis of the post-behaviouralist credo, Ashley launches a broadside, much of which is on target, against neorealism, and especially the Waltzian version of it.

> Although it claims to side with the victors in two American revolutions – the realist revolution against idealism, and the scientific revolution against traditionalism – it in fact betrays both. It betrays the former's commitment to political autonomy by reducing political practice to an economic logic, and it neuters the critical faculties of the latter by swallowing methodological rules that render science a purely technical enterprise. From

realism it learns only an interest in power, from science it takes only an interest in expanding the reach of control, and from this selective borrowing it creates a theoretical perspective that parades the possibility of a rational power that need never acknowledge power's limits. What emerges is a positivist structuralism that treats the given order as the natural order, limits rather than expands political discourse, negates or trivialises the significance of variety across time and place, subordinates all practice to an interest in control, bows to the ideal of a social power beyond responsibility, and thereby deprives political interaction of those practical capacities which make social learning and creative change possible. What emerges is an ideology that anticipates, legitimises, and orients a totalitarian project of global proportions: the rationalisation of global politics.[24]

Much of this cannot be gainsaid, even if the inference of a deliberate attempt to create such a totalitarian project, or its likelihood of success, deserves to be treated with a good deal of scepticism. On the other hand, this is a possible outcome. Ashley's concerns are also with the extent to which structural realism is in fact structural at all in the sense that:

the structuralist posits the possibility of a structural whole – a deep social subjectivity – having an autonomous existence independent of, prior to, and constitutive of the elements. From a structuralist point of view, a structural whole cannot be described by starting with the parts as abstract, already defined entities, taking note of their external joining, and describing emergent properties among them.[25]

We have already noted that Waltz, in effect, denies the autonomy of the whole, a point Ashley emphasises,[26] except in relation to the individual unit which, Ashley concedes, does give structural realism some justification for the appellation.

Ashley castigates structural realism for being 'silent' about 'four dimensions of history . . . process, practice, power, and politics'.[27] As a process structural realism is not open-ended, but circumscribed and limited.[28] In its practice 'people are reduced to some idealized *Homo economicus*, able to carry out, but never to reflect critically on, the limited rational logic that the system demands of them',[29] a charge just as applicable to Gilpin as to Waltz. Both seem to deny the relevance of critical theory, which Ashley rightly deplores. He also suggests that they have 'no comprehension of, and in fact den[y], the social basis and social limits of power'.[30] Power, for Ashley, 'depends on and is limited by the conditions of its *recognition* within a community as a whole',[31] that is, what we called earlier legitimized relationships in which 'actors gain recognition and are *empowered*'.[32] Finally, 'neorealist historicism denies *politics* . . . [because] it reduces politics to those aspects which lend themselves to interpretation exclusively within a framework of economic action under structural constraints'.[33] In short, we can only learn to play the game better, we cannot rewrite the rules. While politics, in this sense of a technical rationality for solving 'puzzles', is also a characteristic of economic reasoning, the essence of politics, which is the realization of 'problems' and their resolution, is lost.[34] This is a charge that Waltz must answer, but what of Gilpin?

Whereas Waltz is pugnacious in his presentation of structural realism, Gilpin is more sagacious, but not bland. Like Waltz, Gilpin uses economic logic or rational choice theory as a technical rationality for dealing with political puzzles. He argues that economic forces are important, more so than Waltz, but in the end, 'they always work in the context of the political struggle among groups and nations.'[35] It is this political struggle that is the subject of *War and Change in World Politics*.[36] The notion of change in the title, and its consideration, is a distinct advance on Waltz and it puts a welcome emphasis on the question of differing rates of change leading to demands by the rising Powers for the revision of the rules of the international structure and practice in their favour. The outcome may well, but not necessarily, be hegemonic war. Gilpin's essay thus has a dynamic quality much wanting, and notable for its absence, in Waltz.

Why then the inordinate attention given to Waltz? Because he makes an admirable stalking horse for the debate about structural realism, which in itself is an attempt to cloak realism in the new-found legitimacy of structuralism. But, in the end, little new is added to the older conceptions of Carr, Schwarzenberger and Morgenthau. Structural realism is a reformulation of realism in a new context – both intellectual, in the form of the world society and structural paradigms, and practical, in the shape of the empirical phenomena including declining state-centricity and the global economic structure that gave rise to these newly relevant paradigms. The intrusion of critical theory also suggests a reversal to the old realist–idealist debate, but in new guise, while a strong resurgence of Marxism gives it an added dimension, as we shall see below.[37] The rigour and parsimony of political rational-choice theory also stimulates comment and debate. But structural realism is still realism in that, as Gilpin states, 'the nature of international relations has not changed fundamentally over the millenia . . . Thucydides . . . would . . . have little trouble in understanding the power struggle of our age'.[38] And it is this power struggle that, for realists of every hue, comes before all else.

Rational choice and world politics

Gilpin begins by contrasting sociological theory with economic or rational-choice theory. In the former the social system is the primary determinant of behavior' and therefore 'the focus of theorizing'.[39] While acknowledging that 'economic and sociological approaches must be integrated to explain international political change',[40] Gilpin puts greater emphasis on economic or rational-choice theory.

> [This] assumes that individual behavior is determined wholly by rationality; that is, individuals seek to maximize, or at least to satisfy, certain values or interests at the lowest possible cost to themselves . . . it holds that individuals will seek to acquire their objectives until a market equilibrium is reached; that is. . . . until the associated costs are equal to the realized benefits.[41]

Gilpin argues that this notion can be used to develop an understanding of international political change, because structures will change when the interests and relative powers of states change. He feels that rational choice 'can draw on a large and well-tested body of economic theory',[42] an assertion of the standing of economic theory that is open to dispute. Although Gilpin does not ignore the sociological perspective within which rational behaviour takes place, he builds his argument on the logic of the latter.

Thus the study of international political change must focus on the international system and especially on the efforts of political actors to change the international system in order to advance their own interests.[43]

In this quest Gilpin rests his argument on five assumptions:

1 An international system is stable (i.e., in a state of equilibrium) if no state believes it profitable to attempt to change the system.
2 A state will attempt to change the international system if the expected benefits exceed the expected costs (i.e., if there is an expected net gain).
3 A state will seek to change the international system through territorial, political, and economic expansion until the marginal costs of further change are equal to or greater than the marginal benefits.
4 Once an equilibrium between the costs and benefits of further change and expansion is reached, the tendency is for the economic costs of maintaining the status quo to rise faster than the economic capacity to support the status quo.
5 If the disequilibrium in the international system is not resolved, then the system will be changed, and a new equilibrium reflecting the redistribution of power will be established.[44]

Gilpin agrees with the Marxist notion that revolutionary or structural change occurs when there are 'differential rates of change in major components composing the social system', otherwise 'there would be incremental evolution of the system'.[45] Where they differ is that Marx sees the engine of change in the economic rather than the political system.

States, because international society is anarchic, must always be expansive for otherwise they risk being the victims of the expansion of others. This, Gilpin suggests, sets in motion a cycle of expansion, consolidation, challenge and decline. Eventually the initial expansion, originally fuelled by economic surplus, meets countervailing forces and the returns to expansion diminish after the initial enjoyment of the economies of scale. An equilibrium is then reached,[46] and there is an erosion of the original élan that supported an aggressive and expansionist foreign policy. The society grows conservative, less innovative, and less willing to run risks . . . society becomes less willing to pay the costs . . . associated with political and economic expansion.[47]

But, owing to the decline of the marginal returns to expansion, the costs of maintaining even the status quo rise, while the will to make sacrifices falls. Consumption, rather than savings, is the order of the day, and comparative advantage declines.[48]

These rising states, on the other hand, enjoy lower costs, rising rates of return on their resources, and the advantages of back-wardness. In time, the differential rates of growth of declining and rising states in the system produce a decisive redistribution of power and result in disequilibrium in the system.[49]

At this point the rising state can seek to change the rules of the international system in its favour.[50] Hegemonic war may result.

The cycle is familiar in its broad outline from many historians, and especially from one of the founders of IR, Arnold Toynbee. Where Gilpin has been innovative is in his explicit use of economic or rational choice theory as a framework for his argument. His view of the world starts from the interests of actors conceived in a Hobbesian dilemma. The interests of actors have consequences for structures, but while structures act as constraints, the system is actor-dominant. We will forbear repeating, but note Ashley's criticism of this economistic, atomistic and, ultimately, closed system. Gilpin's approach to the cycle is dynamic, to a limited extent, and thereby an improvement on Waltz, but George Model-ski puts the cycle in the context of a single structure through several centuries. Modelski, as we have seen, thereby adds a historical dimension, whereas Gilpin only offers historical examples. The phenomena look very different when viewed through opposite ends of the telescope – particular states in a cycle at one end, a long-standing historical structure englobing several cycles at the other. In fixing his eye firmly at the latter end of the telescope, Modelski offers the more satisfactory interpretation of structural realism. In this he is more of a structuralist than a realist. Moreover, to a far greater extent than either Waltz or Gilpin,

Modelski shows how structure relates to the processes of action. He has a place for the 'great men' of history that seems to be singularly lacking in rational choice theory. He may not be so parsimonious or rigorous in his theorizing, but he gives us a better insight into the complexities of structure and process, and in a way that a realist can appreciate, without succumbing to a mindless axiomatic analysis. Rational choice analysis, when applied unthinkingly, can quickly degenerate into this. Moreover, putting the emphasis on the actor, whether in the conception of Waltz or Gilpin, renders the analysis not so much structuralist as realist.

Back to realism

Realism has enjoyed a resurgence in its neorealist or structural mode, but it has also been the object of attention in its more traditional formulation. Realism stems from the mainstream of political thought, and the various debates in IR have created a degree of mutual interest between political theorists and IR theorists, if we can be allowed to distinguish between them. Charles Beitz, in his *Political Theory and International Relations*, has bridged that distinction in an admirable fashion and contributed significantly to the growth of interest in normative theory in contemporary IR.[51]

Beitz denies the contemporary validity of the Hobbesian argument of which realism is a current manifestation. If the Hobbesian argument is to be convincing then, for Beitz,

> it must be the case that international relations is analogous to the state of nature in the respects relevant to the prediction that a state of nature regularly issues in a state of war.

For this analogy to be acceptable, at least four propositions must be true:

1 The actors in international relations are states.
2 States have relatively equal power (the weakest can defeat the strongest).
3 States are independent of each other in the sense that they can order their internal (i.e., non-security) affairs independently of the internal policies of other actors.

NO HOBBES theory of "State of Nature" is WRONG.

4 There are no reliable expectations of reciprocal compliance by
the actors with rules of cooperation in the absence of a superior
power capable of enforcing these rules.[52]

Beitz found that none of these conditions held in contemporary
international relations. The realists are therefore bereft of their
Hobbesian legitimacy. Moreover, John Vasquez has examined the
precepts of realism empirically and found them of little use in
explaining the world as it is. To the extent that Vasquez is correct,
the 'realists' are hoist with their own petard.

Vasquez's approach is very different from that of Beitz and,
indeed, from that of the critics of realism in the 1960s. Vasquez is
a scholar in the behavioural vein and he has put his methodological
skills to good use in a devastating critique of realism. His work,
going back to the 1973 ISA Conference paper, 'Color it Morgenthau', has not had the acknowledgement that it deserves, perhaps
because it is not dealing merely with anomalies. Vasquez is not
crying out that the Emperor has no clothes – which would be an
embarrassment – but that the Emperor is an imposter – which, for
the realists, is treason.

Vasquez himself, however, is careful in his research and modest
in the claims he makes in his conclusions. He points out that:

> The contribution of the realist paradigm to the development of
> a scientific study of international relations has been, first, to
> point out that science must be empirical and theoretical, not
> normative and narrowly historical, and second, to provide a
> picture of the world (i.e., a paradigm) which has permitted the
> field to develop a common research agenda and to follow it
> systematically and somewhat cumulatively.[53]

The essence of this paradigm is based on Morgenthau's three
fundamental assumptions:

1 Nation–states or their decision makers are the most important
actors for understanding international relations.
2 There is a sharp distinction between domestic politics and
international politics.
3 International relations is the struggle for power and peace.

Understanding how and why that struggle occurs and suggesting ways for regulating it is the purpose of the discipline. All
research that is not at least indirectly related to this purpose is
trivial.[54]

Vasquez has no difficulty in establishing the centrality of these
notions in the literature, but their explanatory power proved to be
a different matter. Of the 7,678 hypotheses that were statistically
tested between 1956 and 1970 in the United States, of which 7,158
were realist, 'those that accepted rather than rejected the three
realist assumptions were more frequently falsified . . . of the
statistical findings that did exhibit high correlations, the realist
ones tended to contain more trivial findings than the non-realist
ones'.[55] Thus,

> Power politics is not so much an explanation as a description of
> one type of behavior found in the global political system. If this
> is correct, then power politics behavior itself must be explained;
> it does not explain.[56]

One of the things to be explained, which is largely ignored by
neorealists and structural realists such as Waltz and Gilpin, as well
as by 'classical' realists such as Morgenthau, Carr and Schwarzenberger, is the nature of the state and the domestic determinants and
constraints on state behaviour. Such questions have been 'black-
boxed' by realists and left to political scientists, who examine
domestic politics that, by definition, operate according to different
principles from international relations – politics that are less violent
and more consensual. Others, however, want to 'bring the state
back in.'

Bringing the state back in[57]

Tony Thorndike has described graphically and quoted the traditional starting point of this debate.

> In the crushingly powerful language of the hastily-written
> *Manifesto*: 'The executive of the modern State is but a committee
> for managing the common affairs of the bourgeoisie' . . . and,

as the social revolution progressed towards full equality in the fullness of time, everybody would, in effect, be an administrator and the state – as we know it – would wither away. In Engels' celebrated, if enigmatic, phrase . . . 'the government of man will become the administration of things'.[58]

And that, for a long time, was the end of the matter.

In IR the idealists and realists of the interwar period and beyond took the state for granted. A consideration of the nature and role of the state did not become apposite until world society and structural approaches brought it into question by challenging its centrality in IR theory. The resurgence of realism perforce brings the state back in. However, a reaction to world-system approaches suggested that Marxist-influenced thought is remiss to go no further than portraying the state as the managing committee of the bourgeoisie. This was particularly true of those political scientists and sociologists in the USA who were dissatisfied with pluralist and structural-functionalist approaches and attracted to a neo-Marxist perspective.[59] In none of these approaches did the state seem to some to be given its due: to what extent did it have autonomy from the confines of consensus or class in the respective approaches? In other words, can states 'conceived as organizations claiming control over Territories and people . . . formulate and pursue goals that are not simply reflective of the demands or interests of social groups, classes or society'?[60] In particular, can they do so in such cataclysmic situations as revolution or the change from feudalism to capitalism?[61]

Theda Skocpol, one of the champions of this approach, points to the 'general underpinnings of state capacities':

> Obviously, sheer sovereign integrity and the stable adminstrative–military control of a given territory are preconditions for any state's ability to implement policies. Beyond this, loyal and skilled officials and plentiful financial resources are basic to state effectiveness in attaining all sorts of goals.[62]

But there is no reason why these underpinnings, and thus the state itself, should not be captured by a particular class, an independent civil service, the military or simply be a reflection of societal consensus. Be that as it may, Skocpol suggests further:

> Bringing the state back in to a central place in analyses of policy
> making and social change . . . does not mean that old theoretical
> emphases should simply be turned on their heads. Studies of
> states alone are not to be substituted for concerns with classes or
> groups; nor are purely state-determinist arguments to be
> fashioned in the place of society-centered explanations. The need
> to analyse states in relation to socioeconomic and sociocultural
> contexts is convincingly demonstrated . . . [63]

But what is the state and can it act coherently and autonomously?
Is it greater than the sum of its parts or is it a structure captured by
a bureaucracy, a class or whatever? Can it really command or must
it negotiate? Can it really dispense with legitimacy and, if so, who
guards the guards? Are they, in the last resort, 'the state' and by
their very role do they always have the ability to usurp the state's
'autonomy'? But why, then, are not all states 'garrison states' or
military regimes of an overt or covert sort? Clearly, who controls
the state's legal and administrative structure is an important
question, especially in so far as outcomes are concerned, but it
seems that the notion of autonomy can quickly be pushed too far.
The state may be a vehicle, or a battlefield, but the limits to
'bringing it back in' have also been recognized by Skocpol's fellow
editors, Dietrich Rueschemeyer and Peter Evans.[64] Indeed, the
more the state does in providing services, the more it is a prize to
be fought over and the less it is likely to be autonomous. It does,
however, have structural functions in the supply of collective
goods, and to this extent it is autonomous, but the importance of
such collective goods can vary.

There have been strenuous attempts both in IR through the neorealists, in political science and in historical sociology to re-
establish the state as a central, indeed *the* central concept in the
field. The importance of the state and its degree of autonomy is no
fixed thing. It waxes and wanes over time and in different domains.
It needs to be brought in, therefore, as and when it is relevant, not
as an inescapable starting point or autonomous structure. Can the
same be said of its hereditary analytical rival the mode of production? If political realism, resurgent or traditional, reveals a state-
centricity that passes over much of substance that needs to be
explained, if 'bringing the state back in' has not revealed the extent
to which it is autonomous in performing the functions which it

does in fact fulfil, can a better explanation be found in some form
of Marxism resurgent? In short, should our realism be economic
rather than political in its substance and essence?

Production, power and world order

Robert Cox, in a major project with Jeffrey Harrod, seeks to relate
production and power.

> Production creates the material basis for all forms of social
> existence, and the ways in which human efforts are combined in
> productive processes affect all other aspects of social life, includ-
> ing the polity. Production generates the capacity to exercise
> power, but power determines the manner in which production
> takes place.[65]

Moreover, 'to assert the centrality of production . . . leads directly
to the matter of social classes'.[66] Cox, however, argues that the
state is important because 'the principal structures have been, if not
actually created by the state, at least encouraged and sustained by
the state',[67] be they competitive capitalism and the liberal state,
central planning and the bolshevik state or state corporatism and
the fascist state. Indeed, for Cox, 'production has been more
shaped by the state than shaping of it'.[68] Moreover, 'Class and
party are the channels of encounter between production and the
state. They explain where the balance of influence lies, whether it
comes primarily from the social forces generated in the production
process or from the state.' The class structure determines for the
state's servants what is possible and what is precluded: it acts as a
constraint.[69] But so does the particular world order that is, in its
turn, reflective of the dominant mode of production. Where there
is a hegemonic world Power, there tends to be a linkage between
social classes in different states and connections in production
giving rise to a world economy. Thus an 'incipient world society
grows up around the interstate system . . .'[70] Such linkages do not
flourish in non-hegemonic world orders and states 'advance and
protect the interests of particular national social classes and production organizations, using all the political, economic, and military
means at their disposal as necessary'.[71]

Cox finds 'structures at the three levels of enquiry: modes of social relations of production, forms of state, and structures of world order . . . [as well as] structures of structures linking together these three levels in systems that have had a certain stability for a certain duration'.[72] These structures, which are inferred from 'historical patterns of conduct', rather than being some inner essence of capital, have openings for change.[73] But of the three levels of enquiry the most important one for Cox is the state.

> Although production was the point of departure of this study, the crucial role, it turns out, is played by the state . . . States . . . determine the whole complex structure of production from which the state then extracts sufficient resources to continue to exercise its power. Of course, states do not do this in an isolated way. Each state is constrained by its position and its relative power in the world order, which places limits on its will and its ability to change production relations . . . [Nevertheless] states undoubtedly act with a certain autonomy.[74]

Robert Cox's book *Production Power and World Order* is beginning to have a significant impact because it reflects the diverse face of realism. It is not an ideological book, but an empirical study. It is a genuine resurgence of realism, drawing upon traditional concerns of modes of production and social classes to the extent that Cox expresses fears that he might seem an old-fashioned Marxist, but at the same time 'bringing the state back in' to a central position. This position, although central, is not, however, a determining one since there are constraints, both global and domestic: it is a predominant and influential position. Cox has achieved a new balance between state-centricity, world-system constraints and world society processes. His is not a fusion of the three paradigms that have dominated IR in recent decades, nor is it a return to oversimplified Marxist precepts, but it is a remarkable attempt to construct a whole. Cox's synthesis of power, production and world order is striking and exciting. It represents not so much neorealism or structural realism, but a new realism. The question is whether Cox's three ingredients are the correct ones and whether he has mixed them properly to the right recipe. If realism is to be resurgent, it will be on the basis of such a fecund integrative conception of a living and changing whole rather than a sterile assertion of state-supremacy or stubborn insistence on the rigorous application of the theory of rational choice. The debate upon the ingredients and the recipe has begun. To what extent has the state been brought back in?

Notes: Chapter 11

1 Robert Cox, *Production Power and World Order* (New York: Columbia University Press, 1987), p. 399.
2 It is frustrating that in a subject so riddled with difficulties of nomenclature that we are adding to our burdens by creating more such difficulties. We shall use the term 'structural realism' as a synonym for the term 'neorealism'. We are not alone in this, since Robert Keohane evidently prefers the former term but uses the latter in the title of his well-known and very useful edited volume on the subject: Robert O. Keohane (ed.), *Neorealism and its Critics* (New York: Colombia University Press, 1986).
3 Kenneth Waltz, *Theory of International Politics* (New York: Random House, 1979).
4 Robert Gilpin, *War and Change in World Politics* (Cambridge: Cambridge University Press, 1981).
5 See Yale H. Ferguson and Richard W. Mansbach, *The Elusive Quest* (Colombia, SC: University of South Carolina Press, 1988), Hedley Bull, *The Anarchical Society* (London: Macmillan, 1977) and R. D. McKinlay and R. Little, *Global Problems and World Order* (London: Frances Pinter, 1986) for other statements on this issue.
6 Joseph S. Nye, 'Neorealism and neoliberalism', *World Politics*, January 1988, p. 243.
7 Waltz, *Theory of International Politics*, p. 80.
8 ibid., p. 82.
9 ibid., p. 93.
10 John Gerard Ruggie, 'Continuity and transformation in the world polity', *World Politics*, January 1983.
11 ibid., p. 285.
12 Waltz, *Theory of International Politics*, pp. 95–6.
13 ibid., p. 98.
14 Kenneth Waltz, 'A response to my critics', in Keohane (ed.), *Neorealism*, p. 328.
15 Alexander E. Wendt, 'The agent-structure problem in international relations', *International Organization*, Summer 1987, p. 342.
16 Waltz, 'A response . . .', in Keohane (ed.), *Neorealism*, p. 105.
17 ibid., p. 102.
18 For example, Robert Keohane criticises the notion of perfect rationality which, he rightly suggests, needs ameliorating by considerations of

'satisficing' and near rationality (in 'Neorealism and world politics', in *Neorealism and its Critics*, p. 13 and 'Theory of world politics', ibid., p. 167). He also castigates reliance on a 'single characteristic of the international system (overall power capabilities)' and raises doubts about its fungibility (ibid.). Therefore, its predictive capacity is likely to be over-exaggerated (ibid., p. 191). In short, the realist assumptions are severely questioned and modifications offered (ibid., pp. 193–5). Waltz justifies his position by saying that although 'The state in fact is not a unitary and purposive actor[,] I assumed it to be such only for the purpose of constructing a theory' (Waltz, 'A response, in Keohane (ed.), *Neorealism*, p. 339). Less indulgent critics have not been so kind. Richard Higgott has pointed out that in realist thought the state 'is not *under*theorised so much as *un*theorised' (Richard Higgot (ed.), *New Directions in International Relations? Australian Perspectives* (Canberra: Australian National University IR Department, 1988), p. 7). Richard Ashley is scathing: 'The proposition that the state might be *essentially* problematic or contested is excluded from neorealist theory . . . One simply *assumes* that states have the status of unitary actors . . . In short, the state-as-actor assumption is a metaphysical commitment tied to science and exempted from scientific criticism' (Richard Ashley, 'The poverty of neorealism' in Keohane (ed.), *Neorealism* pp. 269–70). If the assumption is questionable then the viability of the whole edifice is in doubt. Indeed, Ashley points to the significant caveats of many of those who can, nevertheless, remain in broad sympathy with Waltz ('A response' p. 269). For example, Keohane, despite his doubts, can call the structuralist realist research programme 'an impressive achievement . . . elegant, parsimonious, deductively rigorous' (Theory of world politics', in *Neorealism* p. 167)' . . . [and] spare, logically tight . . .' (ibid., p. 197) to which Robert Cox's tart comment is apt: 'One person's elegance is another's oversimplification' (Robert Cox, 'Social forces, states and world orders', in Keohane (ed.), *Neorealism*, p. 244).

19 Gilpin, *War and Change*, p. 91.
20 ibid., p. 91.
21 ibid., p. 93.
22 Nye, 'Neorealism and neoliberalism', *World Politics*, January 1988, p. 244, and Waltz, *Theory of International Politics*, pp. 138–9.
23 Ashley in Keohane (ed.), *Neorealism*, pp. 257–8.
24 ibid., p. 258.
25 ibid., pp. 286–7.
26 ibid., pp. 287–8.
27 ibid., p. 290.
28 ibid.
29 ibid., p. 291.
30 ibid.
31 ibid.
32 ibid., p. 292.
33 ibid.
34 A puzzle is a situation to which it is known there is an answer, even

though the precise answer may not yet be known; a problem is a situation about which it is not known whether there can be an answer. If politics is about solving puzzles, a view to which the structural realists seem to incline, then Ashley is right to suggest that they have no 'hint of politics as a creative, critical enterprise . . . by which men and women might reflect on their goals and strive to shape *freely* their collective will'. ibid., p. 292.

35 Robert G. Gilpin, 'The richness of the tradition of political realism', in Keohane (ed.), *Neorealism*, p. 310.
36 Gilpin, *War and Change*.
37 We are grateful to Roger Spegele for the point.
38 Gilpin, *War and Change*, p. 211.
39 ibid., p. ix.
40 ibid., p. xiii.
41 ibid., p. x.
42 ibid., p. xi.
43 ibid., p. 10.
44 ibid., pp. 10–11.
45 ibid., p. 48.
46 ibid., pp.106–7.
47 ibid., p. 154.
48 ibid., pp. 156–7, 184–5.
49 ibid., p. 185.
50 ibid., p. 187.
51 Charles Beitz, *Political Theory and International Relations* (Princeton, NJ: Princeton University Press, 1979).
52 ibid., p. 36.
53 John A. Vasquez, *The Power of Power Politics* (London: Frances Pinter, 1983), p. 19.
54 ibid., p. 18.
55 Richard Mansbach and John A. Vasquez, *In Search of Theory* (New York: Columbia University Press, 1981), pp. 13–14.
56 Vasquez, *The Power of Power Politics*, p. 216.
57 This is the title of a volume of essays by prominent advocates of this point of view: Peter B. Evans, Dietrich Rueschemeyer and Theda Skocpol (eds), *Bringing the State Back In* (Cambridge: Cambridge University Press, 1985). The starting point for this debate in the North American context was the 1981 convention of the American Political Science Association when, for the first time, the convention was devoted to the theme of 'Restoring the State to Political Science'. However, the state has always been central to the so-called English school of international relations.
58 Tony Thorndike, 'The revolutionary approach: the Marxist perspective', in Trevor Taylor (ed.), *Approaches and Theory in International Relations* (London: Longman, 1978), pp. 64–5.
59 See Theda Skocpol, 'Bringing the state back in: current research', in Evans *et.al.*, *Bringing the State Back In*, p. 4 ff.
60 ibid., p. 9.

61 See Theda Skocpol, *States and Social Revolutions* (London: Cambridge University Press, 1979); Ellen Kay Trimberger, *Revolutions from Above* (New Brunswick, NJ: Transaction Books, 1978); Charles Tilly (ed.), *The Formation of National States in Western Europe* (London: Princeton University Press, 1975). See also Eric Nordlinger, *On the Autonomy of the Modern Democratic State* (Cambridge, Mass.: Harvard University Press, 1981).
62 Skocpol, 'Current research', in Evans *et.al.*, *Bringing the State Back In*, p. 16.
63 ibid., p. 20.
64 Dietrich Rueschemeyer and Peter B. Evans, 'The state and economic transformation', in Evans *et al.*, *Bringing the State Back In*, pp. 47–8.
65 Robert W. Cox, *Production Power and World Order* (New York: Columbia University Press, 1987), p. 1.
66 ibid., p. 2.
67 ibid., p. 5.
68 ibid.
69 ibid., p. 6.
70 ibid., p. 7.
71 ibid., p. 8.
72 ibid., p. 395.
73 ibid., p. 396.
74 ibid., p. 399.

Further reading

Cox, Robert W. *Production Power and World Order.* New York: Columbia University Press, 1987.
Evans, Peter B., Rueschemeyer, Dietrich and Skocpol, Theda (eds), *Bringing the State Back In.* Cambridge: Cambridge University Press, 1985.
Gilpin, Robert. *War and Change in World Politics.* Cambridge: Cambridge University Press, 1981.
Keohane, Robert O. (ed.). *Neorealism and Its Critics.* New York: Columbia University Press, 1986.
Waltz, Kenneth. *Theory of International Politics.* New York: Random House, 1979.

12 *Paradigms in perspective: conflict, international political economy and the return to theory*

> Reality therefore emerges from the abstract as well as the concrete, from the subjective as well as the objective, from invention as well as from understanding, from desire as well as from observation. It is a phenomenon of mind as well as of matter and is certain to be distorted by confinement to any particular theory. (Quincy Wright)[1]

In considering 'IR Now' we have concentrated on three different, competing, but overlapping intellectual maps of an IR universe – those of realism, world society and structuralism. Our justification for proceeding in this manner is that we need to know ourselves, and these three conceptual frameworks, paradigms if you will, provide navigation points for identification of where particular contributions to the literature stand in relation to other contributions. By relating to such points, we may be able better to know where we are and, indeed, who we are, intellectually speaking. Such grand schema perform another function in the present volume: they are a way of reducing an intellectual maelstrom to a simple form in order to enable our readers (we hope and trust) to grasp complexity through simplicity, which is, after all, the hallmark of all theory, science and learning. And we are not the only ones to approach the field in this manner.

This sort of intellectual mapping exercise, while having its most important uses and exciting a continuing fascination, is not, however, the usual endeavour in IR. Most of us, most of the time, carry out research in, and teach, lesser things. We explore islands of theory as a conflict researcher, foreign policy analyst, integration theorist, international political economist or whatever: that is, we specialize in a particular aspect of theory. In the terminology of Thomas Kuhn[2] we are in the business of 'normal science'. We are conducting our research largely within one of the conceptual frameworks previously discussed, because that particular one is the most intellectually congenial for us and most suitable for the subject at hand. But we forget, at our peril, that we are working within a larger framework, the logic of which can have no small influence as we explore our particular 'island of theory'.[3]

The compass of this volume dictates that we can do no more than touch upon a few islands of theory and thus we are giving an unbalanced representation of the discipline (just as our three conceptual frameworks also represent a subjective view of IR). In short, there is far more in terms of quantity, and indeed, often of great quality, in particular islands of theory than there is in the inter-paradigm debate, but there is also a difference in kind between the two. Our concern in this book has been with the big picture; most IR theorists are dealing with miniatures. In this chapter we try to link the two by considering the implications for conflict studies and international political economy (IPE) of the three conceptual frameworks that are the foundation of our analysis of 'IR Now'. Such an analysis serves to illustrate how the same topic can appear to be very different when seen through three different intellectual prisms. An island of theory is the consideration by a group of scholars of a particular range of questions or issues which they have grouped together because they share an inter-subjective view of their coherence and interrelationship. The scholars have become specialists with their own journals, conferences, departments and degrees, and are recognized as such by non-specialists, who may well defer to them on these questions. Yet, despite this collegiality, fundamental differences may persist on the nature of each island. This, in itself, is a stimulus to a renewed consideration of more general theoretical questions. Not surprisingly, given the different approaches set out in previous chapters, the late 1980s saw a new burst of theorizing that now, at the turn of the decade, is in full flood. There has been a return to theory, especially normative theory, among younger scholars, the scale and significance of which we cannot and do not ignore at the end of the chapter.

Conflict

The First World War was, as we have seen, the catalyst for our discipline, and the study of war and conflict permeates virtually every chapter of this book. However, the three conceptual frameworks can often be seen in the writings of times past: the nineteenth century is a case in point. The literature on the Congress and Concert system suggests the realist tradition. Each great Power was seeking to impose its rules of the game – be it Pax Britannica or Napoleon's order – which would protect the interests of the dominant Power and act as a constraint upon the other great Powers. On the other hand, no great Power would submit itself willingly to such constraints. Hence, if it could not 'win', in the sense of laying down the rules of the game, it did not wish to lose. It was amenable, therefore, to cooperating with others to ensure that no Power was able to lay down the rules of the game. The system was, in essence, competitive, being formed by the rivalry between the different world orders of the great Powers, but in order to escape being a victim of the constraints of a world order favourable to the interests of others, a modicum of cooperation among the Powers was necessary. And to secure this degree of cooperation for the management of conflict the Congress and Concert system was devised, as a codification of the balance of power.

The realist tradition was not the only way of seeing things in the nineteenth-century European world system. Whereas some saw self-help in an anarchical society as the dominant characteristic of inter-state relations, others were more impressed by the degree of integration and cooperation in the emerging world society.

The progressive, radical or liberal tradition – in many ways the predecessor of world society approaches – was much more inclined to ascribe behaviour to nurture rather than to nature. It was impressed by the way science and reason had, from the Renaissance by way of the Enlightenment to the agrarian and industrial revolutions of the eighteenth and nineteenth centuries, begun to unlock the 'secrets' of nature. Our lot depended, to a certain degree, on what use we made of this new-found knowledge. Moreover, as knowledge grew in a cumulative manner a sense of competence and confidence grew with it, so that what might not yet be understood would most likely be so in the future. From this, a progression of concerns followed from understanding, and then manipulation, first of the natural environment, thereafter the domestic social, economic and political environment and finally the international environment. In Western Europe and on the Atlantic seaboard of the United States two of the traditional curses of mankind – famine and disease – were in the process of being lifted or there was a prospect that they might be, as scientific agriculture and public health schemes began to have their effect. The third traditional curse now loomed larger, both relatively and absolutely – war. If the agrarian and industrial revolutions, allied to the welfare state with its public health and public education, alongside trades unions and the franchise, were creating a new society in which the notion of war between the civilized Powers seemed to be an anomaly, then by dint of applying the same principles that had led to such progress within society, a similar 'great leap forward' might be envisaged for international society. The need was evident because the two great revolutions of the nineteenth century – the industrial and the French – had made war absolutely more terrible; the industrial revolution by providing the infrastructure and *matériel* to keep armies of millions in the field, if necessary for years at a time, and the French Revolution by giving the fillip to nationalism that enabled those armies to be motivated to fight 'For King and Country' the so-called civilized world over.

In the face of this threat, with the American Civil War as the harbinger of the horrors of the First World War and the limited wars of the Crimea or of Bismarck as a constant reminder of their frail state of grace, groups of individuals began to coalesce in the middle of the nineteenth century into what we would now call a peace movement. Hinsley[4] recounts how gentlemen from Britain, the United States and the Continent began to organize peace congresses and 'working men' set up their own meetings. Their ultimate purpose was no less than social engineering on a grand scale: the control, indeed the abolition, of war between states. Their belief was in the harmony of interests – political no less than economic – and their efforts were not without success, even at the governmental level. The growth of arbitration treaties between states, sometimes with compulsory elements, is a reflection of this intellectual tradition, which led eventually to the forming of the Permanent Court of Arbitration and a welter of similar institutions in the Americas. The Hague Peace Congresses of 1899 and 1907 – the first mainly European, but the second including a significant Latin American representation – gave arms control, disarmament and the codification of the laws of war in a humanitarian direction a great boost, even if the motivation for calling the 1899 meeting had been the Tsar's financial inability to compete in the arms race rather than his wish not to do so. But others responded to his call and made something of it, building on the tradition of middle- and working-class international movements, the arbitration treaties and private institutions such as the International Committee of the Red Cross formed by Swiss personalities.

Their moment came with the First World War. The institutions of the Concert system, and its underlying realist philosophy, had allowed a catastrophic civil war, which had destroyed the moral, physical, social, economic and political fabric of European civilization, broadly construed. It was time to try other ways and the progressive, radical, liberal, social engineering approach had in Woodrow Wilson a political leader of intellectual ability, practical success and great moral stature matched by popular esteem, especially in Europe. Wilson had a diagnosis of the causes of catastrophe and a plan to put them right. The causes lay in the existence of imperfectly representative governments, which stifled legitimate national aspirations and contorted the basic international harmony of interests for their own dynastic purposes. It was necessary to remove these impediments so that the global political system would have a freedom commensurate with the global economic system, to the mutual benefit of both. International society would then become more like national society, with its consensus on basic values and its subsequent willingness to forgo self-help and to permit the establishment and operation of central means of coercion. However, given the high degree of consensus, and with representative government, this did not constitute a serious threat, except to the occasional deviant. Collective security would be 'writ large' to the international level. If all states were both democratic and nation-states, and could take a full and free part in the elaboration of the ground rules on which a system of collective security would be based, then peace was far more likely to be preserved. It was a peace to be buttressed by a League of Nations that not only existed to handle disputes, either by judicial processes, arbitration or conciliation, but also promoted peace in an active manner through the processes of peaceful change. States would come together not merely to deal with problems, but also to take advantage of opportunities. These opportunities would frequently be of a functional nature, as the international public unions had earlier foreshadowed, and they were to blossom in the framework of the League. Thus the League of Nations would develop, sustain and safeguard an international community – a league – of nations. Social engineering at the global level had come of age and with it world society approaches.

We have seen the mixed fortunes that befell this experiment, and with it the academic standing of the embryonic world society or pluralist approach, which subsequently gave way to the establishment of the realist consensus in the 1940s and 1950s. But we must not forget our third framework – that of the structuralist. This received one of its most important formulations in the works of Karl Marx, his contemporaries and successors, such as Lenin, in the nineteenth and early twentieth centuries. As we saw in previous chapters, conflict in the Marxist tradition was due to incompatible interests built into structures, whether between the bourgeoisie and the proletariat in a capitalist state, or between the great capitalist states themselves as a consequence of their highest condition – imperialism. However, this view of conflict and war sank from the mainstream of Western, and especially the English language academic discourse in IR, only to re-emerge recently.

War and conflict were always the subject of courses in IR from the time of the establishment of the discipline. In the beginning they broached the questions of peace and security, with strong institutional and legal overtones, which befitted what the League of Nations became, although Woodrow Wilson himself had strong views supporting the vigorous application of sanctions where necessary. The Hague tradition of disarmament and arms control was developed with new intellectual vigour and a degree of practical success. And there was considerable popular support for collective security and the League in some countries, such as the powerful League of Nations Union in Britain and the 'peace pledge' campaign. But as the thirties brought power politics once again to the forefront of the practical agenda, the academic world followed, but more in the style of current analyses of policy than that of strategic studies. It was with the Second World War, and the notion of 'grand strategy' – an amalgam of political, economic and strategic factors – that strategic questions became ensconced in the lecture halls of the universities as well as those of the military staff colleges.

After the Second World War a curious hiatus occurred, and for several reasons. On the one hand, academic attention was caught by a new attempt at collective security in the form of the United Nations, which quickly came to naught because of the collapse of the wartime Grand Alliance. On the other hand, within two years of the end of the war the Cold War was reaching its climax, so that political and economic relations were uppermost with the formulation and implementation of the Truman Doctrine and the Marshall Plan. It was only with the success of the Marshall Plan, the victory of the Communists in China and the Korean War, necessitating a major rearmament effort, that strategic factors and NATO, as a military organization, came to the fore. There was a mutism, too, on atomic weapons. On the one hand, there were those who reacted to Hiroshima and Nagasaki by thinking that they would change everything, but they were not sure to what, or how, and so they held their peace. Others thought that atomic weapons would not change the traditional military factors at all, so they carried on with 'business as usual'. Moreover, the war had engendered a brutalization of thought and spirit, and violence was endemic globally, whether in the Cold War context or as the struggles for national liberation gained momentum. The debate on atomic weapons was not yet joined and minds were concentrated on the short-term tasks of economic renewal, political and military survival or the struggle for independence.

The intellectual climate began to change in 1949 with Marshal of the Royal Air Force Sir John Slessor's paper, published later as *Defence of the West*,[5] in which he set out the broad lines of the doctrine of massive retaliation. The political climate changed too, with the development of the hydrogen bomb, the testing of which caused public concern. At the other end of the yield spectrum, the promise of nuclear weapons deemed suitable for battlefield use opened up the prospect of limited nuclear war. In Britain a group of academics, journalists, politicians and churchmen, led by Rear Admiral Sir Anthony Buzzard, appalled by the enormity and indiscriminate nature of the hydrogen bomb, began to explore the notion of graduated deterrence,[6] to be followed shortly thereafter by an American study group.[7] There were methodological innovations, too, as Arthur Burns demonstrated when he was one of the first to bring notions of game theory into the mainstream of IR.[8] In short, the nuclear debate was now being joined around the paradox that the more terrible nuclear war is made the less likely it is to occur, whereas the less terrible nuclear war is made the more likely it is to occur, but the more bearable it will be if it does occur. In the late 1950s and 1960s the central ideas of massive retaliation and graduated deterrence – later flexible response – were set out, stimulated enormously by the Institute for Strategic Studies in London and the Rand Corporation in the United States. A good selection of the literature of the time is to be found in John Garnett's well-chosen selection of reprints of the period.[9]

The debate was and remains inconclusive, because no one has been able to present a tested empirical theory of deterrence, at any level, from the individual to nuclear Powers. The manipulation of threats is something that we all do, but with little confidence about the outcome. The subsequent literature gives us scant reason for revising this view.[10] We simply do not have cogent empirical theory that relates what is at stake – the behaviour to be deterred – to the sanction threatened in case of non-observance seen in the context of the likelihood of the behaviour being detected and that of the sanction being applied. Depending on the assumptions being made, both massive retaliation and the graduated deterrence have a degree of plausibility and the choice of assumptions is still largely a question of fashion and political expediency. In the 1950s and 1960s these ideas were explored in their broad outline and could sensibly be taken no further, pending a firm empirical basis. However, in the process of their exploration the approach to an island of theory was formed, which found a central place – as befits its importance, if not its intellectual standing – in the undergraduate and postgraduate IR curricula.

The prospect of a limited nuclear war – limited at least in theory – raised the question of the broader issue of limited war in general and the relationship between conventional and nuclear weapons.[11] However, many of the conflicts of the postwar period were not of the classic type, but unconventional wars part of a revolutionary or national liberation process – a process that included economic, psychological, sociological and political factors as well as the military element. An 'insurgent' literature developed with different schools, such as those of Mao and the Latin Americans, with occasional but important contributions from Africa.[12] A 'counterinsurgency' literature revealed its schools too, as exemplified by the contrast between the 'hearts and minds' approach[13] and those who discounted attitudes in their belief that behaviour could be coerced successfully if the price of pursuing values was made too high.[14] Strategists were being led towards political sociology and conflict research, where Ted Robert Gurr's important *Handbook of Political Conflict*[15] is a very helpful overview. But the more traditional concerns of arms control and disarmament were still being pursued with some useful conceptual contributions being made to a tradition that stretches back into the nineteenth century.[16] Strategic studies had, by the 1960s, established itself in IR as well as, in its more tactical and military aspects, in part of the curricula of the staff colleges. It was a sub-field of the discipline and, for a while, an intellectual growth area. It continues to sustain itself, but not with the *élan* of its halcyon days of the decade beginning in the mid-1950s.

Strategic studies concerns itself with the 'sharp end' of power politics and fits snugly into the realist framework.[17] It is concerned with the manipulation and application of threats, principally between states operating in an anarchical society dominated by the practice and possibility of self-help. While order and stability may be a conceivable goal, peace, in such a situation, in any sense other than the absence of overt violence, is a chimera. The job of the strategist is to identify correctly the current balance of forces so that political settlements may be devised that reflect it. These, however, will change as the balance of forces changes. There is a danger that academic strategists may become thereby too close to status quo governments making their subject an applied science, a mere adjunct of state power, dependent upon the value orientation and policy premises of governments, so that the academic status of strategic studies is put at risk.

A decade after the incorporation of strategic studies into the mainstream of IR came a similar blossoming of conflict research, which reflects more the concerns and conceptual framework of the world society theorist. Although some notable contributors to this approach were already IR scholars, for example John Burton, others came to conflict research, and therefore to IR, from a variety of fields both in the social sciences, such as Kenneth Boulding in economics, and beyond, as in the case of Anatol Rapoport.

Psychologists, sociologists, economists, physicists, mathematicians, all enriched the field not only by asking and seeking to respond to some basic questions, often in reaction to the strategists' conceptions of deterrence theory, but also by bringing with them their methodological proclivities, which changed the face of IR in terms of research techniques. Conflict research was far more than behaviouralism in research methods, but it did provide an important *entrée* into IR for behaviouralist methods.

The founding of a journal is a frequent sign that an 'island of theory' has 'arrived'. The second issue of the *Journal of Conflict Resolution* provides an admirable and still valid visiting card for conflict research.[18] The writings of Johan Galtung and his colleagues in the early years of *Journal of Peace Research* served a similar function. Other names to conjure with as conflict research got under way were Boulding, Burton, Coser and Rapoport.[19] While some of these were attracted to formal models, as in the case of Michael Nicholson, others began to establish problem-solving workshops to bring about controlled communication and in general to facilitate relations.[20] Surveys and textbooks began to appear, so that by the early 1970s there was an abundant literature, the existence of which no serious scholar in IR could any longer ignore, the more so by the end of the decade.[21] This led to a degree of incorporation into the IR mainstream, although not as fully as in the case of strategic studies, perhaps because the ethos of conflict research was more questioning of the establishment – academic, political and state-centric. Nevertheless, there was a convergence with a wider literature, for example, on negotiation, with Fred Iklé in *How Nations Negotiate*,[22] who adopted an essentially zero–sum framework familiar from the strategists, Gilbert Winham[23] being particularly insightful on the multilateral diplomacy of managing conflict, and Adam Curle in *Making Peace*[24] and John Burton in *Resolving Deep-Rooted Conflict* suggesting the modalities for the self-sustaining non–coercive resolution of conflict rather than its mere settlement.[25] The movement from settlement to resolution takes us into the heartland not only of conflict research, but also of the world society approach as in a *Festschrift* for John Burton.[26] How, then, does conflict research relate to the wider conception of world society or pluralism and its historical precedents of Wilsonian thought, social engineering and progressive, radical ideas rooted in some notion of a harmony of interests?

In its most extreme form conflict research has a notion of conflict that is holistic, be it marital, neighbourhood, industrial, ethnic or interstate.[27] It embraces many different levels, crosses disciplinary boundaries without compunction and is non-partisan in spirit. It seeks the goal of resolution by being supportive of all the parties, no matter how seemingly deviant they may be, in a non-judgemental and non-directive manner. It views conflict as endemic and sometimes functional, conflict behaviour as learned, and, although individual conflicts can be resolved, conflict as a phenomenon is considered always to be with us. Moreover, it is a crucial part of the process of learning. It is its *dys*functionalities that are a matter of the greatest concern. The emphasis is upon relationships and their degree of legitimacy in the belief that social intercourse is, in its essence, non zero sum. While it may not always be possible in particular circumstances at a particular time to bring this out, peace is, nevertheless, a practical goal. There is no denial of the importance of power politics, only of its inevitability, and there is a clear recognition that resolution based on legitimized relations is precluded if it masks a situation of structural violence.

Structural violence is a term that Galtung made his own as he traversed the line from conflict research, of which he had been one of the founding fathers, to a form of 'peace research' conceived in the structuralist tradition. While peace can have other conceptions, and to this extent the appellation of peace researcher is a misnomer since it is not a monopoly of the structuralist school, nevertheless the idea that peace is more than the absence of violence, and connotes justice and the absence of structural violence, is a hallmark of peace researchers, but not of them alone. This concern with structural violence, and with action and relevance, was very much evident in the post-behavioural mood of the late 1960s and early 1970s referred to in Chapter 11. Illustrative of this is the well-known article by Hermann Schmid, and Galtung's reaction to it.[28] Thereafter the peace research literature has been both sparse and prolix. It has been sparse in the sense that much of it has been of a practical rather than conceptual orientation. A good source for this literature is Scandinavian journals, such as the *Bulletin of Peace Proposals* and *Instant Research on War and Peace*. But it has been prolix in another sense, since ideas of conflict permeate the structuralist approach, be it in the economic tradition of Frank and Wallerstein or the political one of Modelski. In the economic tradition many detailed studies have been made, indeed they are a major part of the burgeoning literature in international political economy (IPE), to which we shall turn shortly.

Peace research is value promoting, although what those values are, or should be, is not a matter of consensus among peace researchers. Nevertheless, a peaceful society will be one without structural violence, and the way to achieve this is to expose existing structural violence by increasing the polarization within society. This will, it is suggested, have the double benefit of educating those who are the victims of structural violence to their predicament and forcing those who benefit from the structures either to reform, or to defend their privileges. In the latter case, the peace researcher will help the victims to destroy the oppressive structures, by violent means if necessary. The peace researcher is thus on the opposite side of the barricades from the strategist, while the conflict researcher is trying to make such barricades unnecessary.[29]

We can thus see quite clearly that the three conceptual frameworks continue to give rise to very different analyses about the causes and ways of managing conflict and war as well as the promise of very different outcomes. Theory does matter, because we cannot think without a theory that tells us what to look for and how to interpret what we find. Facts do not speak for themselves, they have meaning thrust upon them. It behoves us, therefore, to know our theories as we know ourselves. And this is not only true for conflict and war, but also for IPE.

International political economy (IPE)

IPE has fared differently in Britain from the United States. In Britain it has always been part of mainstream IR, with departments of political economy in universities and courses, for example, on the 'politics of international economic relations' and 'international economic law' in the undergraduate IR degrees at the University of London since the Second World War. At Oxford and Cambridge, PPE (Politics, Philosphy and Economics) at the undergraduate level ensured some juxtaposition of politics and economics. Indeed, there was no difficulty, intellectual or institutional, in exploring the interaction between economic and political questions at all levels. And for a country hard pressed in both domains, internally and internationally, there was a considerable practical incentive for the British academic community to do so. Ironically, one of the earlier excellent books in this genre, Richard Gardner's *Sterling-Dollar Diplomacy* was written by an American.[30] But Keynes has made a well-known contribution in his *The Economic Consequences of the Peace*[31] in the 1920s and the American Eugene Staley's *War and the Private Investor* is still remembered from the interwar period.[32] In the United States, however, the legal tradition in IR to some extent blocked the growth of IPE, until political scientists became fascinated by the emergence of European economic integration and formulated the theory of neofunctionalism. One of the principal figures in Britain and beyond during the last four decades has been Susan Strange.[33] Not only have her writings had a considerable and significant impact in Britain and abroad, especially the United States, but she has founded, animated and acted as *la patronne* for a group of younger British scholars in the area for the best part of twenty years.[34] IPE has thus flourished in Britain as an organic part of IR.

It is, however, the Latin Americans who gave the subject an *éclat* that was previously absent. We have seen in Chapter 10 how the ECLA group led to ideas on *dependencia*, centre–periphery and world-systems and in so doing changed the face of IR by giving a new vitality and validity to structural approaches. Prebisch, Frank, Amin, Emmanuel and Wallerstein are names familiar to any IR scholar, and not only in the English-speaking world. Furthermore, the problems with which they were struggling were centre-stage politically, as well as economically, as demands grew for a New International Economic Order (NIEO). Robert Cox has conveniently identified many of the schools in approaching that topic.[35] Moreover, it was a topic that seized and still excites the public imagination, as the quite astonishing sales figures of the two Brandt Reports indicate.[36] Thus, in Britain and in Latin America, it has been economic woes that have been a catalyst for academic endeavour, and so it is with the United States – the decline of the United States from undisputed global dominance and leadership in economic affairs.[37] This surge of interest has given rise to a demand for textbooks or surveys, and Brett and Spero,[38] among others, have met this need in a satisfactory manner, while Robert Keohane and Robert Gilpin have taken stock in a broader manner. Keohane, building on his work with Nye discussed in Chapter 9 has examined the situation *After Hegemony* from the point of view of the United States and of the vestiges of the Bretton Woods system created by the United States and Britain at the end of the war.[39] It is in this context that regime theorists are relevant, as we saw previously.[40] But Stephen Krasner has gone further and undertaken an 'economic realist' account of the 'third world against global liberalism' in world political economy.[41] Robert Gilpin has built upon the framework of a well-known article 'Three models of the future'[42] to expound upon *The Political Economy of International Relations*.[43] His three models, or in his recent formulation 'three ideologies of political economy', is grist to our mill in a different context.

In 'Three models of the future', Gilpin identified the 'sovereignty-at-bay' or liberal model,[44] the *dependencia* model and the mercantilist or economic nationalist model, which correspond fairly closely to our three general frameworks of 'world society', 'structuralist' and 'realist' in IR. The match is perhaps less close between the liberal model and world society. They share the notion of declining state-centricity and the virtues of interdependence, but the liberal conception of multinational corporations as the acceptable medium of capitalism's 'hidden hand' – Gilpin categorized it as the 'critical transmission belt of capital, ideas, and growth'[45] – might be treated with a degree of scepticism by advocates of the world society approach. There is a shared conception of the possibility of a 'harmony of interests', but many working in the world society paradigm would balk at the nostrums and ideology of an unreconstructed economic liberalism. With the *dependencia* model there is less difficulty, for we have seen how that fits into the structuralist *Weltanschauung*. Gilpin points out that a 'key element missing in both the sovereignty-at-bay and the dependencia models is the nation state',[46] and this is as central to the mercantilist approach as it is to that of the realist.

> By *mercantilism* I mean the attempt of governments to manipulate economic arrangements in order to maximise their own interests, whether or not this is at the expense of others. The interests may be related to domestic concerns (full employment, price stability, etc.) or to foreign policy (security, independence, etc.) . . . The essence of mercantilism . . . is the priority of *national* economic and political objectives over considerations of

global economic efficiency . . . In short, each nation will pursue economic policies that reflect domestic economic needs and external political ambitions without much concern for the effects of these policies on other countries or on the international economic system as a whole.[47]

Since those in the mercantilist school tend to argue that the phenomenal period of economic growth in the developed world has come to an end, the dominance of the liberal thesis (and that of the United States in a hegemonic role) is likely to decline in favour of more mercantilist perceptions. Gilpin identifies two forms of mercantilism in the literature – benign and malign.[48] Both suggest that economic regionalism is re-establishing itself, but thereafter they differ.

Benign mercantilism entails a degree of protectionism that safeguards the value and interests of a society; it enables a society to retain domestic autonomy and possess valued industries in a world characterised by the internationalisation of production, global integration of financial markets, and the diminution of national control. Malevolent mercantilism, on the other hand, refers to the economic clashes of nations characteristic . . . of the 1930s; its purpose is to triumph over other states. The first is defensive; the second is the conduct of interstate warfare by economic means.[49]

The second is clearly a realist conception, and so could be benign mercantilism, although in certain formulations (for example, some regimes) it would sit more easily in the world society framework than 'hard line' nineteenth-century-style economic liberalism.

Gilpin's triptych, and that of the strategist, conflict researcher and peace researcher, do seem to complement our delineation of three conceptual frameworks or intellectual traditions. In so far as IPE is concerned, Gilpin envisages in the future a mixed system of mercantilistic competition, economic regionalism and sectoral protectionism.[50] The extent to which this will materialize, and its degree of benevolence or malevolence, will affect greatly our future wellbeing and not just our economic wellbeing. But so, too, will our ability to analyse, manage, settle or resolve conflict in all manner of human relations. Indeed, politics and economics are both fundamental and interactive since they treat the basic questions of values and resources. To these questions the approach in IR has been diverse, as our three conceptual frameworks suggest. Moreover, they are not the only ones possible.

In the last chapters there has been an endeavour, however sketchily and inadequately, to give an impression of 'IR now'. While attempting to give a judicious sense of the whole, one must, perforce, choose and describe 'IR now' in a subjective manner. Yet if, notwithstanding any inadequacies, misunderstandings, intellectual blindness and failings in presentation, a constructive, if critical, reaction has been stimulated, then, paradoxically, the purpose of provoking a learning process in a fructuous intellectual exercise will have been achieved. Just such a critical reaction is now occurring in what was referred to earlier in this chapter as a return to theory. It is to that which we now return.

A return to theory

Interdependence means that there is a need for norms, rules and practices by which interactions may be governed, hence the relevance of normative theory and the current vogue that it is enjoying. Normative theories were for long, at least in Britain, the principal form of theorizing about IR. They did not have such prominence in the United States and, with the growing dominance of US scholars and institutions in the discipline, normative theorizing became something of a rather antiquarian pursuit – an intellectual backwater. In recent years, however, things have begun to change and there is a new surge of interest on both sides of the Atlantic. Books published in the last five years are now the subject of animated debate[51] and students are choosing the normative theory options in growing and significant numbers. Whereas in the past an IR scholar could 'get by', admittedly badly, with scant knowledge of normative considerations, this is no longer the case. There is an abundant literature which, given the nature of the subject, has a timeless quality about it. It can be set out under four rubrics – the legal, realist, classical and cosmopolitan.

It is sometimes amusing, if shocking, when giving a guest seminar in a political science department that does not have an IR component, to witness the surprise, indeed bewilderment, of the audience when an 'IR man' makes frequent reference to Hobbes, Thucydides, Rousseau, Marx, Kant, Locke and the like. But the roots of normative theory, and indeed of our three conceptual frameworks, lie deep in the classical literature of political philosphy. The perennial questions of justice, rights, duties and obligations permeate the three IR frameworks and it is the responses to them that help to differentiate the paradigms. Moreover, epistemological questions are as fiercely debated in IR as elsewhere and students, at least in reputable institutions, are introduced to them even at the undergraduate level. Credit for some of this must lie in an important heritage for IR – that from international law, which was established as part of the emerging European state system that culminated in the Treaty of Westphalia in 1648. The formative influence of international law on IR was considerable, and it remains, as was seen in 'IR then'.

Codification of actual and desirable practice, institutional frameworks and procedures, conciliation and judicial processes, with political activity to promote peaceful change and functional cooperation, were the hallmarks of the progressive radical approach to the question of international political relations, which culminated in the foundation of the League of Nations. It was peace through law and institutions, and it had its roots in the writings of Saint-Simon, Kant and Grotius. Indeed, one international lawyer, Hersch Lauterpacht, reduced all disputes to legal questions to the exclusion of political questions, [52] while J. L. Brierly, in his magisterial essay *The Law of Nations*, [53] saw international law as underpinning the political order, not preceding it. However, international law gradually became more positivistic and sociological, as the work of Georg Schwarzenberger suggests. [54] International law moved further into the mainstream of IR with the work of Richard Falk, especially in relation to the Vietnam War, [55] and Myers McDougall and the 'Yale school', [56] of which a distinguished exponent in Britain is Rosalyn Higgins. McDougall argues that law is an instrument for the pursuit of goals and it is thus coextensive with politics itself. Indeed, international law was seen by some as a social science[57] and taught as such. The legal aspects of questions, for long hitherto neglected, began to assume a greater salience as, for example, in legal restraints in war[58] and the protection of human rights.[59] In part this reflects a reaction against realism.

Arnold Wolfers[60] has suggested that in so far as continental realists are concerned, *raison d'état* comes before questions of morality, especially in the Germanic tradition. This sits somewhat uneasily in an Anglo–American context, where accepted principles of morality are deemed to inform the foreign policy process, at least in declaratory terms. Hoffman suggests that there are four general arguments, of a Hobbesian nature, which the 'continental hard-liners' adopt – the idea of a moral vacuum, moral relativism, the duality of morality and the primacy of the national interest. Hoffman cites a voluminous literature in support of this analysis.[61]

While many continental refugees to the United States established this tradition there and some, such as Georg Schwarzenberger, planted similar ideas in less fertile soil in Britain, thinking in Britain frequently seeks to relate the natural law tradition[62] to that of the notion of a social contract. If we can reason, so the argument goes, then we can give ourselves guidance on the course of action that we should follow. The application of reason is likely to lead us to the idea that some form of social contract is expedient in terms of mutual wellbeing and thus is established a basis for societal norms and rules on rights, duties and obligations at all levels. In the 'English school' of IR, Roy Jones's call for the closure of which caused a furore,[63] emphasis is put less on *raison d'état* than on the idea of 'international society'. This society has a moral basis in principles such as non–intervention, *pacta sunt servanda* and the like. There is a substantial literature in this vein.[64] In the United States, Michael Walzer's *Just and Unjust Wars*[65] has excited attention and there is a similar interest in the question in Britain.[66] The debate can be pursued advantageously on either side of the Atlantic.[67] But there is also a cosmopolitan approach that is worthy of consideration.

The cosmopolitan approach conceives of morality in global, not state-centric terms. One of the foundation texts of this approach is John Rawls's *A Theory of Justice*[68] – distributive justice. Charles Beitz, among others, has related Rawls's conceptions to IR[69] and in so doing has given the individual, rather than the state, a significant role in the global context. Henry Shue's conception of *Basic Rights*[70] includes economic rights (now recognized in UN formulations), as well as 'Western' civil and political rights, so that the cosmopolitan approach does provide a normative element to both the 'world society' and 'structuralist' frameworks. This is recognized in Andrew Linklater's *Men and Citizens in the Theory of*

IR.[71] It also pushes normative theory in the direction of critical theory, exemplified in IR by Cox and Ashley as we have seen, and more recently by younger scholars such as Linklater and Hoffman.[72] The implications for needs theory or for structural change are obvious.

The question of rationality is important in the context of critical theory, since one of its most pointed criticisms of the conventional language of discourse is that it does not embrace what Ashley called 'rationality proper'. As Hoffman comments,

> The difficulty is not with rationality *per se* but its distorted, partial development through the universalisation of a single form of rationality, namely instrumental, economic and administrative reason. Furthermore, unlike radical interpretivism with its attack on the Enlightenment *as a whole*, critical theory seeks to maintain the link between freedom and reason which has been central to political consciousness; it seeks to critique the development of certain forms of rationality but does not accept the radical interpretivist renunciation of reason itself. It retains a concept of reason which asserts itself simultaneously against both instrumentalism and existentialism, which is exercised in conjunction with normative concerns and which is critically applicable to itself. The essence of rationality, in the context of critical theory, entails a limitless invitation to criticism. In consequence, a complacent faith in *rationalism* is ruled out.[73]

On the other hand, 'Critical theory does not impose a utopian model of emancipated society'[74] – perhaps because critical theorists do not have one, or at least cannot agree upon one. Where then does critical theory leave us? It appears to suggest that we should always be aware of the circumstances in which theorizing takes place. We need to ask ourselves, of ourselves as well as of others, for whom is theorizing taking place as well as by whom it is taking place. In other words, it incites us to a professional awareness of context in the broadest sense, both of the nature of our social product from gestation to all possible uses and in rationality proper. Such an admonition is necessary and salutary, but hardly revolutionary. It suggests that once critical theory has raised consciousness it has achieved its purpose. It is not a theory *of* something, but a way of theorizing about something. However, the very idea of rationality itself is being challenged in IR as elsewhere.

In some insightful papers, Pauline Rosenau has provided the lay IR scholar with a cogent introduction to post modernism and post-structuralism.[75] In the tradition of Nietzsche, Heidegger and others, post-modernists reject reason as the child of the Enlightenment and a legitimizing device for the modern institutions of society and the idea of progress. Truth, for post-modernists, is meaningless, arbitrary or contingent: it is relative and subjective. There is no attempt 'to categorize, classify, simplify, verify and generalise as does science. They, rather, seek to highlight uniqueness, to concentrate on the enigmatic, to appreciate the unrepeatable'.[76] Their method is to deconstruct a 'text'. Through this intellectual dismemberment they seek to get to the very heart of the text and to set it in context by revealing what has been unsaid or concealed. The analysis is fiercely introspective – a withdrawal into self. It proposes nothing, but merely decomposes. As Pauline Rosenau comments:

> They value tension between plot and narrative, elegance of expression and style, seductiveness of content, and simplicity of presentation. They ask what a text tells us in terms of our own experience and discrimination . . . Lacking any confidence in reason, so rationality provides no help to post-modernists in determining comparative excellence of varying perspectives. A denial of universal truth, or even an approximation to it, follows logically. Skepticism about the possibility of knowledge leads the most pessimistic among the post-modernists to question the efficacy of personal action because such intervention implies a goal or project, and some intellectual tools for choosing certain ends over others.[77]

But Rosenau also refers to an affirmative post-modernism which opens up science 'to the metaphysical and the mystical, thus facilitating a synthesis of science and theology'.[78]

Post-modernists live in a closed personal world. We all do. But the modern scientific rational enterprise entails trying to break out of that personal world rather than glorifying and glorying in it. There is a point to the post-modernist position, but acute subjectivism can be transmitted only with great difficulty. It is a solitary exercise. It will therefore have little effect on the discipline (even laying aside the fearsome intellectual problems it is likely to pose most IR scholars). And, if subjectivity is reduced to facilitate transmission by taking a step towards more conventional science, then the point of the post-modernist exercise is diminished. Post-modernists are thus hoist with their own petard.[79] They represent an extreme case of that fundamental bifurcation between subjective and objective, categories of mind and the external world, concept and fact, paradigms and trends, consciousness and objective world that categorizes much of social theory.[80]

IR comes in many forms. There is Academic IR, which develops theory and coherence, and Instrumental IR, which is concerned with utility. Colonial IR is about the domination of the centre and Scientific IR is about method. Reasonable IR values prudence and Providential IR relates to conceptual categories.[81] To this we can add Post-modern IR. The reader is entitled to enquire about the IR of the authors of this survey. This volume is, after all, not an objective survey of 'IR then and now'. It is a survey of the Anglo-American mainstream and what that mainstream acknowledges as its antecedents. It is a view from what is taken to be the centre and reflects values that are liberal, internationalist, Western and bourgeois. *Nolens volens* these values are inculcated into our readers. Moreover, these values are given fuller sway as we undertake our final task – however imperfectly – to broach the future of IR.

Notes: Chapter 12

1 Quincy Wright, *The Study of International Relations* (New York: Appleton-Century-Crofts, 1955), p. 12.
2 Thomas Kuhn, *The Structure of Scientific Revolutions* (Chicago: University of Chicago Press, 1970).
3 The phrase was first given currency in this context by Harold Guetzkow.
4 F. H. Hinsley, *Power and the Pursuit of Peace* (London: Cambridge University Press, 1963).
5 Sir John Slessor, *Strategy for the West* (London: Cassell, 1954), and the famous 'massive retaliation' speech of US Secretary of State John Foster Dulles, Department of State: *Bulletin*, XXX, 761, 25 January 1954.
6 Anthony Buzzard, 'Massive retaliation and graduated deterrence', *World Politics*, January 1956.

7 Henry Kissinger, *Nuclear Weapons and Foreign Policy* (New York: Harper, 1957).

8 Arthur Lee Burns, 'From balance to deterrence', *World Politics*, July 1957.

9 John Garnett (ed.), *Theories of Peace and Security* (London: Macmillan, 1970); Thomas C. Schelling, *The Strategy of Conflict* (Cambridge, Mass: Harvard University Press, 1980); Bernard Brodie, *Strategy in the Missile Age* (Princeton, NJ: Princeton University Press, 1959); Louis J. Halle, *The Elements of International Strategy* (Lanham, Mass.: University Press of America, 1984); André Beaufre, *Deterrence and Strategy* (London: Faber, 1965); Philip Green, *Deadly Logic* (Columbus: Ohio State University Press, 1966).

10 Alexander George and Richard Smoke, *Deterrence in American Foreign Policy* (New York: Columbia University Press, 1974); Patrick Morgan, *Deterrence: A Conceptual Analysis* (London: Sage, 1977); Robert Jervis, 'Deterrence theory revisited', *World Politics*, XXXI, 2, 1979; Richard Rosecrance, 'Strategic deterrence reconsidered', *Adelphi Papers*, No. 116 (London: International Institute for Strategic Studies, November 1975).

11 Ian Clark, *Limited Nuclear War* (Oxford: Martin Robertson, 1982); John Mearsheimer, *Conventional Deterrence* (Ithaca, NY: Cornell University Press, 1983); Paul Bracken, *The Command and Control of Nuclear Forces* (New Haven, Conn.: Yale University Press, 1983).

12 Mao Tse Tung, *Basic Tactics* (New York: Praeger, 1986); Che Guevara: *Guerrilla Warfare* (Harmondsworth: Pelican, 1969); Regis Debray, *Revolution in the Revolution* (London: Greenwood, 1980); Frantz Fanon, *The Wretched of the Earth* (Harmondsworth: Penguin, 1983); Amilcar Cabral, *Unity and Struggle* (London: Heinemann, 1980).

13 Robert Thompson, *Defeating Communist Insurgency* (London: Macmillan, 1975).

14 Nathan Leites and Charles Wolf, *Rebellion and Authority* (Chicago: Markham, 1970).

15 Ted Robert Gurr (ed.), *Handbook of Political Conflict* (New York: Free Press, 1981).

16 Colin Gray, *The Soviet American Arms Race* (Lexington, Mass.: Lexington Press, 1976); Samuel Huntingdon, 'Arms races: prerequisites and results', in George Quester (ed.), *Power, Action and Interaction* (Boston: Little, Brown, 1971); Hedley Bull, *The Control of the Arms Race* (London: Weidenfeld and Nicolson, 1961); Mary Kaldor, *The Baroque Arsenal* (London: Deutsch, 1982).

17 A. J. R. Groom, 'Paradigms in conflict: the strategist, the conflict researcher and the peace researcher', *Review of International Studies*, April 1988.

18 *Journal of Conflict Resolution*, I, 2, Special Issue edited by R. W. Mack and R. C. Snyder.

19 Kenneth Boulding, *Conflict and Defense* (New York: Harper and Row, 1962); J. W. Burton, *Peace Theory* (New York: Knopf, 1962); Lewis Coser, *The Function of Social Conflict* (London: Routledge and Kegan

Paul, 1956); Anatol Rapoport, *Fights Games and Debates* (Ann Arbor, Mich.: University of Michigan Press, 1974).

20 Michael Nicholson, *Conflict Analysis* (London: English Universities Press, 1970); J. W. Burton, *Conflict and Communication* (London: Macmillan, 1969).

21 Louis Kriesberg, *Social Conflicts* (Englewood Cliffs, NJ: Prentice Hall, 1982); C. R. Mitchell, *The Structure of International Conflict* (London: Macmillan, 1981); Jurgen Dedring, *Recent Advances in Peace and Conflict Research* (London: Sage, 1976); C. G. Smith (ed.), *Conflict Resolution* (Notre Dame, Ind.: University of Notre Dame Press, 1971); Morton Deutsch, *The Resolution of Conflict* (New Haven, Conn.: Yale University Press, 1973).

22 Fred Iklé, *How Nations Negotiate* (New York: Columbia University Press, 1971).

23 Gilbert Winham, 'Negotiation as a management process', *World Politics*, XXX, 1, 1977.

24 Adam Curle, *Making Peace* (London: Tavistock, 1971).

25 J. W. Burton, *Resolving Deep-Rooted Conflict* (Lanham, Mass.: University Press of America, 1987); Edward Azar and J. W. Burton (eds), *International Conflict Resolution* (Brighton: Wheatsheaf, 1986); C. R. Mitchell, *Peacemaking and the Consultant's Role* (Farnborough: Gower, 1981).

26 Michael Banks (ed.), *Conflict in World Society* (Brighton: Wheatsheaf, 1984).

27 Groom, 'Paradigms in conflict', *Review of International Studies*, April 1988.

28 Hermann Schmid, 'Politics and peace research', *Journal of Peace Research*, March 1968; Johan Galtung, *Essays in Peace Research*, Vols. I–V (Atlantic Highlands, NJ: Humanities Press, 1975–79).

29 This theme is developed in Groom, 'Paradigms in conflict', *Review of International Studies*, April 1988.

30 Richard Gardner, *Sterling–Dollar Diplomacy* (Oxford: Clarendon Press, 1956).

31 J. M. Keynes, *The Economic Consequences of the Peace* (London: Macmillan, 1920).

32 Eugene Staley, *War and the Private Investor* (Chicago: University of Chicago Press, 1935).

33 Susan Strange, *Sterling and British Policy* (London: Oxford University Press, 1971); *Casino Capitalism* (Oxford: Blackwell, 1986); *States and Markets* (London: Pinter, 1988); (ed.), *Paths to International Political Economy* (London: Allen & Unwin, 1984).

34 Susan Strange and Roger Tooze (eds), *The International Management of Surplus Capacity* (London: Allen & Unwin, 1982); R. J. Barry Jones (ed.), *Perspectives on Political Economy* (London: Frances Pinter, 1983).

35 Robert Cox, 'Ideologies and the new international economic order', in Michael Smith, Richard Little, and Michael Shackleton (eds), *Perspectives in World Politics* (London: Croom Helm, 1981).

36 The Brandt Commission, *North–South* (London: Pan, 1980), and *Common Crisis* (London: Pan, 1983).
37 For an interesting analysis of these debates from an IR perspective see R. D. McKinlay and R. Little, *Global Problems and World Order* (London: Frances Pinter, 1986).
38 E. A. Brett, *The World Economy since the War* (London: Macmillan, 1985); Joan E. Spero, *The Politics of International Economic Relations* (London: Allen & Unwin, 1982).
39 Robert Keohane, *After Hegemony* (Princeton, NJ: Princeton University Press, 1984).
40 Stephen Krasner (ed.), *International Regimes* (Ithaca, NY: Cornell University Press, 1983).
41 Stephen Krasner, *Structural Conflict: The Third World Against Global Liberalism* (Los Angeles: University of California Press, 1985).
42 Robert Gilpin, 'Three models of the future', in Smith, Little and Shackleton (eds), *Perspectives in World Politics*.
43 Robert Gilpin, *The Political Economy of International Relations* (Princeton, NJ: Princeton University Press, 1987). For a discussion of competing typologies of IPE, see Richard Higgot, *Politics of Australia's International Economic Relations* (London: Macmillan, forthcoming).
44 See Raymond Vernon, *Sovereignty at Bay* (New York: Basic Books, 1971).
45 Gilpin, 'Three models of the future', in Smith *et al.*, *Perspectives in World Politics*, p. 402.
46 ibid., p. 404.
47 ibid., p. 405.
48 ibid., p. 406.
49 Gilpin, *Political Economy of IR*, p. 404.
50 ibid., p. 394 ff
51 Alberto Coll, *The Wisdom of Statecraft* (Durham, NC: Duke University Press, 1985); Mervyn Frost, *Towards a Normative Theory of International Relations* (London: Cambridge University Press, 1986); James Mayall (ed.), *The Community of States* (London: Allen & Unwin, 1983); Terry Nardin, *Law, Morality and the Relations of States* (Princeton, NJ: Princeton University Press, 1983); David D. Newsom (ed.), *The Diplomacy of Human Rights* (Lanham, Mass: University Press of America, 1986); N. G. Onuf, *World of Our Making: Rules and Rule in Social Theory and International Relations* (Columbia, SC: University of South Carolina Press, 1989); John Vincent, *Foreign Policy and Human Rights* (London: Cambridge University Press, 1986); Moorhead Wright, *Rights and Obligations in North/South Relations* (London: Macmillan, 1986). These paragraphs draw upon Mark Hoffman, 'Normative theories', in Margot Light and A. J. R. Groom (eds), *International Relations*, with the kind permission of the author.
52 H. Lauterpacht, *International Law* (Cambridge: Cambridge University Press, 1977).
53 J. L. Brierley, *The Law of Nations* (Oxford: Clarendon Press, 1963).

54 Georg Schwarzenberger, *The Frontiers of International Law* (London: Stevens, 1962).

55 Richard Falk, *The International Law of Civil War* (Princeton, NJ: Princeton University Press, 1971); *Legal Order in a Violent World* (Princeton, NJ: Princeton University Press, 1968); *The Status of Law in International Society* (Princeton, NJ: Princeton University Press, 1970); with C. Black (eds), *The Future of the International Legal Order* (Princeton, NJ: Princeton University Press, 1969).

56 M. S. McDougall *et al.*, *Human Rights and World Public Order* (New Haven, Conn.: Yale Univesity Press, 1961); M. S. McDougall, *Studies in World Public Order* (New Haven, Conn.:Yale University Press, 1960).

57 Wesley Gould and Michael Barkun, *International Law and the Social Sciences* (Princeton, NJ: Princeton University Press, 1970).

58 Geoffrey Best, *Humanity in Warfare* (London: Weidenfeld and Nicolson, 1980).

59 Vincent, *Foreign Policy and Human Rights*.

60 Arnold Wolfers, *Discord and Collaboration* (Baltimore, Md: Johns Hopkins University Press, 1966).

61 Hoffman, 'Normative theories', in Light and Groom (eds), *International Relations*, pp. 31–2.

62 E. B. F. Midgley, *The Natural Law Tradition and the Theory of International Relations* (London: Elek, 1975).

63 Roy E. Jones, 'The English school of international relations: A case for closure', *British Journal of International Studies*, 7, 1, 1981.

64 Martin Wight, *Power Politics* (Leicester: Leicester University Press, 1978); *Systems of States* (Leicester: Leicester University Press, 1978); Herbert Butterfield and Martin Wight (eds), *Diplomatic Investigations* (London: Allen & Unwin, 1966); C. A. W. Manning, *The Nature of International Society* (London: Macmillan, 1975); Alan James (ed.), *The Bases of International Order* (London: Oxford University Press, 1973); Hedley Bull, *The Anarchical Society* (London: Macmillan, 1977); Michael Donelan (ed.), *The Reason of States* (London: Allen & Unwin, 1978); James Mayall (ed.), *The Community of States* (London: Allen & Unwin, 1983).

65 Michael Walzer, *Just and Unjust Wars* (New York: Basic Books, 1977).

66 B. Paskins and M. Dockrill, *The Ethics of War* (London: Duckworth, 1979).

67 Geoffrey Goodwin (ed.), *Ethics and Nuclear Deterrence* (London: Croom Helm, 1982); J. E. Hare and Carey B. Joynt, *Ethics and International Affairs* (London: Macmillan, 1982).

68 John Rawls, *A Theory of Justice* (Oxford: Clarendon Press 1972).

69 Charles Beitz, *Political Theory and International Relations* (Princeton, NJ: Princeton University Press, 1979).

70 Henry Shue, *Basic Rights* (Princeton, NJ: Princeton University Press, 1980).

71 A. Linklater, *Men and Citizens in the Theory of International Relations* (London: Macmillan, 1981).

310 *'Now': contending paradigms*

72 Andrew Linklater, 'Realism, Marxism and critical international theory', *Review of International Studies*, October 1986, and Mark Hoffman, 'States, cosmopolitanism and normative international theory', *Paradigms*, 2, 1.
73 Mark Hoffman, 'Conversations on critical international relations theory', *Millennium*, Spring 1988, p. 92.
74 ibid., p. 93.
75 Pauline Rosenau, 'Internal logic, external absurdity: post-modernism and post-structuralism in political science', *Paradigms*, summer 1990, and 'Once again into the fray: International relations confronts the humanities', *Millennium*, spring 1990.
76 P. Rosenau, *Paradigms*. p.42
77 P. Rosenau, *Paradigms*. p.43
78 Pauline Rosenau, 'Modern and post-modern science – some contrasts', article submitted to the Special Issue of the *American Political Science Review* on 'Post-modern science'.
79 Or have they merely perpetrated a gigantic and successful spoof?
80 We are grateful to Osmo Apunen for the categorization.
81 Further thanks are due to Osmo Apunen for the categorization.

Further reading

Garnett, John (ed.). *Theories of Peace and Security*. London: Macmillan, 1970.
Gilpin, Robert. *The Political Economy of International Relations*. Princeton, NJ: Princeton University Press, 1987.
Groom, A. J. R. 'Paradigms in conflict: the strategist, the conflict researcher and the peace researcher', *Review of International Studies*, April 1988.
Gurr, Ted Robert (ed.). *Handbook of Political Conflict*. New York: Free Press, 1981.
Hinsley, F. H.. *Power and the Pursuit of Peace*. London: Cambridge University Press, 1963.
Krasner, Stephen (ed.). *International Regimes*. Ithaca, NY: Cornell University Press, 1983.
Kuhn, Thomas. *The Structure of Scientific Revolutions*. Chicago: University of Chicago Press, 1970.
McKinlay, R. D. and Little, R. *Global Problems and World Order*. London: Frances Pinter, 1986.
Nardin, Terry. *Law, Morality and the Relations of States*. Princeton, NJ: Princeton University Press, 1983.
Schelling, Thomas C. *The Strategy of Conflict*. Cambridge, Mass: Harvard University Press, 1980.
Schmid, Hermann. 'Politics and peace research'. *Journal of Peace Research*, March 1968.

Spero, Joan E. *Politics of International Economic Relations*. London: Allen & Unwin, 1982.

Vincent, John. *Foreign Policy and Human Rights*. London: Cambridge University Press, 1986.

PART THREE

Epilogue

13. *Future imperfectly*

> In short, all too rare are the efforts to confront directly the possibility that world politics are undergoing unprecedented transformation and thus to theorize anew about the organizing structures and processes that underlie the multi-centric world which has evolved to parallel the state-centric world of national actors. Such an avoidance is certainly understandable. Chaos does convey a sense of transition and invites postponing the tasks of theory until stable patterns evolve. (James N. Rosenau).[1]

In a joint effort to show the way, the authors have in fact shown that there is no 'royal road' to knowledge in IR. That is one reason why the subject is fascinating, if frustrating. It is essential to get IR right, not only for its own sake, but because those practitioners who are sensitive to what IR scholars are saying otherwise may so easily get things wrong. A sense of pressing urgency for a scientific understanding of war and peace led to the creation of the new discipline in the first place. It is no less so now than in 1918, even though it may be true that IR specialists still offer practitioners little truly 'scientific' knowledge for guidance through an agenda the calamitous potentialities of which are growing in a seemingly exponential fashion – nuclear war, ecopolitics, the gamut of 'one world' problems, identity issues, human needs. Yet the effort must be made, and it is being made. What (in addition to making themselves better heard by practitioners of their era) are the challenges for the next generation of scholars?

The first half of this book saw two periods of consensus in the development of the study of international relations, bridged by a period of world economic collapse, intellectual confusion, policy contradiction, and war on an unprecedented scale. While no such consensus can be discerned today, the scholarship of the future will, it is argued in the second half, grow out of three dominant paradigms in a sea of diverse assumptions and what have come to be known as 'world views'. We are perhaps too close to events and trends in this second half to be able to be as objective 'now' as in the more distant earlier periods 'then'. It remains to be seen whether the canons of 'normal science' will produce instant objectivity 'next'. It is not likely.

Obviously, any notion of normal science is hardly possible, given the incomplete and inadequate state of knowledge in the three paradigms as here set forth. Moreover, even taken together, the paradigms themselves cannot expect to encapsulate all that is known in the discipline. The realist paradigm is simple, but hardly satisfactory, even after the refurbishment offered by those in other paradigms such as the structuralists. The multifarious world society approaches are complex and ill-focused as they seek, in breaking out of the state-centric mould, to account for and deal with the diversity of the contemporary world. Even with a certain plausibility at one level, the structuralists tend to find it difficult to relate convincingly the whole to the processes between the parts, nor do they demonstrate in any practical manner how the whole is greater than the sum of its parts. For their part, the critical theorists may exhort all three to greater vision and self-knowledge, but at what point do efforts to meet this all-too-often legitimate criticism constitute a hindrance to the possibility of a better world rather than progress towards it?

While a learning process and mutual influence do exist between them, there is little to be gained in an attempt to achieve conceptual paradigmatic complementarity, or even compromise, any more than there is in a bitter intellectual struggle for the survival of the fittest 'paradigm'. Instead of mere debate to win an argument, discussion to define an issue and seek its elucidation reflects the growing conceptual awareness in the discipline. This is an important asset. And what of normal science? Surely, the findings of our research must lead to more appropriate values than the mere accumulation and presentation of data. Has not the apparently traumatic experience of some traditionalists with the behaviouralists' revolution now given way to a wider acceptance – or at least understanding – of their insistence upon an empirical base for reaching conclusions? Like most revolutions, this one has been absorbed into the mainstream in the process of changing it. Once its limitations were recognized by both the challengers and the challenged, it added a new dimension to the classical insistence upon scholarly responsibility.

Towards a research agenda

The question of conflict and war is a perennial one, indeed as Kal Holsti argues, it is the common thread among all the paradigms (of which he prefers one – the classical or realist). Divergent approaches to conflict hold varying degrees of promise. Strategic studies, after a genuine flowering nourished by the Cold War in the 1950s and 1960s, have been overtaken first by routine, then by spectacular change towards freedom and independence, not only among the national components of the Soviet bloc, but among ethnic clusters within the USSR itself.

There are still some areas in strategic studies, particularly in deterrence theory, that require conceptual elucidation and re-examination, notwithstanding the difficulties of empirical verification. Much of the thinking about nuclear deterrence has been in terms of two contending parties with some cognizance of complications inherent in interstate tensions within the respective alliance systems. This bipolar configuration is rapidiy being replaced by a multipolar one, with near-nuclear Powers – India, Israel and South Africa among them, with others – for whom it is a case of 'if they do, we do'. Substantial nuclear weapons' proliferation is not only possible but to be expected. Such a world requires thinking about now, in anticipation of the event, in another burst of creative conceptual thinking about deterrence. At this point, strategic theory has little to say on this new reality of world politics. It is not only a question of the global deterrence system of several actors (Western Europe? China? India? with the two super Powers) but also of regional balances: for example, South Asia with India, Pakistan, China and the USSR.

What then of the relationship between the regional balance and the global system? The emergency of a triad of interlocking systems – global, regional and the interaction between the two – calls urgently for analysis, drawing not only upon traditional sources of nuclear deterrence theory. Indeed, more work is needed on the manipulation of threats at other systems' levels, as well as on the evolution of cooperation as reflected in the kind of innovative research being done by IR specialists such as Robert Axelrod and Kenneth Oye.[2]

The traditional reaction to the problems of armaments has been to pursue ever more actively the quest for disarmament or arms control. Simple action–reaction models seem inadequate to explain the dynamics of such phenomena as the military–industrial complex (MIC) that President Eisenhower warned his countrymen about in his farewell speech. Nor is the equally simple explanation of a conspiracy between industrial, bureaucratic and military elites to create artificial tensions to justify their continued demands upon public treasuries any more convincing. To be sure, manipulation is possible to the degree that governments reign rather than rule. Were it otherwise, the solution would be easier – merely a question of replacing those exerting such malevolent control. To convert the garrison state to a civilian state may not be impossible, but its modalities deserve a higher place on the strategists' agenda. Instead of the emphasis being placed upon capabilities, more attention needs to be paid to intentions in order to be able to reduce the probability that the worst case becomes the most likely case. Happily the super Powers appear to be taking some steps in this direction, urged forward by more outspoken allies insistent upon true consultation.

Strategists have also to come to terms with easier access to effective means of coercion in the contemporary world for desperate individuals as well as small states and other groups obsessed with 'powerlessness'. Expectations between capabilities and outcomes seem less and less clear. In the nineteenth century, a major Power could 'send a gunboat', and the offending weaker state would come to heel, but in the second half of the twentieth century half a million men in Algeria, Vietnam, or Afghanistan proved insufficient to enable a major Power to impose its will. This applies at other levels too. Those with nothing to lose have little compunction about risking everything and no reason to compromise; a party with many assets can forgo the loss of anyone with a fair degree of equanimity. Hence, while the asymmetries of capability may be offset by the asymmetries of commitment, the means available to the weak and dispossessed can impose real costs on the powerful and well-to-do. One reason Western societies are prosperous is because they are open, complex, interdependent and therefore vulnerable. The costs of reducing that vulnerability may be significant in terms of their very wellbeing. Superficially, the alternatives seem to consist of either destroying those who threaten the system or of accommodating them, but neither makes much policy sense. As soon as they have a stake in the existing or reformed order with something to lose they may be more amenable to cooperation. As John Vincent has pointed out in his sober analysis of terrorism,[3] for those vulnerable to 'terrorism' the only bearable strategy is one of incorporation. Peace researchers have provided sobering insights into possible unpleasant alternatives, and the conflict researchers offer ways in which genuine peace may be achieved, partly by utilizing techniques and approaches drawn from society's successful efforts in fields apparently far removed from IR, such as arbitration in industrial disputes, psychological counselling, and criminal rehabilitation.

Ironically, wider access to effective means of coercion opens up what has since the days of Georg Schwarzenberger, Hans Speier and Harold Lasswell been a principal potential growth area in IR – the political sociology of world society. Sociology as a discipline is at last awakening to macrosociological possibilities, which could in effect break down the boundaries between IR, political science, geography, anthropology and other social sciences. In particular, institutional reform, identity studies, international economic issues, the communication/information revolution (including the worldwide explosion in literacy, despite shocking lack of progress in some areas) and ecological/man–milieu issues are not only of greater and greater importance but are – at last – being acknowledged by national decision-makers to be so.

Such questions permeate our field. Take another leading component – IPE. The debt problem is such that some governments have been tempted to opt for financial terrorism, by threatening to default, because they see no possibility of accommodation and, therefore, no incentive for cooperation. If they are going to suffer whatever they do, why should they act in ways likely to enhance the interests of the broader international community? But if they do not act 'responsibly' all suffer, including the huge voting blocs responsive to nationalistic appeals by demogogic candidates. Reincorporation is called for on terms acceptable to all parties, and the techniques of facilitation and problem-solving of the conflict researcher are just as relevant in such cases as they are in violent intercommunal or international disputes. The debt question is only one aspect of the 'North–South' problem or global core–periphery relationships especially when the poverty line and the colour line coalesce, a potential fusion that suggests a global comparison with *Apartheid* 'writ large'. After all, do not immigration policies in Europe, North America and Australasia represent a sort of global

'Group Areas Act' dictating that environmentally dirty, physically dangerous, and economically unpromising work is done in 'black areas' the world over? Several possible broad outcomes do suggest themselves to those sensitive to these concerns, where IPE and problems of participation, identity and structural reform overlap.

Timely reform in *all* of these dimensions seems unlikely. On the other hand, the strategist might take a leaf out of the realists' book, assume that acceptable accommodation is impossible, and argue that the developed North should make more effective coercive use of its capabilities. While the asymmetries are still in its favour, the North might theoretically establish a twenty-first-century form of coercive control to obtain what it needs. In this, Wallerstein might suggest the semi-periphery would be expected by the centre to play a crucial role. Coercive systems, however, are rarely cost-effective in the long run. The colonial Powers conceded this when the 'winds of change' blew their empires away in mid-century. Such costs figure prominently in the decline of Powers in the conceptions, not only of historians like Paul Kennedy, whose *Rise and Fall of the Great Powers*[4] hit like a bombshell those in Washington who read only his chapter on the decline of America, but of political scientists like Gilpin and Modelski as well. If the system simply allows itself to drift, it will slowly disaggregate. In either case revolution or fiscal catastrophe – as a result of increasing costs, declining capabilities and abdication – will force structural change.

That IPE, strategy and conflict are inextricably intertwined relates to a central concern of FPA, namely decision-making. Beyond that is integration theory, which as has been stressed above, must take into account disintegration as well. Even though, as in the case of strategic studies, the heroic era of theorizing (the 1950s and 1960s) is in the past, there is a new agenda for 'integration' theorists which involves institutional change, in particular as a reflection of changing notions of identity, both of which link it to FPA. Frequently, organizations created to minister to a human need come to give equal or even more weight to institutional and even self-seeking needs. To be sure, institutions develop a philosophy and standard operating procedures that enable them to survive in terms of their self-image and their need for public accountability in the fulfilment of their functions. The human need for which they were established may change or come no longer to fit into the requirements of self-image, public responsibility and institutional survival. So it is with states. Some cannot command the statistical services necessary for them to make proper use of, say, the World Bank, IMF or the panoply of international public and private donor institutions designed to assist them. Fortunately, there are some transnational 'Sally Armies' in the shape of Oxfam, War on Want, numerous American and a few European and Japanese foundations, and even some governmental bodies such as the Commonwealth Secretariat, to which they can turn. The discrepancy between human and institutional needs in world society is not the only area of the organizational fabric requiring analysis and renovation – the same is true of participation.

The sharp dichotomy between IGOs and INGOs has the effect of disenfranchising significant actors. For example, UN conferences on North–South or development questions generally are handicapped by the absence of MNCs in the Council chamber. It matters little, in this context, whether MNCs are viewed as benign or malign for the purposes of development; they are important in the process and in affecting and effecting the outcome.[5] The system needs reform in order to promote enfranchisement rather than the reverse. Part of the problem arises from the declining pre-eminence of state-centricity in international relations. Systems of transactions rarely have coterminous boundaries with each other or with state administrative boundaries. Britain is not a security unit, an economic unit or an ethnic unit. On a generous count there may be no more than twenty-eight proper nation-states in the world.[6] How then can such diversity be accommodated in institutional terms in order to reap the benefits of organization as well as those of diversity?

In the section on integration, various ways in which this can be attempted within the existing state system were set forth, including rebuilding it or by going beyond state systems altogether. The work of Stephen Krasner, Joseph Nye and Robert Keohane in regime theory has been very helpful in understanding this phenomenon, even though regime theory seems often to raise more questions than it answers (particularly when one tries to define it convincingly to keen young graduate students). Systems boundaries are getting both bigger and smaller, depending on the issue area. The process is similar, owing to the altering of systems boundaries, even if the effect is opposite. This suggests that the question of governance is primary. To quote James Rosenau:

> Put in more dialectical terms, the organizing principle of realism – that states are endlessly confronting a security dilemma – is conceived to be increasingly in competition with the driving force of the multi-centric world – that systems and subsystems at divers macro-levels are endlessly coping with an autonomy dilemma.

Sovereignty no longer, if indeed it ever did, offers full protection of human relationships in politics, economics, and such social questions as human rights. Moving away from a sovereign state structure seems more likely to take the form of regional structures than toward anything resembling world government. However, systems boundaries are no more coterminous with those, say, of the EC than they are with its individual member-states, and few cogent reasons are put forth for paying the price of forcing them to become so. Nevertheless, what is both often overlooked and occasionally demonstrated is that these larger groupings can even prove useful in providing room for manoeuvre for smaller entities: for example, is it not possible to envisage the sting being taken out of the Northern Ireland and Cyprus disputes by their being ministered to in a European Community setting? In other words, the smaller state, region of a state or transborder grouping may gain more control over matters that most directly concern it, rather than less, as a result of regional integration patterns; thus, citizens in Flanders may be 'free' in Europe in a way that might be more difficult for them to enjoy in Belgium. Within such conglomerations, forms of consociation may be the most appropriate form of governance, but, beyond that, what about the governance of world society as a whole?

World government on the contemporary state model finds little favour. At the other end of the spectrum, global management by functional institutions, of a type and in a sense conceived by David Mitrany, while perhaps less unrealistic, is not very probable. The phenomenon of states simultaneously drifting apart and drifting together suggests a need for flexible and diverse institutional frameworks. It also calls for learning not only to tolerate ambiguity but to derive benefits from it. The challenge is to find ways to be able to associate and disassociate in a common context. These are not beyond mankind's historical experience. Perhaps the medieval world, the Ottoman Empire, the ancient Chinese notion of world order or India before British organizational dominance provide what political scientists might call 'models' for contemporary adaptation. They are unlikely to reproduce at a global level the recent European state system, which is itself fast becoming something quite different. Could it be that there is an even longer cycle than that outlined by Modelski, towards a more ambiguous and complex 'medieval' system of governance and away from the pristine purity of sovereignty?

These thoughts point to a central question of politics, indeed of all social life, that of identity. Who are we, to whom do we relate, and how do we relate to them (which in itself largely determines who we are)? Identity studies, most often in the guise of the study of nationalism, have constituted an essential component of our discipline since its foundation, from Carleton J. H. Hayes to Karl Deutsch. It is easy to forget that the nation-state constituted an underlying feature of the Wilsonian world order; now identity studies need to be conceived in a wider framework. Ethnic politics prevails within the developed world just as it does in the developing world, although the motivation may be different. In the advanced industrial democracies the compartmentalization of the individual into many discrete roles, and the rate of change in each role, is such as to induce a real sense of strain. People in secular *gesellschaftliche* societies, in danger of not knowing who they are because they are rarely treated by others as a whole, cling to ethnicity as a refuge against the impersonal vagaries of modern life. Knowing that one is part of a race, a nation, an ethnic group or whatever one wants to call the identity group, sustains the ability to live such a life by giving a sense of completeness and identity. Such an awareness becomes more acute, particularly in developing countries, when the struggle for resources is decided in the new supra-group centre whose decision-makers determine the allocation of national resources on a countrywide basis, particularly when ethnic loyalties then become the currency of the allocation process.

There are other elements to identity studies. Many societies are now multiracial in a manner hitherto less conspicuous. It is no longer a question of the movement of entire populations but an increase in racial diversity within the former metropoles such as Britain, France, Belgium and Holland, and indeed in the Baltic States, Azerbaijan and Armenia, to say nothing of the hispanicization of much of the American southwest. Contrast this with a growing awareness by indigenous minority populations of resource allocation to be shared with immigrant majorities; the situations in New Caledonia, New Zealand, and Northern Ireland are just as apposite as that of Fiji. Among the most challenging books waiting to be written by the new generation of IR specialists worldwide will reveal the systemic implications of such dilemmas.

Nor is that the end of identity studies, for gender is both a transnational and international issue, albeit most obvious within societies. It is perhaps the single most important root of structural violence in the world. This, in addition to the growing institutional competence and awareness of injustice on the part of women is making gender one of the growing points of the discipline.[8] None of these questions of relevance to governance, to integration and disintegration, and indeed to the international system, have yet been addressed seriously by IR scholars, other than by the occasional pioneers noted. They constitute an exciting, if taxing, agenda-in-waiting.

Rates of change in almost every facet of the contemporary world are quickening. It took a century from the first military use of gunpowder in Europe to its general use, during which there was time for society to adapt to a new technology, but only half a century from man's first powered flight to his landing on the moon. This quickening pace, which has given rise to ecopolitics, has not been accompanied by socio-political change at a commensurate rate. Only reluctantly did the G-7 powers at the Paris summit in 1989 recognize the importance to international security of environmental realities. As it draws to a close, the twentieth century has yet to produce any great 'ism', no overarching social–political–economic doctrine, or even a human needs' equivalent of deterrence theory by which societies may order their lives in a way commensurate with twentieth century technology, with all its health-giving promise and with all its polluted horrors. What do the old 'isms' of capitalism, communism, liberalism, secularism, socialism offer? In short, the scientific and technological problems of the near twenty-first century are still being addressed with the social, political and economic tools of the nineteenth. The gap is widening, as scholars as different as Henry Steele Commager, Andrew Scott, and Joseph Nye have shown in their approaches to interdependence. The need for new and relevant theory is greater than ever.

Towards the future study of international relations

Now what of the discipline itself? From being an Anglo-American speciality, indeed even idiosyncracy, it is becoming worldwide, with a promising body of scholarship already emerging on the Continent, in India, in Japan and not surprisingly now, in Eastern Europe. Before Tiananmen Square, Chinese universities seemed fascinated by neorealism and even by its critics. The United States is pre-eminent in the quantity of research produced; many of the leaders of the field from all over the world have found succour in North American universities – a particularly perverse form of 'brain drain'. Despite all this, some profess to see indications that the profession in the United States (which given the nature of the subject and its worldwide distribution is hardly to be expected) has become more insular, although since Vietnam strong counter-forces against the insularity of the power approach have steadily gained strength.

Intellectual insularity is not characteristic of Britain. Postgraduate study until a generation ago was for British scholars undertaken mainly in the United States, because the UK had neither the postgraduate programmes, adequate financial support, nor the tradition of the doctorate. It now provides several such programmes with significant numbers of students (for example, at LSE and Kent). Moreover, postgraduate studies abroad in IR by British students are no longer exclusively in North America. A substantial proportion go to Continental universities and the LSE has always acted as a magnet for American graduate students in IR.[9] Now there is a more even distribution of American students to the new British centres of IR. Continental students receive their higher training either at home, in Britain or in the United States. There is an important flow of Commonwealth students to Britain, of Latin Americans to North America and, increasingly, to Europe. Intellectually ambitious students from all parts of the Middle East venture to Britain and the Continent, to Canada, Australia and

New Zealand, and in a still never-ending stream to all corners of American academe. One striking statistic to come out of the brouhaha between President Bush and the US Congress about the return of Chinese students in 1989 was that there were then no less than 30,000 Chinese studying in the United States. Teachers and textbooks, as well as students, move around the system on a global basis.

Nevertheless, the discipline is still dominated by the Anglo-American mainstream, particularly since that mainstream has now embraced all three of the paradigms around which we have based the analysis of 'IR now'. Therefore, there seems little to say about those third-world writers who have chosen the morality of international relations as their principal concern. A world figure of the stature of Gandhi is missing. Less surprising, there is little about realistic thinking from a third-world perspective, except in terms of capitalist powers' exploitation. Mao's formulation of the Three Worlds Theory is a case in point. What is happening *within* the considerable world of Japanese IR has remained a closed book. Ignored have been Colonel Kaddaffi's 'Green Book', Islamic 'IR' theory and Baathist philosophy is *IR Now*, though their antecedents received some attention in *IR Then*. To the extent that there has been concentration upon the Western centre our view has been parochial. That is the state of *IR Now*.

Yet it is our fervent hope that the globalization of IR that everyone talks about will come to pass, no matter how uncomfortable this may be for the centre. In *The Dividing Discipline*, Kal Holsti has endeavoured to review some of the trends in non-Western countries,[11] but the catch is still unfortunately fairly meagre, so it is not just a matter of neglecting all but the Anglo-American product. While honouring and cataloguing our own heritage in the discipline, we can learn from others, and deepen our thinking by contributions from other cultural and intellectual traditions, especially from India, China and Japan , to say nothing of other Asian, African or Latin American societies. There are problems enough to go round, and ignorance abounds. With so much at stake, IR scholars can ill-afford to neglect any serious paradigm. The field *has* made strides toward a unified discipline of international relations which Quincy Wright tried to describe in the last four chapters of *The Study of International Relations*,[12] but those strides (or paradigms) take not only one but several zigzag trails up the road that he envisioned at mid-century. That is the history of IR – then and now.

Notes: Chapter 13

1 James N. Rosenau, 'Patterned chaos in global life: structure and process in the two worlds of world politics', *International Political Science Review*, 9, 4, 1988, p. 329.

2 Robert Axelrod, *The Evolution of Cooperation* (New York: Basic Books, 1984); Kenneth A. Oye (ed.), *Cooperation under Anarchy* (Princeton, NJ: Princeton University Press, 1986).

3 John Vincent, *Foreign Policy and Human Rights* (London: Cambridge University Press, 1986).

4 Paul Kennedy, *The Rise and Fall of the Great Powers* (London: Unwin Hyman, 1988).

5 On the role of non-governmental actors in global conferences, see Paul Taylor and A. J. R. Groom (eds), *Global Issues in the United Nations' Framework* (London: Macmillan, 1989).

6 See Gunnar Neilsson, 'Sobre los conceptos de etnicidad, nacion y estado', in Alfonso Perez-Agote (ed.), *Sociologia del Nacionalismo* (Vitoria: University of Basque Country Press, 1989.)

7 James N. Rosenau, 'Patterned chaos in global life: structure and process in the two worlds of world politics', *International Political Science Review*, 9, 4, 1988, p. 330.

8 See Joan Segar and Ann Olson, *Women in the World* (London: Pluto, 1985), a remarkably clear and colourful cartographic demonstration of the status of women throughout the world on the basis of some fifty universal criteria; *Millennium*'s special issue, 'Women in international relations', 17, 3, Winter 1988; Jean Bethke Elshtain and Sheila Thomas (eds), *Women, Militarism, and War* (Lanham, Mass: Rowan and Littlefield, 1989).

9 A personal note may be of interest here: the British member of this team, after a Masters in IR at Lehigh University in Pennsylvania, took his doctorate at the Graduate Institute of International Studies in Geneva, where the American author, who took his early MSc(Econ)-level work at the LSE, taught for several semesters.

10 See Stephen Chan, 'China's foreign policy and Africa', *The Round Table*, 296, 1985; Herbert S. Yee, 'The Three World Theory and post-Mao China's global strategy', *International Affairs*, 59, 2, 1983; Peter Worsley, 'One world or three? A critique of the world-system theory of Immanuel Wallerstein, in R. Milibrand and J. Saville (eds), *Socialist Register 1980* (London: Merlin, 1980).

11 K. J. Holsti, *The Dividing Discipline* (London: Allen & Unwin, 1985).

12 Quincy Wright, *The Study of International Relations* (New York: Appleton–Century–Crofts, 1955).

Further reading

Axelrod, Robert. *The Evolution of Cooperation*. New York: Basic Books, 1984.
Millennium Special Issue: 'Women in international relations', *Millennium*, Winter 1988.
Wright, Quincy. *The Study of International Relations*. New York: Appleton–Century–Croft, 1955.

References

Adams, Brooks. *Law of Civilization and Decay*. New York: Vintage Books, 1955.

Allen, Steven H. *International Relations*. Princeton, NJ: Princeton University Press, 1920.

Almond, Gabriel A. *The American People and Foreign Policy*. New York: Harcourt, 1950.

Almond, Gabriel A. and Coleman, James S. (eds). *The Politics of Developing Areas*. Princeton, NJ: Princeton University Press, 1960.

Almond, Gabriel A. and Powell, G. Bingham (eds). *Comparative Politics*. Boston: Little, Brown, 1966.

Allison, Graham. *The Essence of Decision*. Boston: Little, Brown, 1971.

Angell, Norman. *The Great Illusion*. New York: G. P. Putnam, 1911.

Aquinas, St Thomas. *Summa Theologica*, tr. by Fathers of the English Dominican Province. 5 vols. Westminster, Maryland: Christian Classics, 1981.

Aristotle. *Politics*, tr. by Ernest Baker. Oxford: Oxford University Press, 1946.

Ashley, Richard K. *The Political Economy of War and Peace*. London: Pinter, 1980.

Ashon, Sir George. *The Study of War for Statesmen and Citizens*. London: Longman, Green, 1927.

Augustinus, St Aurelius. [*c.*400]. *Confessions* tr. by R. S. Pinecoffin, 2 vols. Baltimore: Penguin, 1961.

Avery, William P. and Rapkin, David (eds). *America in a Changing World: Political Economy*. London: Longman, 1982.

Axelrod, Robert. *The Evolution of Cooperation*. New York: Basic Books, 1984.

Azar, E. and Burton, J. W. (eds). *International Conflict Resolution*. Brighton: Wheatsheaf, 1986.

Bailey, Stanley H. *International Studies in Great Britain*. London: Oxford University Press, 1933.

Baldwin, David. *Economic Statecraft*. Princeton, NJ: Princeton University Press, 1985.

Banks, Michael H. (ed.). *Conflict in World Society*. Brighton: Wheatsheaf, 1984.

Baran, Paul. *The Political Economy of Growth*. New York: Monthly Review Press, 1957.

Beaufre, André. *Deterrence and Strategy*. London: Faber, 1965.

Beitz, Charles R. *Political Theory and International Relations*. Princeton, NJ: Princeton University Press, 1979.

Bell, Coral. *The Conventions of Crisis*. London: Oxford University Press, 1971.

Benedetti, Vincent. *Studies in Diplomacy*. London: Heinemann, 1896.

Bentham, Jeremy. [1789]. *An Introduction to the Principles of Morals and Legislation*, ed. by J. H. Burns and H. L. A. Hart. London: Athlone Press, 1970.

Bernard, Jessie and Bernard, Luther L. *Sociology and the Study of International Relations*. St Louis, Mo.: Washington University Studies, 1934.

Bercovitch, Jacob. *Social Conditions and Third Parties*. Boulder, Colo: Westview, 1986.

Best, Geoffrey. *Humanity in Warfare*. London: Weidenfeld and Nicolson, 1980.

Bloomfield, Lincoln P. *The Foreign Policy Process*. Englewood Cliffs, NJ: Prentice Hall, 1982.

Boardman, Robert and Groom, A. J. R. (eds.). *The Management of Britain's External Relations*. London: Macmillan, 1973.

Bolingbroke, Henry St John. *Idea of a Patriot King*, 1746.

Boulding, Kenneth. *The Image*. Ann Arbor, Mich.: University of Michigan Press, 1961.

Boulding, Kenneth. *Conflict and Defense*. New York: Harper and Row 1962.

Bourne, Randolph (ed.). Towards an Enduring Peace, A symposium of peace proposals and programs, 1914–1916. New York: Arres Ason for International Conciliation, 1916.

Bowman, Isaiah. [1922]. *The New World: Problems in Political Geography*. New York: World Book Co., 4th edn, 1928.

Boyd, Gavin and Hepple, Gerald. *Political Change and Foreign Policy*. New York: St Martin's Press, 1987.

Bozeman, Adda B. *Politics and Culture in International History*. Princeton, NJ: Princeton University Press, 1960.

Bracken, Paul. *The Command and Control of Nuclear Forces*. New Haven, Conn.: Yale University Press, 1983.

Brailsford, Henry N. *A League of Nations*. London: Headley, 1917.

Brandt Commission. *North–South*. London: Pan, 1980.

Brandt Commission. *Common Crisis*. London: Pan, 1983.

Braybrooke, David and Lindblom, Charles. *The Strategy of Decision*. New York: Free Press, 1970.

Braybrooke, David. *Meeting Needs*. Princeton, NJ: Princeton University Press 1987.

Brett, E. A. *The World Economy Since the War*. London: Macmillan, 1985.

Brewer, Anthony. *Marxist Theories of Imperialism*. London: Routledge & Kegan Paul, 1980.

Brierly, James L. [1936]. *The Law of Nations*, 6th edn. Oxford: The Clarendon Press, 1963.

Brodie, Bernard. *Strategy in the Missile Age*. Princeton, NJ: Princeton University Press, 1959.

Brown, James F., Hodges, Charles, and Roucek, Joseph S. (eds). *Contemporary World Politics*. New York: Wiley, 1939.

Bryce, James. *International Relations*. London and New York: Macmillan, 1922.

Buell, Raymond. *International Relations*. New York: Henry Holt, 1922.

Buell, Raymond. *World Adrift*. New York: Foreign Policy Association, 1935.

Buell, Raymond and Goslin, Ryland Alexander. *War Drums and Peace Plans*. New York: The Foreign Policy Association, 1936.

Bukharin, N.I. *Imperialism and World Economy*, intro. by V. I. Lenin. London: Merlin Press. 1972.

Bull, Hedley. *The Anarchical Society*. London: Macmillan, 1977.

Bull, H. and Watson, A. (eds). *The Expansion of International Society*. Oxford: Oxford University Press, 1984.

Burns, Cecil Delisle. *International Politics*. London: Methuen, 1920.

Burton, J. W. *International Relations*. London: Cambridge University Press, 1967.

Burton, J. W. *Systems, States, Diplomacy and Rules*. London: Cambridge University Press, 1968.

Burton, J. W. *Conflict and Communication*. London: Macmillan, 1969.

Burton, J. W. *World Society*. London: Cambridge University Press, 1972.

Burton, J. W. *Deviance, Terrorism and War*. Oxford: Martin Robertson, 1979.

Burton, J. W. *Dear Survivors*. London: Pinter, 1983.

Burton, J. W. *Global Conflict*. Brighton: Wheatsheaf, 1984.

Burton, J. W. *Resolving Deep-Rooted Conflict*. Lanham, Mass.: University Press of America, 1987.

Burton, J. W., Groom, A. J. R., Mitchell, C. R. and de Reuck, A. V. S. *The Study of World Society: A London Perspective*. Pittsburgh: International Studies Association Monograph No. 1, 1974.

Butler, Harold B. *The Economic Factor in International Affairs*. Manchester: Manchester University Press, 1939.

Butler, Nicholas M. *The International Mind: An Argument for the Judicial Settlement of International Disputes*. New York: C. Scribner's, 1912.

Butler, Nicholas, M. *The Basis of a Durable Peace*. New York: C. Scribner's, 1918.

Butterworth, Herbert and Wight, Martin (eds). *Diplomatic Investigations* London: Allen & Unwin, 1966.

Cabral, Amilcar. *Unity and Struggle*. London: Heinemann, 1980.

Callières, François de. [1716]. *On the Manner of Negotiating with Princes* (1917), tr. by A. F. Whyte. Notre Dame, Ind.: University of Notre Dame Press, 1963.

Carr, Edward H. *The Twenty-Years' Crisis, 1919–1939: An Introduction to the Study of International Relations*. London: Macmillan, 1939.

Carr-Saunders, A. M. *The Population Problem*. Oxford: Clarendon Press, 1922.

Cherrington, Ben M. *Methods of Education in International Attitudes*. New York City, Teachers College. New York: Columbia University Press, 1934.

Choucri, Nazli and North, Robert C. *Nations in Conflict: National Growth and International Violence*. San Francisco: W. H. Freeman, 1975.

Clark, Ian. *Reform and Resistance in the International Order*. Cambridge: Cambridge University Press, 1980.

Clark, Ian. *Limited Nuclear War*. Oxford: Martin Robertson, 1982.

Clark, Ian. *Waging War*. Oxford: Clarendon Press, 1988.

Claude, Inis L. *Power and International Relations*. New York: Random House, 1962.

Clausewitz, Carl von. *On War*, tr. and ed. by Michael Howard and Peter Paret. Princeton, NJ: Princeton University Press, 1976.

Cobden, Richard. *Free Trade as the Best Human Means for Securing Universal and Permanent Peace*, 1842.

Cohen, Benjamin D. *The Question of Imperialism*. London: Weidenfeld & Nicolson, 1980.

Colby, Charles C. (ed.). *Geographic Aspects of International Relations*. Chicago: University of Chicago Press, 1938.

Cole, George D. H. *A Guide Through World Chaos*. New York: Knopf, 1934.

Coll, Alberto. *The Wisdom of Statecraft*. Durham, NC: Duke University Press, 1985.

Comte, Auguste. *System of Positive Polity*. New York: Burt Franklin Research, 1965.

Connor, Walker. *The National Question in Marxist–Leninst Theory and Strategy*. Princeton, NJ: Princeton University Press, 1984.

Coser, Lewis. *The Function of Social Conflict*. London: Routledge & Kegan Paul, 1956.

Cox, Robert W. *Production Power and World Order*. New York: Columbia University Press, 1987.

Crucé, Emeric. *The New Cyneas*, tr. by Thomas Willing Bach. Philadelphia: Allen, Lane, Scott, 1909.

Curle, Adam. *Making Peace*. London: Tavistock, 1971.

Czartoryski, Adam. *Memories of Prince Adam Czartoryski with Alexander I*, ed. by Adam Gielgud. London: Remington, 1880.

Dante Alighieri. *De Monarchia* (On World Government), tr. by Herbert W. Schneider, 1 vol. New York: Liberal Arts Press, 1957.

Davies, David. *Suicide or Sanity? An Examination of the Proposals before the Geneva Disarmament Conference*. London: Williams & Norgate, 1932.

de Reuck, A. V. S. and Knight, Julie (eds). *Conflict in Society*. London: J. & A. Churchill, 1966.

de Rivera, J. *The Psychological Dimension of Foreign Policy*. Columbus, Ohio: Charles E. Merrill, 1968.

Debray, Régis. *Revolution in the Revolution*. London: Greenwood, 1980.

Dedring, Jurgen. *Recent Advances in Peace and Conflict Research*. London: Sage, 1976.

Dell, Edmund. *The Politics of Economic Interdependence*. New York: St Martin's Press, 1987.

Demiashkevich, Michael J. *Shackled Diplomacy*. New York: Barnes & Noble, 1934.

Der Derian, James. *On Diplomacy*. Oxford: Blackwell, 1987.

Deutsch, Karl W. *et al*. *Political Community and the North Atlantic Area*. Princeton, NJ: Princeton University Press, 1957.

Deutsch, Karl W. *The Nerves of Government*. New York: Free Press, 1963.

Deutsch, Karl W. *Nationalism and Social Communication*. Cambridge, Mass.: MIT Press, 1966.

Deutsch, Morton. *The Resolution of Conflict*. New Haven, Conn.: Yale University Press, 1973.

Dickinson, G. Lowes. *The Choice before us*. New York: Dodd Mead, 1918.

Donelan, Michael (ed.). *The Reason of States*. London: Allen & Unwin, 1978.

Dubois, Pierre. *De Recuperatione Terre Sancte*, tr. by Ruth Hardy. Berkeley, Calif. 1920.

Dubois, Pierre. *The Recovery of the Holy Land*, tr. by Walther J. Brandt. New York: Columbia University Press, 1956.

Dutt, R. Palme. *World Politics 1918–1936*. New York: Random House, 1936.

Earle, Edward Meade (ed.). *Makers of Modern Strategy*. Princeton, NJ: University of Princeton, 1943.

Edgeworth, Francis, Y. *Papers Relating to Political Economy*. London: Macmillan, 1925.

Edmonds, Martin. *Armed Services and Society*. Leicester: Leicester University Press, 1988.

Eliot, George F. *Bombs Bursting in Air: The Influence of Air Power on International Relations*. New York: Reynal & Hitchcock, 1939.

Ellsworth, Paul T. *International Economics*. New York: Macmillan, 1938.

Erasmus, Desiderius. *The Education of a Christian Prince*, tr. by P. E. Corbett. London: Grotius Society Publications, No. 1, 1921.

Fanon, Frantz. *The Wretched of the Earth*. Harmondsworth: Penguin, 1983.

Fairgrieve, James. *Geography and World Power*. Chicago: University of Chicago Press, 1924 and later editions.

Faiuries, John C. *The Rise of Internationalism*. New York: W. D. Gray, 1914.

Falk, Richard. *The Promise of World Order*. Brighton: Wheatsheaf, 1987.

Fenwick, Charles. *International Law*, 3rd rev. edn. New York: Appleton–Century–Crofts, 1948.

Ferguson, Y. and Mansbach, R. W. *The Elusive Quest*. Columbia, SC: University of South Carolina Press, 1988.

Foster, John W. *The Practice of Diplomacy*. Boston: Houghton-Mifflin, 1906.

Fox, William T. R. *The Super Powers*. New York: Harcourt-Brace, 1944.

Fox, William, T. R. *Theoretical Aspects of International Relations*. Notre Dame, Ind.: University of Notre Dame Press, 1959.

Fox, William T. R. *The American Study of International Relations*. Columbia, SC: Institute of International Studies, University of South Carolina, 1966.

Frei, D. *Assumptions and Perceptions in Disarmament*. New York: United Nations, 1984.

Fromm, Erich. *Escape from Freedom*. New York: Farrar & Rhinehart, 1941.

Frost, Mervyn. *Towards a Normative Theory of International Relations*. London: Cambridge University Press, 1986.

Fuller, J. F. C. *War and Western Civilization*. London: Duckworth, 1932.

Fuller, J. F. C. *The Conduct of War, 1789–1961*. New Brunswick, NJ: Rutgers University Press, 1961.

Gardner, Richard. *Sterling–Dollar Diplomacy*. Oxford: Clarendon Press, 1956.

Garnett, J. C. *Commonsense and the Theory of International Politics*. London: Macmillan, 1984.

Gathorne-Hardy, G. M. *A Short History of International Affairs 1920–39*, 4th edn. London: Oxford University Press, 1950.

Gellner, Ernest. *Thought and Change*. Chicago: University of Chicago Press, 1963.

Gentili, Alberico. *Three Books on the Law of War*, tr. by John C. Rolfe. 2 vols. Oxford: Clarendon Press, 1983.

George, Alexander and Smoke, Richard. *Deterrence in American Foreign Policy*. New York: Columbia University Press, 1974.

Giddens, Anthony. *The Nation-State and Violence*. Cambridge: Polity Press, 1985.

Gill, Stephen and Law, David. *The Global Political Economy*. Brighton: Wheatsheaf, 1988.

Gilpin, Robert. *War and Change in World Politics*. Cambridge: Cambridge University Press, 1981.

Gilpin, Robert. *The Political Economy of International Relations*. Princeton, NJ: Princeton University Press, 1987.

Goldmann, Kjell. *Change and Stability in Foreign Policy*. Princeton, NJ: Princeton University Press, 1988.

Goldstein, Joshua. *Long Cycles: Prosperity and War in the Modern Age*. London: Yale University Press, 1988.

Goodwin, Geoffrey (ed.). *Ethics and Nuclear Deterrence*. London: Croom Helm, 1982.

Gould, Wesley and Barkun, Michael. *International Law and the Social Sciences*. Princeton, NJ: Princeton University Press, 1970.

Gray, Colin. *The Soviet–American Arms Race*. Lexington, Mass.: Lexington Press, 1976.

Green, Philip. *Deadly Logic*. Columbus: Ohio State University Press, 1966.

Groom, A. J. R. and Taylor, Paul (eds). *Functionalism: Theory and Practice in International Relations*. London: University of London Press, 1975.

Groom, A. J. R. and Taylor, Paul (eds). *Frameworks for International Cooperation*. London: Pinter, 1990.

Grotius, Hugo. [1625]. *The Law of War and Peace*, tr. by Francis W. Kelsey. New York: Bobbs–Merrill Co., 1925.

Guevara, Che. *Guerrilla Warfare*. Harmondsworth: Pelican, 1969.

Gurr, Ted Robert (ed.). *Handbook of Political Conflict*. New York: Free Press, 1981.

Haas, Ernst. *The Uniting of Europe*. London: Stevens, 1958.

Haas, Ernst. *The Obsolescence of Regional Integration Theory*. Berkeley, Calif.: University of California, Institute of International Studies, 1976.

Hall, William Edward. *Treatise on International Law*. 8th edn. Oxford: Clarendon Press, 1924.

Hall, John A. *Powers and Liberties*. Hamondsworth: Penguin, 1986.

Halle, Louis J. *The Elements of International Strategy*. Lanham, Mass.: University Press of America, 1984.

Halliday, Fred. *The Making of the Second Cold War*. London: Verso, 1983.

Halperin, Morton H. *Bureaucratic Politics and Foreign Policy*. Washington: Brookings, 1974.

Hamilton, Alexander; Madison, James and Jay, John. *The Federalist Papers*. Baltimore: Johns Hopkins University Press, 1981.

Handel, Michael. *Weak States in the International System*. London: Frank Cass, 1981.

Hare, J. E. and Joynt, Carey B. *Ethics and International Affairs*. London: Macmillan, 1982.

Harden, Sheila. *Small is Dangerous*. New York: St Martin's Press, 1985.

Harrod, R. F. *The Trade Cycle*. New York: A. M. Kelly, 1936.

Harshorne, Richard. *The Nature of Geography: a critical survey of current thought in the light of the past*. Lancaster, PA.: The Association Press, 1939.

Haushoffer, Karl. *Wehrgeopolitik* Berlin: Junken and Dünnhaupt, 1940

Heatley, David P. *Diplomacy and the Study of International Relations*. Oxford: Clarendon Press, 1919.

Hechter, Michael. *Internal Colonialism*. London: Routledge & Kegan Paul, 1975.

Hechter, Michael. *Principles of Group Solidarity*. Berkeley, Calif.: University of California Press, 1987.

Heraclides, Alexis. *The International Dimension of Secessionist Movements*. London: Frank Cass, 1990.

Hermann, Charles (ed.). *International Crises*. New York: Free Press, 1972.

Herodotus. *History of the Greek and Persian War*, tr. by George Rawlinson. New York: Twayne Publishers, 1963.

Herz, John H. *Political Realism and Political Federalism: A study in Theories and Realism*. Chicago: University of Chicago Press, 1951.

Herze, John H. *International Politics in the Atomic Age*. New York: Columbia University Press, 1959.

Higgins, Pearce. *Studies in International Law*. Cambridge: Cambridge University Press, 1928.

Higgott, Richard (ed.). *New Directions in International Relations? Australian Perspectives.* Canberra: Australian National University, International Relations Department, 1988.

Hinsley, F. H. *Power and the Pursuit of Peace.* London: Cambridge University Press, 1963.

Historicus, Sir William George Harcourt. *Some Questions About International Law.* London: Macmillan, 1863.

Hobbes, Thomas. [1651]. *Leviathan.* Oxford: Oxford University Press, 1952.

Hobson, J. A. *Towards International Government.* New York: Macmillan, 1915.

Hobson, J. A. [1905]. *Imperialism: A Study.* Ann Arbor, Mich.: University of Michigan Press, 1965.

Hodges, Charles. *The Background of International Relations.* New York: Wiley, 1931.

Hodgson, James G. *Economic Nationalism.* New York: H. W. Wilson, 1933.

Hoffmann, Stanley. *Contemporary Theory in International Relations.* Englewood Cliffs, NJ: Prentice-Hall, 1960.

Holbraad, Carsten. *Middle Powers in International Politics.* New York: St Martin's Press, 1984.

Holland, T. E. *Letters to 'The Times' upon War and Neutrality 1881–1920.* New York: Longman, Green, 1921.

Holsti, K. J. *The Dividing Discipline.* London: Allen & Unwin, 1987.

Hopkins, Terence, Wallerstein, I., et al. *World System Analysis: Theory and Methodology.* London: Sage, 1982.

Horowitz, Donald L. *Ethnic Groups in Conflict.* Berkeley, Calif.: University of California Press, 1985.

Huddleston, Sisley. *War Unless –.* London: Gollancz, 1933.

Hudson, Manley O. *The Permanent Court of International Justice.* New York Macmillan, 1937.

Hume, David. [1748; 1751]. *Enquiries Concerning Human Understanding and Concerning the Principles of Morals,* ed. by L. A. Selby Bigge. Oxford: Clarendon Press, 1975.

Huntington, Ellsworth. *The Character of Races as Influenced by Physical Environment, Natural Selection and Historical Development.* New York: C. Scribner's, 1924.

Hyman, Sonia Z. *Economic Security and World Peace.* New York: The League for Industrial Democracy, 1938.

Iklé, Fred. *How Nations Negotiate.* Millwood: Kraus Reprint, 1982.

Ishimaru, Tota. *The Next World War,* tr. by B. Matsuka. London: Hurst & Blackett, 1937.

James, Alan. *Sovereign Statehood.* London: Allen and Unwin, 1986.

James, Alan. (ed.). *The Bases of International Order.* London: Oxford University Press, 1973.

Janis, Irving L. *Victims of Groupthink.* Boston: Houghton Mifflin, 1982.

Janowsky, Oscar I. and Fagen, Michael M. *International Aspects of German Racial Policies*. New York: Oxford University Press, 1937.

Jensen, Lloyd. *Explaining Foreign Policy*. Engelwood Cliffs, NJ: Prentice-Hall, 1982.

Jervis, Robert. *The Logic of Images in International Relations*. Princeton, NJ: Princeton University Press, 1970.

Jervis, Robert. *Perception and Misperception in International Politics*. Princeton, NJ: Princeton University Press, 1976.

Johnson, Chalmers. *Revolutionary Change*. London: Longman, 1983.

Jomini, Baron Antoine Henri. [1838]. *The Art of War*. Westport, Conn.: Greenwood Press, 1972.

Jones, R. J. Barry (ed.). *Perspectives on Political Economy*. London: Pinter, 1983.

Jones, R. J. Barry. *Conflict and Control in the World Economy*. Brighton: Wheatsheaf, 1986.

Jones, R. J. Bary *The Worlds of Political Economy*. London: Pinter, 1988.

Jones, R. J. Barry and Willetts, P. (eds). *Interdependence on Trial*. London: Pinter, 1984.

Jonsson, Christor. *Superpower*. London: Pinter, 1984.

Kalijarvi, Thorsten W. F. and associates. *Modern World Politics*, 3rd edn. New York: Crowell, 1943.

Kant, Immanuel. [1787]. *Critique of Pure Reason*, tr. by Max Mueller, 2nd rev. edn. New York: Doubleday, 1961.

Kant, Immanuel. [1795] *Perpetual Peace*, tr. by Lewis L. Beck. New York: Bobbs-Merrill, Publishers, 1957.

Kaplan, Morton. *System and Process in International Politics*. New York: Wiley, 1957.

Karms, Margaret P. *Persistent Patterns and Emergent Structures in a Waning Century*. New York: Praeger, 1986.

Karsh, Efraim. *Neutrality and Small States*. London: Routledge, 1988.

Kastler, Norman M. *Modern Human Relations: An Elementary Sociology*. Boston: Little, Brown, 1940.

Kautilya. *The Kautilya's Arthasastra*, tr. by N. A. Nikam and Richard McKeon. Chicago: University of Chicago Press, 1959.

Kazancigil, Ali. (ed.). *The State in Global Perspective*. Aldershot: Gower, 1986.

Kegley, Charles W. Jr and McGowan, Patrick J. (eds). *The Political Economy of Foreign Policy Behavior*. Beverly Hills, Calif.: Sage, 1981.

Kelsen, Hans. *The Legal Process and International Order*. London: Constable, 1935.

Kennan, George. *American Diplomacy 1900–1950*. Chicago: University of Chicago Press, 1951.

Kennedy, Paul. *Rise and Fall of the Great Powers*. London: Unwin Hyman, 1988.

Keohane, Robert O. and Nye, Joseph S. Jr (eds). *Transnational Relations and World Politics*. London: Harvard University Press, 1971.

Keohane, Robert O. and Nye, Joseph S. Jr. *Power and Interdependence.* Boston: Little, Brown, 1977.

Keohane, Robert. *After Hegemony.* Princeton, NJ: Princeton University Press, 1984.

Keohane, Robert (ed.). *Neorealism and Its Critics.* New York: Columbia University Press, 1986.

Keynes, J. M. *The Economic Consequences of the Peace.* New York: Harcourt, 1919.

Keynes, J. M. *Unemployment as a World Problem,* ed. by Quincy Wright. Chicago: The University of Chicago Press, 1931.

Kirk, Grayson, L. *The Study of International Relations.* New York: Council on Foreign Relations, 1947.

Kissinger, Henry. *Nuclear Weapons and Foreign Policy.* New York: Harper, 1957.

Kissinger, Henry. *A World Restored.* Boston: Houghton Mifflin, 1957.

Kjellen, Rudolph. *Die Politischen Probleme des Weltkrieges.* Leipzig: B. G. Teubner, 1916.

Knorr, Klaus and Verba, Sidney (eds). *The International System: Theoretical Essays.* Princeton, NJ: Princeton University Press, 1961.

Kolko, Gabriel. *The Roots of American Foreign Policy.* Boston: Beacon, 1969.

Kolko, Joyce and Kolko, Gabriel. *The Limits of Power.* London: Harper & Row, 1972.

Krasner, Stephen (ed.). *International Regimes.* Ithaca, NY: Cornell University Press, 1983.

Krasner, Stephen. *Structural Conflict.* Berkeley, Calif.: University of California Press, 1985.

Kriesberg, Louis. *Social Conflicts.* Englewood Cliffs, NJ: Prentice-Hall, 1982.

Kubalkova, V. and Cruickshank, A. *Marxism and International Relations.* Oxford: Clarendon Press, 1985.

Kuhn, Thomas. *The Structure of Scientific Revolutions.* Chicago: University of Chicago Press, 1970.

Ladd, William.[1832]. *An Essay on a Congress of Nations for the Adjustment of International Disputes without Resort to Arms.* New York: Oxford University Press, 1916.

Lasswell, Harold D. *Propaganda Technique in the World War.* London: K. Paul, Trench, Trubner, 1927.

Lasswell, Harold D. *World Politics and Personal Insecurity.* New York: McGraw-Hill, 1935.

Lauterpacht, Hersch. *The Function of Law in the International Community.* Oxford: Clarendon Press, 1933.

LeBon, Gustave. *The Psychology of Peoples.* New York: G. E. Stechert, 1924.

Leites, Nathan and Wolf, Charles. *Defeating Communist Insurgency.* London: Macmillan, 1975.

Lenin, V. I. [1917]. *Imperialism: The Highest Stage of Capitalism*. New York: International Publishers, 1939.

Levi, Leone. [1866]. Draft Project of a Council and High Court of Arbitration. In A. C. P. Beales, *The History of Peace*. London: G. Bell, 1931.

Levin, N. Gordon, Jr. *Woodrow Wilson and World Politics*. Oxford: Oxford University Press, 1968.

Liddell-Hart, Basil H. *Great Captains Unveiled*. Edinburgh: Blackwood, 1927.

Light, Margot and Groom, A. J. R. (eds). *International Relations: A Handbook of Current Theory*. London: Pinter, 1985.

Lijphart, Arend. *Democracy in Plural Societies*. New Haven, Conn.: Yale University Press, 1980.

Lindberg, Leon. *The Political Dynamics of European Economic Integration*. Stanford, Calif.: Stanford University Press, 1963.

Lindberg, Leon and Scheingold, S. *Europe's Would-Be Polity*. Englewood Cliffs, NJ: Prentice-Hall, 1970.

Lindberg, Leon and Scheingold, S. (eds). *Regional Integration*. Cambridge, Mass.: Harvard University Press, 1971.

Linklater, Andrew. *Men and Citizens in the Theory of International Relations*. London: Macmillan, 1981.

Little, Richard and Smith, Steve (eds). *Belief Systems and International Relations*. Oxford: Blackwell, 1988.

Locke, John. [1690]. *Two Treaties of Government*. New York: Dutton, 1977.

Lorimer, James. *The Application of the Principle of Relative or Proportional Equality to International Organisation* (1867).

Lorimer, Sir James. *Institutes of the Law of Nations*. Edinburgh: W. Blackwood, 1883.

Luttwak, Edward. *Strategy: the logic of war and peace*. Cambridge, Mass.: Belknap Press of Harvard University Press, 1987.

McClelland, Charles. *Theory and the International System*. London: Collier–Macmillan, 1966.

McDougall, Myers S. *Studies in World Public Order*. New Haven, Conn.: Yale University Press, 1960.

McDougall, Myers S. *et al*. *Human Rights and World Public Order*. New Haven, Conn.: Yale University Press, 1961.

McGowan, Patrick and Kegley, Charles Jr (eds). *Foreign Policy and the Modern World-System*. London: Sage, 1983.

Machiavelli, Niccolò. *The Discourses*. New York: The Modern Library, 1950.

Machiavelli, Niccolò. [1513]. *The Prince*. New York: Penguin, 1975.

McKinlay, R. D. and Little, Richard. *Global Problems and World Order*. London: Pinter, 1986.

Mackinder, Halford J. [1920]. *Democratic Ideals and Reality: A Study of the Politics of Reconstruction*. New York: Henry Holt, 1919.

Maclean, Annie, M. *Modern Immigration: A View of the Situation in Immigrant Receiving Countries*. Philadelphia: J. B. Lippincott, 1925.

Madriaga, Salvador de. *Theory and Practice of International Relations*. Philadelphia: University of Pennsylvania Press, 1937.

Magdoff, Harry. *The Age of Imperialism*. London: Monthly Review Press, 1969.

Maghroori, Ray and Romberg, Bennett (eds). *Globalism versus Realism*. Boulder: Colo: Westview, 1982.

Mahan, Alfred Thayer. [1890]. *The Influence of Sea Power upon History 1660–1783*. London: Methuen, 1965.

Maine, Henry Sumner. *Ancient Law, Its Connection with Early History and Its Relation to Modern Ideas*. 4th edn. London: Murray, 1930.

Malthus, Thomas R. [1798]. *An Essay on the Principle of Population*. New York: Modern Library, 1960.

Mander, Linden A. *Foundations of Modern World Society*, rev. edn. Stanford, Calif.: Stanford University Press, 1948 (originally published in 1941).

Mann, Michael. *The Sources of Social Power*. Cambridge: Cambridge University Press, 1986.

Mannheim, Karl. *Man and Society in An Age of Reconstruction*. London: K. Paul, Trench, Trubner, 1940.

Manning, C. A. W. *The Nature of International Society*. London: Macmillan, 1975 (first published in 1962 by G. Bell, London).

Mansbach, Richard W., Ferguson, Yale H. and Lampert, Donald E. *The Web of World Politics*. Englewood Cliffs, NJ: Prentice-Hall, 1976.

Mansbach, Richard W. and Vasquez, John A. *In Search of Theory*. New York: Columbia University Press, 1981.

Mao Tse Tung. *Basic Tactics*. New York: Praeger, 1986.

Marsilus of Padua. *Marsilus of Padua, Defender of Peace*. New York: Columbia University Press, 1951–1956.

Marvin, F. S. *The Evolution of World Peace*. London: Oxford University Press, 1921.

Marx, Karl. *The German Ideology*. New York: A. A. Knopf, 1946.

Marx, Karl. *Das Kapital*, ed. by Friedrich Engels. New York: International Publishers, 1967.

Marx, Karl. *Critique of Political Economy*, tr. by Annette Jolin and Joseph O'Malley. Cambridge: Cambridge University Press, 1970.

Marx, Karl and Engels, Friedrich. [1848]. *The Communist Manifesto*. New York: Russell & Russell, 1963.

Mayall, James (ed.). *The Community of States*. London: Allen & Unwin, 1983.

Mayer, Arno J. *Politics and Diplomacy of Peacemaking*. London: Weidenfeld & Nicolson, 1968.

Meadows, Donella H. *et al. The Limits to Growth*. London: Pan, 1974.

Mearsheimer, John J. *Conventional Deterrence*. Ithaca, NY: Cornell University Press, 1983.

Mencius. *Mencius: A New Translation*, tr. by W. A. C. H. Dobson. Toronto: University of Toronto Press, 1963.

Mendlovitz, Saul and Walker, R. B. S. *Towards a Just World Peace*. London: Butterworth, 1987.

Merritt, Richard L. and Russett, Bruce M. (eds). *From National Development to Global Community*. London: Allen & Unwin, 1981.

Middlebush, Frederich A. and Hill, Chesney. *Elements of International Relations*. New York: McGraw-Hill, 1940.

Midgley, E. B. F. *The Natural Law Tradition and the Theory of International Relations*. London: Elek, 1975.

Midlarsky, Manus. *The Onset of War*. London: Unwin Hyman, 1988.

Mill, James. *Essays on Government, Jurisprudence and Liberty of the Press and the Law of Nations*. New York: A. M. Kelly, 1967.

Miller, J. D. B. *Norman Angell and The Futility of War*. London: Macmillan, 1986.

Mishra, K. P. and Beal, Richard Smith, (eds). *International Relations Theory*. New Delhi: Vikas, 1980.

Mitchell, C. R. *The Structure of International Conflict*. London: Macmillan, 1981.

Mitchell, C. R. *Peacemaking and the Consultant's Role*. Farnborough: Gower, 1981.

Mitrany, David. *A Working Peace System*. Chicago: Quadrangle, 1966.

Mitrany, David. *The Functional Theory of Politics*. London: Martin Robertson, 1975.

Modelski, George. *Long Cycles in World Politics*. London: Macmillan, 1987.

Modelski, George. *Sea Power in Global Politics 1494–1993*. London: Macmillan, 1988.

Moon, Parker T. *Syllabus on International Relations*, issued by Institute of International Education. New York: Macmillan, 1925.

Morgan, Patrick. *Deterrence: A Conceptual Analysis*. London: Sage, 1977.

Morgenthau, Hans J. *Scientific Man vs Power Politics*. Chicago: University of Chicago Press, 1946.

Morgenthau, Hans J. *Politics among Nations: The Struggle for Power and Peace*. New York: Knopf, 1948.

Morgenthau, Hans. J. *Truth and Power*. New York: Praeger, 1970.

Morgenthau, Hans J. [1950]. *Principles and Problems of International Politics*, ed. with Kenneth W. Thompson. New York: Knopf, 1950.

Mowat, R. B. *International Relations*. London: Rivington, 1931.

Muir, Ramsay. *Political Consequences of the Great War*. New York: H. Holt, 1931.

Myndal, Gunnar. *Population: a problem for democracy*. Cambridge, Mass.: Harvard University Press, 1938 (Godkin lecture).

Nardin, Terry. *Law, Morality and the Relations of States*. Princeton, NJ: Princeton University Press, 1983.

Newson, David D. (ed.). *The Diplomacy of Human Rights*. Lanham, Mass.: University Press of America, 1986.

Nicholson, Michael. *Conflict Analysis*. London: English Universities Press, 1970.

Nicolson, Harold. *Diplomacy*. London: Oxford University Press, 1963.

Niebuhr, Reinhold. *Moral Man and Immoral Society: A Study in Ethics and Politics*. New York: C. Scribner's, 1952.

Nordlinger, Eric. *On the Autonomy of the Modern Democratic State*. Cambridge, Mass.: Harvard University Press, 1981.

Notter, Harley. *The Origins of the Foreign Policy of Woodrow Wilson*. Baltimore: Johns Hopkins University Press, 1937.

Nye, Joseph. *Nuclear Ethics*. New York: Free Press, 1986.

Olsen, Mancur. *The Logic of Collective Action*. Cambridge, Mass: Harvard University Press, 1971.

Olson, William C. (ed). *The Theory and Practice of International Relations*. 8th edition. Englewood Cliffs, N. J: Prentice-Hall, 1991 (first edition, 1960, with Fred Sondermann and David S. McLellan).

Onuf, Nicholas G. *World of Our Making: Rules and Rule in Social Theory and International Relations*. Columbia, SC: University of South Carolina Press, 1989.

Oye, Kenneth (ed.). *Cooperation Under Anarchy*. Princeton, NJ: Princeton University Press, 1986.

Padelford, Norman J. and Lincoln, George A. *International Politics*. New York: Macmillan, 1954.

Palme Commission. *Common Security*. London: Pan, 1982.

Palmer, Norman and Perkins, Howard. *International Relations, a World Community in Transition*. Boston: Houghton Mifflin, 1953.

Paret, Peter (ed.). *Makers of Modern Strategy*. Princeton, NJ: Princeton University Press, 1986.

Parker, Geoffrey. *Western Geopolitical Thought in The Twentieth Century*. London: Croom Helm, 1985.

Parker, Geoffrey. *The Geopolitics of Domination*. London: Routledge, 1988.

Parkinson, F. *The Philosophy of International Relations*. London: Sage, 1977.

Paskins, Bary and Dockrill, Michael. *The Ethics of War*. London: Duckworth, 1979.

Pavolich, Michael. *The Foundations of Imperialist Policy*. London: Labour Publ. Col., 1922.

Penn, William. [1693]. *Essays Towards the Present and Future Peace of Europe*. London: Peace Committee of the Society of Friends, 1936.

Petrie, Sir Charles. *Diplomatic History 1713–1913*. London: Hollis & Carter, 1946.

Piscatori, James. *Islam in a World of Nation-States*. London: Cambridge University Press, 1984.

Plato. *The Republic*, tr. by Sir Desmond Lee. Harmondsworth Penguin, 1955, 1974, 1981.

Plato. *The Dialogues of Plato*, tr. by R. E. Allen. New Haven, Conn.: Yale University Press, 1984.

Playne, Caroline Elizabeth. *Neuroses of the Nations*. London: George Allen and Unwin, 1925.

Politis, N. *New Aspects of International Law*. International Law Pamphlet Series No. 49. Washington: Carnegie Endowment of International Peace, 1928.

Potter, Pitman B. *An Introduction to the Study of International Organization.* 4th edn. New York and London: Appleton-Century, 1935.

Potter, Pitman B. *Collective Security and Peaceful Change.* Chicago: University of Chicago Press, 1937.

Pufendorf, Samuel von. [1672]. *The Law of Nature and Nations,* tr. by Walter Simons, 2 vols. Oxford: Clarendon Press, 1934.,

Quester, George (ed.). *Power, Action and Interaction.* Boston: Little, Brown, 1971.

Rapoport, Anatol. *Fights, Games and Debates.* Ann Arbor, Mich.: University of Michigan Press, 1974.

Rawls, John. *A Theory of Justice.* Oxford: Clarendon Press, 1972.

Read, Elizabeth Fisher. *International Law and International Relations.* New York: The American Foundation, 1925.

Reinsch, Paul. *World Politics at the End of the Nineteenth Century as Influenced by the Oriental Situation.* New York: Macmillan, 1900.

Reinsch, Paul. *Public International Unions, Their Work and Organisation.* Boston: Ginn, 1911.

Richardson, L. F. *Arms and Insecurity.* Pittsburgh, Pa: Boxwood Press, 1960.

Robbins, Lionel C. *Economy Planning and International Order.* London: Macmillan, 1937.

Roberts, Morley. *Bio-Politics.* London: J. M. Dent, 1938.

Roberts, Morley. *The Behaviour of Nations.* London: J. M. Dent, 1941.

Rose, Stein. *M-Day, The First Day of the War.* New York: Harcourt, Brace, 1936.

Rosenau, James N. *The Scientific Study of Foreign Policy.* London: Pinter, 1980.

Rosenau, James N. *The Study of Global Interdependence.* London: Frances Pinter: 1980.

Rosenau, James N. *The Study of Political Adaptation.* London: Frances Pinter, 1980.

Rosenau, James N. (ed.). *International Politics and Foreign Policy.* New York: Free Press, 1961, 1969.

Rosenau, James N. (ed.). *The Domestic Sources of Foreign Policy.* New York: Free Press, 1967.

Rosenau, James N. (ed.). *Linkage Politics.* New York: Free Press, 1969.

Rosenau, James N. (ed.). *Comparing Foreign Policies.* New York: Wiley, 1974.

Rothstein, Robert. *Planning, Prediction and Policy Making in Foreign Affairs.* Boston: Little, Brown, 1972.

Rousseau, Jean Jacques. [1762]. *The Social Contract,* tr. by Maurice Cranston. Baltimore: Penguin, 1968.

Ruggie, John. (ed.). *The Antinomies of Interdependence.* New York: Columbia University Press, 1983.

Russell, Bertrand R. *Education and The Modern World.* New York: W. W. Norton, 1932.

Russell, Frank M. *Theories of International Relations*. New York: D. Appleton–Century, 1936.

Russett, Bruce N. *International Regions and the International System*. Westport: Greenwood, 1975.

Sainte-Claire Deville, Henri. *De La Réorganisation de la Société Européenne*. Paris: Mallet-Bachelier, 1859.

St Pierre, Abbé. *A Project for Making Perpetual Peace in Europe*, tr. by H H. Bellot. London: Grotius Society Publication No 5, 1927.

Sandole, Dennis and Sandole-Staroste, Ingrid (eds). *Conflict Management and Problem Solving*. London: Pinter, 1987.

Schelling, Thomas C. *The Strategy of Conflict*. Cambridge, Mass: Harvard University Press, 1980.

Schuman, Frederick L. *International Politics*. New York: McGraw-Hill, 1933, with further editions in 1937, 1941, 1948, 1953 and 1958.

Schumpeter, Joseph A. *Imperialism and Social Classes*. Oxford: Blackwell, 1951.

Schwarzenberger, Georg. *Power Politics: A Study of World Society*. New York: F.A. Praeger, 1941.

Schwarzenberger, Georg. *International Law and Totalitarian Lawlessness*. London: Cape, 1943.

Scott, Andrew M. *The Revolution in Statecraft*. Durham, NC: Duke University Press, 1962.

Scott, Andrew M. *The Dynamics of Interdependence*. London: University of North Carolina Press, 1982.

Senghaas, Dieter. *The European Experience: A Historical Critique of Dependency Theory*. London: Berg, 1985.

Sharp, Walter R. and Grayson, Kirk. *Contemporary International Politics*. New York: Farrar & Rhinehart, 1940.

Shotwell, James T. *On the Rim of the Abyss*. New York: Macmillan, 1936.

Shue, Henry. *Basic Rights*. Princeton, NJ: Princeton University Press, 1980.

Simonds, Frank and Emeny, Brooks. *The Great Powers in World Politics*: *International Relations and Economic Nationalism*. New York: American Book Co., 1935.

Singer, Marshall R. *Weak States in a World of Powers*. New York: Free Press, 1972.

Skocpol, Theda. *States and Social Revolutions*. London: Cambridge University Press, 1979.

Slessor, Sir John. *Strategy for the West*. London: Cassell, 1954.

Smith, Adam. [1776]. *A Wealth of Nations*, ed. by R. H. Campbell and A. S. Skinner. Oxford: Clarendon Press, 1976.

Smith, A. D. *Nationalism in the Twentieth Century*. Oxford: Martin Robertson, 1979.

Smith, A. D. *The Ethnic Revival in the Modern World*. Cambridge: Cambridge University Press, 1981.

Smith, A. D. *State and Nation in the Third World*. Brighton: Wheatsheaf, 1983.

References 345

Smith, C. G. (ed.). *Conflict Resolution*. Notre Dame, University of Notre Dame Press, 1971.

Smith, Michael; Little, Richard and Shackleton, Michael (eds). *Perspectives on World Politics*. London: Croom Helm, 1981.

Smith, Steve (ed.). *International Relations: British and American Perspectives*. Oxford: Blackwell, 1985.

Smith, Steve and Clarke, M. (eds). *Foreign Policy Implementation*. London: Allen & Unwin, 1985.

Snyder, Richard C. *et al*. *Foreign Policy Decision-Making: An Approach to the Study of International Politics*. New York: Free Press, 1962.

Sorokin, Pitrim A. *The Crisis in Our Age*. New York: E. P. Dutton, 1946.

Spero, Joan E. *The Politics of International Economic Relations*. London: Allen & Unwin, 1982.

Spinoza, Benedictus de. *The Collected Works of Spinoza*. tr. by Edwin Corley. Princeton, NJ: Princeton University Press, 1985.

Sprout, Harold and Sprout, Margaret. *Foundations of National Power*. Princeton, NJ: Princeton University Press, 1945.

Sprout, Harold and Sprout, Margaret. *Man–Milieu Relationship Hypotheses in the Context of International Politics*. Princeton, NJ: Center of International Studies, Princeton University, 1956.

Sprout, Harold and Sprout, Margaret. *The Ecological Perspective in Human Affairs*. Princeton, NJ: Princeton University Press, 1965.

Spykman, Nicholas J. *America's Strategy in World Politics*. New York: Harcourt Brace, 1942.

Spykman, Nicholas J. *The Geography of the Peace*, ed. by Helen R. Nicholl. New York: Harcourt Brace, 1944.

Staley, Eugene. *War and the Private Investor*. Chicago: University of Chicago Press, 1935.

Staley, Eugene. *World Economy in Transition*. New York: Council on Foreign Relations, 1939.

Stalin, Josef. *Marxism and The National Colonial Question*. New York: International Publishers, 1935.

Steinbruner, John. *The Cybernetic Theory of Decision*. Princeton, NJ: Princeton University Press, 1976.

Stoddard, Theodore L. *Clashing Tides of Color*. New York: C. Scribner's, 1935.

Strange, Susan. *Sterling and British Policy*. London: Oxford University Press, 1971.

Strange, Susan. *Casino Capitalism*. Oxford: Blackwell, 1986.

Strange, Susan. *States and Markets*. London: Pinter, 1988.

Strange, Susan (ed.). *Paths to International Political Economy*. London: Allen & Unwin, 1984.

Strange, Susan and Tooze, Roger (eds). *The International Management of Surplus Capacity*. London: Allen & Unwin, 1982.

Stratton, George Malcolm. *The Social Psychology of International Conduct*. New York: D. Appleton, 1929.

Strausz-Hupé, Robert. *Geopolitics*. New York: Putnam, 1942.

Suarez, Francisco. *Selection from Three Works*, tr. by Gladys L. Williams, Ammi Brown and John Waldron, 2 vols. Oxford: Clarendon Press, 1944.

Taylor, Paul and Groom, A. J. R. (eds.). *Global Issues in the United Nations' System*. London: Macmillan, 1989.
Taylor, Trevor (ed.). *Approaches and Theory in International Relations*. London: Longman, 1978.
Thakur, Ramesh (ed.). *International Conflict Resolution*. Boulder, Colo: Westview, 1988.
Thompson, Robert. *Defeating Communist Insurgency*. London: Macmillan, 1975.
Thompson, William R. (ed.). *Contending Approaches to World System Analysis*. London: Sage, 1983.
Thucydides. *History of the Peloponnesian War*. tr. by Rex Warner. New York: Penguin, 1954 (reprinted edn, 1985).
Tilly, Charles (ed.). *The Formation of Nation States in Western Europe*. Princeton, NJ: Princeton University Press, 1975.
Touval, S. and Zartman, I. W. (eds). *International Mediation in Theory and Practice*. Boulder, Colo: Westview, 1985.
Tocqueville, Alexis de. *Democracy in America*. New York: Harper & Row, 1966.
Tonnies, Ferdinand. [1887]. *Community and Society*. New York: Harper & Row, 1965.
Toynbee, Arnold J. *The World After the Peace Conference*. London: Oxford University Press, 1925.
Trimberger, Ellen Kay. *Revolutions from Above*. New Brunswick NJ: Transaction Books, 1978.
Tucker, Robert W. *The Radical Left and American Foreign Policy*. London: Johns Hopkins Press, 1971.

Valkenburg, Samuel Van. *Elements of Political Geography*, 2nd edn. New York: Prentice-Hall, 1939.
Van Dyke, Vernon. *Human Rights, Ethnicity and Discrimination*. Westport: Greenwood, 1985.
Vasquez, John A. *The Power of Power Politics*. London: Pinter, 1983.
Vattel, Emeric de. [1758]. *The Law of Nations*. New York: AMS Press, 1987.
Vayrynen, Raimo (ed.). *The Quest for Peace*. London: Sage, 1987.
Vernon, Raymond. *Sovereignty at Bay*. New York: Basic Books, 1971.
Vincent, John. *Foreign Policy and Human Rights*. London: Cambridge University Press, 1986.
Viner, Jacob. *Studies in The Theory of International Trade*. New York & London: Harper and Bros., 1937.

Wallas, Graham. *The Great Society*. New York: Macmillan. 1914.
Wallerstein, Immanuel. *The Capitalist World Economy*. London: Cambridge University Press, 1979.

Waltz, Kenneth N. *Man, The State and War*. New York: Columbia University Press, 1959.

Waltz, Kenneth N. *Theory of International Politics*. New York: Random House, 1979.

Walzer, Michael. *Just and Unjust Wars*. New York: Basic Books, 1977.

Ware, Edith E. (ed.). *The Study of International Relations in the Survey for 1937*. New York: Columbia University Press, 1938.

Ware, Edith E. (ed.). *The Study of International Relations in the United States: Survey for 1937*. New York: Carnegie Endowment for International Peace, 1939.

Webster, C. K. *The Congress of Vienna 1814–1815*. New York: Barnes & Noble, 1963.

Wheare, Kenneth. *Federal Government*. London: Greenwood, 1980.

Wheaton, Henry. *Elements of International Law*. Boston: Little, Brown & Co., 1857.

Whittlesey, D. S. *The Earth and the State; a study of political geography*. New York: H. Holt and Co., 1939.

Wight, Martin. [1946]. *Power Politics*. New York: Penguin, 1978, and Leicester: Leicester University Press, 1978 (originally published by the Royal Institute of International Affairs, 1946).

Williams, W. Appleman. *The Tragedy of American Diplomacy*. New York: Dell, 1972.

Wilson, Thomas Woodrow. *Congressional Government: a Study in American Politics*. Boston: Houghton Mifflin, 1885.

Wolfers, Arnold. *Discord and Collaboration*. Baltimore, Md: Johns Hopkins University Press, 1966.

Wolfers, Arnold and Martin Laurence W. (eds). *The Anglo-American Tradition in Foreign Affairs*. New Haven: Yale University Press, 1956.

Wright, Moorhead. *Rights and Obligations in North/South Relations*. London: Macmillan, 1986.

Wright, Quincy. *A Study of War*. Chicago: University of Chicago Press, 1942.

Wright, Quincy. *The Study of International Relations*. New York: Appleton–Century–Crofts, 1955.

Wright, Quincy. *Research on International Law since the World War*. Washington: Carnegie Endowment, Division of International Law, 1930.

Zagare, Frank. *The Dynamics of Deterrence*. Chicago: Chicago University Press, 1987.

Zartman, I. William (ed.). *Positive Sum*. New Brunswick: Transaction, 1987.

Index

Acton, John Emerich Edward Dalberg, 1st Baron Acton of Aldenham 33
Adams, John Quincy 29
Afghanistan 146, 318
Africa 171, 195, 293
aggression 207
Alexander I of Russia 22, 25
Al-Farabi 4
Algeciras Conference 48
Alger, Chadwick 210, 211, 236
Algeria 318
Allen, S. H. 68
Allison, Graham 166, 168
Almond, Gabriel A. 61, 142, 157, 158, 159, 160
America 20, 22, 31, 57, 58, 100, 146, 268, 302
  higher education 63–8, 75, 91, 118, 139–40, 325
  organizational base for study of international relations 70–1
  post-behavioural criticism 228–31
  public opinion 59, 60
American Civil War 288
American League to Enforce Peace 51, 52
American Peace Society 40
American Political Science Association 56, 226
Amin, I. 235, 297
Amnesty International 145, 165, 205
anarchists 40, 245
Angell, Norman 47, 84
anthropology 66
Appadorai, Dr A. 119
Aquinas, St Thomas 5, 66
Aristotle 2
arms control 289, 290, 293, 317–18
Ashley, Richard 226, 253, 254, 255, 268, 269, 270, 273, 303
Asoka 3
association 172
Aston, Sir George 67
atomic weapons *see* nuclear weapons

Aussenpolitik 45–6
Austria 23, 25
Axelrod, Robert 169, 317

Bacon, Francis, Baron Verulam of Verulam, Viscount St Albans 13, 108
Bailey, S. H. 71, 82
Bailey meetings 73, 86
"balance" 150
balance of power 11–12, 23, 24, 25, 33, 38, 69, 111, 143, 147, 150, 155, 287
Balkans 42
Band Aid 205
Banks, Michael H. 138
Baran, Paul 233
Barnes, Harry Elmer 98
BBC (British Broadcasting Corporation) 165
Beal, Richard Smith 152
behaviouralism 122–6, 138, 142, 144, 150, 163
  post-behavioural revolution 226–31
Beitz, Charles 142, 274–5, 302
Belgium 42
Bellers, John 12, 41
Beloff, Max 60, 120–1
Benedetti, Count Vincent 46
Bentham, Jeremy 19, 20, 41
Bergesen, Albert 240
Berlin, Congress of 29
Bernard, Jessie 94
Bernard, Luther L. 94
Bernard, Montague 27
Beveridge, William Henry Beveridge, 1st Baron 82
Bible 4
bipolarity 265, 266, 267, 268, 317
Birnbaum, Dr Karl 119
Bismarck, Otto Edward Leopold von, Prince Bismarck, Duke of Lauenburg 30, 33, 45, 49
Bluntschli, J. K. 44

Bodin, Jean 6
"body politic" 10
Boer War 47
Bolingbroke, Henry St John, 1st
    Viscount 12
Boulding, Kenneth 150, 157, 166, 293,
    294
Bourne, Randolph 52
Bowman, Isaiah 52, 67
Bozeman, Adda 122
Brailsford, H. L. 52
Brandt Reports 297
Braudel, 203, 227
Braybrooke, David 167
Brecher, Michael 166
Brett, E. A. 297
Bretton Woods 298
Brierly, J. L. 95, 301
Bright, John 30, 39, 42
Britain 23, 48, 58, 100, 146, 302
    higher education 63–8, 75, 117–18,
        139–40, 296–7, 325
    League of Nations 57
    organizational base for study of inter-
        national relations 70–1
    Pax Britannica 25–6, 287
    public opinion 59, 60
    role of government in international
        relations 74–5
British International Studies Association
    73, 124
British League of Nations Society 51
British Peace Society 42
British Society for the Promotion of
    Permanent and Universal Peace 40
Brown, Chris 233, 241
Brown, Phillip 96, 98
Bruce Report 184
Bruch, H. W. 165, 166
Brzezinski, Zbigniew 70
Buddhism 3
Buell, Raymond 52, 80, 84, 98
Bukharin, Nikolay 39
Bull, Hedley 125, 139
bureaucratic politics 166, 168
Burke, Edmund 19, 20, 28
Burns, Arthur 292
Burns, C. Delisle 68
Burton, John 139, 142, 143, 145, 148–9,
    152, 153, 155, 156, 157, 159, 162,
    195, 197, 199, 202, 204–10, 211–17,
    293, 294
Butler, H. B. 95

Butler, Nicholas Murray 53
Buzzard, Sir Anthony 291

Callières, Francois de 12, 46
Cambridge University 65, 296
Canning, George 24
capitalism 39, 47, 52, 144, 226, 227, 228,
    229, 230, 232, 233–42
Carnegie, Andrew 49
Carnegie Endowment for International
    Peace 48, 64, 75, 83
Carr, Edward Hallett 66, 81, 91–3, 95,
    96, 97, 104, 105, 108, 109, 111, 115,
    121, 124, 144, 270, 276
Carr-Saunders, A. M. 66
Castlereagh, Robert Stewart, Viscount
    22, 23–4, 25, 26, 29
Catholic Church 196
centre–periphery relationships 234,
    235–6, 239–40, 241, 297, 319
change *see* homeostasis
Channing, William Ellery 40
Chatham House 70, 71, 72, 74, 89, 96,
    106, 109, 114, 185
Cherrington, Ben 73
Chevalier, Michael 31
Chevallier, V. J. 119
Ch'in dynasty 7
China 2, 58, 291, 325
Choucri, Nazli 226, 253, 254
class struggle 38, 232
Claude, Inis 142, 148
Clausewitz, Karl von 31, 33
Club of Rome 202, 253
Cobden, Richard 30, 39, 40, 42
coercive control 320
Cohen, Benjamin 228, 229, 230
Colby, Charles 94, 97
Cold war 98, 104, 105, 113, 121, 122, 185,
    208, 209, 225, 228, 291
Cole, G. D. H. 95
collective security 289, 290 *see also* League
    of Nations, world society
colonialism 107, 124
    internal 175
Commager, Henry Steele 325
communism 38, 232
comparative politics 157–60
complex interdependence 195, 198, 200,
    216
Comte, Auguste 32
Concert of Europe 13, 26–7, 29, 287, 289
concordance systems 172

Condliffe, J. B. 91
confederalism 44
conferences 71–3, 116–22
conflict research 293–6, 319
conflict resolution 31
Confucius 2, 66
Congress of Berlin 29
Congress of Vienna 21, 23, 26, 29, 56, 57
Connor, Walker 175
consociation 173, 174
coordination 172
Coser, Lewis 294
cosmopolitanism 302–3 *see also* structuralism, world society
Council on Foreign Relations (CFR) 70, 71, 89, 107
Cox, Robert 256, 279, 280, 297, 303
Craig, Gordon 99
Crimean War 27, 39, 147
crisis management 169
critical theory 303, 316
Crowe, Eyre 48
Crucé, Emeric 6
Crusades 5
Cuban missile crisis 166
Curle, Adam 294
cybernetics 160–5
Cyprus 322
Czartowski, Prince Adam 27
Czechoslovakia 90

Dante Alighieri 5
Darby, W. Evans 42
Davies, David 84
de Madariaga, Salvador 88, 96
de Rivera, J. 169
de Vitorio, Francisco 5
debt problems 319
decision-making 320
Declaration of Independence 20
decolonization 171
Delian League 7
demography 19, 66
Denis, Pierre 94
dependencia 227, 232, 233, 234, 297, 298
dependency theory 124, 138
Depression 104
Descartes, René 13, 215
deterrence 291–2, 294, 317
Deutsch, Karl 143, 149, 160–5, 166, 174, 197, 253, 323
developing countries *see* Third World
Dickinson, G. Lowes 51, 53

diplomacy 27, 46–7, 50, 169
  ancient history 1–3
  balance of power *see* balance of power
  New Diplomacy 61
diplomatic history 184–5
disarmament 51, 289, 290, 293, 317
disintegration 171, 174–5, 320
disjointed incrementation 167
Disraeli, Benjamin, 1st Earl of Beaconsfield 43
distributional conflict 197, 198
Djordjević 119
Douhet, Giulio 99
Dubois, Pierre 5
Dunn, Frederick Sherwood 120, 122
Duroselle, J. B. 121, 122
Dutt, R. Palme 88, 96

Earle, Edward Mead 99
East Africa 195
Easton, David 142, 152, 153, 155, 156, 157, 160, 226, 227, 256, 268
ecology 201, 202, 211
economics 19, 27, 66, 84, 95, 96, 116, 120
  see also political economists
  lead economies 248
  rational-choice theory 271–4
Egypt 119
Einstein, Albert 95
Eisenhower, Dwight David 121, 318
Eliot, George Fielding 95
Ellsworth, Paul T. 96
Emeny, Brooks 87, 96
Emmanuel 235, 297
Engels, Friedrich 37, 38
England *see* Britain
Enlightenment 13, 28
Enloe 175
Epictetus 3
equilibrium *see* homeostasis
Erasmus, Desiderius 5, 9
ethnicity 175, 323–4
ethnology 66
European Coal and Steel Community 194
European Community 124, 165, 168, 322
Evans, Peter 236, 278

Fagen, Michael M. 94
Fairgrieve, James 94, 97
Falk, Richard 301
federalism 44, 173, 174
feedback 150, 161, 162

Ferguson, Y. 155
Fichte, Johann 45
flexible response 292
Ford Foundation 75, 196
foreign policy 228 *see also* diplomacy, international relations
foreign policy analysis (FPA) 165–70, 320
Foster, John W. 46
Fox, Anne 124
Fox, Annette Baker 120
Fox, William T. R. 19, 65, 92, 96, 100, 120, 121, 123
France 23, 24, 60, 119, 120, 146
  League of Nations 57
  peace movement 40, 51
Franco–Prussian War 33, 39, 42
Frank, Andre Gunder 234, 295, 297
Frankel, Joseph 166
Franklin, Benjamin 20
free trade 30
French Revolution 49, 50, 288
Freud, Sigmund 95
Frontinus 3
Fuller, J. F. C. 67
functionalism 155, 157–60, 173, 174, 190–5, 322

Galtung, John 210, 211, 235, 236, 253, 294, 295
Gardner, Richard 297
Garibaldi, Giuseppe 39
Garnett, John 292
Garrison, William Lloyd 39
Gathorne-Hardy, G. M. 58, 86
Geldof, Bob 205
gender-specific issues 324
General Systems Theory 150–1, 157
Gentili, Alberico 6, 11
Gentz, Friedrich 26
geography 67, 94–5, 97, 100
geopolitics 45–6, 67, 98, 100, 224, 226, 252–7
Germany 48, 57, 66
Giddens, Anthony 240
Gilpin, Robert 185, 254, 262, 266, 267, 268, 270, 271–4, 276, 297, 298–9, 320
Gladstone, William Ewart 29, 42
global modelling 201–4
"global village" 125, 138 *see also* world society
Godwin, William 40
Gooch, G. P. 88
Goodwin, Geoffrey 116, 118

graduated deterrence 291–2
Grafton, Samuel 100
Great War *see* World War I
Greece 1–2
"Green" movement 211, 241, 251
Greenpeace 205
Greenwood, Arthur 52
Groom, A. J. R. 138
Grosser, Albert 19, 120, 121
Grotius, Hugo 6, 9, 80, 98, 301
Gurr, Ted Robert 293

Haas, Ernst 108, 173–4, 195
Hague Peace Conferences 42, 47, 48, 64, 289, 290
Hall, William 64
Halliday, Fred 230
Halperin, Morton 168
Hamilton, Alexander 20
Harcourt, Sir Vernon 29
harmonization 172
harmony of interest 30, 33, 288, 289, 294, 298
Harold Pratt House 89
Harrod, Jeffrey 279
Harrod, R. F. 95, 96
Hartshorn, Richard 94
Haushofer, Karl 46, 99, 100, 253
Hayes, Carleton J. H. 323
Heatley, David P. 52, 68, 69
Hechter, Michael 175
Hegel, Georg 27, 28
hegemony 199, 200
Heidegger, Martin 304
Henry IV (King of France) 6, 43
Heraclides, Alexis 176
Herodotus 1
Herz, John 170
Higgins, Pearce 63
Higgins, Rosalyn 301
higher education 63–8, 75, 82, 89–90, 91, 116–22, 139–40, 296–7, 325
Hill, Chesney 93
Hinduism 3
Hinsley, Sir Harry 7, 13, 38, 61, 288
historians 32–3, 64–6, 184–5
Hitler, Adolf 46, 80, 90, 91, 98, 100, 253
Hobbes, Thomas 2, 10, 147, 301
Hobson, J. A. 47, 51, 147, 222, 229, 263
Hodges, Charles 81
Hoffmann, Stanley 11, 123, 263, 302, 303
holism 152, 223
Holland, T. E. 44, 64

Holsti, Kal 3, 138, 140, 195, 317, 326
Holy Roman Empire 5, 9
Holzgrefe, Jeff 34
homeostasis 152, 155, 156
Hopkins, Raymond 199, 200
Hudson, Manley O. 71
Hull, Cordell 83
Hume, David 11
hydrogen bomb *see* nuclear weapons
Hyman, Sonia Z. 95

Ibn Khaldun 4, 66
ICI (Imperial Chemical Industries) 165
idealism 42–5, 58, 69, 73–4, 79, 81, 95, 105, 144
identity studies 323–4
Iklé, Fred 294
ILO (International Labour Organization) 165
IMF (International Monetary Fund) 321
immigration 319
imperialism 39, 47, 52, 146–7, 171, 222, 228, 229, 230, 232, 235
import substitution 233–4
India 58, 119, 137, 171, 317
individualism 223
industrial revolution 49, 287, 288
Institute for Strategic Studies 292
integration theory 124, 143, 163, 171–6, 320, 321
interdependence 163–4, 165, 195, 197, 198, 200, 216, 300, 325
internal colonialism 175
"international" 19, 64
International Committee of the Red Cross 289
International Institute of Intellectual Co-operation 71
international law 28–30, 33, 44–5, 51, 63–4, 95, 112, 183–4, 301
    origins 5–7
International League of Peace and Liberty 39
International Olympic Committee 205
International Organization (IO) network 195–200, 216
International Political Economy (IPE) *see* political economists
international relations
    ancient history 1–3
    balance of power *see* balance of power
    comparative politics 157–60
    cybernetics 160–5

diplomacy *see* diplomacy
    early role of government and foundations 74–6
    foreign policy analysis (FPA) 165–70, 320
    future study 325–7
    idealism versus realism 42–5, 79–80 *see also* idealism, realism
    idealist internationalism 73–4, 79, 105, 111
    integration theory *see* integration theory
    international conferences 71–3, 116–22
    Marxism *see* Marxism
    nationalism and *Aussenpolitik* 45–6, *see also* nationalism
    peace movement *see* peace movement
    Peace of Westphalia *see* Peace of Westphalia 8–10
    philosophers 27–8
    political economists and strategists 30–2 *see also* political economists, strategists
    post-World-War I 56–9, 79–80
    power politics *see* power politics
    public opinion *see* public opinion
    religious thought 4–5
    research agenda 317–25
    sociologists and historians 32–3 *see also* historians, sociologists
    state, theory of the 10–11, 33, 38, 276–9
    statesmen–thinkers 22–7
    structuralism *see* structuralism
    systematic study 46–52, 62–3; behaviouralism and quantification 122–6; contrasts in mainstream literature between the World Wars 85–97; defining the subject-matter 82–5; during World War II 98–100; emergence of a consensus 68–70; end of consensus 80–2; organizational base 70–1; post-World War II 104–11; Quincy Wright's contribution 114–16; "scientific" aspects 109–10, 115–16, 316; second consensus 112–14
    systems analysis 149–57
    vision of peace 12–13
    world society *see* world society
International Studies Association 124
internationalism 73–4, 79, 105, 111
Iroquois 4
Ishimaru, T. 95

Israel 236, 317
Italy 6, 42, 57
   Renaissance 7–8

Janis, Irving L. 169
Janowski, Oscar I. 94
Japan 57, 69, 76, 80, 85
Jay, John 20
Jefferson, Thomas 20
Jervis, Robert 169
Johnson, Chalmers 152, 153, 156, 157, 199
Jomini, Baron Antoine Henri 31, 99
Jones, Roy 302
Judge, Anthony 174
jus gentium 3, 6

Kaddafi, Colonel Muammar 326
Kadish treaty 1
Kalijarvi, Thorsten 99
Kant, Immanuel 20, 21, 23, 26, 27, 41, 43, 56, 80, 301
Kaplan, Morton 123, 125, 142, 150, 263
Kautilya 3
Kautsky, Karl 39
Kegley, Charles W. 168
Kelsen, Hans 95, 97
Kennan, George 109
Kennedy, Paul 320
Keohane, Robert 144, 195, 196, 197, 198, 208, 297, 321
Keynes, John Maynard 58, 66, 297
Kirk, Grayson 93, 96, 98, 107, 108
Kisker, George 122
Kissinger, Dr Henry 21, 70, 267
Kjellen, Rudolf 252
Klineberg, Otto 122
Knorr, Klaus 123
Kolko, Gabriel 229
Kondratieff price cycles 250
Koran 4
Korean War 147, 291
Krasner, Stephen 195, 198, 298, 321
Kuhn, Thomas 286
Kung-sun Yang 2

Lacoste, Yves 252
Ladd, William 40
laissez-faire 19
Lampert 155
Lasswell, Harold 67, 95, 100, 114, 122, 319
Latin America 57, 227, 231, 233, 234, 289, 293, 297
Lauterpacht, Hersch 95, 97, 301

law *see* international law
Lawrence, Geoffrey, 3rd Baron Trevithin, 1st Baron Oaksey 52
Le Bon, Gustav 68
lead economies 248
League of Nations 44, 56, 57, 58, 60, 67, 68, 69, 70, 72, 73, 76, 79, 80, 88, 104, 117, 184, 289, 290, 301
legitimacy 145, 149–50, 163, 197, 199, 206, 208–10, 216, 217, 246, 247, 275, 278, 295
Lemonnier, Charles 39
Lenin, Vladimir Ilyich 39, 47, 51, 52, 147, 232, 263, 290
Leninism 222, 230, 231
Levi, Leone 43
Lévi-Strauss, Claude 223
Liddell-Hart, Sir Basil H. 67
Lijphart, Arend 174
Lincoln, George 108, 120
Lindblom 167
Linklater, Andrew 302, 303
Lippman, Walter 51, 61
List, Friedrich 27, 30, 97
Little, Richard 224
Livy 3
Locke, John 10
Lodi, Peace of 7
London School of Economics (LSE) 62, 72, 75, 116, 124, 325
Lorimer, Sir James 29, 43
Ludendorff, Erich von 99

Machiavelli, Niccolò 2, 7, 80, 98, 100
Machtpolitik 45
Mackinder, Sir Halford 46, 67, 99, 252
Macleish, Archibald 32, 123
de Madariaga, Salvador 88, 96
Madison, James 20
Magdoff, Harry 229, 230
Maggi, Ottaviano 6
Mahan, Alfred Thayer 45–6, 67, 99, 252
Maine, Sir Henry Sumner 45
Malthus, Thomas 19
Manchester School 30
Manchuria 69
Mancini, Professor 42
Mander, Linden 94, 96
Mann, Michael 185–9, 225
Mannheim, Karl 93, 94
Manning, C. A. W. 116, 121, 124
Mansbach, Richard W. 143, 155, 156, 170, 195, 199

354 *International Relations then and now*

Mao Zedong (Tse-tung) 293, 326
Marcoartu, Senator 42
Marcus Aurelius 3
Marshall Plan 231, 291
Marsilius of Padua 5
Martens, G. F. de 27
Martin, Laurence 119
Marvin, F. S. 88
Marx, Karl 28, 37, 52, 116, 290, 301
Marxism 34, 37–9, 41, 45, 47, 50, 88, 105,
    109, 125, 139, 222–3, 226, 231–3,
    237, 238, 240, 241, 251, 271, 272,
    277
Massachusetts Peace Society 40
McClelland, Charles 146, 151
McDougall, Myers 301
McGowan 168
Mencius 2
mercantilism 298, 299
Merriam, Charles 120
Metternich, Prince Clemens Lothar
    Wenzel 22, 24, 33
Mexico 119
Middle East 231
Middlebush, Frederich 93
militarism 67
military science *see* strategists
Mill, James 28
minority populations *see* ethnicity
Mitchell, C. R. 215, 216
Mitrany, David 98, 139, 143, 144, 153,
    155, 173, 190, 191, 194, 195, 199,
    202, 322
Modelski, George 185, 225, 226, 228,
    238, 239, 241, 242–52, 254, 273–4,
    295, 320, 323
Molinari, Gustave de 43
Monroe Doctrine 45
Montague Burton Chairs 75
Moon, Parker T. 71
moral relativism 302
moral vacuum 302
Morgenthau, Hans J. 2, 81, 109, 110, 111,
    112, 114, 115, 121, 123, 124, 138,
    142, 144, 145, 146, 147, 148, 190,
    204, 224, 265, 270, 275, 276
Mowat, R. B. 66, 98
Mowlana, Hamid 125
Muir, Ramsay 84
Mukden 80, 85
multipolarity 265, 267, 317
Murrow, Edward R. 71
Myrdal, Gunnar 95

Napoleon I 12, 20, 21, 22, 23
Napoleonic Wars 49
nation states 4, 321, 323
national interest 37, 43, 302
nationalism 39, 45–6, 50, 111, 149, 175,
    268, 288, 323
nationalized industries 165
NATO 112, 291
natural law 302
Nazism 67, 209, 253
Near East 231
needs theory 210–17
Nehru, Jawaharlal 2
neo-functionalism 173, 174, 194, 195
neo-realism 224, 228, 262–71, 325
Netherlands 42, 48, 51
New Diplomacy 61
newly industrializing countries (NICs)
    234
newspapers 60–1
Newton, Sir Isaac 13
Nicholson, Michael 294
Nicholson, Sir Harold 24, 25, 47, 169
Niebuhr, Reinhold 109
Nielsson, Gunnar 176
Nietzsche, Friedrich 304
Nigeria 171
Noble, John 43
non-alignment 137, 143, 149, 162
non-governmental organizations (NGOs)
    205
normative theory 300–1, 302–3
North, Robert 124, 226, 253, 254
Northern Ireland 322
North–South issues 319–20, 321
nuclear weapons 104, 201, 213, 227, 241,
    251, 291–2, 317
Nye, Joseph 2, 144, 195, 196, 197, 198,
    208, 263, 268, 297, 321, 325

Olson, William C. 121
"open covenants" 61
organizational processes 166, 167–8
Oxenstiern, Count Axel Gustafsson 9
Oxfam 321
Oxford University 62–3, 65, 75, 296
    St Anthony's College 106, 122
Oye, Kenneth 317

pacifism 58, 63, 67
Padelford, Norman 108, 120
Paine, Thomas 13
Palmer, Norman 108

Papacy 8, 9
Paris Peace Conference 56
Parker, Geoffrey 252
Parkinson, Fred 2, 28
Parsons, Talcott 151
pattern maintenance 152, 155, 156
Pavlovitch, Michael 66
Pax Britannica 25–6, 287
peace 31, 33, 38, 143, 208, 209, 289
  free trade 30
  international law *see* international law
peace movement 12–13, 27, 39–40, 48, 50, 60, 288
  from opposition to participation 41–2
  post-World War I 56
Peace of Lodi 7
Peace of Westphalia 8–10, 301
peace research 295–6, 319
Pear, Tom H. 95
Pearl Harbor 85, 93
Peirce 214
Peloponnesian War 1
Penn, William 12, 13, 20, 41
peripheries 234, 235–6, 239–40, 241, 297, 319
Perkins, Howard 108
Pharaonic literature 1
philosophy 1–3, 27–8
Pitt, William 22
Plato 2
Playne, C. E. 68
Pol Pot 209
Poland 147
political economists 30–2, 87, 96–7, 296–300, 319–20
political science 62–3, 84, 85, 86–7, 120, 125
Politics, N. 64
Pomona College 121
post-behavioural revolution 226–31
post-modernism 304–5
post-structuralism 304
Potter, Pitman B. 71
power politics 45–6, 106, 107, 111–12, 121, 142, 143, 145, 146–9, 162, 163, 166, 169, 176, 194, 195, 198, 208–10, 216, 246, 247, 265, 290, 293, 295
Prebisch, Raoul 233, 297
problem-solving 143, 162, 213, 294
production 279–81
progress, belief in 50
propaganda 67, 122
Protagorus 2, 106

Proudhon, Joseph-Pierre 44
Prussia 20, 23, 45
psychology 67–8
public opinion 28, 29, 41–2, 53, 58, 59–62, 69, 111
Puchala, Donald 163, 172, 174, 199, 200
Pufendorf, Baron Samuel von 9, 22

Quadruple Alliance 24
quantification 122–6

racial diversity *see* ethnicity
Ramses II 1
Rand Corporation 292
Ransom, Harry Howe 115
Rapoport, Anatol 293, 294
rational actor model 166, 167
rational choice 271–4
rationality 303
Ratzel, Friedrich 45, 252
Rawls, John 302
Ray, James Lee 241
Read, Elizabeth 63
realism 42–5, 58, 79, 80, 81, 95–6, 108, 112, 137, 138, 140, 141, 142, 143, 163, 166, 176, 184, 198, 208, 209, 224, 245, 287, 289, 293, 298, 301–2, 316
  power politics *see* power politics
  production, power and world order 279–81
  rational choice and world politics 271–4
  resurgence 274–6
  role of the state 276–9
  structural realism and neo-realism 262–71
Realpolitik 45, 50
Red Cross 289
regimes 198–200, 321
regionalism 173
Reinsch, Paul 44, 47
religious thought 4–5
Renaissance 7–8
Reynolds, P. A. 121
Ricardo, David 27, 97
Richardson, Lewis F. 95, 123, 184
Richelieu, Armand Jean Duplessis, Cardinal, Duc de 11
Ritter 252
de Rivera, J. 169
Robbins, Lionel 95
Rocquefort, C. de Mougins de 31

Roman Catholic Church 196
Rome 3
Roosevelt, Theodore 51
Root, Elihu 53
Rosecrance 263
Rosenau, James 123, 138, 143, 157, 158, 166, 168, 169–70, 322
Rosenau, Pauline 304
Rousseau, Jean-Jacques 10, 20, 27, 41, 301
Rueschemeyer, Dietrich 278
Ruggie, John 264, 265
Russell, Frank 88, 96
Russett, Bruce 125, 173
Russia 23, 31, 37, 57, 100 *see also* Soviet Union
Rockefeller Foundation 75

Saint Anthony's College, Oxford 106, 122
Saint-Pierre, Charles Irénée Castel, Abbé de 12, 21, 32, 43
Saint-Simon, Claude Henri de Rouvroy, Comte de 40, 41, 301
sanctions 290
Sapin 165, 166
"satisficing" 161, 167
Scandinavia 57
Schmid, Hermann 295
Shue, Henry 302
Schuman, Frederick L. 8, 85, 86, 87, 95, 96, 98, 104, 112, 124
Schumpeter, Joseph A. 146, 147
Schwarzenberger, Georg 7, 95, 98, 106, 144, 208, 270, 276, 301, 302, 319
Scott, Andrew 170, 202–3, 325
Seeley, Sir John 32–3
separatism 175
Sharp, Walter 93, 96, 98
Shotwell, Professor James T. 83, 84
Simon, Herbert 167
Simonds, Frank 87, 96
Singer, David 9, 144, 210
Skocpol, Theda 277
Slessor, Sir John 291
Smith, A. D. 175
Smith, Adam 19, 97, 116
Snyder, Richard 123, 165, 166
social contract 10, 302
sociologists 32–3, 66, 94, 97, 319
Socrates 2
Sorokin, Pitirim A. 66, 94
South Africa 236, 317
sovereign states 8, 9, 322

Soviet Union 57, 58, 146, 175, 222, 268
Speier, Hans 319
Spencer, Herbert 32
Spero, Joan E. 297
Spinoza, Baruch, 8, 22
Sprout, Harold 105, 166, 226, 253
Sprout, Margaret 99, 105, 166, 226, 253
Spykman, Nicholas J. 71, 99, 253
Staley, Eugene 297
Stalin, Joseph 105
Starr, Harvey 125
state, theory of the 10–11, 33, 38, 276–9
state-centricity 120, 122, 125, 138, 142, 143, 144, 149, 150, 153, 155, 159, 160, 166, 175, 176, 195, 196, 198, 207, 216, 250, 265, 278, 298, 321
statesmen-thinkers 22–7
steering 149, 162
Stoddard, Theodore L. 94
Stoics 2
Strange, Susan 297
strategists 45–6, 67, 99, 290–1, 293, 294, 317, 318, 320
Stratton, George 68
Strausz-Hupé, Robert 98
structural realism 262–71
structural violence 295, 324
structuralism 126, 138, 139, 140, 141, 144, 158–60, 166, 222–6, 290, 297, 298, 302, 316
  capitalism as a structure 233–42
  geopolitics 252–7
  long cycles in a global structure 242–52
  Marxist heritage 231–3
  post-behavioural revolution 226–31
Suarez, Francisco 6
Suez 146
Sully, Duc de 7, 12, 21
Summer, Charles 40
Sun Tzu 2
Super Powers 100, 169, 266, 267, 317, 318
"survival of the fittest" 32
Sweden 51, 119
Switzerland 60, 173, 264
systems analysis 149–57

Talleyrand-Périgord, Charles Maurice de, Prince of Benevento 22, 25, 26, 57
terrorism 319
Thatcher, Margaret 168
Third World 193, 227, 229, 230, 233, 234, 235, 236, 319–20, 321, 326

Third World Power Conference 83
Thirty Years War 6, 8, 21
Thompson, Kenneth W. 2, 104, 110, 111, 112, 243
Thoreau, Henry 39
Thorndike, Tony 231, 276
Thucydides 1, 10, 80, 100, 301
Tilly, Charles 159
Tocqueville, Alexis de 31
Tonnies, Ferdinand 39, 66
Toynbee, Arnold J. 8, 70, 88, 95, 109, 114, 185, 273
transactional analysis 163
transgovernmental alliances 165
transnationalism 195, 196
Treaty of Versailles 20, 59, 61
Treaty of Westphalia *see* Peace of Westphalia
Truman Doctrine 291
TUC (Trades Union Congress) 165
Tucker, Robert 228, 229, 230

UN Charter 173
UNESCO 32, 119
United Nations 44, 105, 291, 321
United States *see* America
Universal Peace Conference 40
Universal Peace Congress 48, 49
universities *see* higher education
University College of Wales at Aberystwyth 62, 75, 92
University of Aberdeen 117
University of Cambridge *see* Cambridge University
University of Denver 74
University of London 117, 296
University of Oxford *see* Oxford University
University of Pennsylvania 108
US Council on Foreign Relations (CFR) 70, 71, 89, 107
USSR *see* Soviet Union
utopianism 108, 109, 111, 124

Van Valkenberg, Samuel 94
Vasquez, John 142 143, 156, 170, 195, 199, 275–6
Vattel, Emmerich de 9, 10, 22
Vegitius 3
Verba, Sidney 123, 210
Vernant, M. 119
Versailles, Treaty of 20, 59, 61
Vienna, Congress of 21, 23, 26, 29, 56, 57

Vietnam War 97, 146, 227, 228, 301, 318
Vincent, John 319
Viner, Jacob 95, 117
de Vitoria, Francisco 5
Völkerwanderung 4
Voltaire, François-Marie Arouet de 11

Wall Street crash 80
Wallas, Graham 53
Wallerstein, Immanuel 139, 185, 203, 225, 226, 227, 228, 237, 238–9, 240–1, 242, 243, 244, 251, 254, 295, 297, 320
Waltz, Kenneth 123, 144, 210, 245, 262, 263, 264–6, 267, 268, 269, 270, 273, 274, 276
Waltzer, Michael 302
war 28, 31, 50, 69, 287, 288, 290
War on Want 321
Ward, Lester 32
Ware, Edith 83, 84
Washington, George 20
Webster, Sir Charles Kingsley 23, 26, 58, 62, 65, 66
welfare-maximization *see* functionalism
Wells, H. G. 88
West Africa 171
West Indies 171
Westphalia, Peace of 8–10, 301
Wheare, Sir Kenneth 174
Wheaton, Henry 29
Whiting, Allen 108
Whittlesey, D. S. 94
Wicquefort, Abraham de 11
Wight, Martin 46, 106, 107. 108, 139
Wilson, Sir Harold, Baron Wilson 203
Wilson, Woodrow 2, 21, 56, 57, 61, 62, 289, 290
Winham, Gilbert 294
Wolfers, Arnold 119, 301
Wolff, Christian von 9
women 324
Woolbert, Robert Gale 70
World Bank 321
World Council of Churches 205
World Health Organization 145
World Order Models Project (WOMP) 202, 206, 253
World Peace Foundation 70
world society 125, 138, 139, 140, 141, 144, 145, 153, 155, 157, 158, 161, 163, 165, 166, 170, 176, 183–5, 250, 290, 294, 298, 302, 316

world society (*cont.*)
  domination of Europe as a process
    185–9
  functionalism *see* functionalism
  global modelling 201–4
  International Organization (IO) net-
    work 195–200, 216
  John Burton's contribution 204–10
  needs theory 210–17
world systems *see* structuralism
World War I 50, 51, 56, 287, 288, 289
World War II 97, 98–100, 290

Wright, Quincy 6, 64, 71, 109, 114–16,
  117, 123, 126, 184, 204, 326

Yale Institute of International Studies
  108, 118, 120, 122, 123
Yehia, M. A. 119
Young, Oran 163–4
Yugoslavia 119

Zimmern, Sir Alfred 62, 72, 73, 74, 90,
  94, 95, 96, 97, 110
Zolberg 242